Constantin Freitag

Verb-second as a reconstruction phenomenon

studia grammatica 86

Herausgegeben von Manfred Bierwisch,
Hans-Martin Gärtner und Manfred Krifka

unter Mitwirkung von
Regine Eckardt (Konstanz) und Paul Kiparsky (Stanford)

Constantin Freitag

Verb-second as a reconstruction phenomenon

Evidence from grammar and processing

DE GRUYTER

Free access to the e-book version of this publication was made possible by the 39 academic libraries that supported the open access transformation project in German Linguistics.

ISBN 978-3-11-072493-6
e-ISBN (PDF) 978-3-11-072501-8
e-ISBN (EPUB) 978-3-11-072511-7
ISSN 0081-6469
DOI: https://doi.org/10.1515/9783110725018

Library of Congress Control Number: 2021943618

Bibliographic information published by the Deutsche Nationalbibliothek
The Deutsche Nationalbibliothek lists this publication in the Deutsche Nationalbibliografie; detailed bibliographic data are available on the Internet at http://dnb.dnb.de.

The book is published open access at www.degruyter.com.
Printing and binding: CPI books GmbH, Leck

MIX
Papier aus verantwortungsvollen Quellen
FSC® C083411

www.degruyter.com

Open-Access-Transformation in Linguistics

Open Access for excellent academic publications in the field of German Linguistics: Thanks to the support of 39 academic libraries, 9 frontlist publications from 2021 can be published as gold open access, without any costs to the authors.

The following institutions have contributed to the funding and thus promote the open access transformation in German linguistics and ensure free availability for everyone:

Universitätsbibliothek Augsburg
Universitätsbibliothek Bayreuth
University of California, Berkeley Library
Staatsbibliothek zu Berlin – Preußischer Kulturbesitz
Universitätsbibliothek der Freien Universität Berlin
Universitätsbibliothek der Humboldt-Universität zu Berlin
Universitätsbibliothek der Technischen Universität Berlin
Universitätsbibliothek Bielefeld
Universitäts- und Landesbibliothek Bonn
Staats- und Universitätsbibliothek Bremen
Universitätsbibliothek der Technischen Universität Chemnitz
Universitäts- und Landesbibliothek Darmstadt
Sächsische Landesbibliothek – Staats- und Universitätsbibliothek Dresden
Universitätsbibliothek Duisburg-Essen
Universitäts- und Landesbibliothek Düsseldorf
Universitätsbibliothek Eichstätt-Ingolstadt
Universitätsbibliothek Johann Christian Senckenberg, Frankfurt a. M.
Bibliothek der Pädagogischen Hochschule Freiburg
Niedersächsische Staats- und Universitätsbibliothek Göttingen
Universitätsbibliothek Greifswald
Universitätsbibliothek der FernUniversität in Hagen
Universitäts- und Landesbibliothek Sachsen-Anhalt, Halle (Saale)
Staats- und Universitätsbibliothek Hamburg Carl von Ossietzky
Gottfried Wilhelm Leibniz Bibliothek – Niedersächsische Landesbibliothek, Hannover
Universitäts- und Landesbibliothek Tirol, Innsbruck
Universitätsbibliothek Kassel – Landesbibliothek und Murhardsche Bibliothek der Stadt Kassel
Universitätsbibliothek der Universität Koblenz-Landau
Zentral- und Hochschulbibliothek Luzern
Bibliothek des Leibniz-Instituts für Deutsche Sprache, Mannheim
Universitätsbibliothek Marburg
Universitätsbibliothek der Ludwig-Maximilians-Universität München
Universitäts- und Landesbibliothek Münster
Bibliotheks- und Informationssystem der Carl von Ossietzky Universität Oldenburg
Universitätsbibliothek Osnabrück
Universitätsbibliothek Vechta
Herzog August Bibliothek Wolfenbüttel
Universitätsbibliothek Wuppertal
ZHAW Zürcher Hochschule für Angewandte Wissenschaften, Hochschulbibliothek
Zentralbibliothek Zürich

Dieses Buch ist meiner Familie gewidmet – dem Teil, den ich schon seit einer ganzen Weile kenne und dem, den ich erst kürzlich gefunden habe.

Preface

This book is a condensed version of my doctoral dissertation which I defended in April 2019 at the Department of Linguistics of the University of Konstanz. The dissertation resulted from the AThEME-project (Advancing the European Multilingual Experience). This project has received funding from the European Union's Seventh Framework Programme for research, technological development and demonstration under grant agreement no. 613465.

I am deeply indebted to my supervisor Josef Bayer who committed a great idea to me which laid the foundation of this work and who also supported me thoroughly all along the way to its completion. I am also very grateful that Janet Grijzenhout and Caroline Heycock agreed to be part of my dissertation committee. Without their engagement, feedback, and wit my graduation could not have become such an enjoyment as it has been. I also owe a lot to Sophie Repp for her long-time support and the opportunity to finish my studies in Cologne.

For countless, laughter, discussions, and suggestions, I want to thank my colleagues Yvonne Viesel, Anna Czypionka, and Laura Dörre who made the time in Konstanz unforgettable. Likewise I want to thank my Köln crowd Marlijn Meijer, Katharina Schaebbicke and Max Bonke for the very enjoyable time there.

I am also much obliged to Anne Temme for her stamina and all the effort that she put into the design and the material for Experiment 5.

Thanks to Kathi Fraser, Nathalie Scherf, Anne, Laura, and Yvi for helping me to find English translations for those weird German examples and proofreading the manuscript.

Furthermore, thanks to the people of the linguistic departments and the psycholinguistics labs in Konstanz and Köln, all participants of the experiments, the AThEME-team, Andrea Padovan, Andreas Trotzke, Kleanthes Grohmann, Volker Struckmeier, Tom Roeper, Horst Lohnstein, Lyn Frazier, Hans-Martin Gärtner, Eva Wittenberg, Sten Vikner, Katrine Rosendal Carstensen, Andreas Haida, Halldór Sigurdsson, Thórhallur Eythórsson, Jóhannes Gísli Jónsson, Ingunn Hreinberg Indriðadóttir, Oliver Bott und Fabian Schlotterbeck.

Finally, this work would not have appeared in the Studia Grammatica series without the good will and the commitment of two admirable linguists. I have to thank again Josef Bayer who *lobbied* for me and never let this go out of sight, and Manfred Bierwisch who offered me this opportunity and intensively supported this publication. I am deeply grateful to both of you.

Berlin, 14 June 2021

https://doi.org/10.1515/9783110725018-202

Contents

List of Tables

https://doi.org/10.1515/9783110725018-204

List of Figures

https://doi.org/10.1515/9783110725018-205

Abbreviations

1	first person
2	second person
3	third person
ACC	accusative
ADV	adverb
AUX	auxiliary
DAT	dative
DEF	definite
EC	embedded clause
ERG	ergative
EXPL	expletive
F	feminine
FOC	focus
GEN	genitive
IMP	imperative
INF	infinitive
LIC	licensor
M	masculine
MC	main clause
N	neuter
NEG	negation
NOM	nominative
NPI	negative polarity item
OBJ	object
OV	object<verb
PL	plural
PPI	positive polarity item
PRT	particle
PRS	present
PST	past
PTCP	participle
REFL	reflexive
REL	relativizer/relative pronoun
SG	singular
SOV	subject<object<verb
SUB	subject
SUBJ	subjunctive
SVO	subject<verb<object
V1	verb first
V2	verb second
V-final	verb-final
VO	verb<object

https://doi.org/10.1515/9783110725018-206

1 Introduction

What you see is not what you get, this slogan summarizes the central message that runs through this book. It refers to catchphrases used in computing to distinguish different text-editing systems. Two concepts are frequently opposed. Editors that directly display the final output, like MS-Word, are so-called *what you see is what you get*-editors. Other systems, like LaTeX, require the user to specify the semantic structure and properties of the content by instructions in a markup language. The final output is only perceivable after compiling the code, i. e. the visual feedback of the editor and the printer output may differ significantly. Consequently, these systems are called *what you get is what you mean*-editors. What is the connection to this book? The core of this work is a hypothesis stating that the surface position of the finite verb in verb second (V2) clauses (*what you see*) is not the position in which the finite verb is interpreted (*what you get*). It is now commonly accepted among linguists that the V2-order is a derived order stemming from a transformation of the V-final base order. To my knowledge, Josef Bayer was the first one to observe that finite verbs that appear in the second position of the clause must be interpreted in their clause-final base position in order to comply with well-accepted principles of grammar. He also pointed out that this reconstruction of the finite verb into its base position should be reflected in on-line sentence comprehension. In the tradition of generative grammar such a discrepancy between surface position and underlying interpretation appears very commonly. In the realm of on-line processing, however, this assumption becomes highly significant. Not so much because of the general idea that an element is (re-)interpreted at a distance – a mechanism which is well-accepted for nominal elements in so-called *filler-gap dependencies* – but because the deviation from strict left-to-right processing involves the core element of the clause, the finite verb, which specifies the argument structure, event type, etc. It is hard to believe that the human language processor would not make use of such central information although it is available. This monograph presents a critical investigation of this *V2-Reconstruction Hypothesis* and the consequences for V2-structures. It focuses mainly on German but connections to other V2-languages are made throughout the argumentation. The investigations are carried out on two linguistic areas: grammar and sentence processing. Accordingly, the book is divided into two major parts. In the following, I give a brief outlook of the content of the individual chapters.

Chapter 2 provides the general background for the investigation of the V2-phenomenon by illustrating its three main properties: First, V2-order constitutes a movement dependency between the base position of the verb and the V2-position. Second, V2-movement applies exceptionless, i. e. it cannot be suspended. Third,

https://doi.org/10.1515/9783110725018-001

V2-movement targets one specific position in the left periphery of the clause. The chapter closes with a brief summary of the most important analyses of the V2-phenomenon.

Chapter 3 introduces the basic assumption of what builds the core of this publication, i. e. the V2-Reconstruction Hypothesis. It states that V2-movement targets only the finiteness features of the finite verb, which are represented by inflectional affixes. The lexical part of the verb only moves along because the affixes cannot move on their own. As a consequence, the lexical part has to be reconstructed into its clause-final base position where it is interpreted. Two groups of evidence are presented in support of the V2-Reconstruction Hypothesis: First, I show that the V2-position is systematically filled with surface elements which must not be interpreted and second, I present evidence which indicates that the finite verb has to be interpreted in its base position.

Chapter 4 provides the general background for the experimental investigations by introducing the basic properties of on-line language comprehension with a focus on the syntactic domain. I argue that deviation from strictly incremental processing, as assumed by the V2-Reconstruction Hypothesis, occurs regularly and results in one of two different processing strategies: anticipatory analysis with potential subsequent repairs, or delayed processing. A comparison with well-established manifestations of these two strategies indicates that V2-clauses adhere to delayed processing, as assumed under the V2-Reconstruction Hypothesis.

Chapter 5 provides more specific background for the experimental investigation by reviewing previous findings regarding the processing of the core argument structure in German sentences. Additionally, I review on-line processing experiments on thematic structure, attachment ambiguities and scope computing in German the results of which suggest that verb-related effects only appear at the clause-final position, as predicted by the V2-Reconstruction Hypothesis.

Chapter 6 presents four self-paced reading experiments that test predictions of the V2-Reconstruction Hypothesis concerning on-line sentence processing. The experiments use three different phenomena, NPI-licensing, infinitive selection and thematic-role assignment, to detect the temporal profile of the processing influence of the V2-element. Grammaticality contrasts that are dependent on the interpretation of the finite verb in V2-position show up at the reconstruction site of the verb conforming to the predictions of the V2-Reconstruction Hypothesis.

In Chapter 7, I examine three details of the reconstruction process: First, the special status of subject-initial V2-clauses might be attributable to a more efficient processing route. Second, I argue that verb reconstruction is realized by inserting incoming units directly before the verb, instead of cascadically lowering the verb. Third, I argue that once unambiguous cues for the clause-final base position are encountered, the parse is completed and the core meaning cannot be altered again, as evidenced by restrictions on extraposition.

Chapter 8 summarizes the findings of this contribution. The summary also provides conclusions and open questions for the individual parts and the monograph as a whole.

Additionally, this publication is accompanied by an online appendix that contains supplementary material to the psycholinguistic experiments reported here. There you will find: first, all items and instruction texts, second, the experiment scripts and all stimuli required to replicate the experiments, and third, the results and the scripts used for statistical analysis.

Part I: The grammatical perspective on V2-movement

2 The Syntax of V2

The basis of the verb second phenomenon can be informally described as in (1).

(1) **Description of the verbs second linearization:**
In V2-clauses, the finite verb occupies the second position of the clause.

Obviously, the situation is a little more complicated. The V2-phenomenon can be divided into three core issues: The position of the finite verb, specifying the preverbal element(s) and explaining its root character. The first two issues will be addressed in this chapter. The third one can only be touched because it is a complex topic on its own and not central to the issues in the following chapters of this monograph.

The first section will discuss the core phenomenon and also some cases in which the V2-requirement conflicts with other areas of the grammar. Section 2.2 shows that, due to discourse-pragmatic reasons, sentences may actually show reduced or extended V2-structures. The data in the first two sections is presented with as little theoretical assumptions as possible because these are the empirical observations that must be covered by all syntactic theories. Only in Section 2.3 will I discuss analyses of the generative grammar tradition and highlight the explanatory benefit of the respective accounts.

2.1 Observations: The facts about V2

In this section, I present the basic observations regarding word order regularities in German, representative for V2-languages in general. This is followed by more elaborate discussion of cases in which finite verbs cannot move into the V2-position (Section 2.1.3) and elements that cannot precede the finite verb in V2-clauses (Section 2.1.4). The discussion will show that the regularities of V2 are never suspended but may conflict with other grammatical restrictions.

2.1.1 The core cases: V2, V1 and V-final

V2-order can be best illustrated with declarative and *wh*-interrogative clauses, as in (2) and (3). Either one of the clausal constituents may precede the finite verb, such as the subject in (2a), the object in (2b), or the adverb in (2c). The same holds for the corresponding *wh*-interrogatives in (3).

https://doi.org/10.1515/9783110725018-002

(2) Declaratives

a. Der Junge hat gestern den Kuchen gegessen.
the boy has yesterday the cake eaten
'The boy has eaten the cake yesterday.'

b. Den Kuchen hat der Junge gestern gegessen.
the cake has the boy yesterday eaten
'The boy has eaten the cake yesterday.'

c. Gestern hat der Junge den Kuchen gegessen.
yesterday has the boy the cake eaten
'Yesterday, the boy has eaten the cake.'

(3) *Wh*-interrogatives

a. Was hat der Junge gestern gegessen?
what has the boy yesterday eaten
'What did the boy eat yesterday?'

b. Wer hat gestern den Kuchen gegessen?
who has yesterday the cake eaten
'Who ate the cake yesterday?'

c. Wann hat der Junge den Kuchen gegessen?
when has the boy the cake eaten
'When did the boy eat the cake?'

Two other core sentence types, polar interrogative and imperative rather show V1-patterns with the finite verb in sentence-initial position, as in (4) and (5).[1]

(4) Polar interrogatives

a. Hat der Junge gestern den Kuchen gegessen?
has the boy yesterday the cake eaten
'Did the boy eat the cake yesterday?'

b. # Der Junge hat gestern den Kuchen gegessen?
the boy has yesterday the cake eaten

c. # Gestern hat der Junge den Kuchen gegessen?
yesterday has the boy the cake eaten

1 The sentences in (4b–4d) are syntactically well-formed strings and may even receive an interrogative interpretation. However, these are so-called *declarative questions* that have to be differentiated from true polar interrogatives because they require a very specific utterance context (see Gunlogson 2002, Truckenbrodt 2006a: 259).

d. # Den Kuchen hat der Junge gestern gegessen?
the cake has the boy yesterday eaten

(5) Imperatives

a. Iss heute den Kuchen!
eat today the cake
'Eat the cake today!'

b. * Den Kuchen iss heute!
the cake eat today

c. * Heute iss den Kuchen!
today eat the cake

In subordinate clauses, the finite verb appears only in the clause-final position and not in the corresponding V2/V1-positions, as illustrated in (6).[2]

(6) a. Es it gut, dass der Junge ⟨*hat⟩ gestern den Kuchen gegessen ⟨hat⟩.
it is good that the boy has yesterday the cake eaten has
'It is good that the boy ate the cake yesterday.'

b. Es ist klar, was ⟨*hat⟩ der Junge gestern gegessen ⟨hat⟩.
It is clear what has the boy yesterday eaten has
'It is clear what the boy ate yesterday.'

c. Es ist unklar, ob ⟨*hat⟩ der Junge ⟨*hat⟩ gestern den Kuchen gegessen ⟨hat⟩.
it is unclear whether has the boy has yesterday the cake eaten has
'It is unclear whether the boy ate the cake yesterday.'

This short descriptive sample suffices to conclude that the verb position in German (and other V2-languages) is clause-type specific. We observe a major difference between main and subordinate clauses: In subordinate clauses, the finite verb appears uniformly in the clause-final position. In main clauses, the verb appears always in the left periphery, either in first or second position. In German linguistics, these two verb positions are taken to be the anchor points for a descriptive model that divides the sentences into three fields (Drach 1937): The slot preceding the finite verb in V1/V2-clauses is called the *prefield*, the slot between the finite

2 I will exclude the discussion of embedded V2-clauses because that phenomenon is still discussed controversially and does, as far as I can see, not contribute anything relevant to the central objective of this investigation, the processing of V2. The interested reader is referred to Heycock (2006) and Freywald (2014).

verb and the non-finite verbs in V1/V2-clauses is called the *middle field*, and the slot following the right-peripheral verbal element in main and embedded clauses is called the *postfield*. In the following, I will refer to these fields descriptively in order to avoid specific syntactic analysis, before discussing those in Section 2.3.

(7)

prefield	**V2**	**middle field**	**non-finite verb**	**postfield**
Gestern	hat	der Junge den Kuchen	gegessen,	nachdem ...
Yesterday	has	the boy the cake	eaten	after ...

2.1.2 The prefield: What precedes the finite verb?

Above, we have already seen that the second position is not defined in terms of morphological words but in terms of syntactic constituents, which is also illustrated in (8). The object precedes the finite verb, irrespective of its length.

(8) [Den (mit Schkolade überzogenen) Kuchen] hat der Junge gestern
the with chocolate covered cake has the boy yesterday
gegessen.
eaten
'The boy ate the (with chocolate covered) cake yesterday.'

Consequently, also larger constituents such as VPs and subordinate clauses may occupy the prefield, as is shown in (9).

(9) a. [Gestern den Kuchen gegessen] hat der Junge (sicherlich nicht).
yesterday the cake eaten has the boy surely not
'Yesterday, the boy did definitely not eat the cake.'

b. [Weil er Hunger hatte] hat der Junge gestern den Kuchen
because he hunger had has the boy yesterday the cake
gegessen.
eaten
'The boy ate the cake yesterday because he was hungry.'

In Section 2.1.4, I will discuss restrictions on prefield elements. Some specific forms of complex prefields are presented in Section 2.2.3.

2.1.3 Restrictions on V2-movement

The most robust restriction on V2-movement is a corollary of the V2-generalization: Only finite verbs move, non-finite verbs do not. This restriction appears to be inviolable. Even though German exhibits a range of non-finite matrix clause constructions, as discussed in Gärtner (2013), none of these show a non-finite verb in V2-position. Therefore we may conclude that being some kind of independent clause is not sufficient to trigger verb movement. A necessary requirement for V2-movement is finiteness.

Among the finite clauses, two different restrictions on V2-movement have been observed: An external restriction in which the finite verb is 'trapped' within the surface scope of a comparative operator and cannot be moved. Second, an internal restriction: Complex lexemes with more than one particle attached to the base exhibit a morphological structure that leads to a dilemmatic conflict of morphosyntactic well-formedness conditions under verb movement.

2.1.3.1 External constraint: Configurational restrictions in scope taking comparative operators

Haider (2010: 64–65) observed that verbs which are the target of an adverbial comparison operator cannot move out of the surface scope of such an operator. The verb *verdreifachen* 'triple' is perfectly acceptable as a finite verb in the V-final embedded clause in (10a), and as a participle in the main clause in (10b), irrespective of the presence of the comparative adverbial *mehr als* 'more than'. However, if the verb leaves the surface scope of the comparative operator the structure becomes ungrammatical, irrespective of whether the movement targets the V2-position, as in (10c), or the prefield as in (10d). Additionally, example (10e) shows that movement of the verb is not banned per se. If the comparative operator is topicalized together with the verb, the structure is completely acceptable. The same results are obtained for the equative operator *so gut wie* (*verdoppelt*) 'as much as (doubled)' (Haider 2010: 65).

(10) German

a. ... dass sich der Verlust (mehr als) verdreifachte (soweit ich das
that itself the deficit more than tripled insofar I that
beurteilen kann)
assess can

b. Dann hat sich der Verlust (mehr als) verdreifacht ~~hat~~ (soweit ich das
then has itself the deficit more than tripled insofar I that
beurteilen kann).
assess can

c. Dann verdreifachte sich der Verlust (*mehr als) ~~verdreifachte~~ (soweit
then tripled itself the deficit more than insofar
ich das beurteilen kann).
I that assess can

d. Verdreifacht hat sich der Verlust (*mehr als) ~~verdreifacht hat~~ (soweit
tripled has itself the deficit more than insofar
ich das beurteilen kann)
I that assess can

e. [Mehr als verdreifacht] hat sich der Verlust ~~mehr als verdreifacht hat~~
more than tripled has itself the deficit
(soweit ich das beurteilen kann).
insofar I that assess can
'The deficit has more than tripled, at least as far as I can tell'

A cross-lingustic comparison shows that such comparative structures are movement-phobic also in other, non-V2 languages. The English and Italian paradigms in (11) and (12), respectively, show exactly the same pattern as their German equivalents. As soon as the target of comparison is not within the scope domain of the operator in the surface form, the structure is ungrammatical. Example (11a) shows that a verb like *triple* is fine in the surface scope of an operator like *more than.* (11b) shows that a verb may be fronted, but fronting out of the operator scope in (11c) is deviant.

(11) ENGLISH

a. The value (has) [far more than merely tripled].

b. (He said that the value would triple, and) tripled_1 the value has indeed ~~trippled~~$_1$ within one week.

c. * (He said that the value would more than triple, and) tripled_1 the value has indeed [more than ~~tripled~~$_1$] within one week.

(Haider 2000b: 159, Haider 2010: 64)

Example (12a) presents a similar configuration with the Italian verb *triplicare* "triple" in the scope of a comparative operator. Destroying the surface scope relation results in unacceptability irrespective of whether the verb is fronted as in (12b) or the operator phrase is moved as in (12c).

(12) ITALIAN

a. Il valore si è [molto più che solo triplicato].
the value REFL is much more than only tripled

b. *Il valore si triplica$_1$ [molto più che solo ~~triplica~~$_1$].
the value REFL tripled much more than only

c. *Il valore [molto più che solo]$_1$ si ~~molto più che solo~~$_1$ triplica.
The value much more than only REFL tripled

(Haider 2000b: 159)

Additional support for the assumption that this ban is specific to the comparative environment can be obtained from the inspection of comparative constructions involving non-verbal elements, as illustrated for adjectives in (13), for adverbials in (14), and for DPs[3] in (15).

(13) a. Dann war Christopher mehr als betrunken ~~war~~.
then was Christopher more than drunk
'Then Christopher was more than drunk.'

b. Betrunken$_1$ war Christopher (*mehr als) ~~betrunken~~$_1$ ~~war~~.
drunk was Christopher more than

c. [Mehr als betrunken]$_1$ war Christopher ~~betrunken~~$_1$ ~~war~~.
more than drunk was Christopher

(14) a. Dann wird dieser Kurs mehr als doppelt gewertet ~~wird~~.
then will this course more than double valued
'Then this course will count more than double.'

3 The comparison actually does not target the noun but the numeral. A variant exists that looks like a possible extraction case. However, the fronted noun must be in the plural, see (i.a). Example (i.b) shows that the plural noun cannot originate in the position following the numeral *eine* 'one'. Example (i.c) shows that the plural stems from a position directly following the comparator *mehr* 'more'. These comparative constructions seem to involve two instances of the lexeme MUTTER 'mother' of which maximally one can be spelled out, as illustrated in (i.d). Only the higher instance can be dislocated, the lower one has to remain in the operator scope even if it is not spelled out.

(i) a. *Mütter/ *Mutter hat Christopher offensichtlich mehr als eine.*
mothers mother has Christopher obviously more than one

b. *Dann hat Christopher offensichtlich mehr als eine *Mütter/ Mutter.*
Then has Christopher obviously more than one mothers mother

c. *Dann hat Christopher offensichtlich mehr Mütter als eine (*Mutter).*
then has Christopher obviously more mothers than one mother

d. *Mütter$_1$ hat Christopher offensichtlich mehr ~~Mütter~~$_1$ als eine ~~Mutter~~.*
mothers has Christopher obviously more that one mother
'Christopher has obviously more than one mother.'

b. Doppelt$_1$ wird dieser Kurs (*mehr als) ~~doppelt~~$_1$ gewertet ~~wird~~.
double will this course more than valued

c. [Mehr als doppelt]$_1$ wird dieser Kurs ~~mehr als doppelt~~$_1$ gewertet
more than double will this course valued
~~wird~~.

(15) a. Dann hat Christopher offensichtlich mehr als eine Mutter ~~hat~~.
then has Christopher obviously more than one mother
'Then Christopher has obviously more than one mother.'

b. [Eine Mutter]$_1$ hat Christopher offensichtlich (*mehr als) ~~eine Mutter~~$_1$
one mother has Christopher obviously more than
~~hat~~.

c. [Mehr als eine Mutter]$_1$ hat Christopher offensichtlich ~~mehr als eine Mutter~~$_1$
more than one mother has Christopher obviously
~~hat~~.

Thus, there seems to be a cross-categorial and cross-linguistic restriction on extracting the target of comparison out of the surface scope of the comparative operator. This restriction is arguably so strong that it cannot be violated, not even by a generalized movement operation such as V2-movement.

The following observation sheds some more light on this ban. I assume that the comparison operator is a focus-sensitive operator. The resulting configuration is therefore an *association with focus*-construction (see Section 3.3.1) in which the interpretation changes according to the focus-background structure, as illustrated in (16). The operator needs a focused constituent in its scope.

(16) a. Christopher hat sich mehr als (*nur*) [eín]$_{FOC}$ Auto gekauft. (mindestens
Christopher has REFL more than just one car bought
zwei)
'Christopher bought more than just óne car. (At least two.)'

b. Christopher hat sich mehr als (*nur*) [ein Aúto]$_{FOC}$ gekauft. (Dieser
Christopher has REFL more that just one car bought
Jaguar ist ein Stück Zeitgeschichte)
'Christopher bough more than just a cár. (This Jaguar is a piece of history.)'

The ban on movement, therefore, can be reduced to a requirement of surface focus/accent marking. To demonstrate this, let us first look at the derived/metaphorical use of *mehr als* 'more than', as in (17). In (17a) the whole particle verb *anschreien* 'shout at' is in the surface scope of the operator. Hence, the alternatives to the predicate may include another predicate such as *schubsen* 'shove', as indicated in the continuation in (17a). In (17b), the verbal part is moved to the V2-position and only the particle remains in the surface scope position of the operator. Even though the verb meaning remains intact, the focus-sensitive operator operates on different semantic alternatives, as indicated by the continuations in (17b). A felicitous continuation can only refer to a more extreme alternative of a shouting event. An event of a different type, such as shoving, is excluded. This indicates that the surface element constitutes the basis for the computation of focus alternatives by the focus-sensitive operator *mehr als* 'more than'.

(17) a. Er hat ihn *mehr als* (*nur*) [án-geschrien]$_{\text{FOC}}$. (Er hat ihn mindestens
he has him more than just at-shouted he has him at least
geschubst)
shoved
'He has more than (just) shouted at him. (He has at least shoved him.)'

b. Er schreit ihn *mehr als* (*nur*) [án]$_{\text{FOC}}$ ~~schreit~~. (Er wird ihn #mindestens
he shouts him more than just at he will him at least
schubsen/ regelrecht zusammen-brüllen)
shove downright together-shout
'He is more than (just) shouting AT him. (He will #at least shove him/ downright shout him down.)'

Two predictions follow from the hypothesis that only the surface focus exponent is constitutive for focus-sensitive operators such as *mehr als* 'more than' to generate the relevant alternatives: First, the surface focus exponent must not be null. Second, a meaningful focus alternative to the surface focus exponent must exist. The first prediction is obviously borne out, as illustrated by examples (10)–(15) above. The consequences of the second prediction can be illustrated with idiomatic constructions such as the particle verb *anfangen* 'start' (lit. 'on-catch') in (18). If the whole verb occurs in the focus of the operator, as in (18a), the relevant alternatives depict events that are well beyond the starting point. If the verb is split up by V2-movement, as in (18b), the focus alternatives are computed only with respect to the particle. However, alternative particles do not lead to felicitous alternatives to the idiomatic meaning.

(18) a. Er hat *mehr als* (*nur*) [án-gefangen]$_{FOC}$. (Er ist schon beinahe
He has more than just on-catched he is already almost
fertig.)
done
'He has more than just started. (He's already almost done.)'

b. ??/* Er fängt *mehr als* (*nur*) [án]$_{FOC}$ ~~fängt~~. (#Er wird es auch
He catched more than just on he will it also
beenden)
finish

A similar observation can be made for the idiom *Süßholz raspeln* 'sweet-talk' (lit. 'rasp licorice') in (19). If the entire predicate complex is within the scope of the operator, as in (19a), the alternatives are generated with respect to the idiomatic meaning. In (19b), on the other hand, only the DP of the idiomatic predicate complex is within the surface scope of the operator. Hence, the focus alternatives range only over things that can be rasped, which do not constitute felicitous alternatives to the idiomatic meaning. Example (19c) shows that without the focus-sensitive operator *mehr als*, such predicates may be split by V2-movement without blocking the idiomatic meaning.

(19) a. Er hat mehr als (nur) [Süßholz geraspelt]$_{FOC}$ ~~hat~~. (Er hat sich
He has more than just licorice rasped he has himself
richtig an sie rangeschmissen.)
actually at her at-thrown
'He has more than just sweet-talked. (He actually flinged himself at her.)'

b. Er raspelte mehr als (nur) [Süßholz]$_{FOC}$ ~~raspelte~~. (#Er hat sich
he rasped more that just licorice he has himself
richtig an sie rangeschmissen.)
actually at her at-thrown
'He rasped more than just licorice. (#He actually flinged himself at her.)'

c. Er raspelte (schon den ganzen Tag) Süßholz ~~raspelte~~ (um die alte
he rasped already the whole day licorice for the old
Dame zum Verkauf zu bewegen).
lady to the sale to persuade
'He has been sweet-talking the whole day to persuade the old lady to sell.'

This discussion showed that the restriction on movement out of the surface scope of operators such as *mehr als* 'more than' is so general that it applies to all syntactic categories. Second, the restriction is not a general ban on movement: Movement of a part of the predicate, such as the verbal stem of the particle verb in (17b), is possible. Third, the restriction only excludes movement of the whole focus exponent or parts of a non-compositional element because no meaningful alternatives can be computed for empty elements or non-compositional parts. In essence, even though V2-movement is constrained by this restriction, it is not V2-specific.

2.1.3.2 Internal constraint: Morphological dilemmas of complex verbs

Two different classes of *immobile verbs* can be distinguished in German (and Dutch). These are double-particle verbs and back-transformations. In contrast to the examples of the previous section, the constraint on movement arises from the internal (morphological) structure of the respective predicates. Both classes involve a *morphological* dilemma because the relevant verbs cannot be split up and cannot move as a whole (Haider 1993: 65).

In V2-contexts, German particle verbs split the verbal stem from the particle. The finite verbal part moves to the V2-position and the particle remains behind, as illustrated in (20).

(20) *an-kündigen* 'announce' (lit. 'on-announce')

a. ... dass du uns ankündigst
   that you uns on.announce
   '... that you announce us'

b. Du kündigst$_1$ uns an-t_1.
   you announce us on
   'You announce us.'

c. *Du ankündigst$_1$ uns t_1.
   you on.announce us

There are a few particles, such as *vor* 'before' that combine productively with verbs, even with verbs which are already particle verbs. The result is a double particle verb with two adjacent particles, such as *vor-an-kündigen* 'pre-announce' in (21a). These verbs induce a dilemma in V2-environments: The verb cannot move alone, leaving behind both particles (21b), nor can any of the particles move with the verb (21c–21d), nor can both particles move with the verb (21e), nor can the V2-constraint be ignored and the verb remain in-situ (21f) (Haider 2010: 58–61).

(21) a. ... wenn du uns vorankündigst.
   if you us pre-announce
   '... if you pre-announce us.'

b. * Du kündigst$_1$ uns voran~~kündigst~~$_1$.

c. * Du ankündigst$_1$ uns vor~~ankündigst~~$_1$.

d. * Du vorkündigst$_1$ uns ~~vorankündigst~~$_1$.

e. * Du vorankündigst$_1$ uns ~~vorankündigst~~$_1$.

f. * Du uns vorankündigst.

(see Haider 2010: 60)

Haider (2010: 60–61) lists a number of other combinations to illustrate the productiveness of the pattern, see (22).

(22) a. vor + abdrucken → vorabdrucken 'preprint' (lit. 'pre-off-print')

b. vor + anmelden → voranmelden 'preregister' (lit. 'pre-an-nounce')

c. um + einteilen → umeinteilen 'reorganize' (lit. 're-in-deal')

Haider (2010: 61) also includes examples (23a) and (23b) featuring the initial particle *mit* 'with'. Such examples are exceptional because *mit* is a rather free particle which is located in the right periphery of the middle field (see Bücker 2012: 209-214 for a characterization).[4] The exceptional status is exemplified in (24), showing that *mit* can easily separate from the particle verb without giving rise to this dilemma.

(23) a. mit + einsteigen → miteinsteigen 'get on together' (lit. 'with-in-step')

b. mit + ausdrucken → mitausdrucken 'print out jointly' (lit. 'with-out-print')

(24) a. Dann steigt doch einfach mit-ein~~steigt~~.
then step PRT simply with-in
'Then simply get on together (with the others).'

b. Andrea druckt mir das bereits mit-aus~~druckt~~.
Andrea prints for me that already with-out
'Andrea prints this already for me (jointly with her stuff).'

Moreover, *mit* 'with' may also attach to doubly prefixed verbs as shown in (25). As expected, the resulting complex is unproblematic in V-final position as in (25a), but results in the same dilemmatic situation in (25b) as the doubly prefixed verb alone. Additionally, *mit* must always be the leftmost particle in such constructions.[5]

(25) mit + voranmelden 'jointly preregister' (lit. 'with-pre-announce')

---

4 Sebstian Bücking (p. c.) made me aware of this with his talk at the Universität zu Köln, 10 January 2018.

5 If the meaning allows it, the particle *mit* may occur two times, as in (i), even though this construction is marked because the simpler form with only one *mit* would suffice in this case.

a. Kannst du mich morgen bitte mit-voranmelden? Ich hab keine Zeit.
can you me tomorrow plaese with.pre.an.nounce I have no time
'Can you preregister for me too tomorrow? I don't have time.'

b. * Meldest du mich morgen bitte mit-voran? Ich hab keine Zeit.
nonce you me tomorrow plaese with-pre.an I have no time
'Can you preregister for me too tomorrow? I don't have time.'

I cannot think of a plausible reason why the movement of the finite verb stem should be constraint directly. An explanation of this immobility must rather focus on the clause-final position: Somehow it seems possible to strand one verbal particle alone, but not two particles together (Haider 2010). Clearly, this account remains rather descriptive, which, however, suffices for now.

The second class of verbs, *pseudo-compounds*, shows a very similar pattern (Freywald & Simon 2007).[6] All of these lexemes have a verbal head, the rightmost constituent in German. The first constituent can be of various categories, as shown in (26). The examples illustrate that the verbal lexemes are derived from nominal forms that contained a deverbal head. This modified head is back-transformed[7], which results in a complex verb.

(26) a. N+V
Gen+manipulation → genmanipulieren
gene+manipulation gene.manipulate
'genetic engineering' → 'do genetic engineering'

b. V+V
Mäh+drescher → mähdreschen
mow+thresher mow.thresh
'harvester' → 'use the harvester'

(i) *Wenn du eh schon zum Kiosk gehst, kannst du mir dann auch noch was mit-mitbringen?*
if you PRT already to the kiosk go can you me then also something with-with.bring
'If you are going to the kiosk anyway, could you bring also something for me?'

6 An observation that dates back to Höhle (2018: 370–372).

7 Freywald & Simon (2007) differentiate between *back-conversion* and back-transformation. The only difference is that in conversion no affix is added or removed.

c. A+V
Erst+wähler → erstwählen
first+voter first.vote
'first-time voter' → 'vote for the first time'

d. P+V
Zwischen+landung → zwischenlanden
between+landing between.land
'stopover' → 'stop over'

(Freywald & Simon 2007: 2–3)

However, as illustrated in (27), not all back-transformed verbs are immobile (Fortmann 2007).

(27) a. Theo gewährleistet seine pünktliche Ankunft.
Theo warranty+supplies his punctual arrival
'Theo ensures his punctual arrival.'

b. Eberhardt handhabt Messer und Gabel mit einigem Geschick.
Eberhardt hand+has knive and fork with considerable skill
'Eberhardt handles knive and fork with considerable skill.'

c. Man schlussfolgert oft das Falsche.
one conclusion+deduce often the wrong
'One often reaches the wrong conclusion.'

(Fortmann 2007: 9)

Moreover, Freywald & Simon (2007) present results from a questionnaire study indicating that some of the alleged immobile verbs are not categorically refused by native speakers. Some of them are rated almost as good as the *unproblematic* clause-final variants. Additionally, the decision concerning the (non-)separability of the two constituents of the pseudo-compound seems to be influenced by the category of the first constituent. Prepositions, as in (26d), are more likely to be separated and remain in the clause-final bases position. This is not surprising, considering that the particles of most classical particle verbs are at least homophone variants of prepositions. Furthermore, Freywald & Simon (2007) report that their participants divide into two groups, one accepting back-transformations in V2-contexts and others do not. It seems plausible that the speaker community establishes an acceptance for some verbs, as the ones in (27), over time.[8]

8 The verb *teilnehmen* 'partake' (lit. part+take) seems to be a case in point that most probably results from a back-transformation. Splitting the nominal part, as illustrated in (i), is completely unmarked.

Therefore, the immobility of pseudo-compounds can be reduced to the assumption that the lexical entry of the verbs in question is somewhat defective, which only surfaces when the speaker has to make a decision about separating the verb stem from the modification or not. It also appears possible that lexemes that are currently immobile become mobile in the future.

Comparable cases of immobility of the finite verb due to multiple particle prefixing and back-transformation are also observed in Dutch (Booij 1990, Koopman 1995). However, Vikner (2005) points out that immobile complex verbs are non-existent in Danish despite Danish being a V2-language. He argues that such immobility only occurs in OV-languages like Dutch and German. Vikner (2005) attributes this difference between VO and OV languages to the linearization differences of the resulting phrases. In German and Dutch, particle verbs and back-transformation exhibit a head-final structure, [PRT<V] and [N<V], because the VP and noun composition is head-final. In Danish, noun composition is also head-final resulting in [N<V]-structured back-transformations. Danish particle verbs, on the other hand, show a [V<PRT] pattern due to the VP being head-initial. Interestingly, however, double-particle verbs in Danish show a [PRT<PRT<V] order, which resembles the linearization of noun composition (including back-transformation) and distinguishes double-particle verbs formally from particle verbs. The head-final complexes, back-transformation and double-particle verbs therefore form an inseparable word that moves always as a whole. In V2-contexts, normal particle verbs in Danish split up but retain their relative order (V<PRT), in contrast to German and Dutch. In conclusion it seems that in OV-languages like German and Dutch, the uncertainty of the morphological status is caused by the form identity of the output of morphological and syntactic processes in these languages.[9]

In sum, internal constraints on V2-movement have been identified as conditions on the morphological form, which can be paraphrased as follows: V2-movement is not restricted but the outcome may violate constraints on the morphological representation. We have seen that back-transformations are not categorically excluded from V2-movement and may show each of the two options, movement as a complex or splitting up. Furthermore, it can be expected that the

---

(i) *Er nahm an der Veranstaltung teil~~nahm~~.*
he took at the event part
'He partook in the event.'

9 Following the structure building account of Haider (2012), modification of head-initial phrases is restricted to a single element whereas the modification of head-final phrases is basically unbounded. Multiple-particle verbs are therefore excluded in verb-initial languages.

status of back-transformed lexemes changes over time and that they "develop" unmarked mobility. The comparison with Dutch as another OV-language and Danish as an VO-type V2-language suggested that the OV-property is an important factor for the phenomenon of immobile verbs. In comparison to the generalized ban on movement in the comparative configuration, which was discussed in the previous section, the problems of this section are specifically tied to V2-movement: The separation of verbal parts and particles arises only under head movement. Movement of non-finite forms into the prefield are fine, as shown in (28).

(28) a. Voranmelden kannst du dich ja trotzdem ~~voranmelden kannst~~.
preannounce can you yourself PRT anyway
'You could preannounce yourself anyway.'

b. Genmanipulieren dürfen wir nur wenige Planzen ~~genmanipulieren~~
do genetic engineering may we only few plants
~~dürfen~~.
'We are allowed to do genetic engineering only with few plants.'

2.1.3.3 Summary

I presented two types of restrictions on verb movement, an external and an internal constraint. The external constraint is a generalized ban on moving elements out of a comparative construction if the result is an exponent that does allow the computation of meaningful focus alternatives. This restriction turned out to be not V2-specific because it applies to phrasal movement and head movement alike, applies to other syntactic categories apart from verbs, and is also observed in non-V2 languages. The internal constraint is a specific consequence of applying head movement to double-particle verbs and back-transformations. Such movement leads to separation of the verbal part, stranding the remaining part in the V-final base position. This (non-)separation may lead to conflicts of morphological requirements thereby rendering the output of the head movement unacceptable. Such conflicts seem only to arise in V2-languages of the OV-type like German and Dutch.

I conclude that V2-movement is generalized movement. In specific cases its application can conflict with well-formedness conditions of other grammatical areas. Crucially, however, V2-movement cannot be suspended in those cases. Instead speakers are forced to insert an auxiliary to avoid movement of the problematic element, as in (29b). In any case they can never use the finite verb in the clause-final base position of the matrix clause, as in (29c).

(29) a. ?/??/* Wir genmanipulieren diese Pflanze ~~genmanipulieren~~.
we genetic engineer this plant
'We modify this plant by genetic engineering'

b. Wir haben diese Pflanze genmanipuliert ~~haben~~.
we have this plant genetic engineered
'We modified this plant by genetic engineering'

c. * Wir diese Pflanze genmanipulieren.
we this plant genetic engineer
'We modify this plant by genetic engineering'

2.1.4 Restrictions on prefield elements

Above, I stated that any phrasal element may occupy the prefield. This generalization has to be qualified in two ways. In this section, I will show that some phrasal elements may not occupy the prefield, which seems to be subject to cross-linguistic variation. Cases in which apparent non-phrasal elements occur in the prefield will discussed in Section 2.2.

2.1.4.1 Negation

In German, negation is excluded from topicalization, as shown in (30a). It can only appear in the prefield as part of a larger constituent such as the VP, as in (30b).

(30) Christopher hat das Buch nicht gelesen.
Christopher has the book not read
'Christopher hasn't read the book.'

a. * Nicht$_1$ hat Christopher das Buch ~~nicht~~$_1$ gelesen.
not has Christopher the book read

b. [Das Buch nicht gelesen]$_1$ hat (nur) Christopher ~~das Buch nicht gelesen~~$_1$.
the book not read has only Christopher
'(Only) Christopher didn't read the book.'

Cross-lingustic comparison indicates that negation is not generally excluded from the sentence-initial position in V2-languages. In Swedish, negation can appear in preverbal position in declarative rejections, as in (31b), and in rejection questions, as in (32b). The difference in the felicity conditions between the unmarked position of the negation and the preverbal occurrence is far from trivial and the reader is referred to Seeliger (2015). Fronting of the negation is also possible in Icelandic, Norwegian, and Breton (Holmberg 2015: 350).

(31) SWEDISH: Rejections

a. Han kommer inte till mötet.
he comes not to the.meeting
'He isn't coming to the meeting.'

b. Inte kommer han till mötet.
Not comes he to the.meeting
'He isn't coming to the meeting.'

(Seeliger 2015: 576)

(32) SWEDISH: Rejecting questions

a. Han kommer inte till mötet?
He comes not to the.meeting
'Surely he isn't coming to the meeting?'

b. Inte kommer han till mötet?
Not comes he to the.meeting
'Surely he isn't coming to the meeting?'

(Seeliger 2015: 576–577)

Zeijlstra (2013) discusses two constructions in Dutch in which the negation can be topicalized, as shown in (33).[10]

(33) DUTCH

a. Ik had wel gezien dat Jan aankwam, maar $niet_1$ had ik ~~niet~~$_1$ gezien dat Eddy vertrok.
I had PRT seen that Jan arrived, but NEG had I seen that Eddy left
'I did see that Jan arrived, but I didn't see that Eddy left.'

b. Níet moeten in de lijst worden aangekruist de planten die je al hébt.
NEG must in the list be crossed the plants that you already have
'You must not mark the plants on the list that you already have.'

(Zeijlstra 2013: 893–894)

In O'odham (Papago), an OV-V2 language, the negation can also fill the prefield and precede the auxiliary, as in (34b). Interestingly, in contrast to German[11], the non-finite verb cannot be placed into the prefield and precede the negation, as in

10 Thanks to Heiko Seeliger (p. c.) for pointing that out.

11 An acceptable German equivalent is given in (i).

(34c), whereas example (34d) shows that fronting the verb is fine, without (crossing) the negation (Zepeda 1983: 8–9).[12]

(34) O'ODHAM
  a. ['I:da 'o'odham] 'o pi ñeok.
     this person AUX NEG speaking
     'This person is/was not speaking.'
  b. Pi 'o 'i:da 'o'odham ñeok.
     NEG AUX this person speaking
     'This person is/was not speaking.'
  c. *Ñeok 'o pi 'i:da 'o'odham .
     speaking AUX NEG this person
     'This person is/was not speaking.'
  d. Ñeok 'o 'i:da 'o'odham.
     speaking AUX this person
     'This person is/was speaking.'
  (Zepeda 1983: 8–9)

Three different explanations could cover these cross-linguistic differences: First, negation might be phrasal in some languages, such as Swedish and O'odham, whereas it is non-phrasal in others, such as German. This would allow to maintain the restriction that only phrasal elements occur in the prefield. Second, we might assume that negation is phrasal in all languages and there are independent reasons that restrict negation from being topicalized in German. Third, we might assume that negation is non-phrasal in all languages but there is a mechanism that exceptionally allows topicalization of these elements in languages such as Swedish and O'odham. I leave this open to future research but will come back to this issue in the summary below.

2.1.4.2 Discourse particles

Discourse particles in German cannot appear in the prefield (Zimmermann 2011: 2029, Bayer & Struckmeier 2017b: 7). This is illustrated for the discourse particles

---

(i) *Gesprochen$_1$ hat diese Person nicht ~~gesprochen~~$_1$.*
    spoken has this person not
    'This person has not spoken.'

12 It seems that the negation *pi* in O'odham has its base position right-adjacent to the second position auxiliary. Additionally, there seems to be a requirement that the negation must precede their target (see Zepeda 1983).

wohl and *doch* in (35a) and (35b). In contrast to negation, discourse particles do not move to the prefield as part of a larger unit either, as shown in (36).

(35) Christopher hat wohl/ doch seinem Vater zugehört.
Christopher has PRT PRT his father to-listen
'Christopher listened to his father.'

a. * Wohl hat Christopher ~~wohl~~ seinem Vater zugehört.
PRT has Christopher his father to-listen

b. * Doch hat Christopher ~~doch~~ seinem Vater zugehört.
PRT has Christopher his father to-listen

(36) a. * [Wohl/ Doch seinem Vater] hat Christopher ~~wohl/doch seinem Vater~~ zugehört.
PRT PRT his father has Christopher to-listen

b. * [Wohl/ Doch seinem Vater zugehört] hat Christopher ~~wohl/doch seinem Vater zugehört~~.
PRT PRT his father to-listen has Christopher

Many discourse particles have homophonous counterparts that indeed may occupy the sentence-initial position, as illustrated by the contrast of adverbial *vielleicht* 'perhaps' in (37) and the discourse particle in (38).

(37) *vielleicht* as an adverb

a. Renate ist vielleicht in die Oper gegangen
Renate is perhaps in the opera gone
'Perhaps, Renate went to the opera.'

b. Vielleicht ist Renate in die Oper gegangen.
perhaps is Renate in the opera gone
'Perhaps, Renate went to the opera.'

(Bayer & Struckmeier 2017b: 7, fn. 5)

(38) *vielleicht* as a discourse particle

a. Díe ist vielleicht eingebildet!
she is VIELLEICHT arrogant
'Boy, is shé arrogant!'

b. * Vielleicht ist díe eingebildet!
VIELLEICHT is she arrogant

(Bayer & Struckmeier 2017b: 7, fn. 5)

Zimmermann (2011: 2029) proposes that German discourse particles cannot appear in the prefield position because they cannot bear stress. This may explain why discourse particles do not appear in the prefield on their own but not why they cannot move as part of a larger phrase, as in (36). Additionally, in questions, discourse particles may be fronted along with the *wh*-expression, as in (39) (see Bayer & Trotzke 2015).

(39) a. Wer wohl ist zu spät gekommen?
b. Wie bloß konnte das passieren?

Furthermore, as Zimmermann (2011: 2031-2033) points out, discourse particles may appear in the left periphery in other languages, such as the Swedish particles *nog* and *visst* in (40) (see Scherf 2017).

(40) SWEDISH
Nog/ Visst läser Peter tidningen i köket.
NOG VISST reads Peter newspaper.DEF in kitchen.DEF
'Peter reads the newspaper in the kitchen.' (Scherf 2017: 80)

In sum, discourse particles are heavily restricted in their occurrence in the prefield. A possible explanation has been their inability to bear stress. Concerning the cross-linguistic variation it seems not clear if their distribution is due to their phrase structural status, i. e. being a head vs. a phrase.

2.1.4.3 Verbal particles

It is a well-known fact about German and Dutch that particle verbs may split up in V2-environments, moving the finite verb stem into the V2-position and leaving the particle behind, as shown in (41a) vs. (41b). Fronting the particle verb as a whole, as in (41c), is unproblematic, whereas fronting only the particle, as in (41d), is degraded.

(41) a. ... dass der Vater das Buch vorliest.
that the father the book reads out
'... that the father reads out the book.'

b. Der Vater liest das Buch vor~~liest~~.
the father reads the book out
'The father reads out the book.'

c. Vorgelesen$_2$ hat$_1$ der Vater das Buch ~~vorgelesen$_2$ hat$_1$~~.
read out has the father the book
'The father read out the book.'

d. * Vor$_2$ hat$_1$ der Vater das Buch ~~vor~~$_2$gelesen ~~hat~~$_1$.
out has the father the book read

However, as has been noted by Frey (2004) and discussed by Trotzke & Quaglia (2016) and Trotzke & Wittenberg (2017), some particle verbs allow an emphatic topicalization of the particle, as shown in (42).

(42) a. Rúnter hat sein Chef ihn vor allen Kollegen gemacht!
PRT(down) has his boss him in front of all colleagues made
'His boss put him down/heavily criticized him in front of all his colleagues.' (Trotzke & Quaglia 2016: 118)

b. Áuf hat Otto die Türe gemacht.
PRT(open) has Otto the door made
'Otto opened the door.' (Frey 2004: 32)

Trotzke & Quaglia (2016) argue that the ability to contrast the fronted particle with an alternative particle plays an important role in understanding this restriction.[13] In other words, it seems that it is not the syntactic properties that condition the fronting of the verbal particles but the pragmatic properties that are related to the prefield position.

2.1.4.4 Weak pronouns and expletives

In German, the prefield can be filled by a semantically empty expletive *es* 'there', which is form identical to the neuter pronoun *es* 'it'. The paradigm in (43) illustrates that the expletive can only appear in sentence-initial position, as in (43a), but not in the middle field, i. e. to the right of the V2-position, as in (43b–43d), or after the complementizer, as in (43e), (den Besten 1983: 66–69, Tomaselli 1986, Speyer 2009).

(43) a. Es kann nur eine Konstituente vor dem finiten Verb stehen.
EXPL can only one constituent before the finite verb stand
'Only one constituent may appear in front of the finite verb.'

b. Nur eine Konstituente kann (*es) vor dem finiten Verb stehen.
only one constituent can EXPL before the finite verb stand
'Only one constituent may appear in front of the finite verb.'

c. Wo kann (*es) nur eine Konstituente stehen?
where can EXPL only one constituent stand
'Where does only one constituent may appear?'

13 See also the discussion of examples (17b) and (18b) above.

d. Kann (*es) nur eine Konstituente vor dem finiten Verb stehen?
can EXPL only one constituent before the finite verb stand
'Does only one constituent may appear in front of the finite verb?'

e. ... dass (*es) nur eine Konstituente vor dem finiten Verb stehen
that EXPL only one constituent before the finite verb stand
kann.
can
'... that only one constituent may appear in front of the finite verb.'

The neuter pronoun *es* 'it' frequently appears in the prefield if it represents the subject of the main clause verb, irrespective of whether it is a non-referring element such as the subject of *weather*-verbs in (44) or a referential subject as in (45). The variants in (44b) and (45b) illustrate that these elements may appear in the middle field as well, in contrast to the prefield expletive.

(44) a. Es hat gestern geschneit.
it has yesterday snowed
'Yesterday, it snowed.'

b. Gestern hat es geschneit.
yesterday has it snowed
'Yesterday, it snowed.'

(45) a. Es hat auf dem Tisch gelegen.
it has on the table laid
'It laid on the table.'

b. Auf dem Tisch hat es gelegen.
on the table has it laid
'It laid on the table.'

However, it has been observed that the pronoun *es* may not appear in the prefield if it represents an object, as in (46a), whereas it is fine in the middle field as in (46b) (Travis 1991: 359).

(46) Gestern habe ich ein Buch gekauft.
'Yesterday, I bought a book.'

a. * Es hat mein Vater heute schon gelesen.
it has my father today already read

b. Mein Vater hat es heute schon gelesen.
my father has it today already read
'My father already read it today.'

Closer inspection, however, reveals that there are cases, such as (47), where object-*es* occurring in the prefield is perfectly acceptable (see Lenerz 1994: 162, Frey 2006b, Meinunger 2007).

(47) a. (Gestern bin ich erstmals ohnmächtig geworden.) Es hat zum
yesterday am I for the first time unconscious become it has to the
Glück niemand mitgekriegt.
luck nobody realized
'(Yesterday I fainted for the first time.) (Though) luckily, nobody realized it.'

b. (Wo kommt das Buch her?) Es muss doch jemand dahin gelegt
where comes the book from it must PRT someone there put
haben.
have
'(Where did this book come from?) Someone must have put it there.'

(Meinunger 2007: 555–557)

That the occurrences of *es* are not cases of expletive prefield-*es* can easily be diagnosed by looking at the subordinate clause variants of (47b): As indicated in (48a), the pronoun cannot be left out in the middle field. Moreover, placing the object-*es* after the subject, as in (48b), results in markedness. I suspect that, in order to form a felicitous answer, the pronoun must receive stress, which it cannot. Replacing it by a stressed DP, as in (48c) is fine again.

(48) Wo kommt denn das Buch her?
Where comes PRT the book from
'Where did this book come from?'

a. Ich vermute, dass *(es) jemand dort verloren hat.
I suppose that it somebody there lost has
'Is suppose that somebody has lost it there.'

b. #Ich vermute, dass jemand es dort verloren hat.
I suppose that somebody it there lost has
'Is suppose that somebody has lost it there.'

c. Ich vermute, dass jemand das Búch dort verloren hat.
I suppose that somebody the book there lost has
'Is suppose that somebody has lost the book there.'

Meinunger (2007) observed that the crucial factor for the acceptability of object-*es* in the prefield is the specificity of the subject. With an indefinite unspecific subject as in (49a), object-*es* is fine but with a definite specific subject as in (49b), it is unacceptable and only the demonstrative *das* 'that' is acceptable.

(49) (Wo kommt das Buch her?)
where comes the book from
'Where did this book come from?'

a. Das/ Es muss jemand hier verloren haben.
that it must someone here lost have
'Someone must have lost that/it here.'

b. Das/ *Es muss der Professor hier verloren haben.
that it must the professor here lost have
'The professor must have lost that/it here.'

Similarly, other non-referential pronouns such as the lexical reflexives in (50) and (51) cannot appear in the prefield (see Speyer 2009: 325 fn. 2 and references therein).[14]

(50) a. Ich habe mich getäuscht/ geärgert.
I have REFL been mistaken been upset
'I was mistaken/upset.'

b. * Mich habe ich geärgert/ getäuscht.
REFL have I been mistaken been upset

(51) a. Niemand hat sich das komplett angehört.
nobody has REFL that entirely listened to
'Nobody listened to that entirely.'

---

14 Speyer (2009: 325 fn. 2) also claims that object-expletives are banned from the prefield. However, his contrast pair, given in (i.a) and (i.b), is ill-chosen because it features a specific subject. With an indefinite unspecific subject as in (i.c), the object-expletive is fine in the prefield, thereby paralleling the cases with referential object-*es* discussed above. Example (i.a) shows that the expletive is obligatory also in the middle field.

(i) a. *Karl hat *(es) eilig.*
Karl has it urgent
'Karl was in a hurry.'

b. * *Es hat Karl eilig.*
it has Karl urgent

c. *Es hatte niemand wirklich eilig*
it had no one really urgent
'No one was really in a hurry.'

d. *Niemand hatte *(es) wirklich eilig*
no one had it really urgent

b. * Sich hat das niemand komplett angehört.
REFL has that nobody entirely listened to

Specific non-argumental dative elements (free datives/*Dativus ethicus*) are banned from the sentence-initial position too (Wöllstein-Leisten et al. 1997: 37). These datives are obligatorily realized by a weak pronoun (Mollica 2014: 353).

(52) a. Du bist mir ein Schlingel.
you are me.DAT a rascal
'You're such a rascal.'

b. * Mir bist du ein Schlingel.
me.DAT are you a rascal
(see Wöllstein-Leisten et al. 1997: 37)[15]

The same restriction is observed for a further class of pro-forms: Some verbs which take a clausal complement allow the insertion of the pro-form *es* 'it' or *das* 'that' in the matrix clause, as shown in (53a) and (54a).[16] In (53b), it seems as if the pro-form *es* could occupy the prefield. However, the unacceptability of (54b) and the impossibility of the pro-form *das* in the prefield position in (53c) and (54c) indicate that the *es* in (53b) must be analyzed as expletive prefield-*es*, the occurrence of which is known to depend on the lexical verb (cf. Speyer 2009).[17]

15 Wöllstein-Leisten et al. (1997) state that these datives may not appear in the prefield. Their example, given in (i.a), however, is somewhat confusing because they place the dative pronoun in sentence-initial position of an imperative clause. In imperatives, no constituent is allowed to precede the verb (except for heavy emphasis), as illustrated in (i.c) with the adverbial *heute* 'today'.

(i) a. * *Mir fall nicht hin*
me.DAT fall not down

b. *Fall mir (heute) nicht hin.*
fall me.DAT today not down
'Don't fall down (today).'

c. * *Heute fall mir nicht hin.*
today fall me.DAT not down

16 Reis (1997) calls these pro-forms *Platzhalter-Korrelate* 'placeholder correlates'.

17 Speyer (2009) takes it for granted that the prefield-*es* in clauses such as (53b) is coreferent with the embedded clauses without providing any diagnostic.
Yvonne Viesel (p. c.) does not perceive the contrasts as unacceptable as indicated in (53) and (54). Moreover she provided example (i.a), which also sound very good to me. However, replacing *das*

(53) a. Dem Vater ist es_i/ das_i egal, [dass Christopher zu spät $kommt]_i$.
[the $father]_{DAT}$ is it that equal that Christopher to late comes
'The father doesn't care that Christopher is late.'

b. Es ist dem Vater egal, dass Christopher zu spät kommt.
It is [the $father]_{DAT}$ equal that Christopher to late comes
'The father doesn't care that Christopher is late.'

c. ??/* Das_i ist dem Vater egal, [dass Christopher zu spät $kommt]_i$.
It is [the $father]_{DAT}$ equal that Christopher to late comes
'The father doesn't care that Christopher is late.'

(54) a. Der Vater hat es_i/ das_i geahnt, [dass Christopher zu spät $kommt]_i$.
the father has it that suspected that Christopher to late comes
'The father suspected that Christopher will be late.'

b. ??/* Es hat der Vater geahnt, dass Christopher zu spät kommt.
it has the father suspected that Christopher to late comes
'The father suspected that Christopher will be late.'

c. ??/* Das hat der Vater geahnt, dass Christopher zu spät kommt.
that has the father suspected that Christopher to late comes
'The father suspected that Christopher will be late.'

The reason why all the above mentioned pro-forms cannot appear in the prefield is that they cannot be accented. Without being stressed, only pro-forms that are the highest elements in the middle field can occupy the prefield via an operation which Frey (2004) calls *formal movement*. This is the case for object-*es* with indefinite unspecific subjects. Lexical reflexive pronouns, free datives (Dativus ethicus) and the clausal pro-forms discussed above are never the highest elements of the middle field irrespective of the specificity of the subject. Hence, they can never appear in the prefield, where they must bear stress. Crucially, none of these can

---

by *es* results in unacceptability, shown in (i.b), which indicates that the *es* is rather the prefield expletive than the pro-form of the embedded clause.

(i) a. *Das hab ich (doch) geahnt, dass Christopher wieder zu spät kommt.*
that have I PRT suspected that Christopher again to late comes
'I have suspected that Christopher will be late again.'

b. * *Es hab ich (doch) geahnt, dass Christopher wieder zu spät kommt.*
EXPL have I PRT suspected that Christopher again to late comes

be stressed, which results in their ban from the prefield.[18] In essence, weak pronouns are banned from the prefield because the information structural properties of the prefield position require phonological marking in German, which cannot be realized by these elements for lexico-phonological reasons.

2.1.4.5 Qualificational adverbs

Some adverbials that express the degree to which the event depicted by the predicate holds are quite unacceptable in the prefield, as shown in (55)–(57).[19]

(55) a. Damals hat niemand dem Professor ríchtig zugehört
back then has no one the professor really listened to
'Back then, no one really listened to the professor.'

b. * Ríchig hat niemand dem Professor (damals) ~~ríchtig~~ zugehört
really has no one the professor back then listened to

(56) a. Gestern hast du deinen Bruder káum angeschaut.
yesterday have you your brother hardly looked at
'Yesterday you hardly looked at your brother.'

b. * Káum hast du deinen Bruder (gestern) ~~káum~~ angeschaut.
hardly have you your brother yesterday looked at

(57) a. Angeblich hat der Torwart dem Spieler vóll ins Gesicht geschlagen.
allegedly has the goalkeeper the player right in the face hit
'Allegedly, the goalie hit the player right in the face.'

b. * Vóll hat der Torwart dem Spieler (angeblich) ~~vóll~~ ins Gesicht geschlagen.
right has the goalkeeper the player allegedly in the face hit

---

18 The impossibility of carrying stress has been noted for weak referential pronouns (Travis 1991, Frey 2006b, Meinunger 2007), Dativus ethicus (Mollica 2014: 353), and clausal pro-forms (see Reis 1997: 131).

19 Note that *kaum* can also be used as a temporal conjunction in the sense of 'shortly after', as which it can appear in the prefield as shown in (i). This reading is irrelevant here.

(i) *Kaum hast du deinen Bruder angeschaut, da gab es auch schon Streit.*
shortly after has you your brother looked at, then gave it also already trouble
'As soon as you looked at your brother, the trouble started.'

The a-examples indicate that those adverbials can be accented in their base position in the middle field. At this time, I must leave open why these adverbs are resistant to topicalization.

2.1.4.6 VPs

VPs can be fronted quite easily in German. However, there seem to be language-specific restrictions among the V2-languages. In Icelandic, topicalization of the sole verb as well as a VP (verb plus object) is generally impossible (Thráinsson 2007: 344, 349).[20] Swedish allows VP-topicalization only for certain verb classes like eventives 'read a book' but not for statives like 'know Swedish' (Källgren & Prince 1989: 48–49).

A general observation is that VP-topicalization is heavily restricted if it targets the subject and the verb in intransitive structures and impossible if this leads to the exclusion of other arguments in (di-)transitive structures, in line with classic assumptions about constituency (see De Kuthy & Meurers 2003 for German and Bhatt 1994: 42–43 for Kashmiri). Additionally, the subject included in a topicalized VP may not be definite and the middle field must not be empty (Wöllstein-Leisten et al. 1997: 103–104), as illustrated for the unaccusative *landen* 'land' in the examples in (58b) and (58c). The same contrast is also observable with the impersonal passive in (59) and the unergative verb in (60).

(58) a. ... dass ein/ das Flugzeug gelandet ist.
that a the plane landed is
'... that a plane has landed'

b. * [Das Flugzeug gelandet] ist (auf dem roten Platz noch nie).
the plane landed is on the red square yet never

c. [Ein Flugzeug gelandet] ist *(auf dem roten Platz noch nie).
a plane landed is on the red square yet never
'No plane has ever landed on the Red Square yet.'

(see Haider 1988: 108–109)

(59) a. ... dass ein/ das Flugzeug gesichtet wurde.
that a the plane sighted was
'that a plane was seen'

b. * [Das Flugzeug gesichtet] wurde (dort noch nie).
the plane sighted was there never yet

20 Thanks to Jóhannes Gísli Jónsson (p. c.) for making me aware of this.

c. [Ein Flugzeug gesichtet] wurde *(dort noch nie).
a plane sighted was there never yet
'No plane was ever seen there yet.'
(see Haider 1988: 108–109)

(60) a. ... dass ein Außenseiter gewonnen hat.
that a outsider won has
'... that an underdog has won'
b. * [Dieser Außenseiter gewonnen] hat (dort noch nie).
this outsider won has there never yet
c. [Ein Außenseiter gewonnen] hat *(dort noch nie).
a outsider won has there never yet
'No underdog has ever won there yet.'
(see Haider 1988: 108–109)

It remains puzzling why some material has to follow the finite verb in the c-examples above because the examples in (61) and (62) show that string vacuous movement of the verb is not ruled out generally.[21]

(61) a. Du spinnst.
you spin
'You're nuts.'
b. ... dass du spinnst
that you spin
'... that you're nuts'

(62) a. [Geohrfeigt zu werden] schmerzt.
slapped to be hurts
'It hurts to be slapped.'
b. ... dass geohrfeigt zu werden schmerzt.
that slapped to be hurts
'... that it hurts to be slapped.'
(Haider 1988: 109)

This descriptive presentation will suffice for now, for syntactic analysis of VP-topicalization see Ott (2018) and references therein.

21 Yvonne Viesel (p. c.) suggested that empty middle fields are acceptable only if a lexical verb appears in the V2-position but not if an auxiliary appears there. This appears to be the correct generalization, however, it remains to be investigated why this leads to a contrast in acceptability.

2.1.4.7 Paratactic clauses

Generally, embedded clauses can occupy the prefield as illustrated for complement clauses in (63b) and adverbial clauses in (63c).

(63) a. Sicherlich hat Christopher angenommen, dass wir in die Kneipe gehen,
surely has Christopher assumend that we in the pub go
weil wir das immer so machen.
because we that always so make
'Surely, Christopher assumed that we will go to the pub because we always do that.'

b. [Dass wir in die Kneipe gehen] hat Christopher angenommen, weil
that we in the pub go has Christopher assumend because
wir das immer so machen.
we that always so make

c. [Weil wir das immer so machen] hat Christopher angenommen,
because we that always so make has Christopher assumend
dass wir in die Kneipe gehen.
that we in the pub go

However, some dependent clauses seem to be immobile although they show a typical embedded clause word order, such as the free *dass*-clauses (Reis 1997: 132–138) in (64).

(64) a. Christopher ist ein Idiot, dass er ihr den Pelzmantel bezahlt hat.
Christopher is an idiot that he her the fur coat paid has
'Christopher is such an idiot that he paid for her fur coat.'

b. * [Dass er ihr den Pelzmantel bezahlt hat] ist Chistopher ein Idiot.
that he her the fur coat paid has is Christopher an idiot

A similar observation can be made for the non-finite complementizer *um* (*zu*) 'for' and the corresponding finite complementizer *damit* 'so that': If they introduce final clauses as in (65) and (66), the embedded clauses are completely acceptable in the prefield.

(65) a. Sie nahm den Regenschirm mit, um nicht nass zu werden.
she took the umbrella with for not wet to become
'She took the umbrella with her so that she wouldn't get wet.'

b. [Um nicht nass zu werden] nahm sie den Regenschirm mit.
for not wet to become took she the umbrella with

(66) a. Sie nahm den Regenschirm mit, damit sie nicht nass werden
she took the umbrella with so that she not wet become
würde.
would
'She took the umbrella with her so that she wouldn't get wet.'

b. [Damit sie nicht nass werden würde,] nahm sie den Regenschirm
so that she not wet become would took she the umbrella
mit.
with

However, if these complementizers introduce a prospective clause, fronting of the dependent clauses is impossible, as illustrated in (67) and (68).[22]

(67) a. Sie stellte den Regenschirm neben sich, um ihn dann am Ende
she placed the umbrella next to her for it then at the end
doch zu vergessen.
PRT to forget
'She placed the umbrella next to her only to forget it anyway.'

b. * [Um ihn dann am Ende doch zu vergessen] stellte sie den
for it then at the end PRT to forget placed she the
Regenschirm neben sich.
umbrella next to her

(68) a. Sie stellte den Regenschirm neben sich, damit sie ihn dann am
she placed the umbrella next to her so that she it then at the
Ende doch vergaß.
end PRT forgot
'She placed the umbrella next to her only to forget it anyway.'

b. * [Damit sie ihn dann am Ende doch vergaß] stellte sie den
so that she it then at the end PRT forgot placed she the
Regenschirm neben sich.
umbrella next to her

Similarly, V2-complement clauses cannot appear in the prefield, as shown in (69a) and (69b). Example (69c) illustrates that a canonical V-final *dass*-clause can appear in the prefield in the same environment (see e. g. Reis 1997).

22 Thanks to Łukasz Jędrzejowski (p. c.) for making me aware of the immobility of prospective *um zu*-clauses.

(69) a. Jeder$_i$ möchte gern glauben, er$_i$ sei unheimlich beliebt.
everyone wants gladly believe he is.SUBJ weirdly popular
'Everyone$_i$ wants to believe that he$_i$ is extremely popular.'

b. * [Er$_i$ sei unheimlich beliebt] möchte jeder$_i$ gern glauben.
he is.SUBJ weirdly popular wants everyone gladly believe

c. [Dass er$_i$ unheimlich beliebt sei] möchte jeder$_i$ gern glauben.
that he weirdly popular is.SUBJ wants everyone gladly believe
'Everyone$_i$ wants to believe that he$_i$ is extremely popular.'

(see Reis 1997: 139)

The same argumentation applies also to V2-variants of *weil* 'because' clauses, as shown by the paradigm in (70) (Frey 2012, Antomo & Steinbach 2010).[23]

(70) a. Ich komme nicht mit, weil ich habe kein Geld.
I come not with because I have no money
'I will not join you because I have not enough money.'

b. * [Weil ich habe kein Geld] komme ich nicht mit.
because I have no money come I not with

c. [Weil ich kein Geld habe] komme ich nicht mit.
because I no money have come I not with
'I will not join you because I have not enough money.'

I assume that such clausal elements have in common that they are paratactically connected with the main clause. As a consequence, they are not a proper constituent of the main clause and therefore cannot move to the prefield.

2.1.4.8 Long-distance elements

Typically, only constituents of the main clause can appear in the sentence-initial position. This correctly excludes adverbials of embedded clauses (Frey 2004), as shown by the contrast in (71), and extends to recursively embedded clauses, as in (72) and (73).

(71) a. Ich werde ihr mitteilen, dass der Professor gestern nach ihr gefragt hat.
I will her tell that the professor yesterday for her asked has
'I will tell her that the professor asked for her yesterday.'

---

23 The two variants of *weil*-clauses do not exhibit the same meaning potential. In addition to the literature cited above see Scheffler (2013: 50–55).

b. * Gestern$_1$ werde ich ihr mitteilen, dass der Professor ~~gestern~~$_1$ nach
Yesterday will I her tell that the professor for
ihr gefragt hat.
her asked has

(72) a. Jedoch kann ich noch nicht glauben, [dass Christopher uns
however can I still not believe that Christopher us
gestern erzählt hat, [dass wir das Haus von Oma erben
yesterday told has that we the house of grandma inherit
sollen]].
should
'However, I still can't believe that Christopher has told us yesterday that we should inherit grandma's house.'

b. ??/* [Dass wir das Haus von Oma erben sollen]$_1$ kann ich noch
that we the house of grandma inherit should can I still
nicht glauben, [dass Christopher uns gestern erzählt hat, t_1].
not believe that Christopher us yesterday told has

(73) a. Also ging die Frau nach Hause, [bevor ihr Bruder husten musste,
thus went the woman at home before her brother cough must
[weil er sich verschluckt hatte]].
because he REFL choked on had
'Thus the woman went home before her brother had to cough because he choked on something.'

b. * [Weil er sich verschluckt hatte]$_1$ ging die Frau nach Hause,
because he REFL choked on had went the woman at home
[bevor ihr Bruder husten musste t_1].
before her brother cough must

However, long-distance extraction is possible for *wh*-elements as in (74a), degraded for NPs as in (74b), and strongly degraded for VPs as in (74c), (see Müller 2004). Additionally, such long-distance extractions have been intensively discussed under the term *Syntactic Islands*. It became clear that the overall acceptability of such structures depends on the clause type (see Freitag 2012 and references therein) and is also subject to dialectal variation (Fanselow & Weskott 2010).

(74) a. Wen$_1$ hast du gedacht, dass der Schlagzeuger ~~wen~~$_1$ geküsst hat?
who.ACC have you thought that the drummer kissed has
'Who did you think that the drummer had kissed?'

b. ?/?? [Die Jule]$_1$ habe ich gedacht, [dass der Schlagzeuger ~~the Jule~~$_1$
the Jule have I thought that the drummer
gekūsst hat].
kissed has
'I thought that the drummer had kissed Júle.'

c. ??/* [Die Jule geküsst]$_1$ denke ich, [dass der Schlagzeuger gestern
the Jule kissed think I that the drummer yesterday
~~die Jule geküsst~~$_1$ hat].
has
'I thought that the drummer had kíssed Júle yesterday.'

(see Müller 2004: 201–203)

In sum, some constituents of more deeply embedded clauses are able to move to the prefield. However, long-distance extraction is very restricted.

2.1.4.9 Summary of licit prefield elements

The discussion revealed that the prefield position is a proper syntactic position that must be filled in declarative clauses, as a last resort option even by a semantically empty expletive. Typically any main clause constituent may occupy this position. The restrictions on prefield elements can be divided into three major groups. First, paratactic clauses and constituents of lower embedded clauses are forbidden because they do not count as constituents of the main clause. Furthermore, the sentence-initial position is strongly related to an information structural position of the sentence topic or emphatic contrast. This accounts for the second type of restriction: If an element cannot function as a topic or does not employ a meaningful contrast, the element is infelicitous in the prefield, such as certain verbal particles and presumably qualificational adverbs. The third type of restriction is directly related to the special interpretation of this position: If the element in question is not the highest element in the middle field, it cannot move to the prefield without bearing stress. Weak pronouns cannot bear stress and can therefore only move to the prefield if they are the highest element of the middle field. Three phenomena that have been discussed are not covered by these explanations. These are negation, discourse particles and VP-topicalization. For each of these elements I have noted that there is cross-linguistic variation among the V2-languages whether these elements are allowed in the prefield or not. This indicates that the restrictions are rather language-specific and not a direct property of the V2-configuration as such. I must leave the explanation of these elements for future research.

2.2 Exceptions: Non-V2 structures

Exceptional non-V2-structures come in three main categories: first, clauses with an empty prefield, second, independent clauses in which the finite verb does not move at all, i. e. V-final main clauses, and third, clauses in which more than one constituent appears in the prefield, before the fronted verb.

2.2.1 V-initial clauses

In addition to polar interrogatives, German also exhibits declarative clauses with V1-order. Two forms must be distinguished. The first is the result of *Topic Drop* (see Oppenrieder 2013: 36–39, Trutkowski 2016). As shown in (75a), an argument can be left out if it is a salient topic whereas (75b) illustrates, that deletion of the same element is illicit in the middle field. Hence these structures are underlyingly proper V2-clauses.

(75) Was ist mit den Weingläsern?
'What about the wine glasses?'

a. ~~Die~~ Hab ich schon auf den Tisch gestellt.
them have I already on the table placed
'I've already placed them on the table.'

b. * Ich hab ~~die~~ schon auf den Tisch gestellt.
I have them already on the table placed

However, German exhibits several specific V1-declaratives such as the justification sentence in (76a), which is not only a variant of a V2-clause, as the contrasting example in (76b) shows. Further examples are given in (77) that are typical for narrative style, such as, but not exclusively, jokes (Oppenrieder 2013: 40-42).

(76) Mit dem nahrhaften Blut ihrer Opfer aber schlürfen die Mücken auch Fremdkörper ein, die mitunter eine immunologische Herausforderung sind.
'Together with the nutritious blood of their victims, mosquitoes also suck foreign matter that can be an immunological challenge.'

a. (*Es) Müssen sie sich doch mit ihrem Rüssel durch eine Haut
EXPL must they REFL PRT with their proboscis through a skin
voller Bakterien bohren.
full of bacteria pierce
'Because they must pierce with their proboscis through a skin full of bacteria.'

b. Sie müssen ~~sie~~ sich (*doch) mit ihrem Rüssel durch eine Haut
they must REFL PRT with their proboscis through a skin
voller Bakterien bohren.
full of bacteria pierce
'They must must pierce with their proboscis through a skin full of bacteria.'
(Oppenrieder 2013: 40)

(77) a. (#Es) Kommt ein Mann zum Arzt.
EXPL comes a man to the doctor
'A man came to the doctor.'
b. Ich geh heute auf den Markt. (Da) Kostet ein Bund Petersilie 2 Euro.
I go today on the market there costs a bunch parsley 2 Euro
'I went to the market today. A bunch of parsley cost 2 Euros.' (see Oppenrieder 2013: 41)
c. (*Es/ *So) Sollen sie ihn (doch) haben.
EXPL so should they him PRT have
'They should have him then.' (see Oppenrieder 2013: 42)

These V1-structures also have specific felicity conditions that correlate with their interpretational properties. Syntactically, they might be treated on a par with other V1-structures, such as polar interrogatives.

2.2.2 V-final main clauses

German also exhibits independent clauses in which the finite verb remains in its base position. These either show formal features of interrogative clauses, such the interrogative in (78a) and the exclamative in (78b), or they exhibit a complementizer such as the declarative *dass* in (79a) or the interrogative *ob* in (79b). Truckenbrodt (2013) provides arguments against an ellipsis analysis and details about the felicity conditions and the interpretational potential of independent V-final clauses (see also Oppenrieder 2013: 42–43).

(78) a. Was er wohl eingekauft hat?
what he PRT bought has
'(I wonder) What he might have bought?'
b. Wie schön du doch Klavier spielen kannst.
how beautiful you PRT piano play can
'How beautiful you play the piano.'

(79) a. Dass du mir (ja) nicht zu spät heimkommst!
that you me PRT not to late home come
'Don't be late tonight!' (Truckenbrodt 2013: 238)

b. (X: Peter hasn't written in a long time.
Y: That's true.)
X: Ob es ihm gut geht?
whether it him well goes
'I wonder whether he is doing well.' (Truckenbrodt 2006a: 261)

All V-final main clauses are formally identical to embedded clauses. Hence, the syntactic structure is comparable to regular embedded clauses in German. Clearly, there must exist a pragmatic mechanism to interpreted these dependent clauses as an illocutionary act, a topic which is well beyond the scope of the present discussion (see Bayer 2004: 84–89).

2.2.3 V>2 structures

There are also some structures that (apparently) exhibit more than one constituent before the finite verb. Connectors such as *denn*, *doch*, and *aber* precede the sentence-initial constituent, as in (80), which shows that this also holds for non-subject-initial clauses.

(80) Denn/ doch/ aber [Rosinen] mag Christopher nicht.
because however but raisins likes Christopher not
'Because/However/But Christopher doesn't like raisins.'

A different type of complex prefields are discussed in Müller (2003), Müller (2004: 218–219), and Müller (2005), among others. Examples of characteristic patterns are given in (81). It has been noted that the order of the two prefield elements is fixed (Müller 2005: 307–308), that the fronted elements have to be clause mates (Fanselow 1993: 67)[24], and that the acceptability of examples like (81e) depends on the specificity and definiteness of the fronted DPs (Müller 2004: 218–219). Müller (2005) proposes to analyze the fronted elements as one complex constituent with an empty head, similar to a VP. Under such an analysis, the prefield is only apparently filled with multiple constituents.

24 Note that extraction out of embedded clauses is highly restricted on its own, as discussed in Section 2.1.4.8.

(81) a. [Fast alles] [im Sitzen] bewältigt Fernando Escartin auf dem
almost everything in sitting manages Fernando Escartin on the
Weg zum Gipfel ~~fast alles im Sitzten bewältigt~~.
way to the peak
'Fernando Escartin manages handles almost all passage on it way to the peak seated.' (Müller 2004: 219)

b. [Alle Träume] [gleichzeitig] lassen sich nur selten ~~alle Träume~~
all dream simultaneously let REFL only seldom
~~gleichzeitig~~ verwirklichen ~~lassen~~.
realize
'Only seldom, one can realize all dreams at once.' (Müller 2005: 299)

c. [Zum zweiten Mal] [die Weltmeisterschaft] errang Clark 1965 ...
to the second time the world championship won Clark 1965
~~zum zweiten Mal die Welmeisterschaft errang~~.

'Clark won the world championship in 1965 for the second time.' (Müller 2005: 300)

d. [Von Konstanz] [nach Bern] wird Urs morgen ~~von Konstanz~~
from Constance to Bern will Urs tomorrow
~~nach Bern~~ fahren
drive
'Tomorrow, Urs will drive from Constance to Bern.' (Fanselow 1987: 99)

e. ?? [Kindern] [Bonbons] sollte man ~~Kindern Bonbons~~ nicht geben ~~sollte~~
children sweets should one not give
'One should not give sweet to children.' (Müller 2004: 218)

Grewendorf (2013) argues that German provides a principled option of left-dislocating[25] topic constituents in a position preceding the canonical prefield, as shown for an argument in (82a), also preceding a *wh*-term as in (82b), and for adverbials in (82c) and (82d). Those initial constituents cannot occupy the prefield.[26]

---

25 I will exclude so-called *hanging topics* (*nominativus pendens*) because they are less integrated into the host clauses (see Shaer & Frey 2004, Nolda 2004).

26 Though for different reasons: If the sentence-initial DP in (82a) appears in the prefield, the resumptive pronoun must be deleted. The same applies to (82b), in addition to the complementary distribution with the *wh*-term in the prefield. If the adverbial clause in (82c) appears in the prefield, it is preferably interpreted as an integrated conditional clause which results in an implausible interpretation. The initial constituent in (82d) cannot appear in the prefield at all.

(82) a. [Den Gesetzentwurf zur Armeereform,]$_i$ [den$_i$] lehnte der Senat ab.
the draft bill to the army reform this refused the senat PRT
'The draft bill of the army reform, the senat refused it.'

b. [Den Studenten,]$_i$ [wer] hat den$_i$ gestern kritisiert?
the student who has him yesterday criticized
'This student, who criticized him yesterday?'

c. [Wenn du Durst hast,] [im Kühlschrank] ist ein Bier.
if you thirst has in the fridge is a beer
'In case you are thirsty, there's beer in the fridge.'

d. [Wen immer du einlädst,] [ich] komme nicht.
who ever you invite I came not
'Whoever you will invite, I will not come.'

(Grewendorf 2013: 655–666, 668)

A phenomenon that looks superficially similar is *emphatic topicalization*, described in Bayer & Dasgupta (2016) and illustrated in (83): A constituent of the embedded clause is topicalized in front of the complementizer. As a consequence, the embedded clause must appear sentence-initially. If the analysis of Bayer & Dasgupta (2016) is correct, the prefield is occupied by only one constituent, an embedded clause with a complex prefield of its own.

(83) BAVARIAN

a. [[Da Hans] [ob ~~da Hans~~ kummt]]$_1$ woass-e ned t_1.
the Hans whether comes know-I not
'As for Hans, I don't know whether he will come.' (Bayer & Dasgupta 2016: 5)

b. [[Der] [wenn ~~der~~ das nochmal macht]]$_1$ bin ich echt grantig t_1.
he when this again does am I really pissed
'If he does this again, I'm going to be really pissed.'[27]

Additionally, it has been noted that multiple adverbials can be placed in the prefield, which is known as *adverbial stacking* and illustrated in (84a) for Swedish and in (84b) for German. The German example also illustrates the restrictions on adverb stacking: First, stacked adverbials show the same (language-specific ordering) as in the middle field. Second, only event modifying adverbials take part in the stacking, i. e. they cannot be accompanied by the epistemic adverbial *vermutlich* 'pressumably' or the optional argument *ein Lied* 'a song' although these might

27 From a speaker of Northern Bavarian.

appear in their base position. Even though the adverbials form separate prosodic phrases, it is commonly assumed that they form a kind of cluster that occupies only a single syntactic position (Haider 2000a: 97-102, Holmberg 2015: 353–354).

(84) a. SWEDISH
[I går,] [vid femtiden,] [utanför stationen,] [när jag kom från
yesterday at about.five outside the.station, when I came from
jobbet,] mötte jag en gammal skolkamrat.
work, met I an old schoolmate
'Yesterday, at about five, outside the station, when I came home from work, I met an old schoolmate of mine.' (Holmberg 2015: 353)

b. GERMAN
[Vor zwei Wochen] [in Italien] [am Strand] [als die Sonne
before two weeks in Italy at the beach when the sun
ungerging] ⟨*vermutlich⟩ ⟨*ein Lied⟩ hat der Junge ⟨vermutlich⟩ ⟨ein
sunk presumably a song has the boy presumably a
Lied⟩ gesungen.
song sung
'In Italy, at the beach, two weeks ago, before the sun disappeared, the boy presumably sang a song.'

A further form of complex prefield is currently discussed for urban vernacular varieties of German (*Kiezdeutsch*), Danish, Swedish and Norwegian.[28] Characteristic for this V3-configuration is that exclusively in subject-initial main clauses, one adverb may precede the subject, as shown in (85). For more details see Wiese (2009), Freywald et al. (2015), Walkden (2017), Bonke (2017). Crucially, the fact that this pattern does not extend to object-initial clauses and that it is not obligatory for subject-initial clauses indicates that it is discourse pragmatically driven and does not represent a novel syntactic structure (see especially Freywald et al. 2015).

(85) NON-STANDARD GERMAN (Kiezdeutsch)
a. [ab jétzt] [ich] krieg immer zwánzig euro
from now I get always twenty euros
'From now on, I get always twenty euros.' (Freywald et al. 2015: 89)

b. [danach] [er] sagt zu O., geh mal wég
afterwards he says to O. go PRT away
'Afterwards, he says to O. [=name], go away.' (Walkden 2017: 55)

28 According to Freywald et al. (2015), these structures occur extremely rarely in the corresponding Dutch variant.

In sum, we have seen that there are several cases in which either complex elements occupy the prefield or an additional element precedes a V2-structure for specific discourse pragmatic reasons. However, all these options are highly restricted.

2.2.4 Summary of the non-V2 patterns

In this section, I have presented three classes of deviations from V2-patterns. The first two have been identified as syntactically regular V1-patterns and as embedded clause patterns. What makes them exceptional is not their syntactic structure but their usage as independent utterances. In the third class, apparently more than one constituent precedes the V2-position. Such an extension of the left periphery seems likely for connectors like *aber* 'but' and left-dislocated elements including the examples from the urban vernacular varieties. For the other form of complex prefields, subsuming emphatic topicalization and adverbial stacking, it seems likely that only one constituent, though a complex one, occupies the prefield.

2.3 Explanations: A brief history of syntactic accounts

The core characterization of the V2-phenomenon was already described by Erdmann (1886: 182–185)[29], who states explicitly that the position preceding the finite verb is not a specific subject position but can be freely occupied by other nouns, adverbials, predicative expressions, or even dependent clauses. This description, however, does not explain how this configuration emerges. In the following, I will focus on the productive line of research based on transformational grammar that assumes that the V2-order is a derived order. Opponents of transformational analyses proposed two unrelated ordering sources for matrix and embedded clause order, for instance Bartsch & Vennemann (1972), but see Koster (1975) for a principled criticism. But even within the generative grammar, we find a variety of analyses. Ross (1969: 95) for instance proposed that the base word order of German is SVO and the finite verb is moved into the clause-final position in embedded clauses by a movement rule.

29 Reference found in Haider (1985: 49).

2.3.1 Insertion into the middle field

The insight that German (and Dutch) posess a verb-final basic word order is not very old. Bierwisch (1963: 34) acknowledges that Fourquet (1959) was the first who formulated the observation that the order of subordinate clauses is actually the basic configuration from which the orders of main clauses are derived. Fourquet (1959: 139, fn. 6) also argued that there is one structural position in front of the finite verb which can be filled by subjects and non-subjects alike and that a subject-oriented syntax, does not add any explanatory value, as expressed in the following quote:

> The rule that the subject is inverted after the verb if the first constituent that precedes the finite verb is not the subject is as insightful as the statement that a motorcyclist in France does not give a German a lift if he already has a non-German on the pillion. It is forbidden by law to have more than one person on the pillion: that is all.[30]

Early transformational grammar approaches for German word order have been more or less simultaneously published by Bach (1962) and Bierwisch (1963), even though the latter is far more extensive. The basic derivation of V2-order, however, is almost identical. Both authors propose to derive the appropriate order by placing the finite verb behind the first constituent (Bach 1962: 269, Bierwisch 1963: 111).[31] These approaches could therefore be translated as inserting the verb after the highest element in the middle field, i. e. the sub-CP-domain.[32] That the OV-order is the underlying order and the basis for the transformational rule is motivated by the following observations: All infinitival forms occur in clause-final position as in (86a), and in complex verb forms, only the finite element moves whereas all other elements appear in the clause-final position as in (86b). Fragment answers and lexical mentioning always show verb-final order, as in (86c) and (86d). Furthermore, particles of particle verbs appear in the clause-final position, as in (86e) (see Bierwisch 1963: 35).

---

30 "Die Regel, daß das Subjekt dem Verb nachgestellt ist, wenn das erste Satzglied, auf das das v. f. [verbum finitum] folgt, nicht das Subjekt ist, hat ebensoviel Wert wie die Feststellung, daß in Frankreich ein Motorradfahrer keinen Deutschen aufnimmt, wenn er einen Nicht-Deutschen auf dem Soziussitz hat: gesetzlich darf er nicht zwei Personen auf den Soziussitz nehmen, das ist alles." (Fourquet 1959: 139, fn. 6, translation C. F.)

31 V1-structures are the result of placing the finite verb behind a phonologically empty element. Interrogatives, imperatives and prefield expletive-*es* are generated by morphophonemic rules (Bierwisch 1963: 112).

32 It must be noted that a mapping onto a modern sentence skeleton is not unproblematic.

(86) a. Er *versprach* einen Teller zu *kaufen*.
he promised a plate to buy
'He promised to buy a plate.'

b. Er *hätte* einen Teller *gekauft haben sollen*.
he had a plate bought have should
'He should have bought a plate.'

c. A: Was machst du?
'What do you do?'
B: Zigaretten *holen*./ **Holen* Zigaretten.
cigarettes get get cigarettes
'get cigarettes'

d. jemandem etwas *schenken*/ *jemandem *schenken* etwas/
somebody something donate somebody donate something
**schenken* jemandem etwas
donate somebody something
'donate somebody something (as a present)'

e. Ich *höre* morgen mit dem Rauchen *auf*./ *Ich *aufhöre* morgen
I listen tomorrow with the smoking up I up listen tomorrow
mit dem Rauchen.
with the smoking
'I will quit smoking tomorrow.'

Additional support for the underlying V-final order comes from verbs that cannot undergo movement to the V2-position, as discussed in Section 2.1.3: All verbs that can appear in V2-position do also appear in clause-final position but not vice versa.

To prevent verb movement in embedded clauses, Bach (1962: 269) included a clause boundary symbol into the definition of the transformation rule by stipulation.

2.3.2 V-to-C movement (plus phrasal movement)

Within the sentence skeleton of the X-bar theory, the restriction of V2-movement to main clauses could receive a principled explanation. Emonds (1970: 10–12) noticed that V2 is only one of several syntactic transformations that apply only in root clauses, hence the term *root transformations*. den Besten (1983) attempted to generalize the notion of root transformations even further and identified two crucial insights for the analysis of V2-clauses: First, V2-movement (and likewise all root transformations) targets the clause-initial COMP-position.[33] The verb thereby moves into a fixed position with the consequence that, in subject-initial clauses, the subject has to be preposed like all other initial constituents. den Besten (1983: 56–60) provides the following arguments in favor of the positional identity of the V2-position and the COMP-position. Weak pronouns in Dutch appear right-adjacent to the finite verb in main clauses and right-adjacent to the complementizer in subordinate clauses.[34] Additionally, the positional identity of V2 and COMP accounts for the complementary distribution of verb movement and overt complementizer in German and Dutch (den Besten 1983: 17–18). Furthermore, den Besten (1983: 115–117) introduces the idea that verb movement is triggered by a morphosyntactic feature. Motivated by the selectional differences of complementizers like *dass* 'that', which combines with finite (tensed) VPs, and complementizers like *um* 'for', which combines with non-finite (untensed) VPs, he labels this feature *tense*. This labeling is somewhat surprising considering that non-finite forms may express temporal relations and that, in complementizer agreement, only subject-agreement morphemes show up at the complementizer, as den Besten (1983: 119) even notes himself. To account for the movement of the sentence-initial phrase, den Besten (1983: 60–61) formulates a Wh-*Movement Rule* and a *Constituent Preposing Rule* in the fashion of the transformational grammar. Generally this mechanism has been retained, even though it is currently assumed that the movement is triggered by specific features on the C head that may be more directly connected to interpretational aspects like in *wh*-questions[35], or must be formally enforced by an EPP-feature[36]. A simple scheme of the V-to-C analysis is given in (87).

33 As den Besten (1983: 51,107) acknowledges, the idea that V2 is generated by verb movement and (subsequent) movement of one constituent (including the subject) in front of the verb has also been assumed around the same time by Higgins (1973: 152, fn. 5), Williams (1974), Koster (1975), and Emonds (1976: 40).

34 Similar restrictions on the placement of pronouns hold for German too (see Haider 2010: 131–141).

35 Following Cheng (1991), movement of a *wh*-phrase into the left periphery is one way to execute *clausal typing* (see also Brandner 2004).

36 The *Extended Projection Principle* (Chomsky 1981) captures the observation that some heads (such as I in English) require an overt constituent, in this case a subject, which may also be a semantically empty expletive. A similar regularity holds for the prefield element in V2-languages. In the minimalist framework this EPP-feature corresponds to a strong feature (Chomsky 1995: 232). However, the relatively free choice of constituents which may satisfy this feature in V2-clauses is much more problematic than for subjects.

(87)

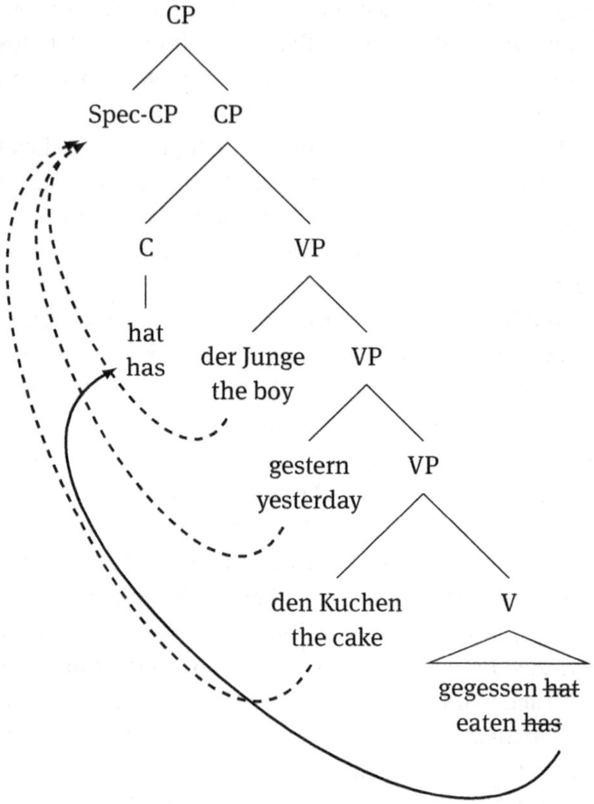

2.3.3 (A)symmetric V2: V-to-I movement in subject-initial clauses

Within the Principles and Parameters approach, scholars tried to account for the word order variation within the Germanic V2-languages with different phrase structure parameters, namely V-to-I and I-to-C movement (see e. g. Platzack 1986, Vikner 1995). Some authors have doubted that all V2-clauses are derived by V-to-C movement. Two popular proposals of this kind are Travis (1991) and Zwart

(1994).[37] The interesting departure from the *traditional* analysis is that they assume that V2-movement does not target a uniform position within the clause structure but that subject-initial clauses are generated by movement of the verb to the phrase-initial I-head[38], as shown in (88). Non-subject-initial clauses are analyzed as V-to-C movement as in the traditional account, as in (89).

(88) Subject-initial clause

a. Der Junge hat gestern den Kuchen gegessen ~~hat~~.
[the boy].NOM has yesterday [the cake].ACC eaten
'The boy has ate the cake yesterday.'

37 These two accounts differ with respect to the headedness of the VP: Travis (1991) assumes a head-final VP for German and Dutch whereas Zwart (1994) assumes a head-initial VP following the *antisymmetry* approach of Kayne (1994). In a nutshell, Zwart (1994) proposes that the basic underlying word order of Dutch (and German) is SVO, from which a second order, namely SOV is derived by raising the subject and the object to higher functional positions (Spec-AgrObjP and Spec-AgrSubP). Note the criticism of antisymmetry approaches to SOV-languages in Haider (2012).

38 In Zwart (1994), this head is identified as the AgrSubj-head of a split-IP model.

b.

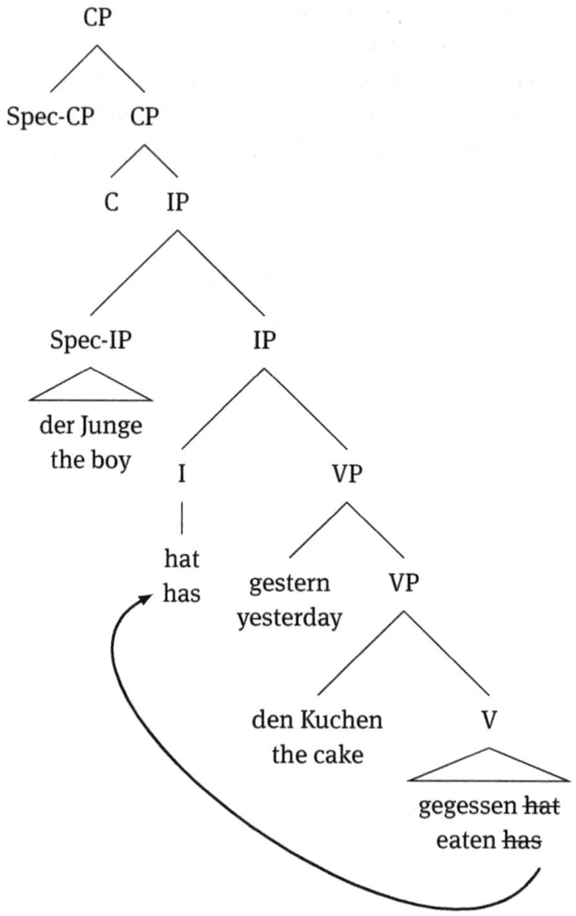
CP
Spec-CP
CP
C
IP
Spec-IP
IP
der Junge
the boy
I
VP
hat
has
gestern
yesterday
VP
den Kuchen
the cake
V
gegessen ~~hat~~
eaten ~~has~~

(89) Non-subject-initial clause

a. Den Kuchen hat der Junge gestern ~~den Kuchen~~ gegessen ~~hat~~.
[the cake].ACC has [the boy].NOM yesterday eaten
'The boy ate the cake yesterday.'

b.

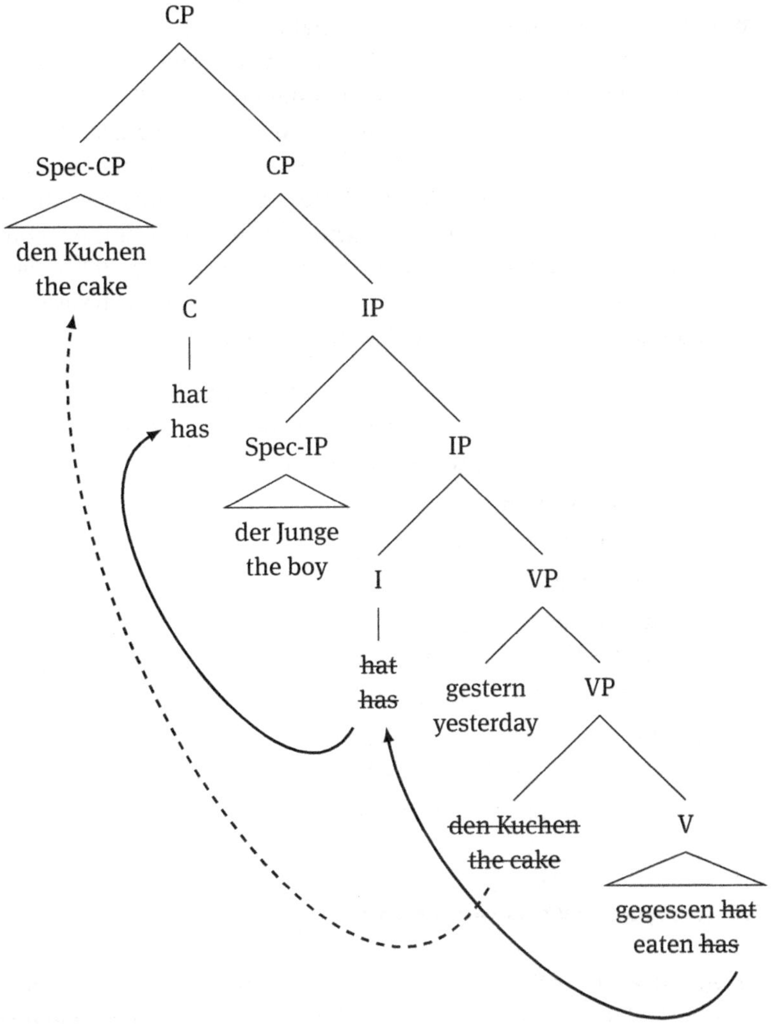

I will not go into detail of the theoretical arguments concerning the contemporary models at that time but rather focus on the empirical arguments in favor of a distinction between subject-initial and non-subject-initial clauses (for an extensive discussion with counterarguments see Schwartz & Vikner 1989 and Schwartz & Vikner 1996). The main evidence comes from the distribution of clitics and weak pronouns. The observation is that there is an asymmetry that allows weak pronouns to appear in the prefield only if they are subjects and not if they are objects (Travis 1991: 359). The example is illustrated for the neuter German weak pronoun *es* 'it' in (90). Taking the sentence in (90a) as an illustration of the base order, it is possible to express the subject by a weak pronoun, as in (90b), but unacceptable for the object, as in (90c). As I have discussed in Section 2.1.4.4, this asymmetry is only apparent and depends on the definiteness and specificity of the other arguments in the middle field. As Travis (1991: 359) partly suggests, the problem of putting *es* into the prefield position seems to correlate with the incompatibility of stressing *es*. Consequently, changing the sentence as in (90d) allows an unstressed object-*es* in the prefield. Hence, there is no empirical basis to postulate a more elaborate syntactic structure than the V-to-C model.

(90) a. ... dass das Kind gestern das Buch gelesen hat
that the child yesterday the book read hat
'... that yesterday the child read the book.'

b. Es hat gestern das Buch gelesen.
it has yesterday the book read
'Yesterday it read the book.'

c. * Es hat das Kind gestern gelesen.
it has the child yesterday read
'Yesterday the child read it.'

d. Es hat noch niemand gelesen.
it has yet nobody read
'Until now, nobody read it.'

2.3.4 Two types of V2-movement: Force and Fin

Following the influential article of Rizzi (1997), the C-domain has been divided into an articulated structure with functional layers, that are related to specific information structural properties on the one hand, such as frame setting, topic, and focus, and two positions that are related to the clause-internal structure and the superordinate structure, namely Fin and Force. Such an articulated periphery may look like in (91). Each of the layers provides a head position and a specifier position. Intuitively, FinP has been associated with V2-movement because

V2-movement only affects finite verbs. The additional positions have been used to account for systematic extensions of the V2-constraint to V3(+n) structures, especially in North Italian dialects (Poletto 2002) and Medieval Romance (Wolfe 2016). To account for typical V2-languages which provide only one position in front of the finite verb, Poletto (2002) and Wolfe (2016) propose that verb movement targets different final landing sites in those languages: In all V2-languages, in order to check the finiteness feature, the finite verb moves to FinP, which is also the final landing site in Fin-V2 languages. As a consequence, more than one element may precede the moved verb. In Force-V2 languages on the other hand, the Force-head has a strong feature that attracts the finite verb in Fin. Consequently, only frame setters or hanging topics may precede the V2-position (Poletto 2002: 237–238).

(91) $[_{\text{HangingTopic/FrameP}}\ [_{\text{ForceP}}\ [_{\text{TopP}}\ [_{\text{FocP}}\ [_{\text{FinP}}\ [_{\text{TP}} \ldots]]]]]]$

The *Split-V2* approach offers a way to account for cross-linguistic variation of the number of elements preceding the finite verb in (apparent) V2-languages. However, it does not provide any insight as to why the verb moves and what triggers this movement to FinP. On the contrary, this account introduces a further puzzle, namely a second abstract feature in ForceP that attracts the finite verb in FinP. In sum, we see that in such a two-stage system, we have to duplicate the stipulated trigger for V2-movement which is already problematic in the classical V2-system.

2.3.5 Remnant movement

Müller (2004) proposes a remnant movement account for V2 in German. In this account, the V2-configuration does not result from two different movements into the C-domain but from only one phrasal movement operation of vP into Spec-CP. Müller (2004) assumes a structural analysis of a simple German sentences as in (92).

(92) a. (dass) der Junge gestern den Kuchen gegessen hat
that the boy yesterday the cake eaten has
'that yesterday, the boy ate the cake.'

b.

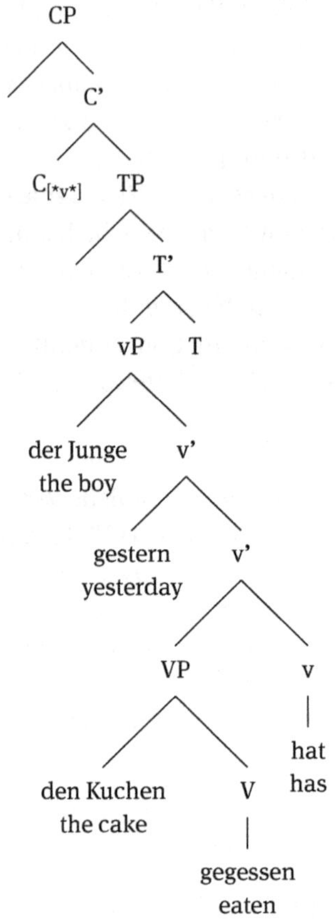

At this stage, all surface constituents are inside vP. Moving vP to Spec-CP would therefore not change the order of the constituents. To obtain the V2-order, all elements that should not appear in the C-domain must be evacuated from vP, as shown in (93). Subsequently, the vP moves to Spec-CP and yields a subject-initial V2-clause, as in (94).

(93)

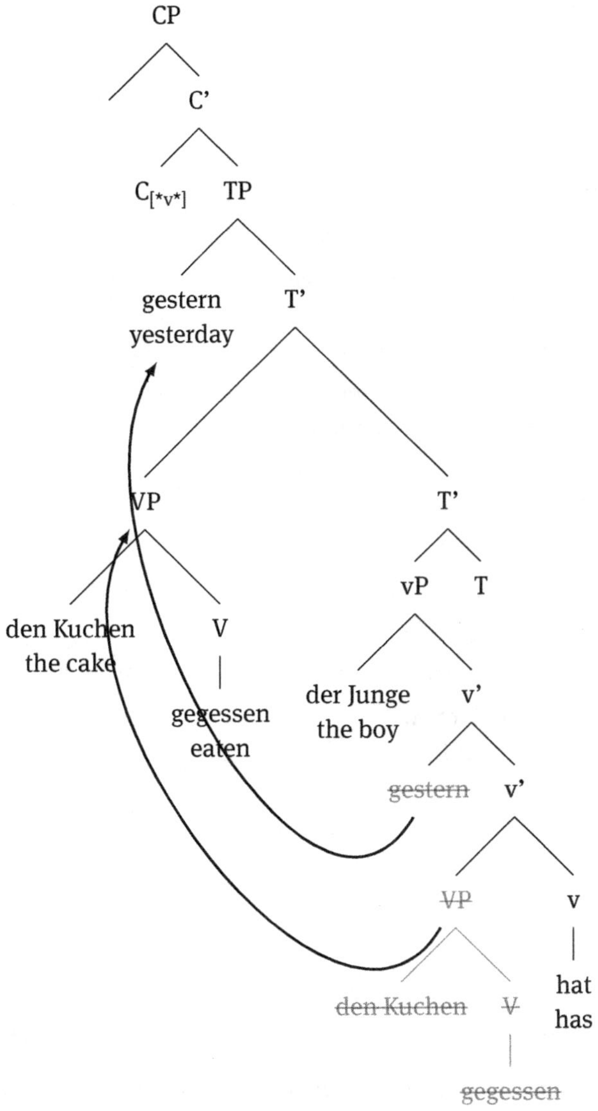
CP
C'
C[*v*]
TP
gestern
yesterday
T'
VP
T'
den Kuchen
the cake
V
gegessen
eaten
vP
T
der Junge
the boy
v'
gestern
v'
VP
v
den Kuchen
V
gegessen
hat
has

(94)

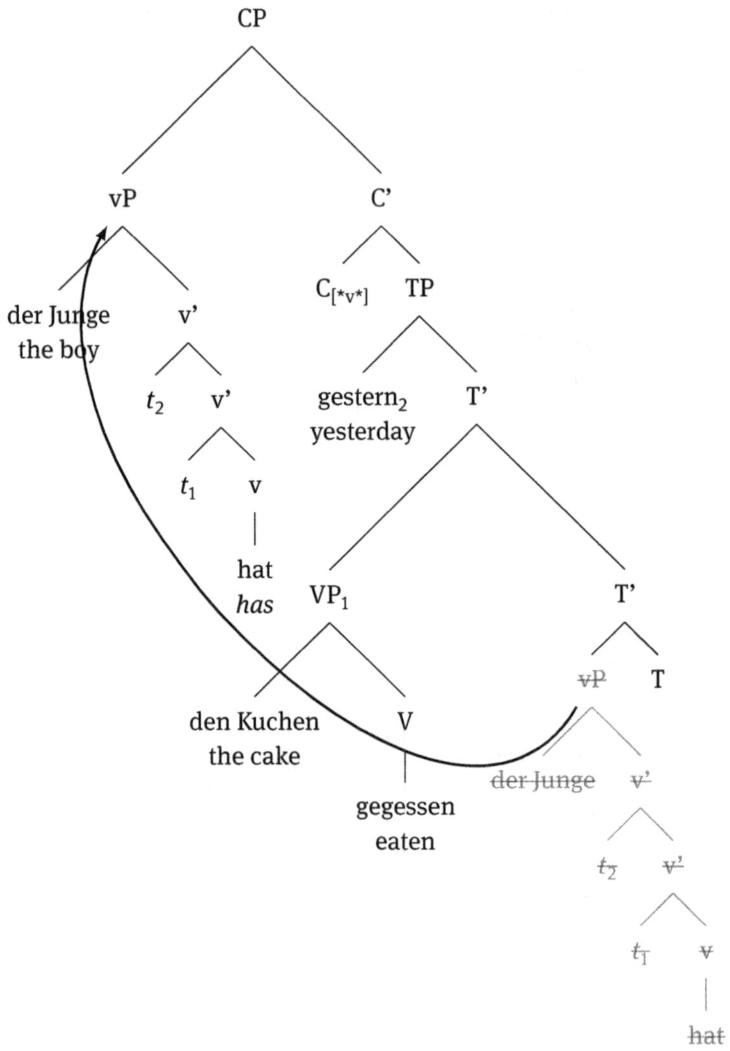

The derivation of object-initial V2-clauses is even more complicated, as shown in (95). Only after a cascade of evacuation movements, the vP is prepared to move to Spec-CP: First, the object is scrambled to the edge of vP. Afterwards, the remaining VP, the adverbial, and the subject are raised to specifiers in the T-domain.

(95)

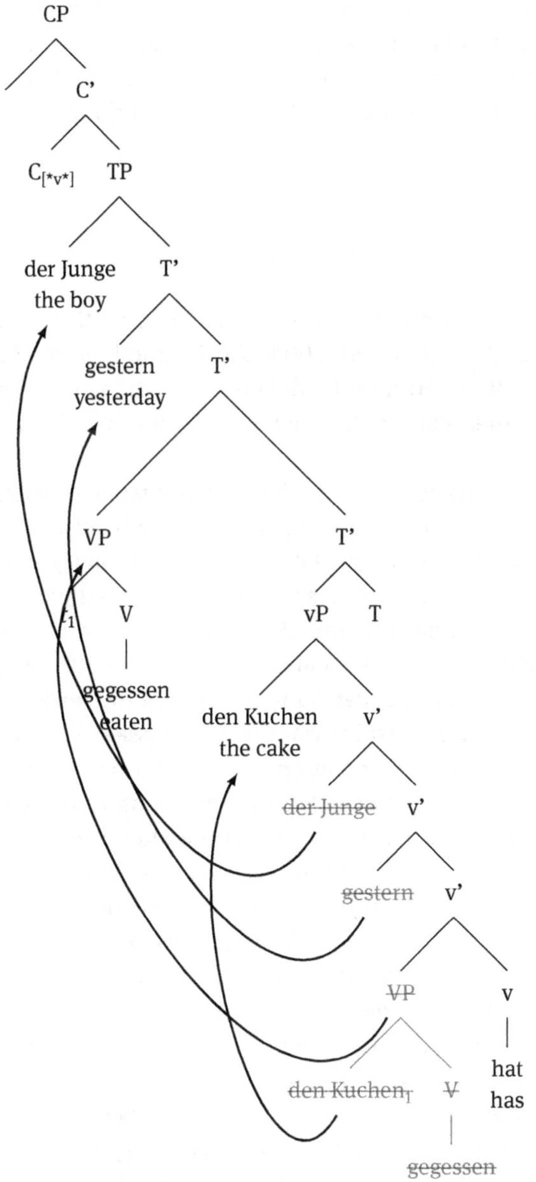

I will not discuss further sentence types but rather focus on the mechanism. Movement is feature driven. Therefore, the movement of vP to Spec-CP must be induced by a feature. Müller (2004) assumes that the C-head bares a strong feature [*v*]

which attracts vP. In this respect, the remnant movement account has to stipulate the attraction mechanism in the same way as the traditional account does for the head movement. Furthermore, Müller (2004) has to assume additional movement triggers to enable the evacuation of the vP, such as an optional [*D*] feature on T (Müller 2004: 189).

2.3.6 Semantico-pragmatic accounts of V2

Semantico-pragmatic accounts of V2 received a lot of attention in the last thirty years (e. g. Wechsler 1991, Brandner 2004, Truckenbrodt 2006a,b, Julien 2015, Lohnstein 2020). I will not go into the details of the differences between these formalizations but rather focus on the common core and sketch two problematic issues.

The history of these accounts starts with the observation of Hooper & Thompson (1973) that root transformation apply only in *asserted* clauses. Common to the above-mentioned accounts is that they derive the illocutionary force in a combinatorial fashion in which verb movement plays an essential part. Truckenbrodt (2006a), for instance, assumes that the CP bears context indices which must be checked via verb movement. These context indices specify the deontic aspect of the speech act, i. e. what the speaker wants in uttering the sentence. Imperative morphology specifies that the speaker wants the addressee to perform what is denoted by the clause. Declaratives and interrogatives are used in acts to change the epistemic states of the interlocutors: Declaratives are used to assert something, i. e. the addressee should accept the content of the utterance. Interrogatives are used to ask the addressee for information. Whereas in −WH clauses, verb movement is essential for evaluating the epistemic component, the crucial effect in +WH clauses reduces to addressee-specification. This already indicates that the ascribed function of computing the illocutionary potential is non-trivial and verb movement does not serve only one purpose. The two effects are devoted to different properties of the verb: verbal mood for the epistemic component and subject-verb agreement for addressee-specification.

Semantico-pragmatic accounts are very attractive because they provide an explanation for why the verb actually has to move. They have in common that they assume that verb-movement is triggered by the need to type a clause, i. e. to express some kind of illocutionary force. And while there seems to be a strong correlation between verb position and clause types, there remain two major issues that relate to the cross-linguistic, the inter-linguistic, and the intra-linguistic level. The first issue concerns the cross-linguistic generality of the claim that illocutionary force has to be marked explicitly by a syntactic mechanism such as verb movement. Proponents of these accounts must explain why (probably) a majority of languages does not show explicit marking for declarative assertions, i. e. how illocutionary force is activated in these cases and why this presumably more economic mechanism is not available in V2-languages. The second issue concerns the correlation between formal properties of sentences (V1, V2, etc.) and their illocutionary force, which is not as uniform as we would expect. On the one hand, we have seen in Section 2.2 that German also exhibits independent utterances without verb movement (see Bayer 2004: 88–89). On the other hand, the mechanism seems to be language-specific because in Kashmiri several types of subordinate clauses (e. g. complement clauses and causal clauses) show obligatory V2-movement without being independent illocutions (Bhatt & Yoon 1991, Bhatt 1995, Koul & Wali 2015). If, however, the effect of verb movement is not uniform, it begs the question why V2-languages show such a similar behavior in root clauses.

2.3.7 Summary of the explanatory accounts

The accounts for V2 that have been discussed in this section can be divided into two groups. The syntactic accounts focus on the mechanisms that derive the correct word order patterns by specifying appropriate features in the respective positions. The semantico-pragmatic accounts, on the hand, try to connect these movement-triggering features with specific aspects of illocutionary properties of the sentences.

2.4 Chapter summary

The review of the observations about the V2-phenomenon showed that movement of the finite verb in main clauses can never be suspended. In Section 2.1.3, I discussed two configurations in which specific verb forms cannot move into the V2-position. Crucially, however, even in these configurations they cannot remain in their clause-final base position. Movement of phrasal constituents, on the other hand, seems to be much less general. V2-languages exhibit regular V1-structures as well as structures in which more than one element precedes the finite verb. Additionally, phrasal movement seems to be directly related to interpretational properties of the elements involved, such as topicality, contrast, etc. Verb movement, in contrast, does not seem to have such a specific meaning component.

The examination in this chapter also showed that V2-order is only the most frequent pattern in main clauses but V1- and V3-orders also occur regularly in the languages at hand. The review of the theoretical accounts revealed that a more precise definition is that the finite verb moves to a certain position. This position is definable in relation to other constituents such as subject and topic, and we might call it the C-position. Constitutional for V2-languages is therefore the relation between the base position of the verb (V) and the high, left-peripheral position (C). This is the core insight of the den Besten (1983) analysis which remains the most accurate and economic analysis until today. I have indicated that a class of accounts try to establish a connection between the movement trigger and the illocutionary potential of matrix clauses. The hypothesis that will be presented in the next chapter complements these observations insofar as it indicates that V2-movement is triggered by an abstract feature which is tied to finiteness inflection in German. However, the remainder of this book does not double down on the cause of V2-movement but focuses on the consequences especially for processing V2-clauses.

3 The V2-Reconstruction Hypothesis

In this chapter, I argue that verbs which are attracted by V2-movement have to be reconstructed into their base position for interpretation. Consequently, the lexical meaning of the finite verb is never interpreted in the overt V2-position. I start by motivating and specifying this hypothesis. Thereafter, I present empirical observations in support for the claims that verbs are not interpreted in V2-position (Section 3.2) but that the verb must be interpreted in its base position (Section 3.3). In Section 3.4, I present the results of an acceptability study which investigates claims concerning periphrastic *tun*, thereby backing up the analysis of Section 3.2. The last section summarizes the results and addresses its consequences.

3.1 Defining the V2-Reconstruction Hypothesis

3.1.1 Introduction

Based on the well-know and solid generalization that only finite verbs are subject to V2-movement, Bayer & Freitag (2020) argue that V2-movement is essentially feature movement. The crucial features that are attracted are the finiteness features which are encoded by the inflection at the finite verb. The inflection, however, cannot be separated from the verb for reasons of morphological integrity. Therefore, the verbal stem that carries the inflection has to move as a whole: The verb is pied-piped. Crucially, even though the verb moves to a higher position, it is interpreted in its base position. This *V2-Reconstruction Hypothesis*[1] is given in (1).

(1) *V2-Reconstruction Hypothesis*
The finite verb that appears in 2nd position in a V2-language is in this position only for the reason of generalized pied-piping. Even when it is perceived in V2-position, its lexical part is evaluated in its base position, i. e. in German in clause-final position.
(Bayer & Freitag 2020: 79)

After a short note that clarifies the necessary concepts in relation to movement, reconstruction, and pied-piping, I will present empirical evidence in support for the V2-Reconstruction Hypothesis in the following two sections. In Part II of this book, I will show that the V2-Reconstruction Hypothesis makes very accurate predictions for the processing of German V2-clauses.

1 *Conjecture about V2* in Bayer & Freitag (2020).

https://doi.org/10.1515/9783110725018-003

3.1.2 Understanding *movement, reconstruction,* and *pied-piping*

Movement can be considered as the establishment of a dependency between two syntactic positions. Such dependencies can be categorized along two parameters: first, movement which is accompanied by an amendment or a change in meaning and second, movement which has no identifiable effect on meaning. In the Minimalist framework (Chomsky 1995), the division between the two interface levels, the Phonetic Form (PF, perceptual-articulatory dimension) and the Logical Form (LF, the conceptual dimension), has been proven to be very useful for the understanding of such dependencies. The types of movement are assumed to exhibit different requirements at the interfaces, such that the meaning-sensitive movement takes place also at LF, whereas the meaning-insensitive movement only takes place at the PF-interface. The four possible combinations of these interface requirements are summarized in Table 3.1.

Table 3.1: Types of movement

		PF	
		moved	**in-situ**
LF	**moved**	classical overt movement	covert movement
	in-situ	PF-movement (pied-piping)	in-situ-elements

Why do elements move? In the minimalist framework, movement (or more appropriately *attraction/internal merge*) must be triggered by a strong uninterpretable feature. Such an [–interpretable] feature attracts the closest element that bears the appropriate feature to delete the [–interpretable] feature. In this way, an element is *moved* from its original position to the target position, where it is in some local relation to the attractor. The division of features into movement triggering [–interpretable] and non-triggering features [+interpretable] originates from a conceptual necessity of the derivational model. One should not be confused by the terminology (±interpretable) and assume that movement does not affect interpretation. Right the opposite is the case. Usually, movement is necessary to yield a grammatical/interpretable structure at all.

We can understand movement, or the establishment of a dependency between two syntactic positions, as a way to express two aspects of meaning with one syntactic object. For illustration, take the case of *wh*-fronting in (2). A declarative sentence, such as (2a) can be transformed into a *wh*-question by replacing a syntactic element by a respective *wh*-term, such as the subject in (2b) or the object in (2c) (the translations indicate the parallel structures in English). In *wh*-fronting languages, such as German and English, the highest *wh*-term must be placed in clause-initial position.

(2) a. Also hat der Junge diesen Mann gekannt.
thus has the boy this man known
'Thus, the boy knew this man.'

b. *Wer* hat ~~wer~~ diesen Mann gekannt?
who.NOM has this man known
'Who knew ~~who knew~~ this man?'[2]

c. *Welchen Mann* hat der Junge ~~welchen Mann~~ gekannt?
which man has the boy known
'Which man did the boy know ~~which man~~?'

Examples (2a) and (2b), however, show that an object can be interpreted in the post-subject position. Therefore, the only properties that need to be interpreted clause-initially in (2c) are the ones that are tied to the interrogative meaning. Following standard assumptions, I assume that quantificational properties are computed at the fronted position, e. g. scope. At the base position, the thematic properties of the object are interpreted, as schematized in (3), see also Sportiche (2006: 40–41).

(3) $[\text{WH+Object}]_1$ Subject Verb_{eng} ~~Object~~$_1$ Verb_{deu}
quantificational properties thematic properties

Example (4) illustrates the effect of scope marking: In both variants, the *wh*-term is related to the object of the embedded clause. In (4a), the *wh*-element only scopes over the embedded clause. Hence, the matrix clause is still declarative. In (4b), on the other hand, the *wh*-element is moved to the sentence-initial position where it scopes over the matrix and the embedded clause. Hence, the whole sentence is interrogative. Due to the identical base position of the *wh*-elements in both sentences, the difference in meaning stems from the different target positions of the moved elements.

(4) a. Also hat die Professorin erzählt, *welchen Mann* der Junge ~~welchen Mann~~
thus has the professor told which man the boy
gekannt hat.
known has
'Thus the professor told which man the boy knew ~~which man~~.'

2 Clearly, the verb moved at least from V-to-I in English subject-questions. Whether it also moves from I-to-C or not is of no particular interest here.

b. *Welchen Mann* hat die Professorin erzählt, dass der Junge ~~welchen Mann~~
which man has the professor told that the boy
gekannt hat?
known has
'Which man did the professor tell that the boy knew ~~which man~~?'

Overt movement results in a situation in which we have multiple positions for interpretation but only one position in which the respective element is spelled out. This connection has been covered by all theories of movement but is handled most elegantly by the copy theory of movement: Movement creates a copy of the moved material in the target position. Usually, only one of this copies is spelled out at PF – under normal conditions the highest of all copies.

Now, we can evaluate whether there is movement only at PF without a semantic motivation. The answer is yes. It is actually very common that movement affects larger parts than only the element which bears the attracted feature. This phenomenon is known under the term *pied-piping* (going back to Ross 1967: 196–240). As I have shown above, the nominal object [$_{\text{DP}}$ Det *boy*] can be interpreted in-situ, i. e. in its post-subject base position. The reason why *wh*-terms such as *which boy* move is that *which* has to move and *which* and *boy* have to be connected by some mechanism. What would be minimally needed for a structure as (5a) is something like the structure in (5b), where the indices indicate the association of the two elements.

(5) a. *Welchen Mann* hat der Junge ~~welchen Mann~~ gekannt?
which man has the boy known
'Which man did the boy know ~~which man~~?'

b. * *Welchen*$_i$ hat der Junge ~~welchen~~ Mann$_i$ gekannt?
which has the boy man known
'*Which did the boy know ~~which~~ man?'

However, frequently, we observe that movement affects larger parts than actually expected, such as in (5a). In such cases, we say that *boy* is pied-piped by the element *which*. The element *boy* does not move because it bears the attracted feature but because it stands in a relation with an element that bears such a feature. The reason why *boy* moves together with *which* is that the relation between these two elements must not be broken by destroying their local configuration. In (5a) the pied-piping element is the phrase structural head that takes its complement along. The same element may also pied-pipe an exponent of a higher structure, such as in (6). The determiner *which* is a complement to the head *mit* 'with'. Nevertheless, in German, such a preposition cannot be left behind as in (6b) but must be fronted along with the DP, as in (6c). The rationale is the same here: The local relation between the preposition and its complement DP must not be destroyed (see Bayer & Bader 2007). Under certain conditions, however, we observe *split phenomena*, for example preposition stranding in English (Hornstein & Weinberg 1981), indicated by the grammatical translation in (6b), or *was-für*-splits in German (den Besten 1985).

(6) a. Dann hat der Junge mit diesem Mann telefoniert.
Then has the boy with this man called
'Then the boy talked to this man over the phone.'

b. * *Welchem Mann* hat der Junge [mit ~~welchem Mann~~] telefoniert?
which man has the boy with called
'Which man did the boy talked to ~~which man~~ over the phone?'

c. *Mit welchem Mann* hat der Junge [~~mit welchem Mann~~] telefoniert?
with which man has the boy called
'To which man did the boy talked ~~to which man~~ over the phone?'

If an element has moved but is interpreted in a position in which it has been "before", we say it has been *reconstructed.* Reconstruction has been discussed almost exclusively for phenomena including binding and scope relations (i. e. quantificational operators), and this for a good reason: binding and scope require a c-command relation between two elements, i. e. a specific hierarchical configuration. This requirement for c-command acts as a robust diagnostic for the actual position of interpretation. Therefore, reconstruction might apply in many more cases for which we just lack a diagnostic to properly identify it (see Chomsky 1976: 332–336, Huang 1993, Bayer 1993: 23–27, and Sportiche 2006 for a comprehensive overview of reconstruction).

Classic examples to illustrate reconstruction effects are condition C violations.[3] Consider example (7). In (7a) the pronoun *ihn* 'him' can be coreferent with *Uwe* because only the phrase containing the R-expression *Uwe* c-commands the pronoun. In (7b), on the other hand, the subject pronoun *er* 'he' cannot be coreferent with *Uwe* because the pronoun now asymmetrically c-commands the R-expression, which violates principle C.

(7) a. Also hat [[Uwes_i] Chefin] $\text{ihn}_{i/j}$ angerufen.
thus has Uwe's boss him called
'Thus Uwe's_i boss called $\text{him}_{i/j}$.'

3 This refers to Principle C of the Binding Theory: R(eferential)-expressions, such as the proper name *Uwe*, must be free, i. e. must not be c-commanded by a coreferential element (Chomsky 1981: 101–103, 188).

b. Also hat er$_{*i/j}$ [[Uwes$_i$] Chefin] angerufen.
thus has he Uwe's boss called
'Thus, he$_{*i/j}$ called Uwe's$_i$ boss.'

Now, consider example (8), in which the complex DP *Uwes Chefin* 'Uwe's boss' is fronted into Spec-CP (topcalized). In (8a), the fronting does not alter the c-command relation between the R-expression and the object pronoun: Spec-CP as well as the subject position c-command the object position. In (8b), on the other hand, the overt position of the R-expression, Spec-CP, is not in the c-command domain of the subject pronoun *er* 'he' but only the base position of the object. Nevertheless, we observe the same coreference options as in (7b), which indicates that binding is evaluated with respect to the base position of moved constituents.

(8) a. [Uwes$_i$ Chefin] hat [~~Uwes$_i$ Chefin~~] ihn$_{i/j}$ angerufen.
Uwe's boss has him called
'Uwe's$_i$ boss called him$_{i/j}$.'
b. [Uwes$_i$ Chefin] hat er$_{*i/j}$ [~~Uwes$_i$ Chefin~~] angerufen.
Uwe's boss has he called
'It was Uwe's$_i$ boss he$_{*i/j}$ called ~~Uwe's boss~~.'

Also relevant in the context of the V2-Reconstruction Hypothesis is the observation that movement which involves (parts of) predicates must obligatorily reconstruct, also in cases of phrasal A-bar movement such as VP-topicalization or topicalization of a predicative adjective (Heycock 1995, Sportiche 2006: 61–62). Hence, V2-moved finite verbs are in good company. Furthermore, Sauerland & Elbourne (2002) argue that (total) reconstruction applies only to cases of PF movement, such as pied-piping. Therefore, two aspects of the V2-Reconstruction Hypothesis receive independent support: Verbs as well as pied-piped elements reconstruct, therefore it is very likely that pied-piped verbs will do so too.

Movement which takes place at both levels, on the surface (PF) and accompanied by a change in meaning (LF), triggers two interpretation processes in language comprehension. In the literature on sentence processing this has been extensively studied under the term *filler-gap dependency* (see Section 4.2.2). Oversimplified, the processor computes one set of properties in the target position and another set of properties in the base position, as illustrated for quantificational properties and thematic properties in (3) and (4).

3.1.3 Outlook

The V2-Reconstruction Hypothesis actually consists of two interrelated claims: First, the lexical content of the finite verb is only pied-piped to the C-position. Second, the finite verb undergoes obligatory reconstruction, i. e. it is interpreted in its base position. In the following, I will list several empirical phenomena in support of the V2-Reconstruction Hypothesis by providing independent evidence for the validity of both claims.[4] The arguments of the first class support the claim that only the finiteness features are attracted by V2-movement and not (the lexical content of) the verb (Section 3.2). I discuss particle verbs, periphrastic-*tun* constructions, verb doubling constructions, Frisian *wer*-insertion, and complementizer agreement. They all have in common that finiteness features are expressed in the C-domain although the lexical verb (or parts of it) is present in the clause-final base position or in Spec-CP. The second class of observations, Section 3.3, contains association with focus, verbal negative polarity items, and sentential negation. These have in common that they require configurations in which the finite verb must be c-commanded by a certain operator. Crucially, only the clause-final base position but not the C-position lies within the c-command domain of the respective operators. This indicates that the meaning of the verb is interpreted in the clause-final position. Thus, these two complementary classes of arguments provide support for the two basic assumptions of the V2-Reconstruction Hypothesis: Movement only targets the finiteness features and the verb has to be reconstructed for semantic interpretation.

3.2 The C-position: Challenging a lexical contribution at the surface position

3.2.1 Particle verbs: V-to-C as movement of phonological words

German exhibits a class of complex verbs, so called particle verbs, which consist of a verbal base and a prefixed particle, usually of prepositional origin. If V2-movement applies to a finite particle verb, only the inflected verbal base moves to the V2-position. The particle remains stranded in the base position, as illustrated in (9a) and (9b). The combination of particle and verb can be transparent,

4 The arguments in Section 3.2 and Section 3.3 have already be published in Bayer & Freitag (2020). Some of those observation were adapted from an earlier manuscript (Bayer 2008), namely periphrastic *tun* (Section 3.2.2), verb doubling (Section 3.2.3), association with focus (Section 3.3.1), and negative polarity items (Section 3.3.2).

as in (9), and related lexemes, such as *abkaufen* (of+buy 'buy from so.'), *ankaufen* (on+buy 'purchase'), or *zukaufen* (to+buy 'buy in addition'), which are all flavors of buying. The particle verb in (10) is an example of a non-compositional meaning, *auf-führen* (on-lead) 'perform'.

(9) a. Uwe kauft einen Apfel ein.
Uwe buys an apple in
'Uwe buys an apple.'

b. ... dass Uwe einen Apfel einkauft.
that Uwe an apple in.buys
'... that Uwe buys an apple.'

(10) Nicole führt eine Oper auf.
Nicole leads an opera on
'Nicole performs an opera.'

The contrast pair in (11) shows that one and the same combination of particle and verb *abhauen* (off+chop) can have a compositional meaning 'chop off' as in (11a) or it can have an idiosyncratic meaning 'leave quickly' as in (11b).

(11) a. Sie haut den Ast mit einer Axt ab.
she chops the branch with an axe off
'She chops off the branch with an axe.'

b. Sie haut vor der Polizei ab.
she chops from the police off
'She leaves quickly from the police.'

All the examples above illustrate that V2-movement does not target the semantic word but a smaller unit. This implies that the verb cannot be interpreted in C because it is incomplete. Kremers (2009) proposes to capture the regularities of particle verb movement by mapping rules between the syntactic and the phonological structure.[5] The relevant units for the mapping in the present discussion are phonological phrases (φ), which typically correspond to syntactic phrases, and prosodic words (ω), which typically correspond to syntactic heads. Kremers (2009) assumes that particle verbs consist of two separate prosodic words, one for the verb and one for the particle, as illustrated in (12) as an analysis of (9b). The particle verb as a whole is a phonological phrase.[6]

---

5 In Chapter 4, I will introduce a similar mapping for language processing (comprehension).

6 Kremers (2009) formulates conditions and mapping restrictions to cover the observation that particles of particle verbs behave like phrases if they are separated from the verbal base, as indi-

(12) Uwe einen Apfel ein kauft
{ ω }$_{\varphi}$ { ω ω }$_{\varphi}$ { ω ω }$_{\varphi}$

The analysis of particle verbs as two separate prosodic words also offers an explanation for the observation that inflectional morphemes, such as the infinitive marker *zu* 'to', may attach directly to the verb, thereby intervening between particle and verb, as shown in (13).

(13) ohne einen Apfel ein-zu-kaufen
without an apple in-to-buy
'without buying an apple'

---

cated by adverbial modification, whereas they behave like heads if they appear adjacent to the verbal base, where they cannot be modified, as shown in (i.b) and (ii.b). Note, however, that additional movement of the particle (verb raising) is necessary to yield this contrast in (ii.b), i. e. modification of the particle is fine in the non-derived base position, as in (ii.a) and (iii.a). The respective contrasts in German, however, seem to be very subtle if at all present, as indicated in (iii).

(i) a. *John threw the ball (right) in.*
b. *John threw (*right) in the ball.*
(see Kremers 2009: 86)

(ii) DUTCH
a. ... *dat Jan de bal (vlak) over geschoten heeft*
that Jan the ball right over shot has
'... *that John kicked the ball just over the goal*'
b. ... *dat Jan de bal* t_1 *heeft [(*vlak) over geschoten]*$_1$
that Jan the ball has right over shot
c. ... *dat Jan de bal (vlak) over* t_1 *heeft [geschoten]*$_1$
that Jan the ball right over has shot
(see Kremers 2009: 86)

(iii) GERMAN
a. ... *dass Jan den Ball (richtig) drübergeschossen hat.*
that Jan the ball right over shot has
'... *that Jan shot the ball right over (the goal)*'
b. *[(Richtig) drüber]*$_1$ *hat Jan den Ball* t_1 *geschossen.*
right over has Jan the ball shot.
'*Jan shoots the ball right over (the goal).*'
c. *[(?Richtig) drübergeschossen]*$_1$ *hat Jan den Ball* t_1.
right over shot has Jan the ball

The observation that V2-movement only targets the verbal base of particle verbs can now be expressed by a mapping rule, as in (14). This rule states that the C-position is a head position that may only be filled by a single head that maps onto a single prosodic word (ω). There is no room for two prosodic words or a phonological phrase. Hence the particle must remain in its underlying position.

(14) C ↔ ω
(Kremers 2009: 92)

In this section, I have pointed out two generalizations concerning particle verbs: First, the separability of particle verbs by V2-movement is independent of semantic compositionality. Second, V2-movement targets only the smallest possible unit, i. e. a prosodic word. These two generalizations indicate that V2-movement is a semantics-free operation based on morphophonological properties (more on the perspective of interpreting particle verbs is discussed in Section 4.3.4). The conclusion about particle verbs is in line with the V2-Reconstruction Hypothesis in (1): V2-movement is a mechanism to bring finiteness features into the C-position. Aspects of the lexical verb are of no importance. Consequently, the meaning of particle verbs, compositional or idiomatic, is interpreted in the clause-final base position.

3.2.2 Semantically empty host I: Periphrastic *tun*

German exhibits several constructions with the verb *tun* 'do'. Very common are light verb constructions as in (15).

(15) a. einen Gefallen tun
a favor do
'do a favor'

b. Leid tun
sorrow do
'be/feel sorry'

Despite these expressions, certain registers and dialectal variants also allow the *tun*-periphrasis. In such constructions, *tun* cooccurs with another verbal element and functions as a finite auxiliary (Fischer 2001). It has been noted that, in some dialectal variants, the *tun*-periphrasis may be used to express conjunctive and to mark aspect (Abraham & Fischer 1998, Kölligan 2004, Schwarz 2004). I will exclude those cases from the discussion and focus solely on the indicative use.

The *tun*-periphrasis is more frequent with *tun* in V2-position[7], as in (16a), but is also acceptable in V-final position, as in (16b).

(16) a. Der Junge tut gerade die Wand streichen.
the boy does currently the wall paint
'Currently the boy is painting the wall.'

b. Ich glaube, dass der Junge gerade die Wand streichen tut.
I believe that the boy currently the wall paint does
'I believe that boy is currently painting the wall.'

It must be noted that the periphrastic construction is a fully optional variant[8] to an inflected lexical verb. Abraham & Fischer (1998) assume that the *tun*-insertion is primarily a means of receiving neutral accent on the clause-final verb. This explains why *tun* appears more frequently in V2-position than in V-final position. Accordingly the *tun*-periphrasis is quite unacceptable in combination with periphrastic tense forms that already involve an auxiliary (Abraham & Fischer 1998: 37).

Crucially, the use of periphrastic *tun* is semantically/pragmatically restricted. The exact classification in the literature differs slightly: agentive vs. non-agentive verbs (Fischer 2001: 40), eventive vs. stative verbs (Maienborn 2003: 54–63, Rothmayr 2009: 28–31, Hoekstra 2016: 342), telic vs. atelic verbs (Schönenberger & Penner 1995: 318–319), and individual-level vs. stage-level predicates (Bayer & Freitag

7 The *tun*-periphrasis also occurs in the C position in V1-clauses, such as in the imperative and interrogative clauses in (i), see also Erb (2001: 183-191) for the compatibility with any sentence type.

(i) a. *Imperative*
Tut euch nich bekleckern
do you not blot
'Don't blot yourselves!'

b. *Interrogative*
Tust du pflügen?
do you plow
'Do you plow?'

(Abraham & Fischer 1998: 38, 40)

8 Despite its superficial similarity, the *tun*-periphrasis is not comparable to the English *do*-support. They have in common that they are elements for the realization of finiteness features and can be replaced by modal verbs or other auxiliaries, thereby receiving a different interpretation. They differ in their distribution: English *do*-support (in absence of another non-thematic verb) is obligatory in *wh*-questions and with sentential negation. In German there is no need for an expletive auxiliary in those environments. German requires an expletive auxiliary in case of a topicalized verb to satisfy the V2-requirement, which lacks an equivalent in English.

2020). The discussion and the results of Experiment 1 (Section 3.4) will reveal that the situation is more complex than a 2-way distinction. It will turn out that only a subgroup of stative verbs do contrast significantly with agentive verbs, as predicted by Maienborn (2003) and Rothmayr (2009). The validity of the present argument, however, does not hinge on the exact characterization of the predicate classes. For simplicity, here, I will follow the characterization of Bayer & Freitag (2020) that periphrastic *tun* is compatible with stage-level predicates but incompatible with individual-level predicates.[9] The incompatibility of individual-level predicates *own*, *resemble* and *lie on a lake* is illustrated in (17) in contrast to the non-periphrastic equivalents in (18).

(17) a. * Der Junge tut einen guten Charakter besitzen.
the boy does a good character own
'The boy has a good character.'

b. * Der Junge tut seinem Vater ziemlich ähneln
the boy does his father much resemble
'The boy resembles his father quite a lot.'

c. * Konstanz tut am Bodensee liegen
Constance does at the Lake Constance lie
'Constance lies on Lake Constance.'

(18) a. Der Junge besitzt einen guten Charakter.
the boy owns a good character
'The boy has a good character.'

b. Der Junge ähnelt seinem Vater ziemlich.
the boy resembles his father much
'The boy resembles his father quite a lot.'

c. Konstanz liegt am Bodensee.
Constance lies at the Lake Constance
'Constance lies on Lake Constance.'

The same effect can be observed for VP-pronominalization (Hoekstra 2016: 342). In coordinations, the VP of the second conjunct can, under identity, be expressed by a weak pronoun *es* or a d-pronoun *das*. The position of the finite verb in the second conjunct is filled with a periphrastic *tun*, as shown in (19) with the stage-level predicate *paint*.

---

9 In a nutshell, *stage-level predicates* describe temporary or transitory properties, such as *jump* or *being hungry*, whereas *individual-level predicates* denote rather permanent properties, such as *being smart* (see Kratzer 1995).

(19) Der Junge streicht [$_{VP}$ gerade die Wand ~~streicht~~]$_i$ und seine Nachbarin
the boy paints currently the wall and his neighbor
tut es$_i$/das$_i$ auch.
does it/that too
'The boy paint the wall and his neighbor does so/it too.'

The examples in (20) show that this very construction is impossible with individual-level predicates. Furthermore, the contrast in (21) shows that individual-level predicates are not incompatible with VP-pronominalization as such. If periphrastic *tun* is replaced by an auxiliary or modal verb, VP-pronominalization is acceptable.

(20) a. Der Junge besitzt [einen guten Charakter ~~besitzt~~]$_i$ (*und seine Freundin
the boy owns a good charackter and his girlfriend
tut es$_i$/das$_i$ auch).
does it/that too
'The boy has a good character and his girlfriend (*does so) too.'

b. Der Junge ähnelt [seinem Vater ziemlich ~~ähnelt~~]$_i$ (*und sein Bruder
the boy resembles his father much and his brother
tut es$_i$/das$_i$ auch).
does it/that too
'The boy resembles his father quite a lot and his brother (*does so) too.'

c. Konstanz liegt [am Bodensee ~~liegt~~]$_i$ (*und Friedrichshafen
Constance lies at the Lake Constance and Friedrichshafen
tut es$_i$/das$_i$ auch).
does it/that too
'Konstanz lies on Lake Constance and Friedrichshafen (*does so) too.'

(21) a. Der Junge könnte [einen guten Charakter besitzten]$_i$ (und seine
the boy could a good charackter own and his
Freundin müsste es$_i$/das$_i$ auch).
girlfriend must it/that too
'The boy could have a good character and his girlfriend should have one too.'

b. Der Junge hat [seinem Vater ziemlich geähnelt]$_i$ (und sein Bruder hat
the boy has his father much resembled and his brother has
es$_i$/das$_i$ auch).
it/that too
'The boy resembled his father quite a lot and his brother did too.'

c. [In a guessing game or riddle]
Konstanz muss [am Bodensee liegen]$_i$ (und Friedrichshafen
Constance must at the Lake Constance lie and Friedrichshafen
muss es$_i$/das$_i$ auch).
must it/that too
'Constance have to lie on Lake Constance and Friedrichshafen have to too.'

A similar contrast arises in pseudoclefts.[10] Again, stage-level predicates, as in (22), are fine, whereas individual-level-predicates in (23) are out.

(22) Was der Junge tat, war die Wand streichen.
what the boy did was the wall paint
'What the boy did was paint the wall.'

(23) a. * Was der Junge tat, war einen guten Charakter besitzen.
what the boy did was a good character own
'What the boy did was have a good character.'

b. * Was der Junge tut, ist seinem Vater ziemlich ähneln.
what the boy does is his father much resemble
'What the boy does is resemble his father quite a lot.'

c. * Was Konstanz tut, ist am Bodensee liegen.
what Constance does is at the Lake Constance lie
'What Constance does is lie on Lake Constance.'

The data indicates that periphrastic *tun* is not completely semantically empty but retains some meaning that renders it incompatible with individual-level predicates. This is the result of an automatic reconstruction into its clause-final position where the semantic restriction is evaluated in the verbal complex.

Crucially, however, the semantics of *tun* can be suspended. This is the case in VP-topicalization, as shown in (24) with individual-level predicates.

(24) a. [$_{VP}$ Einen guten Charakter besitzen] tut der Junge auf alle Fälle.
a good character own does the boy in any cases
'The boy has a good character in any case.'

b. [$_{VP}$ Seinem Vater ähneln] tut nur der Junge.
his father resemble does only the boy
'Only the boy resembles his father.'

10 See Iatridou & Varlokosta (1998) for an overview of this construction.

c. [$_{VP}$ Am Bodensee liegen] tut Stuttgart zum Gück nicht.
at the Lake Constance lie does Stuttgart luckily not
'Luckily, Stuttgart does not lie on Lake Constance.'

What is the difference between these constructions and the other uses of periphrastic *tun*? In VP-topicalization, the thematic verb and, optionally, also other elements within the VP move to Spec-CP. This is unproblematic with analytic verb forms, as in (25). Here, the auxiliary carries the finiteness features and moves to C. Things are different with synthetic verb forms. When the predicate has been moved to Spec-CP, no finite verb is left to satisfy the V2-requirement, as illustrated in (26b). The finiteness features also cannot occupy the C-position alone, as indicated in (26c), because of morphological integrity. In this case, *tun* is inserted as a host for the finiteness features as a *last resort operation*, yielding (26d). In contrast to the optional cases of periphrastic *tun* above, *tun*-insertion to satisfy the V2-requirement in VP-topicalization is obligatory.

(25) [Gestrichen]$_1$ hat$_2$ der Junge die Wand ~~gestrichen~~$_1$ ~~hat~~$_2$.
painted has the boy the wall
'The boy painted the wall.'

(26) a. (dass) der Junge die Wand streich-t
that the boy the wall paint-3SG

b. * [$_{Spec\text{-}CP}$ streich-t$_1$] [$_C$ ∅] der Junge die Wand ~~streich-t~~$_1$.
paint-3SG the boy the wall

c. * [$_{Spec\text{-}CP}$ streich$_1$] [$_C$ ∅-t$_2$] der Junge die Wand ~~streich~~$_1$ ~~-t~~$_2$.
paint 3SG the boy the wall

d. [$_{Spec\text{-}CP}$ streich$_1$-en] [$_C$ tu-t$_2$] der Junge die Wand ~~streich~~$_1$ ~~-t~~$_2$.
paint-INF do-3SG the boy the wall
'The boy paints the wall.'

The VP is fronted for information structural reasons, such as emphasizing a contrast, as illustrated in (27).[11] *Tun* must be inserted into C in order to satisfy the

11 Parts of the verb can also receive information structural marking in canonical word order, such as contrastive focus on the thematic verbs in clause-final position in (i.a). Even *tun* can receive the main accent to mark verum focus, as shown in (i.b). The semantics of *tun*, however, is still active, as illustrated in (ii).

(i) a. *Contrastive focus*
Wir tun heut noch SÄEN, PFLÜGEN und FÜTTERN.
We do.1PL today still sow.INF plow.inf and feed.inf
'Today we still do sow, plow, and feed.'

V2-requirement. It does not originate from a lower projection and cannot be reconstructed into the clause-final position. Therefore, no semantic incongruity with individual-level predicates arises. VP-topicalization thus further supports the hypothesis that *V2* is actually *Features2*. No lexical verb has to take part in V2-movement.

(27) Ich liebe dich noch immer, aber [mögen]$_1$ tu ich dich schon lang
I love you still but like.INF do.1SG I you for a long time
nicht mehr ~~mögen~~$_1$.
not anymore
'I still love you but I stopped liking you a long time ago.' (http://www.neon.de/artikel/fuehlen/liebe/am-ende-bleibt-nur-das-vermissen/1013639, access: 02.08.2017)

3.2.3 Semantically empty host II: Verb doubling

A peculiar variant of VP-topicalization is found in a number of German dialects. In contrast to VP-topicalization with *tun*-insertion, the fronted infinitive is accompanied by the finite form of the same lexical verb in V2-position, as illustrated in (28). Fleischer (2008) call this construction *topikalisierende Infinitivverdoppelung* 'topicalizing infinitive doubling'.

(28) a. VP-topicalization with verb doubling (NON-STANDARD GERMAN)
Trink-en trink-t er nicht, aber rauch-en rauch-t er.
drink-INF drink-3SG he not but smoke-INF smoke-3SG he
'He doesn't drink but he smokes.' (Fleischer 2008: 247-248)

b. VP-topicalization with *tun*-insertion (STANDARD GERMAN)
Trink-en tu-t er nicht, aber rauch-en tu-t er.
drink-INF do-3SG he not but smoke-INF do-3SG he
'He doesn't drink but he smokes.'

---

b. *Verum focus*
Ich TU ja schreiben.
I do.1SG PRT write.INF
'I do write.'
(Abraham & Fischer 1998: 41 nach Eroms 1984)

(ii) * *Der Junge TUT ja einen guten Charakter besitzten.*
the boy do.3SG PRT a good character own.
'The boy does have a good character.'

Note that modals, auxiliaries, and periphrastic *tun* allow the embedding of infinitives. These infinitives may be lexically identical to the embedding predicate, as in (29a). Accordingly, such self-embedding leads to patterns that are superficially very similar to cases of verb doubling. Self-embedding can, however, be differentiated by examples like (29b), which show that it may also appear in a V-final clause. In contrast, the doubled verbs in (28a), *trinken* 'drink' and *rauchen* 'rauchen' do not allow embedding of infinitives at all. Thus, verb doubling does not occur in clause-final position.

(29) a. Könn-en kann er, aber woll-en will er nicht.
can-INF can.3SG he but want-INF want.3SG he not
'He could be able to do it but he is not willing to want to do it.' (Fleischer 2008: 246)

b. Es ist doch klar, dass ein Kind in dem Alter das noch nicht könn-en kann.
It is PART clear that a child in this age that yet not can-INF can.3SG
'It is obvious that a child of this age cannot be able to do this.'

In his detailed survey, Fleischer (2008) reports that this construction was spread over the German language area: The northern end consists of the Berlin dialect as well as archaic peripheral varieties of Prussian. On the southern end it is attested in High Alemannic of Grisons (Switzerland), where it seems to be restricted to auxiliaries, mostly *be*, as in (33) (see also Glaser & Frey 2007). Additionally, the phenomenon is attested in several diasporic German minority dialects, which have survived in the former Soviet Union.[12]

The use of the VP-topicalization with verb doubling is the same as with *tun*-insertion. Fleischer (2008) states that verb doubling is functionally equivalent to *tun*-insertion, i. e. it is assigning a special information structural status to the

12 Koopman (1984: 37–38, 151–186) describes a very similar phenomenon under the term *predicate cleft construction*. She notes that this construction can be found in many African languages and many Caribbean creoles (Koopman 1984: 154). In the Kru lanaguage Vata, for example the verb gets focused by placing it in clause-initial position. Crucially, a copy of the verb is present in its unmarked position within the clause, as shown in (i). Note that the fronted verb may appear in the imperfective form *lē*, as in (i.a), or in the base form *lī*, as in (i.b), but never in the perfective form *lì*, as in (i.c). This parallels the verb doubling cases: In the left periphery only a base form is required, which represents the lexical meaning of the verb. The lower copy is the host for the phi-features. Note further that in Vata, too, only one of the verb forms can be semantically active because 'eat' does not embed clausal units, i. e. the predicate cleft construction is independent of the argument structure of the verb involved (Koopman 1984: 157).

fronted VP. This is further supported by examples that show both forms contrasting in one sentence, as in (30).

(30) a. PRUSSIAN

Schnuw-e	schneff-t	he	nech,	aber	preem-e	dei-t	he	färchterlich.
Schnupf-en	schnupf-t	er	nicht	aber	priem-en	tu-t	er	fürchterlich.
snuff-INF	snuff-3SG	he	not	but	chew tobacco-INF	do-3SG	he	horribly

'He doesn't snuff but he chews tobacco horribly.'

b. ISSIME (HIGH ALLEMANNIC)

Tringe	tringt=er	nöid,	wa	röike	tut=er.
trinken	trinkt=er	nicht,	aber	rauchen	tut=er
drink.INF	drinks=he	not	but	smoke.INF	does=he

'He doesn't drink but he smokes.'

(Fleischer 2008: 252)

In Yiddish, a V2-language with partial German origin, verb doubling is attested too. As can be seen in (31a), only the verb or larger parts of the VP may be topicalized, as in (31b).

(i) VATA

a. *lē à lē sȧká*
eat we eat rice
'We are really EATING *rice.'* or *'We are eating rice.'*

b. *lī Ȯ dā sȧká lī*
eat she/he AUX.PERF rice eat
'She/He has EATEN *rice.'*

c. *lī Ȯ lì sȧká*
eat she/he ate rice
'She/He ATE *rice.'*

(Koopman 1984: 38)

Katja Jasinskaja (p.c.) pointed out that verb doubling constructions are also common in Slavic languages (see Karagjosova & Jasinskaja 2015 and references therein) and crosslingustically, their presence may be rather the rule than the exception (see also Jouitteau 2012: 155–157 and references therein).

(31) YIDDISH

a. Ess-en es-t Maks fish.
eat-INF eat-3SG Max fish
'As for eating, Max eats fish'

b. [Ess-en fish] es-t Maks.
eat-INF fish eat-3SG Max
'As for eating fish, Max eats them'

(Cable 2004: 2)

Yiddish also exhibits a particular phenomenon that sheds light on the mechanism underlying the doubling mechanism. For verbs whose paradigm involves suppletive forms or ablaut, the topicalized infinitive may be realized as a *pseudo-infinitive*, which consists of the stem variant of the inflected form to which the infinitive suffix is added, as illustrated in (32) (Fleischer 2008: 260–261).

(32) YIDDISH

a. gib-n gib ikh (correct infinitive: *geb-n*)
give-INF give.3SG I
'I give'

b. veys-n veys ikh (correct infinitive: *vis-n*)
know-INF know.1SG I
'I know'

c. bin-en bin ikh (correct infinitive: *zay-n*)
am-INF am I
'I am'

d. iz-n iz er (correct infinitive: *zay-n*)
is-INF is he
'He is.'

(Fleischer 2008: 260)

These pseudo-infinitives indicate that the source of the fronted infinitive is the finite verb from the V/I position. As I have exemplified in (26), the verb stem moves to Spec-CP, where the infinitive suffix is added. Somehow certain languages seem to apply a filter that excludes illicit infinitives, as shown in (33), whereas Yiddish seems to lack such a *smoothing device*.

(33) ALEMANNIC

a. Syn bischt schoon albig der glych verdamt Schelm!
be.INF be.2SG still always the same damned rogue
'You are still the same old rogue!' (Fleischer 2008: 248) (area: Splügen, Davos)

b. Sii bisch scho en Flissige.
be.INF be.2SG certainly a hard working
'You certainly work hard.' (Glaser & Frey 2007: 5) (area: Grisons)

The inevitable conclusion from verb doubling in the context of VP-topicalization is that the finite verb in the V2-position is a semantically empty copy which is inserted only to enable the spell-out of the finiteness features in C in order to satisfy the V2-requirement. Let's recapitulate the arguments: First, both copies of the verb cannot be semantically active because verb doubling does apply to verbs that do not allow the embedding of (bare) infinitives. Second, the topicalized phrase must not be semantically empty, otherwise the topic of the sentence would be empty. Third, the finite verb in V2-position can be replaced by an inserted *tun*, by modals, or auxiliaries, whereas the topicalized verb has to be proper lexicalized. Forth, Yiddish pseudo-infinitives provide empirical support for the assumption that the topicalized infinitive is the dislocated finite verb. In sum, the verb doubling phenomenon indicates that the V2-position must only be filled with finiteness features. This may be achieved by inserting semantically empty copies of the verb to provide a host for the relevant features. Thus, this adds further support to the V2-Reconstruction Hypothesis by indicating that the V2-requirement does not involve targeting a meaningful verbal element. Consequently, it is predicted that verb doubling cannot occur in the verb's base position, i. e. the position in which the semantics of the verb is active, such as the clause-final position in (34). This prediction is borne out because such cases seem to be non-existent (Bayer & Freitag 2020: 88).

(34) GERMAN
*Ich glaube, dass ihm das nichts schaden schadet.
I believe that him this nothing harm harms
'I believe that it doesn't harm him'. (Bayer & Freitag 2020: 88)

A somewhat comparable phenomenon are dummy auxiliaries, which are observed in L2-acquisition, shown in (35). They also seem to be semantically empty elements that are inserted in C. In contrast to verb doubling, dummy auxiliaries are only quasi-finite elements that do not show proper subject agreement.

(35) a. L2 GERMAN
Ein Junge is die Fußball spielen.
a boy is the football play.INF
'A boy is playing (with the) football.' (L1 Turkish, ca. 6 years) (Haberzettl 2003: 45)

b. L2 DUTCH
Zij is ligt in de boot
she is.3SG lies.3SG in the boat
'She is lying in the boat.' (L1 Turkish) (van de Craats 2009: 77)

These patterns seem to appear more frequent in L2 Dutch (Coenen & Klein 1992, Verhagen 2009: 58-62, van de Craats 2009) but are also reported for L2 German (Haberzettl 2003, Chilla et al. 2013).

3.2.4 Semantically empty host III: Frisian *wer*-insertion

In another West Germanic variety, we find additional evidence which indicates that the lexical content of the verb does not need to appear in the C-domain but only the finiteness features. Karrharde North Frisian[13] exhibits a periphrastic verb construction with a finite auxiliary *wer-* in V2-position and a thematic verb in base position. Like the *tun*-periphrasis, this construction appears in declaratives, *wh*-interrogative, polar interrogatives, and imperatives, as shown in (36). Moreover, this construction does generally not appear with other auxiliaries or modals. In contrast to the *tun*-periphrasis, the thematic verb in clause-final position is finite too. According to Hoekstra (2016), *wer-* insertion does not show semantic or pragmatic restrictions on the co-occurring verb classes. The syntactic distribution of *wer-*, however, is restricted to the V2-position. It never occurs in clause-final position. Hoekstra (2016) argues that *wer-* is not of verbal origin but stems from the interrogative complementizer *wer* 'if, whether'. The assumption that *wer-* is a reanalyzed complementizer that functions as a semantically empty auxiliary does account for all its properties: restriction to V2-position (C-position), complementary distribution with other auxiliaries in V2-position, no semantic/pragmatic restriction, and the double marking of finiteness on the auxiliary and the thematic verb. Due to its origin as a finite complementizer, *wer-* selects a finite VP, even in last resort cases, such as VP-topicalization in (37), whereas German *tun* selects a non-finite VP. Hoekstra (2016) calls the phenomenon *finite verb doubling* what I consider to be a misnomer for the following reasons: The only thing that appears twice is the finiteness morpheme. The thematic verb, however, appears only once, in contrast to *real* doubling of the verb stem as described in the previous section. Furthermore, *wer-* is actually not of verbal origin, which is (presumably) the crucial prerequisite for the double marking of finiteness.

---

13 Frisian is closely related to low German and Dutch. It is a V-final V2-language that is spoken in the coastal area of the German Bight.

(36) KARRHARDE NORTH FRISIAN

a. Tėth-üttīnen wer-t er kan-d.
Teeth-pulling WER-PRS.3SG he know-PRS.3SG
'He knows how to pull teeth.' (Hoekstra 2016: 322)

b. Wat wer-e jem der apfask-e?
what WER-PRS.2PL you there up.fish-PRS.2PL
'What are you fishing up there?' (Hoekstra 2016: 323)

c. Denn wer-e man eg aw't Håd fāl-e.
then WER-IMP.PL only not on=the head fall-IMP.PL
'Then don't fall on your head.' (Hoekstra 2016: 325)

(37) KARRHARDE NORTH FRISIAN
He es fallight ferkimen, an lait je sagt wer krōnk,
he is maybe come down and lays really perhaps somewhere ill
an $[_{VP}$ sturwe-d$]_1$ wer-t ham niman t_1.
and nurses-PRS.3SG WER-PRS.3SG him no one
'Maybe he has come down in the world and is perhaps ill in bed somewhere with nobody nursing him.' (Hoekstra 2016: 341)

Frisian *wer*-insertion therefore shows that the V2-position does not have to be filled with a genuinely verbal element. A suitable host for the inflectional affix appears to be sufficient. This fact agrees perfectly with the results of periphrastic *tun* and verb doubling.

3.2.5 Complementizer Agreement: Inflection on non-verbal C-elements

Another configuration, the so-called *complementizer agreement*, can be observed in embedded clauses of German and Dutch dialects. As with Frisian *wer*-insertion, the inflectional affix appears at the clause-final verb and on C-elements, i. e. complementizers and *wh*-pronouns as illustrated in (38).[14] Crucially, the subject agreement does not replace the verbal agreement affixes but appears additionally (Bayer 1984, Bennis & Haegeman 1984).

14 This phenomenon therefore has to be distinguished from other instances of *complementizer agreement*. Kawasha (2007) for example describes a phenomenon in Bantu languages in which complementizers agree in person and noun class with the subject of the matrix clause. Furthermore, superficially similar phenomena in non-V2 languages differ considerably. Complementizer agreement in Nadji Arabic, as discussed in Lewis Jr. (2013), occurs only on specific lexical items, is optional, and uses non-verbal agreement morphemes.

(38) BAVARIAN
I frog' me, ob-sd ned du des mocha kan-sd.
I ask myself, whether-2SG not you this make could-2SG
'I ask myself, whether you could not do this.' (Weiss 2005: 148)

The geographical distribution seems to be restricted to Continental West Germanic languages, i. e. varieties of German and Dutch. Most prominently, this phenomenon has been described for Bavarian (Bayer 1984), West Flemish (Haegeman 1992, Shlonsky 1994), and Frisian (de Haan 2010). Weiss (2005: 149–153) notes that in most dialectal variants (of German and Dutch) at least some kind of complementizer agreement can be observed even though there are dialects that lack this phenomenon entirely (see also Zwart 1993, Hoekstra & Smits 1998). The V2-property is commonly assumed to be a necessary prerequisite for complementizer agreement. Nevertheless, being a V2-language does not seem to be a sufficient condition because complementizer agreement has not been reported for Scandinavian languages, North Italian varieties (Rhaeto-Romance), and Kashmiri.[15]

In most dialects, the agreement is paradigmatically defective (see Weiss 2005: 150–152 for an overview). Bavarian and Frisian, for example, display inflectional morphems only for 2nd person singular/plural. West Flemish, on the other hand, shows inflectional markers for all combinations of person and number, and distinguishes even gender in the 3SG (Bennis & Haegeman 1984: 41). Importantly, inflectional morphemes on the complementizers are restricted to categories of subject agreement (person and number) and never involve any tense features (den Besten 1983: 119). Moreover, complementizer agreement seems to be dependent on the formal marking of agreement on verbs: Hoekstra & Smits (1998) state that complementizer agreement only shows up for person/number combinations that exhibit the same person/number agreement morpheme in present and preterite forms of auxiliaries. This condition accounts for paradigmatic gaps of the individual dialectal variants.

Despite the term *complementizer agreement*, the inflectional affixes do not exclusively combine with complementizers but with the lowest element in the left periphery (Bayer 1984: 235). These might be complementizers, such as *dass* 'that'

15 It must be noted, however, that some North Italian dialects, such as Cimbrian, show subject clitics at complementizers that introduce non-V2 clauses whereas enclisis is blocked in subordinate clauses with V2-order (Bidese et al. 2012, 2013). Kashmiri exhibits V2-order in most types of embedded clauses, which therefore are incompatible with complementizer agreement.

in (39a), *wenn* 'if' and *weil* 'because'. In absence of an overt complementizer, the affix may also attach to a *wh*-element, as shown in (39b) and (39c).[16]

(39) BAVARIAN

a. Du sollst song an wäichan Schua dass-st du wui-st
you should say a which one shoe that-2SG you want-2SG
'You should say which one of the shoes you want.' (Bayer 1984: 235)

b. Du sollst song wann-st du komm-st
you should say when-2SG you come-2SG
'You should say when you are going to come.'

c. I frog' me, warum-sd des ned moch-sd.
I ask myself, why-2SG this not make-2SG
'I ask myself why do you not do this.' (Weiss 2005: 148)

The relation of complementizer agreement and V2-movement can be captured by two generalizations: First, complementizer agreement is not optional but obligatory in dialects that allow it.[17] Second, complementizer agreement and verb movement are complementary distributed. The following examples from Bavarian with the causal complementizer *weil* 'because' illustrate the complementary distribution of inflectional morpheme and verb movement. If the complementizer is inflected for 2nd person, as in (40a), V2-order is impossible. With a non-inflected complementizer, as in (40b), verb movement is required.

(40) BAVARIAN

a. Des is schood, weil-st du ⟨*bist⟩ gestern a scho
That is disappointing because-2SG you are yesterday also already
nit kemma ⟨bist⟩.
not come are
'That is disappointing since you already didn't show up yesterday.'

b. Des is schood, weil du ⟨bist⟩ gestern a scho nit
That is disappointing because you are yesterday also already not
kemma ⟨*bist⟩.
come are
'That is disappointing since you already didn't show up yesterday.'

16 Bayer (2014: 41–44) states that only word-size *wh*-operators receive inflection suffixes. In case of phrasal *wh*-elements, insertion of the default complementizer *dass* 'that', as in (39a) provides a licit host for the inflectional morpheme.

17 To my knowledge only Bayer (2014: 41) states explicitly that the complementizer agreement is obligatory in Bavarian. The same can (only) be inferred for the other dialects.

Even though we may assume that complementizer agreement originates from subject clitics, two properties distinguish them robustly: First, clitics are never obligatory whereas complementizer agreement is. Second, clitics do not double, whereas complementizer agreement usually cooccurs with overt subjects (Bayer 2014: 41–43), as shown in (39a) and (39b).

It is still debated whether complementizer agreement involves some kind of copy mechanism of the T-head's phi-features onto C (Fuß 2014), or whether it expresses a separate agreement relation between C (Fin) and the subject (Carstens 2003, Haegeman & van Koppen 2012). One observation, however, indicates that complementizer agreement cannot involve a *simple* copy mechanism of the verbal affix onto the complementizer. Some East Netherlandic dialects and Brabants show non-identical agreement morphemes on the complementizer and the verb (Zwart 1993, Hoekstra & Smits 1998), as illustrated by the contrasting morphemes -*(d)e* and -*t* in (41).

(41) a. EAST NETHERLANDIC
... datt-e wij speul-t.
that-1PL we play-1PL
'... that we play.'

b. BRABANTS
... dad-de gullie kom-t.
that-2PL you come-2PL
'... that you come.'

(Zwart 1993: 253)

Interestingly, the distribution of these two morphemes[18] is not lexically specified. The examples in (42) and (43) show that both endings might appear on the verb. In non-subject-initial V2 matrix clauses, the finite verb in V2-position in (42a) and (43a) shows the same agreement morpheme (-*e*/-*de*) as the complementizers in the subordinate clauses in (41). In subject-initial V2 matrix clauses, as in (42b) and (43b), however, the inflectional morpheme is invariably -*t*, like on the clause-final verb in subordinate clauses in (41).

(42) EAST NETHERLANDIC
a. Waar speul-e/*-t wij?
where play-1PL we
'Where do we play?'

18 As long as we cannot specify any additional semantic contribution to the element in C, I assume that the C-inflection morpheme is an allomorph of the V-inflection morpheme. However, since the C-domain is a functional domain, we might expect some abstract semantic contribution to be there.

b. Wij speult-t/*-e.
we play-1PL
'We play.'

(Zwart 1993: 254)

(43) BRABANTS

a. Waneer kom-de/*-t gullie?
when come-1PL you
'When do you come?'

b. Gullie kom-t/*-de.
you come-1PL
'You are coming.'

(Zwart 1993: 254)

A similar dual agreement morpheme system is also found in Lower Bavarian for first person plural only (*-ma* vs. *-n*), as in (44a). In contrast to the Dutch variants above, the V2-verb exhibits the agreement morpheme of the complementizers (*-ma*) in both non-subject-initial clauses and subject-initial clauses, as shown in (44b) and (44c).

(44) LOWER BAVARIAN

a. ... dass-ma mir noch Minga fahr-n/*-ma.
that-1PL we to Munich drive-1PL
'... that we drive to Munich.'

b. Fahr-ma/*-n mir noch Minga?
drive-1PL we to Munich
'Do we drive to Munich?'

c. Mir fahr-ma/*-n noch Minga.
we drive-1PL to Munich
'We drive to Munich.'

(Bayer 1984: 251, Weiss 2005: 153–154)

Consequently, it is not evident what the contrast of the inflectional morphemes in East Netherlandic and Brabant indicate, given that we assume a basically identical syntactic structure as in Bavarian.

I interpret the inflectional morphemes on the complementizer as spell-out of the finiteness features of the verb, or more precisely the subset of subject-agreement features. The complementary distribution of complementizer agreement and V2-movement suggests that both satisfy the same requirement, i. e. the requirement for phi-features in the C-domain. Complementizer agreement shows that checking the phi-features in C does not have to be realized by verb movement: If the C-head is filled by a suitable host for the agreement features, verb movement is suspended. Thus, this observation provides further support for the V2-Reconstruction Hypothesis: V2-movement is not related to the meaning of the verb but only the phi-features of the finite verb are attracted and the lexical part of the verb is pied-piped.

3.2.6 Summary: Only agreement features in C

In this section, I have discussed four phenomena which illustrate that V2-movement is a semantics-free operation in the sense that the lexical content of the verb is not interpreted in C. The discussion of particle verbs revealed that V2-movement actually targets sub-semantic units, namely prosodic words. For reasons of economy, only the smallest part that can carry the finiteness feature moves to C, which is the prosodic word in case of particle verbs. The following three subsections illustrated alternative solutions for how semantically empty hosts for the agreement features can be provided if the lexical verb is not available, for example because of verb topicalization. One possibility is the insertion of a generalized, semantically empty dummy verb, such as the German *tun* 'do'. The second option is the doubling of the lexical verb. Crucially, those elements are only a host for the verbal agreement in C, as evidenced by their semantic emptiness: In the C-position, these elements do not contribute their lexical meaning component and do not require that their argument frame must be satisfied. A third option is the insertion of the complementizer-like Frisian *wer*. In sum, these C-elements can be characterized as PF-related hosts for the verbal agreement features which have to be realized in the C-position, but due to their affixal nature (bound morphemes) they cannot appear in C on their own.[19] The last phenomenon, complementizer agreement, shed

19 This correctly predicts that languages which encode finiteness not by affixes do not show movement of lexical verbs. This is the case in the *finiteness second* language Warlpiri as described by (Hale 1983), in which finiteness is obviously morphologically disconnected from the verb. The 2nd position is taken by finiteness morphology whereas the verb can be elsewhere, as shown in (i). Legate (2008) argues that the aspect and agreement markers in Warlpiri are (second position) clitics which attach either to auxiliaries or complementizers.

(i) *Ngajulu-rlu ka-rna-ngku nyuntu nya-nyi*
I-ERG PRS-1SUB-2OBJ you see-NON.PST
'I see you' (Hale 1983: 18)

Tohono O'odham (Papago) is another *finiteness second* language in which the finiteness marking is always realized as an auxiliary in second position and never through inflectional affixes on more light on that observation. In a suitable environment, the verb does not move at all. In presence of a complementizer, as in subordinate clauses, the verbal inflection appears at the complementizers, i. e. in C, without displacing the verb. In these cases the finiteness features are present on both, the C-head and the V-head. It became evident that the relevant part of the finiteness inflection is only the subject agreement, which must be realized at the C-head.

3.3 The base position: Arguments for the necessity of reconstruction

This section concentrates on the second claim of the V2-Reconstruction Hypothesis, namely that the finite verb is obligatorily interpreted in its base position. This is obviously true in V-final clauses. I will argue that, in V2-clauses, the finite verb obligatorily has to be reconstructed into its base position in order to be interpreted correctly with respect to the scope of semantic operators, such as focus-sensitive operators (Section 3.3.1), NPI-licensors (Section 3.3.2), and sentential negation (Section 3.3.3).

3.3.1 Association with focus

A first diagnostic which shows that the finite verb must be interpreted in the base position is *association with focus*. Semantic operators operate on elements in their scope domain. Focus-sensitive operators do even interact with the focus-background structure within their arguments. Focus particles such as *nur* 'only', *lediglich* 'solely', and *negative constrastive construction* (Drubig 1994: 28–37) are examples for such an association with focus, as shown in (45). Crucially, the truth conditions of the sentences change as a function of the associated focus phrase of the focus-sensitive operator, as indicated by the focus alternatives in brackets.

(45) a. dass das Kind *nur* [eine kleine Cóla$_{\text{FOC}}$ getrunken hat].
that the child only a small Coke drunk has
'that the child only drank a small Cóke (and not a beer).'

b. dass das Kind *nur* [eine kleíne$_{\text{FOC}}$ Cola getrunken hat].
that the child only a small Coke drunk has
'that the child only drank a smáll Coke (and not a large one).'

the lexical verb. Consequently in O'odham, the lexical verb never occupies the second position (Zepeda 1983, Miyashita 2006).

c. dass das Kind *lediglich* [eine kleine Cola bestéllt$_{FOC}$ hat].
that the child solely a small Coke ordered has
'that the child only órdered a small Coke (she didn't drink it).'

d. dass das Kind *nicht* [die kleíne$_{FOC}$ Cola getrunken hat].
that the child not the small Coke drunk has
'That the child didn't drink the smáll Coke (but the large one).'

It is still debated how the mechanics of association with focus work in detail (see e. g. Krifka 2006 and Wagner 2006). It is, however, widely accepted that a basic requirement is that the focus-sensitive operator must have scope over the focus, i. e. the operator must c-command the focus constituent (Rooth 1985: 40, König 1993: 985, Bayer 1996: 15, Büring & Hartmann 2001: 237, Krifka 2007: 27).

If the focused constituent is moved to the prefield, the focus particle can be moved along with it, as shown in (46). In this way the c-command requirement remains satisfied.

(46) a. [*Nur* [der Doktoránd]$_{FOC}$] hat ~~nur der Doktorand~~ die Arbeit geschrieben ~~hat~~.
only the PhD candidate has the thesis written
'Only the PhD candidate has written the thesis.'

b. [*Nur* [die Arbeít]$_{FOC}$] hat der Doktorand ~~nur die Arbeit~~ geschrieben ~~hat~~.
only the thesis has the PhD candidate written
'The PhD candidate has written only the thesis.'

c. [*Nur* geschríeben$_{FOC}$] hat der Doktorand die Arbeit ~~nur geschrieben~~ ~~hat~~.
only written has the PhD candidate the thesis
'The PhD candidate has only written the thesis.'

Because c-command commonly implies precedence, the focus particle usually precedes the focus constituent. Under certain conditions, however, the order of focus particle and focus constituent can be reversed, as shown in (47). Crucially, the inverted order leads to marked constructions that receive an emphatic exclamative flavor or are even judged as unacceptable (e. g. Büring & Hartmann 2001: 240). Jacobs (1983: 95–101) adds two more observations regarding the markedness of postfocal particles: First, the productivity of this pattern is lexically restricted, i. e. it is, for example, acceptable with *nur* 'only' but ungrammatical with *lediglich* 'solely', as shown in (47b) vs. (47c). Second, even for particles that allow the inverted order, it occurs preferably in the prefield. In the middle field it needs stronger intonational means (accent, pause) to avoid an association with subsequent constituents, as in (47d–47e).

(47) (The superscript M indicates the marked character of the sentence.)

a. M [Geschríeben$_{FOC}$] hat der Doktorand die Arbeit *nur* ~~geschrieben~~
written has the PhD candidate the thesis only
~~hat~~.

b. M [[Der Doktoránd]$_{FOC}$ *nur*] hat ~~der Doktorand nur~~ die Arbeit geschrieben
the PhD candidate only has the thesis written
~~hat~~.

c. * [[Der Doktoránd]$_{FOC}$ *lediglich*] hat ~~der Doktorand nur~~ die Arbeit
the PhD candidate solely has the thesis
geschrieben ~~hat~~.
written

d. M [Der Doktoránd]$_{FOC}$ hat [*nur* ~~der Doktorand~~] die Arbeit geschrieben
the PhD candidate has only the thesis written
~~hat~~.

e. M ... dass [[der Doktoránd]$_{FOC}$ *nur*] die Arbeit geschrieben hat.
that the PhD candidate only the thesis written has

If the inverted order of focus particle and focus constituent is caused by V2-movement, however, no markedness is induced, as illustrated in (48b) (Büring & Hartmann 2001: 241, fn.9). Note also that no lexical restrictions are observable, as it was the case for the marked inverse order above.[20]

(48) a. Wir sahen, dass der Hund sich *nur*/ *lediglich* verteídigte$_{FOC}$.
we saw that the dog REFL only solely defended
'We saw that the dog did only defend itself (it didn't attack those guys).'

b. Der Hund verteídigte$_{FOC}$ sich *nur*/ *lediglich* ~~verteidigte~~.
the dog defended REFL only solely
'The dog did only defend itself (it didn't attack those guys).'

This apparent irregularity is readily explained by the V2-Reconstruction Hypothesis. From the perspective of interpretation, only the finiteness features move to second position whereas the focused verb is only interpreted in its clause-final base position, in which it is c-commanded by the focus particle. At LF, the structure in (48b) actually looks like (49).

(49) Der Hund -te sich *nur* verteídig$_{FOC}$~~te~~
the dog 3SG.PST REFL only defend

20 This indicates that *lediglich* 'solely' does not belong to the class of focus-sensitive operators that require a focus exponent in its surface scope, as described for *mehr als* 'more than' in Section 2.1.3.1.

In sum, the investigation of association with focus indicates that finite verbs in V2-clauses are interpreted only in their base position: Derived word order, in which the focused constituent is outside of the c-command domain of the focus sensitive operator, leads to a strong markedness. This markedness is absent if a focused verb is moved outside the c-command domain of a focus sensitive operator by V2-movement. Hence, I conclude that V2-moved finite verbs are only interpreted in their clause-final base position. In this position, the verb is within the c-command domain of the focus-sensitive operator.

3.3.2 Verbal negative polarity items: Only licensed in the base position

A similar argument can be constructed for negative polarity items. Polarity items are linguistic elements whose interpretation and grammaticality is dependent on the polarity of their minimal syntactic environment, for simplicity, the minimal clause in which they occur. This is illustrated for the negative polarity item (NPI) *jemals* 'ever' in (50a) and the positive polarity item (PPI) *durchaus* 'certainly' in (50b). The NPI is only grammatical with the negative subject *niemand* 'nobody' whereas the pattern is exactly the opposite for the PPI. The translations indicate that the same contrast is also observed for the English equivalents.

(50) a. Niemand/ *Walter hat die Absicht *jemals*$_{\text{NPI}}$ eine Mauer zu bauen.
nobody Walter has the intention ever a wall to build
'Nobody ever$_{\text{NPI}}$ intended to build a wall.'/'*Walter ever$_{\text{NPI}}$ intended to build a wall.'

b. *Niemand/ Walter hat *durchaus*$_{\text{PPI}}$ die Absicht eine Mauer zu bauen.
nobody Walter has certainly the intention a wall to build
'*Nobody certainly$_{\text{PPI}}$ intended to build a wall.'/'Walter certainly$_{\text{PPI}}$ intended to build a wall.'

Despite the term *negative*, NPIs are not only licensed by anti-additive operators, such as negation, but also by downward-entailing operators such as *few* and *hardly*, in interrogative clauses, in antecedents of conditional clauses, and in complement clauses of adversative predicates such as *doubt* or *refuse* (Progovac 1994, Richter & Radó 2014).[21]

21 NPIs can be divided into strong NPIs, which need to be licensed by anti-additive operators (negation), and weak NPIs, which are also licensed by downward entailing operators. I will not elaborate on this distinction because it bears no relevance for the present argument. For a detailed discussion and experimental confirmation of the licensing requirements of strong and weak NPIs see Richter & Radó (2014).

Progovac (1994) proposes to analyze polarity items with the principles of the binding theory. Negative polarity items resemble reflexives such that both are *dependent*: NPIs must be in the scope of an appropriate licensor, as reflexives must be bound by their antecedent. Positive polarity items and pronouns, on the other hand, are *anti-dependent*: PPIs must be interpreted outside of the scope domain of a downward entailing operator (or the particular clause types which have been mentioned above) as pronouns must be interpreted outside of the scope domain of their local antecedents. The configurations of the licensing requirements/ restrictions are illustrated in (51).

(51)

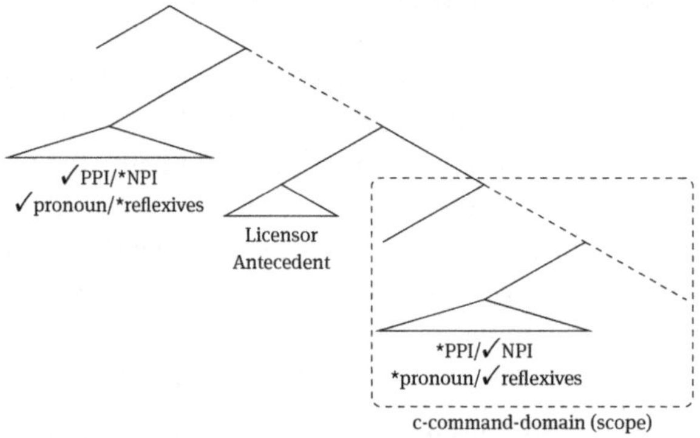

Adverbial NPIs in German indicate that NPI-licensing has to be satisfied at the surface structure. Adverbial NPIs cannot move out of the c-command domain of their licensor, as illustrated by the contrast between (52) and (53). Even though adverbials can normally be placed freely into the prefield, illustrated by *sicherlich*, *gestern*, and *oftmals* in (52), fronting of adverbial NPIs results in ungrammaticality, as shown in (53).[22]

(52) a. Sicherlich hat niemand$_{LIC}$ jemals$_{NPI}$ eine Mauer zu bauen beabsichtigt.
certainly has nobody ever a wall to build planned
'Certainly, nobody ever planned to build a wall.'

b. Gestern haben [nur wenige]$_{LIC}$ überhaupt$_{NPI}$ mitgemacht.
yesterday have only few at all participated
'Yesterday, only few have at all participated.'

22 Note that *überhaupt* can be used as a clausal linker in the sense of 'actually/generally'. Under that reading, sentence (53b) is grammatical but *überhaupt* is a different lexical item and not an NPI.

c. Oftmals hat [kein Student]$_{LIC}$ [auch nur ein bisschen]$_{NPI}$ gelernt.
oftentimes has no student also only a bit studied
'Oftentimes, no student has learned only a tiny bit.'

(53) a. *Jemals$_{NPI}$ hat niemand$_{LIC}$ ~~jemals~~ eine Mauer zu bauen beabsichtigt.
ever has nobody a wall to build planned

b. *Überhaupt$_{NPI}$ haben [nur wenige]$_{LIC}$ ~~überhaupt~~ mitgemacht.
at all have only few studied

c. *[Auch nur ein bisschen]$_{NPI}$ hat [kein Student]$_{LIC}$ ~~auch nur ein bisschen~~
also only a bit has no student
gelernt.
studied

There are two exceptions to this ban on movement, in which an NPI can be fronted: First, the NPI may be contained in a larger constituent that presumably undergoes reconstruction into its base position and thereby restores the licensing relation, as in (54), see also Meinunger (2004: 54).

(54) a. [Jemals$_{NPI}$ eine Mauer zu bauen]$_{VP}$ hat niemand$_{LIC}$ ~~jemals eine Mauer zu~~
ever a wall to build has nobody
~~bauen~~ beabsichtigt.
planned
'Nobody ever planned to build a wall.'

b. [Überhaupt$_{NPI}$ nur eine Prüfung]$_{NP}$ haben [nur wenige Studenten]$_{LIC}$
at all only one exam have only few students
~~überhaupt nur ein Prüfung~~ bestanden.
passed
'Only a few students have passed even one exam.'

c. [Auch nur$_{NPI}$ eine Frage]$_{NP}$ hat [kein Student]$_{LIC}$ ~~auch nur eine Frage~~
also only one question has no student
beantwortet.
answered
'No student has answered even one question.'

The second option is lexically and morphologically very restricted: Some NPIs can combine with their licensor on the morphological level. Similar to other German indefinites, where we observe that *nicht* 'not' and *ein* 'a' combine to *kein* 'no', or *nicht* and *jemand* 'someone' combine to *niemand* 'no one', I assume that *nicht* and *jemals* 'ever' combine to *niemals*.[23] Example (55) illustrates this *morphological pied-piping* process: In (55a), the subject indefinite combines with the negation and becomes the NPI-licensor. In (55b) the NPI moves to the prefield position, thereby pied-piping the negation.[24] The complex that ends up in the prefield is a self-satisfying construction that combines both, the element to be licensed and the licensor in one word.[25]

(55) ∅ hat NEG$_{LIC}$ jemand jemals$_{NPI}$ eine Mauer zu bauen beabsichtigt.
has NEG somebody ever a wall to build planned

a. Anscheinend hat niemand$_{LIC}$ jemals$_{NPI}$ eine Mauer zu bauen beabsichtigt.
apparently has nobody ever a wall to build planned
'Apparently, nobody ever planned to build a wall.'

b. Niemals$_{LIC+NPI}$ hat ~~NEG$_{LIC}$~~ jemand ~~jemals$_{NPI}$~~ eine Mauer zu bauen beabsichtigt.
Never has somebody a wall to build planned
'Never did anyone plan to build a wall.'

With this background on NPIs, we now inspect the exceptional German verb *brauchen* 'need'. Despite its transitive use, *brauchen* also functions as a modal

23 Penka (2011) provides arguments for the separation of the negation and the indefinite meaning, even though her view on the lexical and syntactic analysis of these elements differs from the present one.

24 It is always the highest (leftmost) indefinite that combines with the negation. The negation probably marks the right edge of the existential closure domain because, if an indefinite precedes the negation, it receives an existential interpretation, as in (i), see Diesing (1992) for more on this.

(i) a. *Wahrscheinlich hat niemand die Blumen gegossen.*
probably has no one the flowers watered
'It's possible that no one watered the flowers.'

b. *Wahrscheinlich hat jemand die Blumen nicht gegossen.*
probably has someone the flowers not watered
'It's possible that a specific person whose name I will not say, has not watered the flowers.'

25 Note that these cases resemble the examples in (46) where the focus sensitive operators move with the focus constituent to the prefield.

verb on a par with *müssen* 'must', where it has the meaning 'need to/be obliged to'.[26] As a modal verb, *brauchen* is an NPI, as shown in (56).[27]

(56) Er weiß, dass er dem Studenten *(nicht$_{LIC}$) zu drohen braucht$_{NPI}$.
he knows that he [the student].DAT not to threaten needs
'He knows that he doesn't need to threaten the student.'

In V2-clauses, such as (57), *brauchen* appears in second position, where it precedes the negation. In this constellation, the NPI *brauchen* is outside of the c-command domain of its licensor *nicht*. It is obvious that *brauchen*, in (57), does not employ one of the above mentioned exceptions: It has not been moved to C as part of a larger constituent and it does not morphologically combine with its licensor. The NPI *brauchen*, therefore, seems to be the only NPI that can violate its licensing condition.

(57) Er braucht$_{NPI}$ dem Studenten *(nicht$_{LIC}$) zu drohen ~~braucht~~.
he needs [the student].DAT not to threaten
'He doesn't need to threaten the student.'

The V2-Reconstruction Hypothesis provides a solution to this paradoxical situation. At surface structure (PF), the finite verb moves to second position (C), only to deliver the finiteness feature. The semantic interpretation of the verb, however, takes place in its base position, where it is c-commanded by the NPI-licensor. The finite verb undergoes reconstruction in the same way as the phrasal elements in (54). Hence, no exception to the licensing mechanism of NPIs has to be assumed. The conclusion is that what we see is not what we get at the LF-side of the grammar: At LF, the structure of (57) actually turns out to be as in (58).

(58) Er -t dem Studenten nicht$_{LIC}$ zu drohen brauch$_{NPI}$~~t~~.
he 3SG.PRS [the student].DAT not to threaten need
'He doesn't need to threaten the student.'

---

26 Barbara Tomaszewicz (p. c.) pointed out that the English modal *need* (without *to*) is also an NPI that necessarily scopes under negation to be proper licensed, such that the sentence in (i), only allow the reading in (i.a) but the surface scope order as in (i.b) is not available.

(i) *You need*(n't) shout*

a. *You don't need to shout.* (*NEG > MODAL*)

b. # *You need to not shout.* (*MODAL > NEG*)

27 Dutch exhibits an equivalent NPI modal verb *hoeven* 'need' (see Lin et al. 2015 and references therein). Because of the extensive similarities between Dutch an German, in particular being V2 and OV-languages, the argument for *brauchen* is valid for *hoeven* as well.

This argument is not restricted to a single lexical item. German exhibits several verbal NPIs. A natural example is given in (59a) and three additional constructed examples in (60). The (un)grammatical alternatives in each case illustrate that the verbs, or rather verb frames, are NPIs.

(59) Raketentests sind Nordkorea per UN-Resolution verboten.
'For North Korea it is forbidden to conduct missile tests by UN-resolution.'

a. Aber das schert$_{NPI}$ Machthaber Kim Jong-un wenig$_{LIC}$/ nicht$_{LIC}$/ *ein
but this bothers potentat Kim Jong-un little not a
bisschen/ *∅ ~~schert~~.
bit
'But this bothers potentate Kim Jong-un little/not/a bit/∅.' [ZDF (TV), Morgenmagazin, 29.08.2017]

(60) a. Zumindest verhehlt$_{NPI}$ Julius die Verachtung für seinen Vater nicht$_{LIC}$/
at least concealed Julius the contempt for his father not
*schon/ *∅ ~~verhelt~~.
indeed
'At least Julius did(n't) (indeed) conceal the contempt for his father.'

b. Ich verdenke$_{NPI}$ es niemandem$_{LIC}$/ *jedem, der so etwas
I blame EXPL nobody everybody who so something
erlebt hat, ~~verdenke~~ (dass er enttäuscht ist).
experienced has that he dissapointed is
'I blame nobody/erverbody who has experienced such things (for being disappointed).'

c. Das vergesse$_{NPI}$ ich dir nie$_{LIC}$/ nicht$_{LIC}$/ *morgen/ *sicherlich ~~vergesse~~.
that forget I you never not tomorrow certainly
'I will (∅/forever/certainly) keep that in mind (until tomorrow).'

Most verbal NPIs in German, however, occur in one of two forms that exclude or mask the reconstruction effect: Verbal NPIs of the first type are accompanied by (finite) auxiliaries/modal verbs (mostly idiomatically), which has the effect that the non-finite verbal NPI remains in its base position in V2-clauses, as in (61a). The second type comprises particle verbs where only the inflected stem moves to the V2-position while the particle remains in the clause-final base position, as in (61b). For particle verb NPIs, the argument from Section 3.2.1 becomes relevant: The moved part of the verb must be reconstructed into the base position, next to the particle, in order to allow the interpretation of the complex verb and to evaluate the NPI-specific meaning.[28]

(61) a. Trotzdem konnte ich diese Person niemals$_{LIC}$/ *immer schon [ausstehen ~~konnte~~]$_{NPI}$.
although could I this person never always stand
'Although I could never/*always stand this person.'

b. So komme ich nicht$_{LIC}$/ *sehr wohl [umhin~~komme~~]$_{NPI}$, meine Drohung wahr zu machen.
so come I not very well PRT my threats true to make
'So I'm bound to deliver on my threat.'

Summing up, the argument of this section extends the claim of the previous section that verbs must be interpreted in their base position in order to be within the domain of scope taking operators such as negation. Building on the well-known principles of NPI-licensing, I have shown that the German verbal NPIs, such as *brauchen*, apparently violate this licensing conditions when they have undergone V2-movement. Under the V2-Reconstruction Hypothesis, however, the situation is readily solved because the finite verbal NPI is interpreted in its base position, where it is properly licensed. In Chapter 6, I present two experiments investigating the verbal NPI *brauchen*, which further corroborate the argument of this section.

3.3.3 Sentential negation: C-commanding the verbal base-position

Negation allows us to construct an even more general argument for obligatory reconstruction: As I will show, only obligatory reconstruction of the finite verb explains how sentential negation in V2-clauses with a single verbal element can be derived.

Negation may vary in its scope domain, as roughly indicated by the brackets in (62). Only the negation in (62a) can receive wide scope as sentential negation with the effect of reversing the truth value of the respective affirmative sentence. The

28 Many thanks to all researchers that contributed to *the Collection of Distributionally Idiosyncratic Items* (CoDII). The website hosts a rich data base of German polarity item which makes reasearch on these guys a lot easier. It is available at https://www.english-linguistics.de/codii/index.html, where more information about contributors, research institutes, and funding are available. For references and several other German NPIs that are not yet included in the CODII data base see Richter et al. (2010).

negation in (62b) takes only narrow scope (constituent negation) and excludes the respective constituent from the otherwise positive statement.[29]

(62) a. [Letztlich hat Christopher seinen Bruder *nicht* besucht].
finally has Christopher his brother not visited
'Eventually, Christopher didn't visit his brother. (But he will go for breakfast with his aunt today.)'

b. Letztlich hat Christopher [*nicht* seinen Bruder] besucht.
finally has Christopher not his brother visited
'Eventually, Christopher visited not his brother (but his girl friend).'

From a semantic perspective, it is somewhat surprising that sentence negation is not realized by an initial negation that takes surface scope over the entire clause structure, as noted by Zeijlstra (2007). In the German examples in (62) it even seems that the sentential negation occurs very low in the structure. How can this be explained? The expression of negation in natural languages shows considerable typological variation (Zanuttini 2001, Miestamo 2007) but one generalization seems to hold: sentential negation must c-command the highest verbal element of the clause.[30] Haider (2012: 138–139) states that negation (and high adverbials) must c-command the element that situates the event variable in order to receive wide scope. This element is the finite verb in finite clauses and the highest non-finite verb in non-finite clauses. Accordingly, the negation in (62a) must have scope over the finite auxiliary *hat* or the whole verbal complex *besucht hat* respectively. Example (63) demonstrates that the base position of the negation is within the VP, in a preverbal position. Note that the order of arguments and negation reflects the base generated order because *wh*-indefinites do not scramble.

(63) Da hat [$_{VP}$ wer wen nicht besucht ~~hat~~].
there has someone.NOM somebody.ACC not visited
'Someone didn't visit somebody.' (see Haider 2012: 138)

The negation scope becomes even more evident in (64a). Here the sentence contains only one verbal element. This verb must be finite and therefore moves to the V2-position. Hence it left the c-command domain of the negation. The structure in (64a), however, is still interpreted as sentence negation. Under the assumption

29 Constituent negation may be ultimately subsumed as an association with focus phenomenon (see Section 3.3.1). I will not go into detail here.

30 In verb-initial languages, the negation therefore occurs in pre-VP positions, whereas in verb-final languages negation either occurs as a preverbal particle (German) or as postverbal particle or an affix (Korean, Turkish) (Zanuttini 2001, Miestamo 2007).

that the finite verb is reconstructed and interpreted in its base position, this fact is readily explained. In its base position, the verb *besuchte* in (64a) is within the scope of the negation. Note that this mechanism was crucial to explain the licensing of the NPI-verb *brauchen* in the previous section. In a simplified matter, we might say that the negation must precede the head of the phrase over which it scopes.[31]

(64) a. Letztlich besuchte Christopher seinen Bruder nicht ~~besuchte~~.
finally visited Christopher his brother not
'Finally Christopher didn't visited his brother.'

b.

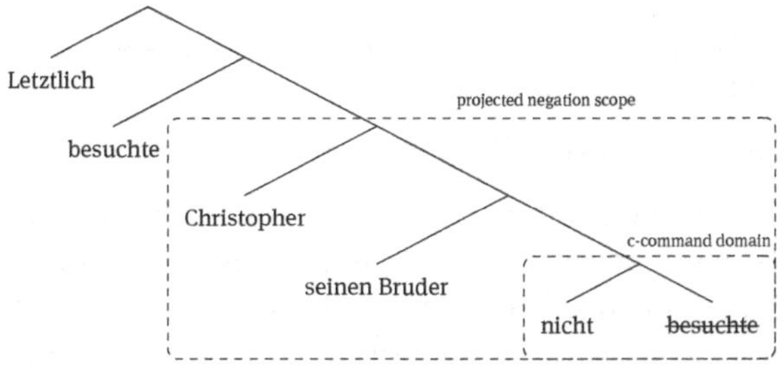

Note further that covertly raising sentential negation to a higher position in which it scopes over the V2-verb, as in (64a), is not a valid option. Such raising would predict that, under sentential negation, all NPIs that occur in a position lower than the V2-position should be licensed, contrary to the fact. (65a) shows that the NPI *jemals* 'ever' is ungrammatical in a position lower than the V2-position but higher than the sentential negation. In contrast, (65b) shows that *jemals* can be licensed in this very position by a licensor that scopes over the V2-position, here, the negative phrase *auf keinen Fall* 'in no way' in Spec-CP.[32]

---

31 Clearly this simplification ignores independent morphosyntactic restriction on the occurrence of negative markers (particles, affixes or auxiliaries, etc.). The shell structure of head-initial projection may induce additional problems. The reader is referred to Haider (2012) for a detailed discussion of these sort of configurational aspects.

32 Under such a raising account, the surface position of negative operators becomes irrelevant for the identification of their scope domain. Hence, we loose the ability to explain the differences in negation placement in OV- vs. VO-languages. This difference, however, appears to be very robust, even in the Scandinavian languages, which combine both properties, being V2-languages and VO-languages. Hence, we must reject accounts that rest on LF-raising of the sentential negation.

(65) a. Letztlich besuchte Christopher (*jemals$_{\text{NPI}}$) seinen Bruder nicht$_{\text{LIC}}$ ~~besuchte~~.
finally visited Christopher ever his brother not

b. [Auf keinen Fall]$_{\text{LIC}}$ besuchte Christopher jemals$_{\text{NPI}}$ seinen Bruder ~~besuchte~~.
at no case visited Christopher ever his brother

'In no way did Christopher ever visit his brother.'

Since the negation does not raise, the only explanation for sentential negation in sentences like (64a) is that the lexical verb reconstructs into its base position where it is within the scope of the negator, as illustrated in (66).

(66) Letztlich -te Christopher seinen Bruder nicht besuch~~-te~~.
finally 3SG Christopher his brother not visit
'Finally, Christopher didn't visit his brother.'

The generalization about negation in German also correctly captures the observation that, in constituent negation, the negation directly precedes the negated constituent: This is illustrated for head-initial phrases, such as the PP (the locative adverbial) in (67a), and the DP (the object) in (67b), as well as for bare heads, such as the pronoun in (67c), and the adjective inside the object-DP in (67d).[33] Additionally, the generalization correctly predicts that preverbal negation in German is superficially ambiguous between sentential negation in (67e) and verb negation in (67f), even though both cases may be distinguished by phonological means.

(67) a. Gestern hat er den jungen Professor [nicht [in der Universität]] gefunden ~~hat~~.
yesterday has he the young professor not in the university found

'Yesterday he did'nt find the young professor in the university.'

b. Gestern hat er [nicht [den jungen Professor]] in der Universität gefunden ~~hat~~.

33 Peter Culicover (p. c.) and Josef Bayer (p. c.) noted that the situation is a little more complex, because there are examples in which the negator is embedded within PPs or complex DPs, as in (i), and still scopes out of these complexes to licence NPIs in the c-command domain of the head node of these complexes (see also Bruening 2014):

(i) a. *[[Not many professors']$_{LIC}$ students] expect anything$_{NPI}$ when the professors retire.*
b. *I talked [to [no one]$_{LIC}$] about any$_{NPI}$ of the problems.*

Josef Bayer pointed out that the problem disappears if the feature of the negator is properly activated via agreement, as proposed in Bayer & Bader (2007).

c. Gestern hat [nicht er] den jungen Professor in der Universität gefunden ~~hat~~.
d. Gestern hat er [den [nicht jungen] Professor] in der Universität gefunden ~~hat~~.
e. Gestern hat er den jungen Professor in der Universität [nicht [gefunden ~~hat~~]].
f. Gestern hat er den jungen Professor in der Universität [nicht gefunden] ~~hat~~.

This *projection of negation scope* can be illustrated even more explicitly by *clause union effects* with German verb clusters (Haider 2010: 19, 272–292), an observation that dates back to Bech (1955). Consider the ambiguous sentence in (68), for example. The preverbal negation can either be interpreted as applying only to the adjacent infinitive, as in (68a), or as scoping over the whole verb cluster, thereby receiving wide scope, as in (68b). If the non-finite complement is extraposed, the scope of the negation is unambiguous: Preceding the infinitive, it only scopes over the embedded clause, as in (68c), whereas it has matrix scope when it precedes the matrix verb, as in (68d).

(68) Der Vater hat ihn nicht zu stören versucht.
the father has him not to disturb tried

a. Der Vater hat ihn [*nicht* zu stören] versucht.
the father has him not to disturb tried
'The father tried not to disturb him.'

b. Der Vater hat ihn [*nicht* [zu stören versucht]].
the father has him not to disturb tried
'The father did not try to disturb him.'

c. Der Vater hat t_1 versucht, [ihn [*nicht* zu stören]]$_1$.
the father has tried him not to disturb
'The father tried not to disturb him.'

d. Der Vater hat t_1 [*nicht* versucht], [ihn zu stören]$_1$.
the father has not tried him to disturb
'The father did not try to disturb him.'

Further support for the reconstruction of the finite verb comes from VP-topicalization patterns. Huang (1993: 132–135) noted that topicalized VPs in German reconstruct (see also Bayer 1993: 7–8, fn. 10), as evidenced by binding facts in (69).[34] The

34 Pronouns in German tend to appear early in the middle field, i. e. preceding the adverbials and particles in (69). I will ignore this for the moment.

reciprocal pronoun *einander* 'each other' in (69a) must be c-commanded by the antecedent *die Raufbolde* 'the roughecks' in order to be properly bound. The personal pronoun *ihm* 'him' in (69b), in contrast, must be c-commanded by the antecedent *Christopher* in order to exclude co-reference, as indicated. In both cases, the topicalized VP must reconstruct into its base position.

(69) a. [Einander$_{i/*j}$ verziehen] haben die Raufbolde$_i$ dann doch noch
each other forgive have the roughnecks then PRT PRT
~~einander$_{i/*j}$ verziehen haben~~
'Eventually the roughnecks did forgive each other.'

b. [Ihm$_{*i/j}$ verziehen] hat Christopher$_i$ dann doch noch ~~ihm$_{*i/j}$ verziehen~~
him forgiven has Christopher then PRT PRT
~~hat~~
'Eventually Christopher did forgive him.'

Verb topicalization, as in (70a), may only front the non-finite verb and leaves the sentential negation behind. This structure still has both readings, with either constituent negation of the lexical verb, comparable to (67f), or sentential negation, comparable to (67e). If the negation, however, is fronted with the non-finite verb, as in (70b), it can only have narrow scope over the verb, as constituent negation. Interestingly, (70c) shows that, if a larger VP is topicalized, the sentential negation remains in its base position. In this way, it is ensured that the negation c-commands the whole verb complex, in which both the finite and non-finite verb are reconstructed, and thereby enabling sentential negation.[35] In sum, these patterns show that under sentential negation elements of the verbal complex may be moved out of the c-command domain of the negation because they are reconstructed into these base positions (Haider 2012: 138–139).

(70) a. Besucht hat [$_{VP}$ der Junge den Vater *nicht* ~~besucht hat~~].
visited has the boy the father not
'As for visiting, the boy didn't visit the father.' WIDE SCOPE/
'The boy didn't VIsited the father.' NARROW SCOPE

35 Note that this is different for at least *wh*-indefinites. There, the indefinite must be reconstructed below the negation. The interpretation of (i) means that there was no one that the boy has visited, not that there was one specific person that he did not visit, see also Footnote 24 in Section 3.3.2.

(i) *Wen besucht hat [$_{VP}$ der Junge (jedenfalls) nicht ~~wen besucht hat~~].*
someone visited has the boy PRT not
'Finally, the boy didn't visit anyone.'

b. [*Nicht* besucht] hat [$_{\text{VP}}$ der Junge den Vater ~~[*nicht* besucht]~~ ~~hat~~],
not visited has the boy the father
sondern angerufen.
but called
'Not visited, that was what the boy did with the father, but called.'

c. [Den Vater besucht] hat [$_{\text{VP}}$ der Junge ~~den Vater~~ (jedenfalls) [*nicht*
the father visited has the boy PRT not
~~besucht hat~~]].
'The boy did not visit the father.'

Haider (2012) argues that a very similar argument can be made for *high* sentence adverbials, such as *leider* 'unfortunately'. He claims that adverbials must c-command their modification domain or at least the head of the respective projection. This leads to the same typological difference as with negation: In OV-languages, like German, *high* sentence adverbials can appear VP internal but in VO-languages, such as English, sentence adverbial must precede the VP. A detailed discussion of the placement of adverbials would go beyond the scope of this section. I therefore refer the reader to Haider (2012: 139).

Summing up: The argument of this section is based on the assumption that semantic operators, such as negation, must c-command the head of their scope domain. For sentential negation this domain consist of the whole VP in VO-languages but only the verbal complex in OV-languages. In V2-clauses (of OV- and VO-languages alike) the finite verb, however, is moved out of the scope domain of the sentential negation. The V2-Reconstruction Hypothesis offers an explanation why this does not affect scope relations: The finite verb is reconstructed into its base position for interpretation. In its base position, the finite verb is within the c-command domain of the sentential negation. Scope taking therefore applies in the same way as in verb-final subordinate clauses. The V2-Reconstruction Hypothesis therefore offers a principled account of the computation of the scope domain of sentential negation in V2-clauses.

3.3.4 Summary: Lexical interpretation only in the base position

In this section, I have presented three phenomena in favor of an obligatory reconstruction of the finite verb in V2-contexts. The two phenomena verbal NPIs and sentential negation showed that the finite verb has to be interpreted in the clause-final position to license the NPI and to enable wide scope of the negation, respectively. The discussion of focus-sensitive operators associated with focused finite verbs went even further and suggested that the finite verb is interpreted only in its base position, which is indicated by the absence of an emphatic markedness which is observed in all other configurations of an inverted order of focus-sensitive operator and focus constituent.

3.4 Experiment 1: The lexical meaning of periphrastic *tun* (acceptability judgments)

3.4.1 Rationale

Introductory information about the *tun*-periphrasis in German is given in Section 3.2.2. There, I noted that a number of authors have stated that certain verbs are incompatible with periphrastic *tun* for semantic reasons, even though the characterization of the verb classes vary: agentive vs. non-agentive verbs (Fischer 2001: 40), eventive vs. stative verbs (Hoekstra 2016: 342), telic vs. atelic verbs (Schönenberger & Penner 1995: 318–319), and individual-level vs. stage-level predicates (Bayer & Freitag 2020). Clearly, all these characterizations build on the intuition that *tun* 'do' specifies an activity. However, as Bayer & Freitag (2020: 83) note, also stative verbs seem quite acceptable with periphrastic *tun*, as long as they can be interpreted as stage-level predicates, i. e. denoting a temporary property/state, as in (71).

(71) Die Clarissa tut den ganzen Tag auf dem Sofa liegen.
the Clarissa does the whole day on the sofa lie
'Clarissa is lying on the sofa the whole day.' (Bayer & Freitag 2020: 83)

Rothmayr (2009) provides a detailed investigation of stative verbs, building on earlier work by Maienborn (2003, 2005, 2007). She distinguishes two different kinds of stative verbs: D(avidsonian) statives and K(imian) statives.[36] The two classes differ with respect to the ontological type of argument they take. D-states, such as *sleep*, contain an event argument, whereas K-states, such as *weigh*, exemplify a property P at a particular time. Some typical representatives are given in (72).[37]

(72) a. **Davidsonian statives:**
sitzen 'sit', *stehen* 'stand', *liegen* 'lie', *schlafen* 'sleep', *warten* 'wait', *leuchten* 'gleam'

36 The terminology refers to work by Davidson (1967) and Kim (1976).

37 Clearly, some verbs can have more than one meaning, thereby occurring in more than one class, such as *Clarissa lies on the couch* as D-state (an event), and *Constance lies on a lake* as a K-state (a property), see Rothmayr (2009: 37–107) for more on these stative/eventive ambiguities.

b. **Kimian statives:**
intelligent sein 'be intelligent', *müde sein* 'be tired', *wiegen* 'weigh', *kennen* 'know', *wissen* 'know', *ähneln* 'resemble'
(see Rothmayr 2009: 7)

Rothmayr (2009: 28–36) presents several diagnostics to distinguish D-states from K-states. Most relevant in the current context is the compatibility with periphrastic *tun*, which she judges perfectly fine with activity verbs as in (73a), clearly unacceptable with K-states as in (73b), and marginal with D-states as in (73c).[38]

(73) a. Josef tut gerade diese Doktorarbeit lesen.
Josef does right now this dissertation read
'Josef is reading this dissertation right now.'

b. * Josef tut diese Oper gut kennen.
Josef does this opera well know

c. ?/?? Josef tut verlegen in der Ecke stehen.
Josef does bashfully in the corner stand

(see Rothmayr 2009: 30–31)

A further diagnostic is that event nominalizations in German can be formed with the suffix *-erei* or the circumfix *Ge-...-e*, which is possible with activity verbs as in (74a) and D-states as in (74c). With K-states, on the other hand, such nominalizations are out, as shown in (74b), because they do not contain an event argument.

(74) a. lesen – Les-erei – Ge-les-e
read reading reading

b. kennen – Kenn-erei – *Ge-kenn-e – z. B. *das Opern-Gekenne
know knowing knowing e. g. the opera-knowing

c. stehen – Steherei – Ge-steh-e
stand standing standing

Additionally, Rothmayr (2009) exemplifies three diagnostics that are based on adverbial modification with manner adverbials, locative modifiers, and degree readings of *ein bisschen* 'a little bit'. The rationale is the same for these three diagnostics: The modification targets an event. Hence, they are incompatible with K-states. I will only illustrate this for manner adverbials with the unavailability of manner modification for K-states in (75b), in contrast to activity verbs and D-states in (75a) and (75c), respectively.

---

38 Rothmayr (2009: 31) marked the example with a D-stative, corresponding to (73c), only with an asterisk, although she describes it as *marginal* in the text. Maienborn (2003: 63, ex. 41) marks these sentences with a ?. I therefore changed the judgement marking accordingly.

(75) a. Josef liest diese Doktorarbeit aufmerksam/ gründlich.
Josef reads this dissertation attentively thoroughly
'Josef reads this dissertation attentively/thoroughly.'
b. Josef kennt diese Oper *aufmerksam/ *gründlich.
Josef knows this opera attentively thoroughly
'Josef knows this opera *attentively/thoroughly'[39]
c. Josef steht bewegungslos/ aufrecht in der Ecke.
Josef stands motionless upright in the corner
'Josef stands motionless/upright in the corner'
(see Rothmayr 2009: 30–31)

In contrast to the distinction of stage-level/individual-level predicates, the division of statives into D-states and K-states refers to the internal structure of the predicates and not to their discourse status. The crucial observation for this claim is that in copular constructions both stage-level and individual-level predicates express a K-state (see Rothmayr 2009: 3–28 for a comprehensive overview of the accounts of event semantics). As for the purpose of this section, this classification provides the basis for the following experiment, in which I will test the predictions regarding the varying compatibility of K-states and D-states with periphrastic *tun*, illustrated in (73). Additionally, I will test the prediction from Section 3.2.2 , i. e. that such incompatibilities are absent in VP-topicalizations, where *tun* is directly inserted in C to satisfy the V2-requirement.[40]

3.4.2 Method

3.4.2.1 Participants

In this experiment, 49 participants (19–37 years, mean 23 years; 8 male; 4 left handed) were tested, all self-declared native speakers of German (5 bilinguals) and students of the University of Cologne. Participants either received course credits or 4 € for participation.

39 *Thoroughly* seems to be unmarked in this context. I suspect that this is because it can have a meaning in which it describes the property of the state of knowledge in the sense of 'know st. very good'. It therefore does not count as a manner modification in the intended sense, in contrast to German *gründlich* or *reading thoroughly*. Thanks to Katie Fraser (p.c.) for sorting this out.

40 The observation that the aspectual incompatibility vanishes in VP-topicalization is also noted by Maienborn (2003: 62, fn. 12), however, without offering any explanation for it.

3.4.2.2 Materials

Materials consisted of 36 experimental items interspersed with 44 fillers (28 from a different experiment) resulting in a total of 80 stimuli per participant. Every stimulus was introduced by a short context (1–3 sentences). The experimental items varied in two factors, VERB TYPE and CLAUSE TYPE. The VERB TYPE was fixed for the lexical variants. CLAUSE TYPE varied within the lexical variants, as illustrated by the sample items in (76)–(78). For each VERB TYPE, at least three structural variants, as exemplified in Table 3.2, were tested to obtain a representative sample of the verb class. In the VP-TOPICALIZATION condition, for most items, the whole VP, including complements, is fronted whereas in others only the infinitival verb appeared in initial position. All items are given in the online appendix.

(76) ACTIVITY

a. Context:
Derzeit geht es ihr zu langsam voran. Also wirft die Chefin der Autowerkstatt einen Blick durch die Scheibe in den Werkstattraum.

'At the moment, she considers the progress to be too slow. So the boss of the garage takes a look through the window into the workroom.'

b. LEXICAL V2
Der Lehrling repariert immer noch den alten Golf.
the apprentice repairs still the old Golf
'The apprentice is still repairing the old VW Golf.'

c. TUN-PERIPHRASIS
Der Lehrling tut immer noch den alten Golf reparieren.
the apprentice does still the old Golf repair
'The apprentice is still repairing the old VW Golf.'

d. VP-TOPICALIZATION
Den alten Golf reparieren tut der Lehrling immer noch.
the old golf repair does the apprentice still
'What the apprentice is still repairing is the old VW Golf.'

(77) K-STATES

a. Context:
Taucher haben das Wrack eines uralten Schiffes gefunden. Es scheint beinahe senkrecht nach unten gesunken zu sein.

'Scuba divers have found the wreck of a very old ship. It seems to have sunk almost upright.'

b. LEXICAL V2

Die Bugspitze steckt jedenfalls metertief in dem schlammigen
the nose sticks in any case meters deep in the muddy
Meeresboden.
sea ground

'The nose sticks in any case several meters deep in the muddy sea ground.'

c. TUN-PERIPHRASIS

Die Bugspitze tut jedenfalls metertief in dem schlammigen
the nose does in any case meters deep in the muddy
Meeresboden stecken.
sea ground stick

'The nose sticks in any case several meters deep in the muddy sea ground.'

d. VP-TOPICALIZATION

Metertief in dem schlammigen Meeresboden stecken tut die
meters deep in the muddy sea ground stick does the
Bugspitze jedenfalls.
nose in any case

'What the nose does is stick meters deep in the muddy sea ground.'

(78) D-STATES

a. Context:

Eine Patientin wird mit hohem Fieber ins Krankenhaus eingeliefert. Allerdings sieht man ihr die Temperatur kaum an.

'A patient is brought to the hospital suffering from intensive fever. However, the high temperature is hardly noticeable when looking at her.'

b. LEXICAL V2

Die Patientin schwitzt lediglich an den Beinen.
the patient sweats solely at the legs

'The patient sweats only from her legs.'

c. TUN-PERIPHRASIS

Die Patientin tut lediglich an den Beinen schwitzen.
the patient does solely at the legs sweat

'The patient sweats only from her legs.'

d. VP-TOPICALIZATION
Schwitzen tut die Patientin lediglich an den Beinen.
sweat does the patient solely at the legs
'The patient sweats only from her legs.'

Table 3.2: Structural variant of the verb types used in experiment 1

subtypes	n	example
		ACTIVITY
inanimate object	(4/12)	*das Auto reparieren* 'repair the car'
animate object	(4/12)	*den Sohn umarmen* 'hug the son'
PP-complement	(4/12)	*über die Bahn schimpfen* 'grumble about the railroad'
		K-STATES
position	(4/12)	*im Boden stecken* 'stick in the ground'
ES possesor	(4/12)	*dem Vater ähneln* 'resemble the father'
measure	(4/12)	*2 € kosten* 'cost 2 €'
		D-STATES
position	(4/12)	*im Weg stehen* 'stand in the way'
internal cause	(4/12)	*grün leuchten* 'glow green'
PP-complement	(1/12)	*auf den Anruf warten* 'wait for the call'
other	(3/12)	*an den Beinen schwitzen* 'sweat on the legs'

3.4.2.3 Procedure

The experiment was conducted as a rating task with a reference sentence (anchor) and an open scale, similar to thermometer judgments (Featherston 2008, 2009). The current task design was as follows: Participants were provided with a single reference sentence (79), a declarative with a center-embedded object clause, which is possible but dispreferred to the variant with the embedded clause right-extraposed. This reference sentence was associated with a score of 0. Participants were asked to judge the acceptability of the target sentences in comparison to the reference sentence. Instruction asked if sentences are better or worse, easier or harder to understand. It was stated explicitly that it is not asked for prescriptive rules or "good" writing style. The instructions also provided some examples with respective proposals for scores.

(79) Die Angestellten haben, dass der Chef Probleme hat, nicht sofort
the employees have that the boss problems has not immediately
bemerkt.
noticed
'The employees did not immediately notice that the boss has problems.'

If a target sentence was worse than the reference sentence, participants should associate a negative score. If it was better, they should assign a positive score. The number range was open but only integers allowed.

The procedure was programmed in the python experiment suite PsychoPy (Peirce 2007) and run on a PC in a psycholinguistic lab. Participants saw four practice items to get acquainted with the task. The experimental stimuli were randomized according to a partial Latin square design,[41] so each participant saw each of the 36 items in exactly one of the three structural variants. The total list of stimuli was randomized by the experiment software. The experiment took approximately 20 minutes.

3.4.2.4 Predictions

According to the claims in the literature and the argumentation above, I expect an interaction of VERB TYPE and CLAUSE TYPE that looks as follows: No verb-specific effect should appear in the LEXICAL V2 condition because V2-movement is insensitive to the lexical meaning of the verb. In the TUN-PERIPHRASIS condition, I expect an effect of verb type with clearly higher acceptability ratings for ACTIVITY in comparison to the other two verbs. Additionally, D-STATES should be a little more acceptable than K-STATES. Furthermore, no verb-specific effect is predicted in the VP-TOPICALIZATION condition because the *tun* is semantically empty. However, the ratings for VP-TOPICALIZATION should be higher than for the TUN-PERIPHRASIS because VP-TOPICALIZATION does not contain a semantic incompatibility. This prediction is restricted to the K-STATES and D-STATES verb, that are marked in the TUN-PERIPHRASIS construction. Obviously, the LEXICAL V2 condition is expected to receive higher ratings because it is an unmarked construction with respect to pragmatics and information structure, whereas the TUN-PERIPHRASIS and the VP-TOPICALIZATION are marked in this respect.

3.4.2.5 Data analysis

Prior to statistical analysis, all emtpy cells have been removed (n=21, 0.5 % of the data). Additionally, I excluded 4 extreme values after data inspection. These val-

41 The Latin square was restricted because VERB TYPE was fixed per item, as noted above.

ues are all singular outliers, which are more than 4 standard deviations away from the participants' mean and therefore most likely constitute typos. I analyzed the data using the statistical software package R (R Core Team 2015), applying linear mixed-effects models of the *lme4* package (Bates et al. 2013) to analyze the Z-transformed response scores. Following arguments in Barr et al. (2013) and Bates et al. (2015), I fitted maximal justified random effect structures for the LME-models. I performed a model criticism as recommended in Baayen & Milin (2010) by excluding absolute standardized residuals exceeding 2.5 standard deviations. I report the results of the criticized model, taking effects as significant if the respective t-value exceeds an absolute value of 2.

In response to the predictions above, I will employ separate analysis of subsets of the data. In a first analysis, I will compare the syntactic configurations (Clause Type). The second analysis will investigate the effect of Verb Type within each of the three configurations. The third analysis will test for each verb type, whether the syntactic configuration correlates with the acceptability.

3.4.3 Results

A graphical summary of the results is presented in Figure 3.1 The primary analysis revealed a main effect of Clause Type with much higher values for lexical V2 structures than for tun-periphrasis and VP-topicalization ($t = 29.91$), see Table 3.3. No difference between the two latter condition could be detected. The secondary analyses detected Verb Type-specific effects only within the tun-periphrasis condition, but no differences in the lexical V2 or the VP-topicalization group. Within the tun-periphrasis group, the activity verbs received significantly higher ratings in comparison to the K-states verbs ($t = -2.126$). Mean rating for the D-states ranges between the two other conditions and is not significantly different from either of them, at least after model criticism ($t = -1.237$), which indicates that the significance in the raw model is driven by outliers, see Table 3.4. The tertiary analysis of the D-states and the K-states condition confirmed the above results. Within both groups, only the extreme difference of the lexical V2 condition in comparison to the other two constructions yields significance. All other contrasts remain non-significant.

3.4.4 Discussion

The results match most of the predictions. Foremost, the expected interaction of Clause Type and Verb Type could be detected. tun-periphrasis received

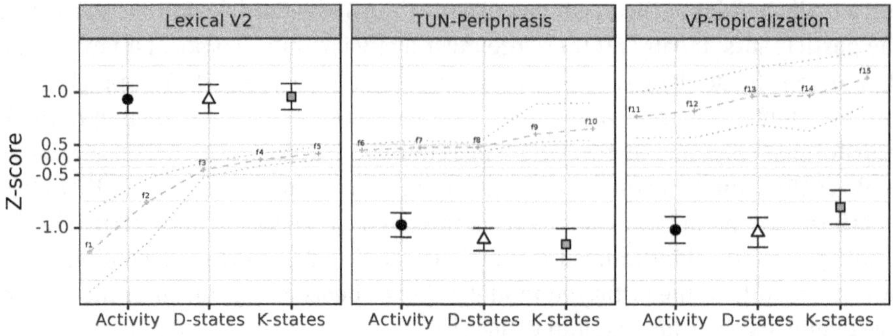

Figure 3.1: Mean Z-scores of the acceptability ratings of experiment 1. The background shows the acceptability of the independent fillers (all errorbars show 95 % CIs). Note the compressed scale in the middle of the Y-axis.

Table 3.3: Output of the LME model for the CLAUSE TYPE-analysis in experiment 1
`lmer(Z.score~clause.type+(1+clause.type|participant.ID)+`
`(1+clause.type|stimulus.ID))`

	criticized model			raw model		
	Estimate	SE	t	Estimate	SE	t
Intercept (TUN-PERIPHRASIS)	−1.06	0.05	−22.07	−1.05	0.05	−19.07
LEXICAL V2	2.04	0.07	29.91	2.01	0.07	26.92
VP-TOPICALIZATION	0.07	0.07	0.98	0.07	0.07	0.98

Table 3.4: Output of the LME model for the TUN-PERIPHRASIS-analysis in experiment 1
`lmer(Z.score~verb.type+trial+(1+verb.type+trial|participant.ID)+(1|stimulus.ID))`

	criticized model			raw model		
	Estimate	SE	t	Estimate	SE	t
Intercept (ACTIVITY)	−1.024	0.049	−20.727	−0.971	0.059	−16.500
D-STATES	−0.038	0.031	−1.237	−0.100	0.043	−2.322
K-STATES	−0.086	0.040	−2.126	−0.114	0.052	−2.191
trial	−0.001	0.001	−1.224	−0.001	0.001	−0.842

higher ratings if combined with ACTIVITY verbs in clause-final position. This indicates that *tun* still retains its agentive meaning in these constructions. Hence, K-STATES receive the lowest rating because they do not exhibit a Davidsonian event argument. As predicted by Rothmayr (2009: 30–31), D-statives are marginal, i. e. they receive intermediate ratings. This differences between ACTIVITY and K-STATES is absent in the construction without *tun*, LEXICAL V2, and in the VP-TOPICALIZATION, in which *tun* is semantically empty. These two comparisons show that the difference cannot be attributed to the verbs per se but is also construction specific. Furthermore, the LEXICAL V2 condition was rated much higher than the other conditions. The only prediction that could not be confirmed, is that the VP-TOPICALIZATION should receive higher ratings than the TUN-PERIPHRASIS group, at least for the stative verbs. However, VP-topicalizations are information structurally very marked. Their acceptability is therefore highly dependent on the licensing by the discourse. The context sentences of the current experiment were constructed with the goal to allow VP-topicalization without, or at least with a small penalty. The results indicate that this goal has not been accomplished.

In sum, experiment 1 was successful, in confirming that *tun* interacts with the meaning of the lexical verb in *tun*-periphrasis but not in VP-topicalizations. It provides a reliable data basis for the discussion of periphrastic *tun*, which often leads to diverging intuitions due to dialectal and register variation interacting with the sometimes subtle differences (see e. g. Erb 2001: 191–197).[42]

This experiment is only a first step in investigating the fine nuances of periphrastic *tun*. However, it provides a starting point for follow-up studies investigating more verb types, such as eventive verbs (*erkennen* 'realize'), configurational verbs (*umgeben* 'surround'), and experiencer verbs (*interessieren* 'interest'), as well as other syntactic constructions, such as VP-pronominalizations and pseudoclefts. Additionally, the overall acceptability of VP-topicalizations should be addressed by providing more supportive contexts in future experiments.

3.5 Chapter summary

In this chapter, I introduced the V2-Reconstruction Hypothesis which says that a V2-moved verb appears in an early position in the clause only to deliver finiteness features, but is always interpreted in its clause-final base position, which is known as reconstruction. I also exemplified that reconstruction is a quite frequent phenomenon in syntax that appears whenever a syntactic element is pied-piped

42 I thank Hans-Martin Gärtner for bringing Erb (2001) to my attention.

by another element, i. e. it does not move because of its own features. The subsequent sections presented empirical evidence for the validity of the two subclaims of the V2-Reconstruction Hypothesis.

Section 3.2 showed that German exhibits systematic cases in which the lexical content of the finite verb is not interpreted in the V2-position, such as the stem of idiomatic particle verbs, *tun*-insertion in VP-topicalizations, and verb doubling. Additionally, Frisian *wer*-insertion and complementizer agreement illustrated that, if a complementizer is present in C, the inflectional affixes attach to these complementizers without moving a verb into C, and in fact, even blocking verb movement. This proves that not the verb has to move to C but only the finiteness features, thereby supporting the first subclaim of the V2-Reconstruction Hypothesis.

In Section 3.3, I presented three phenomena which reveal that the V2-moved verb must be interpreted in its clause-final base position. Association with focus was used to show that only V2-movement can apparently invert the order between the focus-sensitive operator and the focus constituent without introducing markedness. The problem is solved under the assumption that the finite verb is only interpreted in it clause-final base position. Licensing of verbal NPIs construct a similar argument. V2-moved NPIs are apparently the only NPIs that may escape the c-command domain of their licensor. Again this behavior is readily explained under reconstruction analysis. Third, I have shown that the V2-Reconstruction Hypothesis explains why finite verbs precede sentential negation without escaping its scope. These phenomena show that the finite verb of V2-clauses is interpreted only in its clause-final base position, backing the second subclaim of the V2-Reconstruction Hypothesis.

In Section 3.4, I presented experimental evidence which supports the claims about the different semantic contribution of *tun* 'do', in periphrastic *tun* and VP-topicalization. The results show that *tun* leads to a semantic incompatibility with verbs that denote Kimian states, indicating that *tun* still retains some meaning. Such an incompatibility was not detectable for VP-topicalization indicating that, here, a semantically empty *tun* is inserted as a last resort operation to provide a host for the finiteness affixes in C.

In sum, this chapter introduced the main topic of this investigation, the V2-Reconstruction Hypothesis, and provided a range of empirical phenomena for its validity. Note that the assumption of a generalized reconstruction of the finite verb also allows a systematic simplification of the linguistic description of German clauses because explanations for all V-final counterparts of V2-clauses are needed anyway to analyze embedded clauses. In Part II of this monograph, I will illustrate that the predictions of the V2-Reconstruction Hypothesis concerning online sentence comprehension are borne out, too.

Part II: The role of V2-movement in sentence processing

4 Basics of sentence processing

It is widely assumed that, during sentence processing, the meaning is constructed incrementally from left to right. The comprehension process thereby forms incomplete representations in a top-down approach that is guided by grammatical knowledge (*competence*) (Bierwisch 1983, Crocker 1994, Phillips 2003, Haider 2012). In the beginning of this chapter, I will review general properties of the processing apparatus, some specifics of syntactic parsing and its connection to semantic interpretation. The second section focuses on the concept of incrementality and the strict on-line nature of processing procedures. In Section 4.3, I will discuss four classes of V2-constructions in German that provide a challenge for strict online processing: (i) auxiliary verbs, (ii) modal verbs, (iii) cluster triggering verbs, and (iv) particle verbs. For sentences in which these types of verbs occur in V2-position, the human parser cannot predict the argument structure, which follows the finite verb. Hence, these sentences constitute a structural configuration in which the full interpretation has to be delayed until end of the clause.

4.1 Sentence processing: Apparatus and procedures

This section contains considerations about the basic architecture of a language comprehension device, basically following the argumentation in Bierwisch (1983). The processing of natural languages involves a number of subroutines which identify meaningful units such as phonemes syllables etc. from the constant input stream.[1] The processor then combines these units in a non-trivial way which results in a mental representation of the communicated input. I will restrict the discussion to the comprehension process. I assume that, in speech production, similar procedures must apply in reverse order, even though this is by no means an approximate description of speech production, a topic so complex on its own that I could not do it justice here.

4.1.1 Levels of representation

The overall communication process aims to transmit information from one interlocutor to another. The transmission process can be modeled in a similar way as

1 Clearly, similar processes must apply in the visual domain, where an input string of signed or written language has to be segmented into morphosyntactic units.

https://doi.org/10.1515/9783110725018-004

for technical communication systems (Shannon & Weaver 1949). Figure 4.1 illustrates a language-based communication, which will be explicated in the following. I will assume that the endpoints of the communication process consist of mental representations that may be envisioned or approximated as activation patterns, i. e. as a specific network activation in the human brain. I assume that this mental representation is not ordered in the hierarchical or linear dimension. The audio signal, however, is time-dependent and thereby inherently linear though it does not posses an inherent hierarchical structure. Between these two poles, speaker and addressee, a complex mapping process takes place, which corresponds to the language production and language comprehension devices respectively.

Following Bierwisch (1983: 135), with only slight modifications, I assume four necessary levels of representation of linguistic structure, as given in (1)–(4).[2]

(1) Phonological representation (PR): a sequence of (bundles of) phonetic attributes, grouped in terms of perceptually accessible larger units such as syllable, phonological word, intonation group, etc.

(2) Syntactic representation (SR): a categorized, ordered binary tree imposed on syntactic formatives, which correspond to subsequences of PR (including the empty string for syntactic traces *t*). The hierarchical structure yields unambiguous c-command relations.

(3) Logical representation (LR): a categorized, unordered tree imposed on semantic primes, which are either constants or variables, organized according to functor-argument relations with variable binding.

(4) Contextual Representation (CR): a set-theoretical structure not subject to ordering and tree conditions, determined by the inherent ontology of the mental world (whatever that turns out to be).

In addition, I must assume mapping functions, as in (5)–(8), that relate the levels of representation with its dimensional characteristics, linear order and hierarchical order, to each other. The bracketed terms following the mapping functions should be understood rather as a mnemonic than as a proper description. The mapping functions are sequentially ordered from PR to SR, from SR to LR, etc. Each higher representation includes the mapping processes of the lower orders (s = signal and c = context).

2 First, I changed the labels of the levels of representation, Bierwisch (1983) uses *P*, *S*, *LF*, and *C* instead. Second, for the syntactic level, I inserted the additional condition that trees have to be binary because these show unambiguous c-command relations. There, the notion of *c-command* also replaces the notion of *binding*.

(5) H(s) = PR (Hearing)

(6) P(PR) = SR (Parsing)

(7) I(SR) = LR (Interpretation)

(8) V(LR,c) = CR (Verification)

For the comprehension cascade, we can summarize that the time-dependent speech signal *s* is first enriched with hierarchical information, and, in the next steps, pruned from linear order and hierarchical order. Idealizing even further and neglecting the last transformation to mental states, the comprehension process can be seen as the reconstruction of the hierarchical dimension from a sequential object, as illustrated in Figure 4.1. Likewise, production corresponds to a compression process that maps a hierarchical object onto a sequential order (Kural 2005, Haider 2012).

In the following, I will use two terms that must not be confused: The first is the entirety of the devices that take part in the production and comprehension process of natural language, the *human language-processing mechanism*, or short *processor*, which equals the complete mapping function (8). The second is the *parser*, the device that handles the morphosyntactic analysis, which equals the mapping function *P* in (6). In this publication, I will primarily focus on the parser and its relation to the higher order representations, mostly to LR. The classical example in (9) illustrates that a linear string is not unequivocally linked to a single hierarchical representation but may give rise to structural ambiguities. Even though the two structures might be differentiated by intonational means such as pauses, they don't have to be.

(9) The girl saw the boy with the telescope.
  a. The girl saw [the [boy with the telescope]].
    ↦ the boy has a telescope
  b. The girl saw [the boy] [with the telescope].
    ↦ the girl has a telescope

The brackets and the comments in (9a) and (9b) indicate that the difference in meaning correlates with the hierarchical order which is imposed on the input and not of properties of the linear order of the elements in the input string.

4.1.2 Some thoughts about the architecture of the processor

The aim of providing a detailed description of the architecture of the human language-processing mechanism is a too ambitious one for the present book.

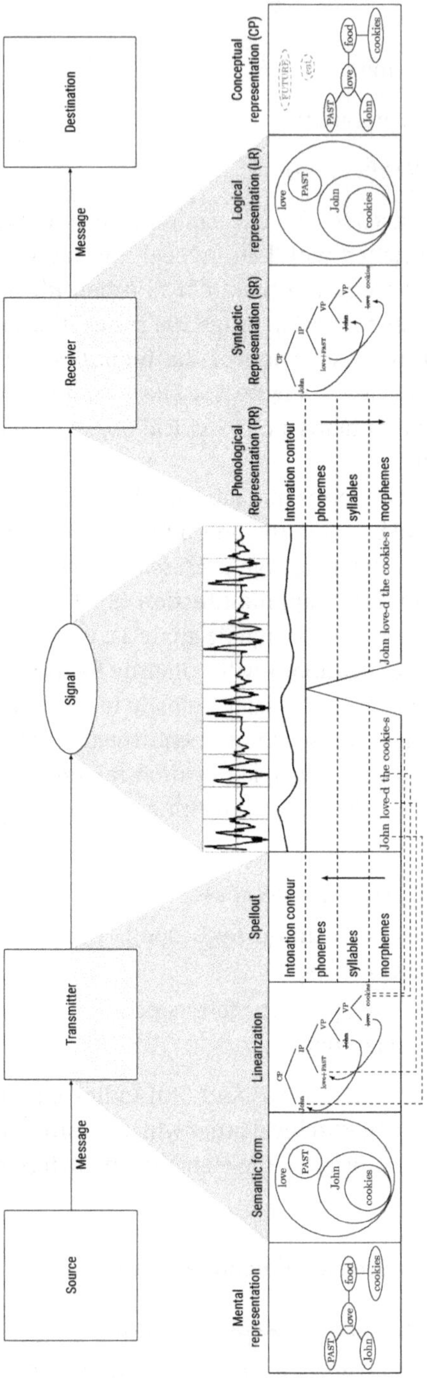

Figure 4.1: Schematic of the language-based communication process

First and foremost, there is no doubt that the language processor is part of the general cognitive system, hence I must give a description of this even larger system. For considerations of the broader perspective the reader is referred to Fodor (1983) and Anderson et al. (2004). Second, the number of possible variations of model parameters is enormous, whereas the predictions and the empirical coverage are often only subtle (Crocker 1994: 246). I will therefore concentrate on a few phenomena that help us to identify some basic parameters that are relevant for the discussion of the processing of V2-structures below.

The two main characteristics of a cognitive processing device can be described with the oppositions *modular* vs. *interactive*, and *serial* vs. *parallel*. Modularity means that the respective procedure will be carried out autonomously, for example, that syntactic analyses are not influenced by the meaning of the constituents but solely guided by syntactic principles. Serial processing defines that only one analysis at a time is generated. Parallel processing, on the other hand, allows that multiple analyses are generated in parallel, of which one will be selected.

The overall picture will surely be a mixed system in which some domains are more interactive whereas others are more autonomous (modular) and some allow for parallel processing while others do not. In accordance with the mainstream literature, I will assume that the human language-processing mechanism is, at least in parts, a serial, modular system. Evidence for the serial nature of syntactic analyses comes from experimental investigations of locally ambiguous structures, such as the famous garden path sentence in (10a). The string *the+horse+raced+past+the+barn* immediately receives a structural analysis. When the last word *fell* is encountered, it does not fit the current analysis and a reanalysis process is triggered, which can be measured in (prolonged) reading times, (lowered) acceptability judgments, etc. For sentences as in (10a), the garden path may be so severe that no reanalysis is triggered and the string is discarded as gibberish.

(10) a. The horse raced past the barn fell.
b. meaning: The horse that was raced past the barn fell.
(Bever 1970: 316)

Reanalysis procedures have been found for a range of constructions cross-linguistically. The pure existence of preferences for structural analyses disfavors a parallel account in which several different parses are developed simultaneously. Crain & Steedman (1985), however, demonstrate that the severity of the garden path can be induced, modulated, or canceled by semantic and contextual factors. Crain & Steedman (1985) argue for a weak interaction of the syntactic and the semantico-pragmatic component: The syntactic analysis operates purely on syntactic principles but the semantico-pragmatic component checks the analyzed chunks in certain intervals and may induce a reanalysis. They demonstrate that even severe garden paths can be avoided by providing an appropriate context. More aspects of the relation between syntactic parsing and interpretation will be discussed in the following sections.

4.1.3 The role of grammar in a processing model

Before I will elaborate on the processing routines, a note on the role of grammatical knowledge in language processing seems in order. The different levels of grammar (phonology, syntax, etc.) provide well-formedness conditions on the levels of representation given in (1)–(4) above (PR, SR, etc.). The grammatical rules specify the targets of the mapping functions. Note that this is not the same as identifying rules of grammar with processing operations (Bierwisch 1983: 158).

Why do we need grammatical rules? Cases of misanalysis are invariably cases in which a locally well-formed structure turns out to be globally ill-formed, such as garden path sentences in (10) or attachment ambiguities, as in (9). However, we do not observe that the parser builds up structures that do not even locally obey the rules of grammar, such as the ungrammatical structure (11b), in which the determiner and the adjective form a constituent with the exclusion of the noun, in contrast to (11a).

(11) the+wild+animal
  a. [the [[wild] animal]]
  b. *[[[the] wild] animal]

Under the assumption that language processing involves several subsequent mapping procedures, grammatical rules operate as check sums on each representation level which ensure that the input for the next mapping function is well-defined. Otherwise every noise that obscures part of the signal will lead to defective mappings and hence to a loss in understanding. But in fact, we observe that also defective signals show a comparably good recoverability, such as utterances in noisy environment, by speakers that show diminished abilities caused by nervousness, drugs, etc., or by non-native speakers that are not in full command of the well-formedness rules. This is explainable if each mapping process has to create a well-formed representation on the next higher level. The specifics of this mechanism is not in the focus of the present discussion but I will assume that a mapping will be attracted by the nearest possible well-formed representation.[3] Two more remarks:

3 The sketch of relating semi-grammatical sentences to a well-formed correspondent structure in Chomsky (1964) could provide an avenue to a formalization.

The application of such intermediate repairs may ensure comprehensibility but may also lead to reduced acceptability. Second, there is certainly a threshold of defectivity beyond which no recovery is possible. If the output of a mapping function is too far from a well-formed representation the input cannot be mapped onto higher representations.

4.1.4 On-line processing and incrementality

After sketching the general architectural properties of the processor, I must give a more detailed description of how parsing and other processing procedures apply. There is consensus that any parser must, at least partially, employ incremental left-to-right (top-down) parsing. The opposite position would be a strictly head-driven (bottom-up) parsing account in which structures are only projected from the heads. It would predict that arguments and modifiers remain unattached until the governing head is encountered (for a more elaborate discussion see Crocker 1994).

The well-documented subject-first preference in German, a head-final language, is a showcase example for an argument against strictly head-driven parsing, a detailed discussion will follow in Chapter 5. In sentences such as (12), increased reading times are observed for the second noun phrase, if it is a nominative *der Gärtner* (12b). This indicates that the case ambiguous first noun phrase is analyzed as subject and has to be reanalyzed as a scrambled object as soon as a nominative NP is encountered. The fact that the reanalysis effect occurs before the subcategorizing verb has been read implies that the arguments are assigned to structural positions before the head of the structure, here V, is encountered. The subject-first effect therefore provides solid counter-evidence against strictly head-driven (bottom-up) accounts.

(12) GERMAN

a. ... dass die Direktorin den Gärtner besucht hat.
that [the director.F]NOM/ACC [the gardener]ACC visited has
'...that the director visited the gardener.'

b. ... dass die Direktorin der Gärtner besucht hat.
that [the director.F]NOM/ACC [the gardener]NOM visited has
'...that the gardener visited the director.'

The example in (12) also illustrates an important point regarding the incrementality of processing: In the course of left-to-right processing, the interpretation will not always be built up fully incrementally but involves deviation from strict online processing. Such deviations are mainly caused by two properties, *underspec-*

ification and *dependence*. Underspecification is a temporal ambiguity of inherent features: The particular element possesses all necessary properties for a mapping to the next higher representation but the properties do fully specify more than one category. Syncretic case-marking would be an example, as exemplified in (13). Case-marking might not be fully unambiguous but the mapping potential of a case-marked DP is inherent. The specific mapping of an underspecified element might be disambiguated later, but the mapping potential does not dependent on the disambiguation, i. e. the phrase *das Buch* in (13a) might be nominative or accusative but never dative or genitive, irrespective of the environment. The mapping potential of the masculine phrases in (13b), in contrast, is restricted to exactly one case, i. e. those DPs are not underspecified with respect to case-marking. A dependent element, in contrast, does not posses all the information for a complete mapping but is contingent on the assignment by another element. Theta roles are a case in point. They are assigned by the predicate. Even with unambiguous case marking the argument is incomplete in this respect, as shown in (14).

(13) *Underspecification*

a. das Buch
   the book.NOM/ACC

b. der Roman vs. den Roman
   the novel.NOM the novel.ACC

(14) *Dependence*

a. weil der Vater dem Jungen.BENEFICIENT ein Buch mitbringt.
   because the father.NOM the boy.DAT a book brings along

b. weil der Vater dem Jungen.EXPERIENCER gefällt.
   because the father.NOM the boy.DAT appeals

Deviations from strict on-line processing can be overcome by two strategies: *anticipation* ("decide for one interpretation even though there is a chance it might be wrong") and *delay* ("let's wait and see"). Before I am going to discuss these strategies in more detail, I will show that linearity-breaking effects take place on all levels of representation.

4.1.4.1 Generality of non-linear processing

I will begin with the phonological representation (PR). The strings in (15a) and (15b) are initially identical, see (15c), and will only be unambigously identified after the relative clause. It is evident that the initial analysis at PR has immediate consequences for the mapping onto the syntactic and semantic structure. In (15a) the initial string is identified as a sequence of a possessive pronoun and an NP.

The initial string in (15b), however, consists of a pronoun and an reduced auxiliary followed by an adjective. Thus, in the first case, the initial string is a complex NP, whereas the string in (15b) is a clause.

(15) Ambiguity at PR
  a. Their plane, which is unusual, is going to be late.
  b. They're plain, which is unusual but good.
  c. [ðeər+pleɪn+wɪtʃ+s+ʌnˈjuː.ʒu.əl+...]

The clauses in (16) illustrate deviations from strictly linear processing on the syntactic level (SR). The *wh*-phrase cannot immediately be interpreted as it is encountered. The two variants show that the dislocated element may either act as object, as in (16a), or as subject as in (16b). This string, however, cannot be disambiguated relying on syntactic cues alone.

(16) Ambiguity at SR
  a. Who_1 did Josef [promise t_1] [Janet will submit the thesis on time]?
  b. Who_1 did Josef [promise Janet] [t_1 will submit the thesis on time]?

Similarly, scope ambiguities are examples on the level of the logical representation (LR). The examples in (17) show that even though both quantifiers and the relating predicate are encountered the scope domain may not be uniquely identified until the appositive clause of the indefinite is processed.

(17) Ambiguity at LR
  a. $\forall > \exists$: Every man loves a woman, namely his mother.
  b. $\exists > \forall$: Every man loves a woman, namely Brigitte Bardot.

Likewise, cases of underspecification can also be demonstrated for the contextual representation (CR), as shown in (18). The identification of the referent of the pronoun *she* does not rely on syntactic or semantic conditions but rather on the contextual information that is presented in the infinitive at the end of the sentence. Clearly, at the time when the pronoun is encountered, an unambiguous identification is not possible.

(18) Ambiguity at CR
  Mary_m asked Sally_s where to go, but, you know, ...
  a. ... she_m isn't the right person to wait for an answer.
  b. ... she_s isn't the right person to give a clear answer.
  (Bierwisch 1983: 119)

I have briefly illustrated that non-linear processing is observable on all levels of representation. As already noted, in an incremental comprehension process these cases of non-linearity can be overcome by two mechanisms: anticipation and delay. These two strategies are coupled with two states of the mapping functions which I have defined above. Following Bierwisch (1983: 136–149), I will call these two states *maximal* and *complete* and define them (19) and (20), respectively (see Crocker 1994 for a similar but less elaborate notion).

(19) *Maximality*
$F(s,c)$ is *maximal* in relation to a grammar G and the respective mapping function H, P, I, or V iff it is fully specified with respect to the input s (the context c), the grammar G and other principles of contextual interpretation.

As we have already seen above for cases of ambiguity, maximality does not mean that the respective structure will not be altered at a later point. For any initial substring s' of s, such that $s = s's''$ we can define completeness in the following way:

(20) *Completeness*
$F(s',c)$ is complete with respect to a grammar G, the respective mapping function H, P, I, or V and the signal s iff the maximal $F(s,c)$ neither modifies nor further specifies the representations that resulted from $F(s',c)$.

Three noteworthy consequences emerge from these definitions: First, maximality and completeness can be achieved at different levels of representation, i. e. the string in the syntactically ambiguous sentence in (16) is complete with respect to the PR mapping, and the initial strings of (17) and (18) are complete with respect to the PR and the SR mapping. Second, logically, a mapping that is complete is also maximal but not vice versa. Third, it is obvious that ambiguous structures allow a maximal mapping whereas dependent structures do so only if the assigner precedes the dependent. I suggest that these two states also correlate with the two resolution strategies: anticipation generally applies to maximal mappings, whereas delay applies to non-maximal mappings. I will illustrate this association below, mainly for the syntactic mapping.

4.1.4.2 Causes for non-linearity

Before we proceed to the parsing strategies, I will suggest a tentative motivation for linearity-breaking properties of language structure. Miyamoto & Takahashi (2002) propose the following insight for the difference between *wh*-in-situ and *wh*-ex-situ constructions. They assume that *wh*-arguments need to satisfy two needs: As arguments, they must receive a theta role, in their base position. As quantifiers, they need to mark their clausal scope. Miyamoto & Takahashi (2002) assume that in Japanese these two functions are realized by two lexical items, as shown in (21). The in-situ *wh*-phrase *nani-o* receives the theta role in clause internal position and the scope is marked by the interrogative particle *-ka* in the clausal periphery. In *wh*-ex-situ languages, such as English, both requirements are satisfied by one lexical item. The *wh*-element is dislocated from its theta-position into its scope marking position in the clausal periphery, as illustrated by the translations in (21) and the examples in (22).

(21) a. Mary-ga **nani-o** katta-to John-ga itta-**ka** watasi-wa kikimasita
Mary-NOM what-ACC bought-DECL John-NOM said-Q I-TOP asked
'I asked what John said Mary had bought'

b. Mary-ga **nani-o** katta-**ka** John-ga kiita-to watasi-wa iimasita
Mary-NOM what-ACC bought-Q John-NOM asked-DECL I-TOP said
'I said John asked what Mary had bought'

(Miyamoto & Takahashi 2002: 143)

(22) a. **What**$_1$ did John say [that Mary had bought t_1]?

b. John said [**what**$_1$ Mary had bought t_1]?

Clearly, this example is not intended to give an explanatory insight into the diverse topic of *wh*-(non-)movement. It should rather illustrate the important point that satisfying multiple requirements of higher order (semantic and contextual interpretation) in a linear string may lead to delayed processing of one of them. In fact, this idea can be generalized: Displacement is the syntactic reflex of satisfying multiple requirements of higher order. This subsumes also cases of topic and focus marking, in which the displacement is information structural tagging. Note, that this perspective on displacement resembles the idea of the Minimalist Program that movement is feature driven (Chomsky 1995: 297–316).

4.2 Incrementality in parsing

In the preceding section, I have presented general ideas about the processing apparatus, the status of syntactic parsing, and the generality of deviation from strict on-line processing. In this section, I will examine parsing procedures during incremental processing in more detail. I will discuss the anticipation strategy in cases of local ambiguity and the delay strategy in filler-gap dependencies. The evidence from parsing suggests that structure building procedures apply locally.

4.2.1 Anticipation: Parsing heuristics

In accordance with most psycholinguistic models, I assume that parsing generates phrase structure left-to-right and top-down (Kimball 1973, Frazier & Fodor 1978, Crocker 1994). This includes that structural assignment/attachment of constituents may begin before the subcategorizing heads are encountered. In such cases, the parser has to predict a structural analysis which may have to be reanalyzed later. This conforms to the strategy that I called anticipation. The mapping that is created hereby is *maximal*, because it conforms to a full-fledged representation of one possible analysis. If, however, more than one mapping is compatible with the full specification of the input, the behavior of the parser must rely on a decision mechanism which can be described by heuristics.

Two heuristics that have been proven to be very adequate are *Minimal Attachment* and *Late Closure* (Frazier 1978), given in (23) and (24). Similar principles have been proposed under different names (see Kimball 1973) but they can be subsumed under these two notions. Both principles are essentially economy principles: Minimal Attachment prevents the postulation of unjustified structure and Late Closure prevents the anticipation of unjustified interpretation domains.

(23) Minimal Attachment
Attach incoming material into the phrase-marker being constructed using the fewest nodes consistent with the well-formedness rules of the language under ananlysis.
(Frazier 1978: 24)

(24) Late Closure
When possible, attach incoming material into the clause currently parsed.
(Frazier 1978: 20)

Clearly, the Minimal Attachment strategy is the only practical assumption, as Frazier (1978: 25) puts it: "Actually, it is difficult to imagine a parser which does not make use of something like the Minimal Attachment strategy. Such a parser might postulate a monstrous structure [...] upon realizing the word *the*." Even if the assumption of a minimal structural link to the existing structure may leads to a revision process, the prediction of a more elaborated structural link would lead to revision even more often.

The Late Closure principle is actually rather an interpretational than a syntactic principle. From a rigid phrase structure perspective, the attachment of a node within the current clause must be less or equally costly than attaching it to another clausal projection (higher or lower). From a syntactic perspective, it would therefore only be an instance of minimal attachment. For cases in which attachment to the same or to a higher clause is equally costly, as for the embedded clauses in (25), experimental investigation indicated that the parser tends to integrate all possible elements (here *the story*) into the current clause, as in (25a), (Frazier 1978).

(25) a. [Though George kept on reading the story] Sue bothered him.
b. Though George kept on reading [the story still bothered him].
(Frazier 1978: 81)

I will discuss this point in more detail in Section 4.2.4 but for now it shall suffice to say that in absence of specific information, the parser prefers to integrate all possible constituents within the current interpretational unit (the clause), and favors a potential reanalysis, over closing an interpretational unit too early.

4.2.2 Delay: Filler-gap dependencies

A typical instance of delayed syntactic processing involves dislocated elements, i. e. elements that do not appear in their canonical base position[4]. Dislocated DPs have been intensively studied in English, German and several other languages, both theoretically and experimentally, but there are many other syntactic categories that occur dislocated. The primary focus of dislocation research lied on *wh*-movement, i. e. the fronting of interrogative elements, but also relativization, and DP-preposing (topicalization or scrambling) have been investigated. In psycholinguistics, the relation between a dislocated element and its base position is called *filler-gap dependency*, following Fodor (1978). The underlying assumption is that the displaced element, the filler, will be associated with the gap during on-line processing. The filler will be reactived and *inserted* at the gap site. With reference to transformational grammar, Fodor (1978: 427) calls it a *detransformation.*

The model of filler-gap dependencies resembles the concept of empty categories/traces in competence grammars. Psycholinguistic research over the past 30 years has yielded reliable support for the assumption that the dislocated element is reactivated at the base position (e. g. Bever & McElree 1988, MacDonald 1989, Osterhout & Swinney 1993, Shapiro 2000, Omaki et al. 2015), even though counter proposals have been made (Pickering & Barry 1991, Traxler & Pickering 1996). Classical arguments in favor of a filler-gap model are the filled-gap effect and filler reactivation in verb-final languages, which I will review below.

4 Clearly, in mainstream phrase structure grammars which assume a binary branching structure, any dislocation must correlate with a different hierarchical position. Usually, this comes on a par with a different linear position, except in cases of string-vacuous dislocation.

There is wide consensus that the parser posits gaps for fillers as early as possible. This strategy has been most famously phrased by Frazier & Clifton (1989) in their *Active Filler Hypothesis*, given in (26).

(26) *Active Filler Hypothesis*
When a filler has been identified, rank the option of assigning it to a gap above all other options.
(Frazier & Clifton 1989: 95)

This preference is illustrated by example (27). As Clifton & Frazier (1989) report, the preferred reading is the one given in (27a) in which the gap is posited earlier than in the alternative in (27b).

(27) Who did Fred tell Mary left the country.
a. Who_1 did Fred tell t_1 Mary left the country.
b. Who_1 did Fred tell Mary t_1 left the country.
(Clifton & Frazier 1989: 292)

Direct experimental support for the active filler strategy is widely known as the *filled-gap effect* (Crain & Fodor 1985, Stowe 1986). In (28c) the filler *who* has to be related with the object position. Under the active filler hypothesis it is predicted that the processor will initiate the association also in cases like (28d). However, with encountering the lexical element *us*, the assignment has to be revised and the filler must be associated with a later gap. This prediction is born out. Longer reading times on the object have been found in (28d) in contrast to both control conditions, (28a) in which no filler-gap dependency is involved, and (28b) in which the filler has already been assigned to the subject position.

(28) My brother wanted to know ...
a. ... if Ruth will bring us home to Mom at Christmas.
b. ... who_1 t_1 will bring us home to Mom at Christmas.
c. ... who_1 Ruth will bring t_1 home to Mom at Christmas.
d. ... who_1 Ruth will bring us home to t_1 at Christmas.
(Stowe 1986: 234)

Several studies have shown that the automated gap-filling effect does only occur at grammatically licit positions and that it is sensitive to lexical and semantic information, such as transitivity and plausibility (Stowe 1986, Stowe et al. 1991, Traxler & Pickering 1996, Wagers & Phillips 2014).

Neurolinguistic research identified two direct neurological correlates that support the establishment of filler-gap dependencies. On the region spanning from the filler until the gap site, left anterior negativities (LAN) have been found, which are typically associated with higher working memory demands that assumably stem from keeping the filler active for integration (Kluender & Kutas 1993b, Kluender & Kutas 1993a, Fiebach et al. 2001). At the gap site, P600 effects have been detected which are modulated by complexity parameters of the filler (subject vs. object and *who* vs. *which NP*), indicating the integration of the filler , i. e. gap-filling (Kaan et al. 2000, Fiebach et al. 2001).

I summarize that the processor integrates phrasal fillers at the earliest position, i. e. a structurally and semantically potential gap site. The (full) interpretation of the filler is therefore delayed until its integration, i. e. the filler cannot be fully interpreted in its surface position. Nevertheless, the gap-filling occurs anticipatory, before the subsequent segment is processed and explicit evidence for the gap is encountered. The processor therefore seeks to keep the processing delay minimal, adhering to a maxim of economy.

4.2.3 Consequences of incremental structure building: Constituency vs. c-command

Phillips (2003) illustrates how incremental structure building diverges from a head driven competence grammar representation. He demonstrates that if syntactic structure is built incrementally in a strict left-to-right order during the course of derivation, the parser may initially create constituents that have to be altered (destroyed) later on. The temporal constituent status of sequences that do not form constituents at a later stage of the derivation, explains why different constituency tests yield conflicting results, as formulated in the predictions in (29).

(29) a. Prediction 1: A constituency test may refer only to those strings that are constituents at the point in the incremental derivation when the test applies.
(Phillips 2003: 47)

b. Prediction 2: Contradictions between constituency tests arise when those tests apply at different stages in the incremental derivation of a sentence.
(Phillips 2003: 51)

c. Prediction 3: Constituents become invisible to syntactic processes as soon as they have been destroyed. (Phillips 2003: 55)

Phillips (2003) argues that coordination is the most liberal diagnostic because coordination applies immediately at the right edge of the first conjunct string: Any constituent that is created during the derivation may be coordinated, as the examples (30)–(32) show.

(30) a. [Wallace will]
b. Wallace will and Wendolene probably won't give Gromit crackers before breakfast.
(Phillips 2003: 47)

(31) a. [Wallace [will give]]
b. Wallace will give and Wendolene will send some crackers to Gromit for his birthday.
c. Wallace will design but won't actually build an exciting new invention for his dog's birthday.
(Phillips 2003: 48)

(32) a. [Wallace [will [give Gromit]]]
b. Wallace will give Gromit and Wendolene will give Preston a shining new collar for walking about town.
c. Wallace will give Gromit and (will) send Preston a shining new collar for walking about town.
(Phillips 2003: 48)

The examples also illustrate how constituency changes over the course of derivation. In (30), the subject and the auxiliary form a constituent (for lack of alternatives). In (31), this constituency is destroyed and the auxiliary forms a constituent with the lexical verb. In (32), this constituency is again disposed because the lexical verb forms a constituent with the indirect object. Example (33) shows that not any arbitrary string can be coordinated.

(33) *Wallace gave his [dog half a dozen] and [sheep a handful of] crackers for breakfast.
(Phillips 2003: 49)

The same accessibility as for coordination does not hold for other constituency diagnostics such as ellipsis (deletion) and topicalization (movement). Phillips (2003) argues that these transformations apply at a later stage of the derivation and therefore can only access currently existing constituents. The example in (34) illustrates such contradictory results for constituency. The two objects of the double object construction may be coordinated[5] as shown in (34a), but the same string cannot be topicalized, i. e. moved to clause-initial position, as in (34b), in

5 Crucially, the constituent status in coordination only holds for the first conjunct. The second conjunct must take part in later reanalysis procedures as in non-coordinated structures.

contrast to the VP in (34c). The conclusion is that topicalization can only apply at a point at which the temporary constituency between the two objects *Gromit + a biscuit* has already been destroyed.

(34) a. Wallace gave [Gromit a biscuit] and [Shawn some cheese] for breakfast.
b. *[Gromit a biscuit]$_1$ Wallace gave t_1 for breakfast
c. [Like cheese]$_1$ though Gromit does t_1, he can't stand Brie.
(Phillips 2003: 38–40)

The approach of Phillips (2003) demonstrates that principles of grammatic competence are subject to structural properties that result from incremental structure building. Phillips (2003) highlights that, whereas constituency is build and rebuild incrementally, hierarchy (c-command) is maintained monotonically, i. e. no obvious c-command test mismatches occur. In other words, as assembly takes place from left to right, a once established c-command relation will not be destroyed. Such a parsing-compatible phrase structure assembly is only efficient for genuine right branching structures (Kimball 1973, Phillips 1996, Haider 2012).

4.2.4 Incrementality and interpretation

I assume that semantic interpretation must follow the (sometimes incomplete) syntactic analysis. Additionally, I presume that the interpretation ensues the analyses of lower levels as closely as possible. Crocker (1994) proposes the *Principle of incremental comprehension*, which is given in (35).

(35) Principle of incremental comprehension (PIC)
The sentence processor operates in such a way as to maximize the interpretation and comprehension of the sentence at each stage of processing (i. e., as each lexical item is encountered). (Crocker 1994: 251)

This principle involves the notion of *maximality* I have introduced in Section 4.1.4.1. There, I have stated that *maximal* processing does not need to be *complete*. As it stands, the PIC predicts that the finite verb in V2-clauses participates in incremental interpretation, in the same way as in English clauses. And indeed, Crocker (1994: 261) states that the selectional properties of the finite verb in V2-position can be consulted immediately. Although I generally agree with the considerations in Crocker (1994), I deviate with respect to V2-parsing. I will show that unambiguous thematic information of the finite verb can only be extracted in a restricted number of V2-clauses (Section 4.3). Additionally, in Chapter 5, I will review the literature on German sentence processing with the conclusion that evidence for access of the thematic structure of the verb is only found at the clause-final position.

Independent of V2-movement, we can, however, assert an asymmetry with respect to the incremental interpretation of verbal arguments in head-initial VPs in contrast to head-final VPs. In head-initial VPs, intransitive predicates are complete with encounter of the verb, i. e. an SV string. Even in transitive structures, the objects usually follow the verb directly. Consequently, with the encounter of the object(s), the structure can receive an immediate interpretation. In head-final structures, on the other hand, all arguments can only receive their complete interpretation when the verbal subcategorizer is encountered. This asymmetry between verb-initial and verb-final structures is observable in parsing effects that have been labeled as *shortsightedness of the parser* by Frazier & Fodor (1978). They deduce the specific parsing behavior (shortsightedness) from the architecture of their two-stage parsing model (*sausage machine*). They assume that the first stage parser is a device with an upper limit of approximately seven segments (≈words). It forms phrase structure packages which are pushed down to the second stage parser. Due to its limited size, the first stage parser cannot attach elements outside of its scope. The second stage parser, on the other hand, integrates the phrase structure packages into the complete phrase marker. The model predicts that attachment preferences can be modulated by two parameters: first, the size of intervening material between attachment site and element to be attached, and second, the size of the unit to be attached. The effects of the two parameters are illustrated in (36) and (37). With increasing length of the material intervening between *read* and *to Mary*, the preference for a local attachment of *to Mary* to the preceding *the letter* increases in contrast to an attachment to the verb *read*. The reason for this is that the high attachment site (*read*) has left the scope of the first stage parser, as indicated by the dashed box. This preference also leads to misanalysis in cases in which low attachment is illicit, as in (36e).[6]

(36) a. [John *read* the letter *to Mary*.]

b. [John *read* the memo and the letter] *to Mary*.

c. John *read* [the note, the memo and the letter] *to Mary*.

d. John *read* the postcard, the note, [the memo and the letter *to Mary*.]

e. John *read* the postcard, the note, [the memo and the newspaper *to Mary*.]

(Frazier & Fodor 1978: 302, 297)

6 The phrase [*letter* [*to Mary*]] with the indicated structural analysis receives an interpretation such as ‘the letter that is intended for Mary/the letter of which Mary is the addressee’. The string *newspaper to Mary* does not allow such an interpretation.

A compensating effect emerges for increasing length of the phrase to be attached. Example (37) shows that small elements are likely to be grouped together with immediately preceding material, as in (37a) in which *out* is preferably attached to *rotten* resulting in the non-existing verb *rot out*, instead of attaching *out* to *threw* resulting in *throw out*. If the new phrase exceeds a certain threshold (length), the preceding constituent and the constituent to be attached will both be sent to the second stage parser separately, as in (37b). As a consequence *out of the window and into the rosebush* will be attached to *threw* by the second stage parser without giving rise to an erroneous attachment to *rotten*.[7]

(37) a. John *threw* the apple [that Mary had discovered was rotten *out*.]

b. John *threw* the apple that Mary had discovered
was rotten [*out of the window and into the rosebush.*]

(Frazier & Fodor 1978: 304)

This grouping mechanism motivates the stylistic preference of placing short constituents before long constituents. In absence of explicit grammatical markers, this helps to avoid misanalyses by the parser, even though the dispreferred order would not violate grammatical rules.

Crucially, such misanalyses and garden path structures are very rare in German. I assume that due to its head-final VP structure, the thematic properties are assigned later which seems to be a more robust mechanism in this respect. As example (38) shows, the initial string can form two different structures: an embedded relative clause with the string *die* being a relative pronoun, that refers to *Maria*, as in (38a), or an embedded non-finite clause in which *die* is the determiner for *Hunde*, as in (38b). Even without explicit prosodic marking the two structures are both easy to comprehend.

(38) Dann sahen wir Maria die Hunde überraschenderweise ...

a. [Dann sahen wir [Maria, [die Hunde überraschenderweise nicht leiden
then saw we Maria REL dogs surprisingly not like
kann,]] dort sitzen].
can there sit
'Then we saw Maria who surprisingly doesn't like dogs sitting there.'

b. [Dann sahen wir [Maria [die Hunde] überraschenderweise streicheln]].
then saw we Maria the dogs surprisingly pet
'Then we saw Maria surprisingly petting the dogs.'

7 Certainly, the relation between the matrix verb and the particle in (37a) can be marked by prosodic means in speech. This possibility is available for most if not all attachment ambiguities.

The natural finding in (39) shows that, in German, the verb *schließt* (literally 'lock, close') and its corresponding particle *ein* (literally 'in', yielding *einschließen* 'include') can be separated by comparably long intervening material. Those sentences do not exhibit attachment problems, which are expected within the two stage parsing model of Frazier & Fodor (1978), as has been illustrated for English in (37a).

(39) Der Begriff Schriften-Software *schließt* jegliche Updates, Upgrades, Erweiterungen, veränderte Versionen und Arbeitskopien der Schriften-Software, an denen dem Lizenznehmer, d.h. einer natürlichen Person und juristischen Person bzw. innerhalb der juristischen Person einer Tochtergesellschaft mit Mehrheitsanteil, hiernach ein Nutzungsrecht eingeräumt wird, *ein*.
'The term font software includes all updates, upgrades, extensions, changed version and working copies of the font software for which the licence taker, i. e. a natural person and legal person or rather within the legal person of an associated company with majority share herewith receives a right to use.'
(from a font license agreement by Elsner+Flake Type consulting, 2008)

However, this asymmetry between English and German seems to be restricted to the domain of predicates and its arguments and not to hold for the languages as a whole. Looking at the nominal domain, we find that both languages pattern alike. The attachment of (non-adjacent) adjuncts seems to give rise to the same problems in English (Frazier & Fodor 1978) and German (Hemforth et al. 2000), as illustrated in (40). In both clauses, the relative clause is initially preferably connected to the plural object, which leads to reanalysis as soon as the singluar verb is encountered.

(40) a. The girl applied for the jobs that was attractive.
(Frazier & Fodor 1978: 297)

b. GERMAN
Die Frau bewarb sich auf die Stellenanzeigen, die attraktiv
the woman applied REFL on the job announcements REL attractive
war.
was.SG

Crucially, the nominal phrase is head-initial in both English and German. Therefore, I tentatively conclude that headedness of the phrase structure categories is the defining factor that drives the exemplified (mis)interpretation effects.

I summarize that strictly incremental interpretation can be detected for head-initial phrases such as the VP in English, whereas it seems to be absent in the

German head-final VP. As a consequence the verb-argument processing of English and German differ, which results in specific misanalyses that are present in English but typically absent in German. This may generalize to head-initial and head-final phrase structures, even within one language as sketched for German VP vs. NP.

4.3 Configurationality of V2: The discrepancy between finite verb and lexical head

In Chapter 2, I argued that V2-structures involve two displaced elements, the preverbal constituent and the finite verb itself. Consequently, we expect that German sentence processing must involve the resolutions of these two distance dependencies.

The first dependency concerns the preverbal element. This is the classic case of a phrasal filler-gap dependency, such as for *wh*-elements in English. Because I have assumed that the preverbal element is moved from a clause-internal position below the C-domain, I predict that these elements always have to be connected to their clause-internal positions. In Chapter 7, I will discuss the special status of subject-initial clauses.

The second dependency concerns the finite verb, which originates in its clause-final base position. Similar to the dislocated DPs, I assume that the finite verb has to be reconstructed into the clause-final position. But even if this turns out to be accurate, the question remains whether the verb is actually fully interpreted in its dislocated position. There are two main options: First, the parser uses all information on-line in order to compute a (partial) interpretation of the sentence. Second, the parser relies on a uniform mechanism to generate interpretations for matrix and subordinate clauses, and therefore processes both as V-final structures. At first glance, the first option seems to be more efficient. Why should the processor ignore information that is already available? The answer is that V-final parsing is actually less error prone than the strict incremental approach.

I have assumed that the finite verb only moves to the C-position because the finiteness features cannot move separately without taking the verb along. As a result, verbal elements of different kind may appear in the V2-position. Only thematic verbs in synthetic tense forms provide morphosyntactic elements that are specified for finiteness and provide unambiguous lexical information about the thematic frame that would allow the prediction upcoming elements. In the following, I will present four classes of verbal elements, auxiliaries, modals, cluster verbs, and particle verbs, that may appear in the V2-position and are considerably defective with respect to thematic information. I will illustrate that a predictive processing would lead to severe garden paths which are, however, not observable. I will exclude cases of lexically ambiguous verbs because different meanings are often derived and do not show a divergent thematic structure. Additionally, in comparison to the configurational cases below, lexical ambiguity is assumably low frequent.

4.3.1 Auxiliary verbs

German only exhibits two synthetic tense forms, the present and the simple past (*Präteritum*). All other tense forms, as well as all passive constructions, involve auxiliary verbs. The highest auxiliary verb carries finiteness inflection and is placed in the V2-position. Some auxiliary verbs take part in more than one verb form, such as *werden* 'will', which is involved in future tense (41a), passive (41b), future perfect (41c), or in its lexical meaning 'become' (41d).

(41) a. Dann wird Peter in die Kneipe gehen.
then becomes Peter in the pub go
'Then Peter will go to the pub.'

b. Dann wird Peter in die Kneipe eingeladen.
then becomes Peter in the pub invited
'Then Peter is invited into the pub.'

c. Dann wird Peter in der Kneipe seinen Spaß gehabt haben.
then becomes Peter in the pub his fun had have
'Then Peter will have had his fun in the pub.'

d. Dann wird Peter in der Kneipe zum Mann.
then becomes Peter in the pub to the man
'Then Peter becomes a man in the pub.'

Similarly, the two auxiliaries *haben* 'have' and *sein* 'be' feature in a range of construction such as copula constructions, past tense, modal use, etc. As is evident by the paradigm in (41), the sentences are identical until the post subject region. Even after the PPs *in die/der Kneipe* no robust prediction can be generated about the thematic structure, depending on the finite verb.

4.3.2 Modal verbs

Modal verbs may also be finite and target the V2-position. As Parodi (2000) notes, modal verbs have a lexical meaning[8] and agree with the subject but they do not project their own argument structure[9]. Modals rather parasitically use the argument structure of the verb in its scope. The examples in (42) show that the subcategorization, i. ė. the number of arguments and the morphological marking of the arguments exclusively depend on the lexical verbs, which appear clause-finally.

(42) a. Dann muss der Student schlafen.
then must the student sleep
'Then, the student hase to sleep.'

b. Dann muss der Student einem Professor ein Buch in das
then must [the student]NOM [a professor]DAT [a book]ACC in the
Büro bringen.
office bring
'Then, the student has to bring a book to the professor in the office.'

c. Dann müssen dem Studenten die Bücher gefallen.
then must.PL [the student]DAT [the books]NOM please
'Then, the books have to appeal to the student.'

d. Dann muss es den Studenten frieren.
then must EXPL [the student]ACC be cold
'Then, the student has to be cold.'

We can conclude that also modal verbs in V2-position do not allow to make predictions about the arguments to follow. These arguments exclusively depend on the clause-final lexical verb.

---

8 The type of modality (epistemic, denontic, etc.) may vary depending on the context.

9 Josef Bayer pointed out that modals could be analyzed on a par with raising verbs: Such verbs take a propositional complement that may receive a theta role, as indicated in (i).

(i) a. *MODAL [PROPOSITION]*$_\theta$

b. *Also muss [Schelli einen Rausch gehabt haben]*$_\theta$.
thus must Schelli a intoxication had have
'Thus, Schelli must have had a buzz on.'

Even under this analysis, the crucial argument, that the number and type of arguments to come are not predictable by interpreting the modal verb, remains unaffected. The argument structure within the propositional complement of the modal is solely dependent on the predicate inside the complement.

4.3.3 Clustering verbs: Selecting non-finite complements

In German, as in other V-final languages, some verbs may take non-finite complements with which they form a verb cluster (Haider 2010). As an infinitive, the embedded verb shares the subject with the higher predicate (raising) but may selects additional arguments. Those other arguments are not selected by the higher verb, as shown in (43).

(43) a. Dann versucht der Professor zu schlafen.
then tries the professor to sleep
'Then, the professor tries to sleep.'

b. Dann versucht der Professor seinen Studenten anzusprechen.
then tries the professor his student to address
'Then, the professor tries to address his student.'

c. Dann versucht der Professor dem Studenten die Veranstaltung zu empfehlen.
then tries the professor the student the event to recommend
'Then, the professor tries to recommend the event to his student.'

Haider (2010: 276) notes that most cluster triggering verbs do not even thematically specify a subject, as shown in the raising constructions in (44a) and (44b). The number of arguments, case requirements and unmarked word order are solely specified by the embedded verb, as shown by the comparison with the embedded clause in (44c) that lacks the raising predicate *drohen*. Note that the raising verbs in (44a) and (44b) nevertheless agree with the nominative argument. For a thorough overview of German infinitival constructions see Haider (2010: 272–292).

(44) a. Jetzt droht der Wind die Blätter wegzuwehen.
now threats.SG the wind.NOM the sheets.ACC to blow away
'Now, the sheets are in danger of getting blown away by the wind.'

b. Jetzt drohen dem Mann die Zähne auszufallen.
now threaten.PL the man.DAT the teeth.NOM to fall out
'Now, the man is in danger of loosing his teeth.'

c. ... dass dem Mann die Zähne ausfallen.
that the man.DAT the teeth.NOM fall out
'... that the man looses his teeth.'

With regard to cluster triggering verbs, I likewise conclude that substantial predictions regarding the argument structure to follow cannot be achieved by relying on information provided by the finite verb in second position.

4.3.4 Particle verbs

A further important instance of discontinuous verb forms are particle verbs. They are morphologically complex and consist of a stem plus a prefixed particle (separable prefix). Crucially, if such a verb is targeted by V2-movement, only the verb stem moves to the left periphery and the particle remains in the clause-final position, as in (45). Particle verb formation is a productive process which can also apply recursively although not without serious consequences (see Haider 2010: 58–61 and Section 2.1.3.2). Several verb particle combinations obtain an idiosyncratic reading, as the one in (45).

(45) a. ..., dass wir mit dem Rauchen aufhören.
that we with the smoking up hear
'... that we quit smoking.'

b. Dann hören wir mit dem Rauchen auf.
then hear we with the smoking up
'Then we quit smoking.'

Clearly, in sentences with idiosyncratic particle verbs, the meaning of the sentence is not predictable at the point at which the finite verb stem is reached, as shown by the contrast of the word pair *mitbringen* 'bring along' and *umbringen* 'kill' in (46).

(46) a. Judith brachte ihre Mutter am Sonntag [...] einfach mit.
Judith brought her mother on Sunday simply with.PRT
'Judith simply brought her mother along on Sunday.'

b. Judith brachte ihre Mutter am Sonntag [...] einfach um.
Judith brought her mother on Sunday simply for.PRT
'Judith simply killed her mother on Sunday.'

The productive cases do not have such drastic differences in meaning but the combination with the particle can change the argument structure of the verb, as in the examples in (47), which resemble structures that have been investigated by Czypionka et al. (2016).

(47) a. transitive with accusative object
Dann hört die Polizei die Telefongespräche der Verbrecher
then hears the police [the telephone calls of the criminals]ACC
∅/an/mit/ab.
∅/on/with/off
'Then the police hears/listens to/listens in/wiretaps the phone calls of the criminals.'

b. transitive with dative object
Dann hört die Polizei den Telefongesprächen der Verbrecher zu.
then hears the police [the telephone calls of the criminals]DAT to
'Then the police listens to the phone calls of the criminals.'

c. intransitive
Dann hört die Polizei (bei den Telefongesprächen der Verbrecher)
then hears the police at the telephone calls of the criminals
weg.
away
'Then the police listen uncarefully/turn a deaf ear to the phone calls of the criminals.'

Another facet of the argument structure of particle verbs is illustrated in (48). This example is actually presented by Crocker (1994: 261) to argue that after encountering the strings *Das Mädchen sah* or *Das Buch sah*, the parser could determine the subject position for *Das Mädchen*, as in (48a) and determine that *Das Buch* cannot be an agentive subject of the verb *sehen* 'see'.[10] However, as the example in (48b) shows, there is a particle verb *aussehen* 'appear' that does not require an agentive subject. Hence, the parser cannot draw any robust conclusion that is exclusively based on the initial string, at least not without unambiguous case marking, restricting context etc.

(48) a. Das Mädchen sah das Buch.
the girl saw the book
'The girl saw the book.'

b. Das Buch sah alt und wertvoll aus.
the book saw old and valuable out.PRT
'The book appeared to be old and valuable.'

As indicated in example (46), the distance between the verb stem and the particle can theoretically be of any length due to intervening modifiers, see Bierwisch (1983: 146–147) and also (39). Consequently no solid prediction regarding the content to follow can be made for particle verbs, and in many cases it is not even predictable whether a particle will follow at all.

10 Both nouns are neuter in German. Neuter nouns show case syncretism of nominative and accusative singular (see Section 5.1.1).

4.3.5 Summary: A uniform parsing mechanism for V2-clauses

In sum, we have seen that in many cases in which a finite verb appears in V2-position, it does not allow substantial predictions about the arguments to come because these are selected by the corresponding non-finite verb that is located in clause-final position. This configuration was shown for non-thematic verbs that take part in all but two tense forms in German and all passive structures, for modal verbs, and for clustering verbs. These three groups can be subsumed under one structural analysis, namely the verb cluster formation. The higher verbal element bears finiteness features and moves to the V2-position in matrix clauses. The lower verb provides the argument frame and selects the arguments. Crucially, in all cluster formations, the lexical head that determines the argument structure is always in the clause-final position, due to its non-finiteness. Additionally, I discussed particle verbs which share one property with verb cluster patterns, namely that they form a discontinuous verb form. Only the finite verb moves to V2-position and the particle remains in the final position. Hence, lexical specification can only be achieved after combining verb and particle, i. e. at the end of the clause.

In addition, it must not be neglected that all embedded clauses in German conform to a verb-final structure.[11] Hence, I presume that the processing of German sentences must be able to cope with V-final structures in an efficient way. Now, considering the cases discussed above, in which a full interpretation is delayed until the clause-final position, it seems intuitive that these structures do not impose a problem, because V-final parsing is a necessary part of the processing device anyway. Instead, the following question suggests itself: Why should the processing mechanism make predictive use of elements that are rather useless or even misleading in a large number of cases instead of relying on a uniform verb-final parsing mechanism? Exactly that latter consideration is central to the reconstruction hypothesis.[12]

11 Embedded V2-clauses are ignored here.

12 Although he rejects that conclusion, Crocker (1994: 260–261) suggested a delayed processing of the finite verbs in V2-structures: "If we assume the traditional gap-filling strategies, then German and Dutch hearers would be forced to delay the use of verb's selectional information until the end of the sentence, after all the complements have been parsed, the verb's trace identified, and thematic assignment performed."

4.4 Chapter summary

In this chapter, I introduced the basic ingredients for the investigation of how V2-clauses are processed. The first section introduced the basic considerations regarding the processing device of human language. I concluded that such a system must operate on several levels of linguistic representations. The mapping from the input signal onto the final level of interpretation proceeds mostly incrementally, and on-line. A closer inspection, however, revealed that deviation from strict on-line processing may affect all levels of representation. I have characterized two types of such deviations: underspecification and dependence.

In the second section, I focused on processing routines that are involved in incremental structure building. Within the syntactic domain, I discussed two processing strategies, which each relate to one of the two groups of deviations from on-line processing: *Anticipation* subsumes parsing heuristics that allow premature decisions for underspecified (ambiguous) structures. The attachment preferences can be modeled by only two principles: *Minimal Attachment* and *Late Closure*. The strategy for incomplete dependence structures is *Delay*. I discussed filler-gap dependencies as a prototypical case in which the interpretation of a dislocated element is delayed until its reactivation at its base position. Furthermore, I reported that constituency diagnostics indicate that structure building in English proceeds incrementally, whereby some elements may form a constituent only temporarily, whereas c-command relation are maintained monotonically. With reference to classical examples of misanalysis (garden path sentences), I argued that interpretation in English head-initial VPs may proceed highly incremental which causes these robust misanalyses. The fact that comparable garden path effects are basically absent in German is a first indication that structure building and interpretation routines in German may not be identical to the ones in English. I suggested that these differences originate from the contrary headedness of the VPs in German and English.

In the third section, I emphasized that V2-clauses in particular would give rise to frequent misanalyses under an incremental processing hypothesis. Such misanalyses, however, are basically absent in German. I discussed four frequent configurations: non-thematic verbs, modal verbs, clustering verbs and particle verbs. In all configurations, the verbal complex consists of a finite verb in V2-position and an element in the clause-final base position. The interpretation of the predicate is contingent on the element in the clause-final position. I therefore suggested that V2-clauses in German are processed in the same way as V-final clauses.

In sum, this chapter introduced the concept of on-line language comprehension. I illustrated that deviations from strict on-line processing occur regularly and give rise to two processing strategies, *anticipation* and *delay*. I argued that processing of English clauses builds on anticipation which may result in distinct misanalyses (garden path). From the absence of comparable misanalyses in German V2-clauses, I concluded that processing of German main clauses resorts to delayed interpretation of the verb at the clause-final position. This hypothesis of obligatory verb reconstruction will be checked against experimental results of German sentence processing in the following chapters.

5 Processing of German clauses

In this chapter, I review the literature about sentence processing in German. I will first discuss effects of argument ordering in the middle field (scrambling), mostly in V-final clauses. Subsequently, I will discuss effects of XP-fronting, i. e. moving one argument into the prefield of V2-clauses. The discussion of these two instances of argument dislocation in German will provide the baseline for the inspection of verb-related processing effects in Section 5.3. The gathered experimental findings indicate indicate that meaning-related information of the verb does not influences the processing of arguments in German but rather support the hypothesis that the full interpretation of the verb is delayed until the clause-final position.

5.1 Scrambling

Scrambling is a term for the reordering of constituents within the clausal domain (middle field), notably the extended VP (incl. vP and IP). It therefore contrasts with the placement of constituents into the clausal left periphery (*wh*-movement, topicalization, fronting, etc.) and into the right periphery (extraposition).

First, I want to ensure that scrambling in German is an instance of displacement, comparable to filler-gap dependencies, which shows reactivation effects of the displaced element at the base position. For short scrambling Clahsen & Featherston (1999) and Featherston (2001) report results from two cross-modal lexical priming studies which indicate that dislocated NPs are reactivated at their base position. In both structures, (1) and (2), the probe, which is identical to the dislocated element, received shorter reaction times at the gap site (#2), in comparison to the control site (#1). The shorter reaction times for the matching target indicate that the filler is reactivated at the gap site (#2) which facilitates the lexical activation of the probe and reduces the reaction time in the lexical decision task[1].

1 In a lexical decision task, participants have to decide whether a given string is an actual word or a non-word. For the here presented target items both, identical and unrelated, probes are actual words, the filler items contained also non-words.

https://doi.org/10.1515/9783110725018-005

(1) a. Nach zwei Tagen Streit sprach der Richter [das Geschäft]$_1$ [dem
after two days dispute awarded the judge the business the
ziemlich überraschten #1 Andreas] #2 t_1 zu.
rather surprised Andreas to
'After two days of dispute the judge awarded the business to the rather surprised Andreas.'

b. identical probe: *Geschäft* 'business', unrelated probe: *Wagen* 'car'
(Clahsen & Featherston 1999: 426)

(2) [[So ein Haus]$_1$ [einer völlig normalen #1 Kundin] #2 t_1 verkaufen]$_{VP2}$
Such a house a totally normal customer sell
konnte nur Maria t_2.
could only Maria
'Only Maria could sell such a house to a totally normal customer.'
– only identical probes, such as *Haus* 'house' – (Featherston 2001: 94)

In the following, I will look at the specific processing effects that arise from non-canonical argument ordering. For this, I divide the discussion into cases in which the arguments show unambiguous case marking, which allows immediate identification of non-canonical order, and cases with ambiguous case-marking, which gives rise to (temporary) ambiguities. We will see that the (lack of) unequivocal formal marking modulates the temporal locus of the experimental effects.

5.1.1 Unambiguous case marking

The linear order of arguments in the German middle field shows a linearization preference in which the subject is realized as the first argument. Subsequent arguments are preferably realized in the order *dative (indirect object) before accusative (direct object)* (see the *linear precedence rules* in Uszkoreit 1986). The validity of these linearization preferences have been empirically confirmed with reaction times and accuracy measures in comprehension and production studies, and in acceptability judgments (Bayer & Marslen-Wilson 1992, Pechmann et al. 1996, Rösler et al. 1998, Röder et al. 2000, Bornkessel et al. 2002). On-line methods have revealed prolonged reading times on initial unambiguously case-marked objects (Scheepers 1997).

Several ERP studies investigated transitive (3) and ditransitive clauses (4) with scrambled, unambiguously case-marked arguments and provide robust evidence for the processing difficulties of non-canonical argument ordering. On the first argument position, initial dative or accusative objects result in a negativity which is located in fronto-central or anterior sites (Rösler et al. 1998, Bornkessel et al. 2002, 2003a, Schlesewsky et al. 2003, Bornkessel & Schlesewsky 2006b). This negativity emerges shortly after the onset of the case-marked determiner (350-400ms), and is absent for case marked pronouns (Schlesewsky et al. 2003). It is commonly interpreted as a reflection of an increased processing load (Bornkessel & Schlesewsky 2006b) and, more specifically, as a reflection of working memory demands due to the storing of the argument for later integration (Rösler et al. 1998). On the second NP, non-canonical orders evoke a posterior positivity (300–400ms) which is detectable for DAT<NOM order (Bornkessel et al. 2002, 2003b), and more pronounced for other non-canonical orders such as ACC<NOM, DAT<ACC, and ACC<DAT (Rösler et al. 1998). Bornkessel et al. (2003b: 286-290) interpret this positivity as an indication of thematic reanalysis induced by a non-canonical argument order.

(3) a. NOM<ACC
... dass der Jäger den Gärtner besucht.
that [the hunter]NOM [the gardener]ACC visits
'...that the hunter visits the gardener.'

b. ACC<NOM
... dass den Jäger der Gärtner besucht.
that [the hunter]ACC [the gardener]NOM visit
'... that the gardener visits the hunter.'

c. NOM<DAT
... dass der Jäger dem Gärtner hilft.
that [the hunter]NOM [the gardener]DAT helps
'... that the hunter helps the gardener.'

d. DAT<NOM
... dass dem Jäger der Gärtner hilft.
that [the hunter]DAT [the gardener]NOM helps
'... that the gardener helps the hunter.'

(Bornkessel et al. 2002: B24)

At the third argument position of ditransitive structures as in (4), Rösler et al. (1998) report a long-lasting posterior positivity and a fronto-central negativity (357–625ms) for the non-canonical order NOM<ACC<DAT (in contrast to NOM<DAT<ACC) on the determiner and the noun. At the clause-final verb, non-canonical orders lead to a posterior negativity (31–500ms) (Rösler et al. 1998: 166).

(4) Dann hat [der Vater] [dem Sohn] [den Schnuller] gegeben.
then has [the father]NOM [the son]DAT [the pacifier]ACC given.
'Then the father gave the pacifier to the son.'
(Rösler et al. 1998: 153)

I summarize that explicitly marked non-canonical argument order gives rise to immediate processing responses with initial negativities in response to the mismatch and later positivities indicating a reanalysis.

5.1.2 Ambiguous case marking

Many studies have investigated the processing of clauses with (partially) case-ambiguous arguments. In German, only masculine singular nouns show morphologically distinct forms for nominative and accusative, as shown in Table 5.1.

Table 5.1: Case marking and syncretism in German

	NOMINATIVE	ACCUSATIVE	DATIVE	GENITIVE
MASCULINE DP	der/ein Mann	den/einen Mann	dem/einem Mann	des/eines Mannes
NEUTER DP	das/ein Ding		dem/einem Ding	des/eines Dinges
FEMININE DP	die/eine Frau		der/einer Frau	
proper name	Josef			Josef's
PLURAL DP	die Männer/Frauen/Dinge		den Männern/Frauen/Dingen	der Männer/Frauen/Dinge
bare PLURAL (M, N)	Männer/Dinge		Männern/Dingen	∅
bare PLURAL (F)	Frauen			∅

Due to this case syncretism, we can investigate the default parsing process by constructing initially ambiguous clauses that will be disambiguated at a later point. I noted that German shows a subject-first preference, which is indicated by processing difficulties for initial non-nominative arguments. Unsurprisingly, this preference prevails also with case-ambiguous arguments. If the first encountered argument is case-ambiguous, though compatible with nominative case, it will be initially interpreted as a subject. This subject-first preference is indicated by reanalysis processes that occur if the unambiguous nominative-marking of another argument, as in (5a), or the agreement on the verb, as in (5b), resolve the ambiguity towards a non-subject interpretation of the first argument.[2] At the point of such a *late* disambiguation, a structural reanalysis has to take place. This is detectable by increased reaction times and decreased acceptability judgments (Bader & Meng 1999, Scheepers et al. 2000, Bader & Bayer 2006). Generally, disambiguation through the clause-final verb (agreement) is more severe than dis-

2 Bader & Bayer (2006: 87-104) refer to these two types as *nominal disambiguation* and *verbal disambiguation*, respectively.

ambiguation by arguments (Bader & Bayer 2006: 103). In on-line measures, these reanalysis effects manifest in form of longer reading times for object-initial orders immediately at the disambiguating element (Bayer & Marslen-Wilson 1992, Bader & Lasser 1994, Scheepers et al. 2000, Kretzschmar et al. 2012). Similarly, in ERP experiments, such effects turn up immediately at the disambiguating region as well. In an initially ambiguous object-initial clause, a P600 (Friederici et al. 2001), an N400 (Schlesewsky & Bornkessel 2004: 1217), and both (Mecklinger et al. 1995) are reported at the disambiguating clause-final verb. The effects are interpreted as the reflection of a reanalysis process.[3]

(5) a. ... dass die Mutter der Schüler angeschrien hat.
that [the mother]NOM/ACC [the pupil]NOM shouted at has.3SG
'... that the pupil shouted at the mother.'

b. ... dass die Mutter die Schüler angeschrien haben.
that [the mother]NOM/ACC [the pupils]NOM/ACC shouted at have.3PL
'... that the pupils have shouted at the mother.'

In sum, we observe immediate local responses that correspond to reanalysis processes during the parsing of non-canonical argument orders. These effects either turn up at the point of disambiguation or at the unambiguously case-marked, non-initial arguments. In unambiguous cases, the reanalysis is preceded by an increased processing load at the first argument. Such mismatch or memory stacking effects are logically absent in ambiguous clauses.

5.2 XP-fronting

In addition to scrambling, German exhibits a second kind of argument reordering, to which I will refer here as *XP-fronting*. In contrast to scrambling, the leftward moved constituent targets a clause peripheral position, i. e. a specifier position in the C-domain. This position may be typically occupied by (topicalized) DPs, *wh*-elements, or adverbs but, as has been discussed in Chapter 2, basically every phrasal constituent may occupy this position. The location of this position is indicated by the two following observations: In V2-(main) clauses, the fronted element obligatorily precedes the finite verb and in embedded clauses it obligatorily precedes the subject. This position also marks an important contrast to scrambling. Following our assumptions above, the Spec-CP position is a position that

3 For arguments in favor of an interpretation of the N400 component as reanalysis, see Schlesewsky & Bornkessel (2004: 1218, fn. 2).

is usually filled through movement.[4] Hence, the processor may immediately start the filler-gap parsing by encountering this position. There is simply no possibility for assuming that the fronted element is in its base position. I will restrict the discussion to cases of argument fronting. Clearly, the specifics of (un)ambiguous case marking of DPs in the prefield are identical to those of the scrambled DPs discussed in Section 5.1 above, see especially Table 5.1. As in the preceding section, I will first discuss cases of unambiguous marked arguments before I will examine cases with an ambiguous initial argument.

5.2.1 Unambiguous case marking

Sentences with object-before-subject order show longer reaction times and lower acceptability judgments than sentences with canonical subject-before-object order (Hemforth 1993: 157-170). In on-line measures with simple transitive sentences, as in (6), the following effects are reported: Object-initial orders evoke longer reading/reaction times on the first DP, the verb, and the second DP (Bayer & Marslen-Wilson 1992, Hemforth 1993: 157-170, Konieczny 1996, Fanselow et al. 1999, Weskott 2003). Scheepers (1997: 147–160) notes that the effect on reading times for unambiguously accusative-marked initial DPs is larger in scrambling contexts than for XP-fronting.

(6) a. Der kluge Onkel besuchte den kleinen Jungen.
[the smart uncle]NOM visits [the small boy]ACC
'The smart uncle visits the small boy.'

b. Den klugen Onkel besuchte der kleine Junge.
[the smart uncle]ACC visits [the small boy]NOM
'The small boy visits the smart uncle.'

(Hemforth 1993: 158)

In ERP, sentences with non-canonical word order and unambiguously case-marked arguments show a lasting left anterior negativity (LAN) starting from the first dislocated element until the end of the second noun phrase (Matzke et al. 2002, Felser et al. 2003). This negativity is interpreted as an increased working memory demand caused by holding material in working memory for delayed integration. Matzke et al. (2002) report an additional N400 at frontotemporal sites on the second DP. Felser et al. (2003) report a similar early frontal negativity on the clause-final verb. The interpretation of this negativity remains inconclusive.

4 The only unequivocal exception in which Spec-CP is filled by an element lacking a base position, is the case of expletives, see Section 2.1.4.4.

In sum, unambiguously case marked object-initial clauses show long-lasting processing difficulties that last until the base position of the fronted element. This is reflected by increased reading times and LAN-effects.

5.2.2 Ambiguous case marking

Similar to the scrambling cases above, the processor shows a preference for analyzing case-ambiguous fronted XPs, such as in (7), as subjects by default. This subject-first preference is evident in prolonged reaction times and lowered acceptability judgments for non-canonical orders (Bader & Bayer 2006). Analogously, in on-line measures, prolonged reading times are found immediately at the disambiguating element in declarative clauses (Bayer & Marslen-Wilson 1992, Hemforth 1993), *wh*-interrogatives (Schlesewsky et al. 2000), and relative clauses (Schriefers et al. 1995). In ERP studies with ambiguous intial arguments, the following effects were found: At the disambiguating second argument the non-canonical order evoked a frontotemporal N400 and a posterior positivity (Matzke et al. 2002, Bornkessel 2002, Frisch et al. 2002, Mecklinger et al. 1995)[5].

(7) a. Die kluge Tante besuchte den kleinen Jungen.
[the smart aunt]NOM/ACC visits [the small boy]ACC
'The smart aunt visits the small boy.'

b. Die kluge Tante besuchte der kleine Junge.
[the smart aunt]NOM/ACC visits [the small boy]NOM
'The small boy visits the smart aunt.'

(Hemforth 1993: 158)

The subject-first preference is not restricted to German but has also been detected in other languages, such as Dutch (Kaan 1997) and Basque (Erdocia et al. 2009). Moreover, Weskott (2003) shows that this preference can be mitigated by increasing the inferability of the fronted object from the context and that the effect can even be canceled through syntactic priming of an object-before-subject structure.

In sum, I conclude that XP-fronting results in long-lasting processing demands which indicate a restructuring process that needs to hold the displaced element (filler) active in memory until the reconstruction site (gap). This is reflected by prolonged reading times and a LAN effect in ERPs. Scrambling, on the

5 The topography of the negativity reported in Mecklinger et al. (1995) is different: right lateralized, posterior. However, Mecklinger et al. (1995) used material in which the syntactically disambiguating auxiliary was preceded by a semantic disambiguation caused by the lexical meaning of the participle, which induced the N400.

other hand, is more local. The reordered constituents never left the head domain, i. e. the extended VP. Therefore, no heavy restructuring has to take place but only local reranking/reordering. In case of local ambiguities, however, the results of both structures are almost identical. This is not surprising if we consider the process in detail. After encountering an ambiguous prefield argument, the processor will reconstruct it immediately into the highest VP internal position, i. e. the subject position. After this operation, all subsequent reanalysis processes are identical to scrambled orders in the middle field.

5.3 The processing influence of the verb

Processing effects of verb movement are considerably understudied. Evidence for the processing impact of verbs is mostly indirect and falls in two main classes: first, the interaction of the verb position with effects of argument processing and second, the influence of verb position on more general sentence processing routines, such as attachment and scope computation. In the last subsection, I will review the few direct investigations of processing verbs in sentences.

5.3.1 Thematic processing

The most direct role that the verb may play in on-line processing is the assignment of thematic roles to its arguments, thereby predicting the number and type of arguments and integrating these based on the verb frame. Hence, German V2-clauses could contrast quite sharply with their V-final counterparts because, in the former, the verb information may be early available for incremental processing. In the latter, the verbal elements follow all of the arguments. Hence, the verb frame cannot be accessible during the processing of the arguments. In this respect, experiencer object verbs, such as *verblüffen* 'baffle', constitute useful test cases because they have shown to exhibit an argument ordering that deviates from agentive verbs, such as *zerreißen* 'ripp up'. Experiencers are preferred to be linearized as the first argument, although they show the same case marking as objects of canonical agentive verbs, i. e. accusative or dative.[6] In contrast to the subject-first preference, these verbs are said to exhibit an *experiencer-first* preference (see Verhoeven

6 Whether the argument order for experiencer object verbs really show a inherent preference for object-initial ordering is still a matter of current research. At least we can state that the subject-first preference for these verbs is significantly weaker than for agentive verbs (see Temme & Verhoeven 2016 and references therein).

2015, Temme & Verhoeven 2016). Building on the reliable effect of non-canonical word order (scrambling) reported in Section 5.1, Schlesewsky & Bornkessel (2004) discuss the influence of verb specific information on argument ordering. In sentences, as in (8), they contrast agentive verbs (*folgen* 'follow'/*drohen* 'threaten'), which show an unmarked subject-before-object order (8a), with experiencer object verbs (*gefallen* 'please'), which have an unmarked object-before-subject order (8b). At the clause-final verb, they report higher processing costs (early parietal positivity) for experiencer object verbs, which is detectable with both argument orders subject-before-object, and object-before-subject. Schlesewsky & Bornkessel (2004) conclude that at the clause-final verb, the exceptional thematic hierarchy of experiencer object verbs induces a revision process.

(8) a. ... dass der Mönch dem Bischof folgt/gefällt, obwohl ...
that [the monk].NOM [the bishop].DAT follows/appeals, although
'... that the monk follows/is appealing to the bishop.'

b. ... dass dem Mönch der Bischof folgt/gefällt, obwohl ...
that [the monk].DAT [the bishop].NOM follows/appeals, although
'... that the bishop follows/is appealing to the monk.'

(Schlesewsky & Bornkessel 2004: 1215)

Bornkessel (2002: 99–116) investigates the same argument order contrast for V2-clauses in which the verb information is present in advance of the arguments, as in (9). Hence, under the assumption of incremental processing, we expect that the argument order and the verb classes will interact, i. e. that subject-before-object order is preferred after agentive verbs and object-before-subject order is preferred after experiencer object verbs.

(9) a. Vielleicht droht/gefällt der Bäcker dem Regisseur seit der Party.
perhaps threatens/pleases [the baker]NOM [the director]DAT since the party

b. Vielleicht droht/gefällt dem Bäcker der Regisseur seit der Party.
perhaps threatens/pleases [the baker]DAT [the director]NOM since the party

c. Vielleicht droht/gefällt Stefan dem/der Regisseur seit der Party.
perhaps threatens/pleases Stefan.NOM/ACC/DAT the.DAT/the.NOM director since the party

(Bornkessel 2002: 100)

Bornkessel (2002) reports that there are no effects detectable at the verb. This means either, that the differences of the two verb classes are too small to detect, or that the two verb classes are not processed differently at this point. In the unambiguously case-marked conditions, the initial dative DP (9b) elicited a positivity in the 300–900 ms window in contrast to the nominative DP (9a). Crucially, this effect was present for both verb types, and showed only slight topographical variation with respect to the verb types. For the initially case-ambiguous clauses, the dative-before-nominative order elicited a robust N400 effect at the disambiguating NP2 for both verb types. Agentive verbs additionally showed a weak P600 effect for dative-before-nominative order which indicates that after disambiguation a reanalysis of the object-before-subject order is initiated. This reanalysis is absent for experiencer verbs. In sum, the experiment showed a robust nominative-first preference for both verb types. The results of the first experiment suggest that the thematic structure of experiencer verbs is exceptional. This is further supported by a thematic reanalyses process that was detected only for agentive verbs at the clause-final position. However, the results of the experiment do not indicate that the verb information guides the process of constructing a thematic hierarchy. Crucially, the results suggest that even though the verb information is available before the arguments are processed, the effects are identical to the verb-final structures with respect to the components as well as in their temporal occurrence. "Therefore, the mechanisms responsible for the establishment of thematic relations between arguments also appear to operate without drawing upon verb-specific information, even when this information is available" (Schlesewsky & Bornkessel 2004: 1227).

In a similar way, Scheepers et al. (2000)[7] investigated the influence of verb-mediated thematic information on argument ordering. They contrasted experiencer subject verbs, such as *fürchten* 'frighten', with experiencer object verbs, such as *ängstigen* 'fear', in V2 and V-final clauses, as shown in (10).[8] In both clause types, the NP1 *die strenge Lehrerin* 'the strict teacher' is case-ambiguous between nominative and accusative. In acceptability judgment studies, Scheepers et al. (2000) stated that the object-before-subject order gave rise to higher acceptability judgments for experiencer object verbs and that the acceptability could even be enlarged by using an inanimate subject. This indicates that experiencer object verbs have a stronger tendency for object-before-subject order than experiencer

7 The reported experiments are also published in Scheepers (1997: 123-146).

8 Scheepers et al. (2000) refer to experiencer subject verbs with with *psychological statives* and to experiencer object verbs with *psychological causatives*.

subject verbs, which might be reflected in on-line measures as well. The predictions concerning (10) were tested in an eye tracking study.

(10) a. V-final–S<O vs. O<S
Dass |$_{NP1}$ die strenge Lehrerin |$_{NP2}$ den stillen Schüler/ der stillen
that the strict teacher [the quiet pupil]ACC/ [the quiet
Schüler |$_{ADV}$ ein wenig |$_{Verb}$ ängstigte/ fürchtete, | hatte der Psychologe
pupil]NOM a bit fears/ frightens had the psychologist
von einigen Klassenkameraden erfahren.
from some class mates get to know
'That the strict teacher frightened the quiet pupil a bit, the psycologist learned from some of the class mates' or
'That the quiet pupil feared the strict teacher a bit, ...'

b. V2–S<O vs. O<S
Offenbar |$_{Verb}$ ängstigte/ fürchtete |$_{NP1}$ die strenge Lehrerin |$_{NP2}$ den
obviously fears/ frightens the strict teacher [the
stillen Schüler/ der stille Schüler |$_{ADV}$ ein wenig, | was der
quiet pupil]ACC/ [the quiet pupil]NOM a bit what the
Psychologe von einigen Klassenkameraden erfahren hatte.
psychologist from some class mates get to know had
'Obviously the strict teacher frightened the quiet pupil a bit, ...' or
'Obviously the quiet pupil feared the strict teacher a bit, ...'

(Scheepers et al. 2000: 115–117)

In V2-clauses, experiencer subject verbs elicited longer reading times in early (first pass reading times) and late measures (regression path duration). Expectedly, no effect turned up at the case ambiguous NP1. In both clause types the object-before-subject order evoke longer reading times in early measures (first path reading times) only on the disambiguating NP2. The late measures (regression path duration) revealed longer reading times for the object-before-subject order on the disambiguating NP2, the following adverb and the verb in V-final clauses. Additionally, the late measures also revealed an interaction of verb type and argument ordering on the clause-final element, i. e. the adverbial in V2-clauses and the verb in V-final clauses. This interaction points in the expected direction, namely that the preference for SO and the dispreference for OS is more pronounced in experiencer subject verbs. This late effect is still visible in the answer accuracy of the comprehension question which followed the items: Whereas no differences were detected within canonical subject-initial sentences, answer accuracy after object-initial clauses were significantly lower only for the experiencer subject verbs, irrespective of the verb position (V2 vs. V-final). This indicates that the thematic information of the verb influences processing only at a late point during processing

German clauses – in fact, so late that it spills over to subsequent tasks. That these effects turn up at the end of the clause also in V2-clauses is unexpected under an incremental processing hypothesis, but matches the V2-Reconstruction Hypothesis.

Scheepers (1997: 171-186) investigates the processing of thematic hierarchies by constrasting verbs that take a goal-PP, like *werfen* 'throw', with verbs that select a theme-PP, such as *bewerfen* 'pelt', as shown in (11). An acceptability pretest indicated that verbs which take theme-PPs show a stronger preference for an NP<PP order in (11c), compared to verbs which take a goal-PP.

(11) a. PP-goal–NP<PP
Der Junge warf den spitzen Stein gestern auf die neue Garagentür, ...
the boy threw the pointed stone yesterday at the new garage door

b. PP-goal–PP<NP
Der Junge warf auf die neue Garagentür gestern den spitzen
the boy threw at the new garage door yesterday the pointed
Stein, ...
stone

c. PP-theme–NP<PP
Der Junge bewarf die neue Garagentür gestern mit dem spitzen
the boy pelt the new garage door yesterday with the pointed
Stein, ...
stone

d. PP-theme–PP<NP
Der Junge bewarf mit dem spitzen Stein gestern die neue Garagentür, ...
the boy pelt with the pointed stone yesterday the new garage door

e. V-final scheme
Der Junge hat [NP/PP]1 gestern [NP/PP]2 geworfen/beworfen, ...
the boy has [NP/PP]1 yesterday [NP/PP]2 thrown/pelted

(Scheepers 1997: 172)

The self-paced reading experiment revealed a general NP<PP preference (shorter reading times) on the first argument and the sentence-final spillover region. This preference was more pronounced for verbs with theme-PPs, which is in accordance with the acceptability judgments. However, the effects were independent of the verb position and therefore plausibly stem from properties of the arguments. No effects could be detected at the second argument. At the clause-final verb, Scheepers (1997) detected an interaction of argument order and verb type: Goal-PP verbs (*werfen*) show shorter reading times after PP<NP order whereas Theme-PP verbs (*bewerfen*) show shorter reading times after NP<PP order. Thus, process-

ing advantages due to argument order which is consistent with the thematic frame of the verb are detectable only for clause-final verbs. The experiment did not indicate advantages during processing of the argument patterns matching the thematic frame, which could be accessible early on in V2-clauses.

To account for this asymmetry Scheepers (1997) and Scheepers et al. (2000) assume that syntactic and thematic processing are (perhaps modularly) separated, which has the consequence that information about the thematic roles (linking) is not available until the clause-final wrap-up process. In a similar way, Schlesewsky & Bornkessel (2004) account for the above mentioned ERP results. They propose the *argument dependency model* (ADM), for which they assume two independent processing pathways: a syntactic pathway and a thematic pathway. Schlesewsky & Bornkessel (2004) argue that unambiguous case marking and animacy information feed into the thematic pathway, while in case of morphological ambiguity, linear order feeds into the syntactic pathway.[9] They conclude that both pathways operate independently of (potentially) available verb meaning. More explicitly, even if the lexical verb appears in the V2-position in German, there is no indication that the meaning of the verb influences the incremental interpretation process. The availability or operatibility of the two pathways is dependent on language-specific parameters: If a language does not provide enough morphological case information, the syntactic pathway will most likely dominate (e. g. English). In sum, both accounts attribute the absence of verb-specific processing influences until the clause-final position to a modular separation of syntactic and thematic processing. The V2-Reconstruction Hypothesis provides a principled explanation for this separation which otherwise has to be stipulated.

5.3.2 Attachment ambiguities

Further evidence in support of the V2-Reconstruction Hypothesis comes from attachment ambiguities of PP-adjuncts that can either modify the VP or the preceding NP. Konieczny et al. (1997) investigate the role of the lexical verb on structural attachment of NPs and PPs in German. They constructed experimental sentences in which the PP is either attached low, i. e. internal (as daugther node) to the previously processed phrase, as in (12a), or high-attached, i. e. external to the previously processed phrase, as in (12b).

9 Several authors also have stressed that in absence of case marking thematic ranking can be guided by animacy (contrasts) of the arguments in German (MacWhinney et al. 1984, Schlesewsky & Bornkessel 2004, Czypionka 2013).

(12) $[_{VP}$ NP + NP + PP$]$

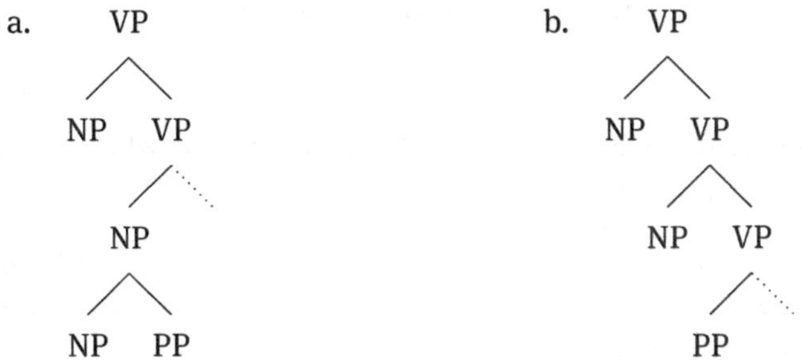

In a series of three eye-tracking studies, Konieczny et al. (1997) investigate the attachment strategy and the potential garden-path effect that may result from erroneous attachment in German. They contrast clauses with the lexical verb in V2-position, as in (13a) and (13b), and clauses with the lexical verb in clause-final position, as in (13c) and (13d). Evidently, if the lexical verb occurs in clause-final position, it cannot aid the parser in resolving the attachment problem. However, if the lexical verb precedes the arguments, the parser may be biased towards high or low attachment. Konieczny et al. (1997) tested two different verb classes, one class with a strong preference for PP-adjuncts, such as *beobachten* 'watch', and one class without a preference, such as *erblicken* 'catch sight of', to amplify the impact of the verb.

(13) a. V2–VP-biased PP
Marion *beobachtete* [das Pferd] [mit dem neuen Fernglas].
Marion watched the horse with the new binoculars
'Marion watched the horse with the new binoculars.'

b. V2–NP-biased PP
Marion *beobachtete* [das Pferd mit dem weißen Fleck].
Marion watched the horse with the white patch
'Marion watched the horse with the white patch'

c. V-final–VP-biased PP
Ich habe gehört, dass Marion [das Pferd] [mit dem neuen Fernglas]
I have heard that Marion the horse with the new binoculars
beobachtete.
watched
'I have heard that Marion watched the horse with the new binoculars.'

d. V-final–NP-biased PP
Ich habe gehört, dass Marion [das Pferd mit dem weißen Fleck]
I have heard that Marion the horse with the white patch
beobachtete.
watched
'I have heard that Marion watched the horse with the white patch.'
(cf. Konieczny et al. 1997: 317)

The results show essentially three effects: First, in V-final clauses, reading time measures are shorter for NP-biased PPs (*with the white patch*), which indicates that low attachment to the immediately preceding phrase seems to be the default. Second, in the V2 condition, on the other hand, reading times for VP-biased PPs (*with the new binoculars*) were shorter than for NP-biased PPs. Third, reading times on the PP-segment are longer in V2-clauses than in V-final clauses (Konieczny et al. 1997, Konieczny & Völker 2000). The first effect is straightforward: In V-final clauses, the parser adheres to the principle of Minimal Attachment[10] and initially attaches the PP to the last active node, i. e. the object NP.[11] After the attachment, the phrase will be interpreted. In case of a VP-biased PP (13c) the structure has to be reanalyzed such that the PP will be high-attached to the VP. This reanalysis is visible as prolonged reading times. What is the difference in V2-clauses? After encountering the object NP *das Pferd* 'the horse' the verb is reconstructed into the final position and the clause is complete for interpretation, as illustrated in (14a). In contrast to the V-final counterpart, the NP-node is already closed, because the structure is well-formed for interpretation. Now, when the parser encounters a PP, it adheres to late closure and tries to integrate this PP into the current clause. But it will do so in accordance with minimal attachment, i. e. with the structurally most parsimonious operation, i. e. high attachment to the VP, as shown in (14b). If this is the correct structure, as in (13a), the processing is complete. In case the high attachment is semantically ill-formed, as in (13b), the structure has to be revised again, as illustrated in (14c). This account perfectly explains the effect of the PP-attachment experiments. The V-final attachment strategy is the default strategy that prefers low attachment. Reading times on the PP are longer in V2-clauses because in these configurations the structure that is already pushed to interpretation has to be reopened to include the PP. Furthermore, low attachment in V2-clauses involves an additional repair process which results in even longer reading times.

10 See Section 4.2.1

11 In contrast to Konieczny et al. (1997), I assume that a VP is postulated in a top down fashion. In V-final clauses, the V-head of this VP, however, is not or at least less active than the NP node because it has not been encountered yet.

(14)

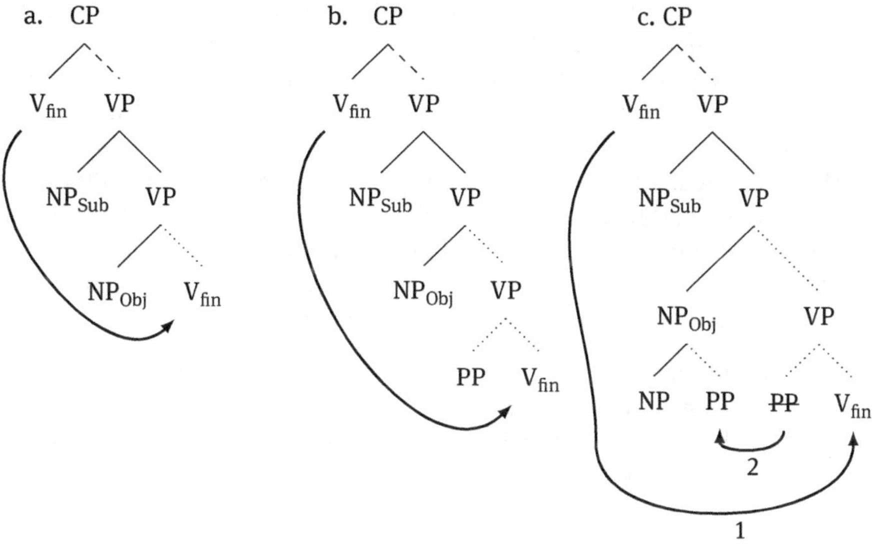

Konieczny et al. (1997) provide a different interpretation of the results in a head-driven approach. They assume that phrases are only postulated if a head has been encountered. As a consequence, the PP is not attached to the VP in V-final clauses because the VP is not postulated until the final verb is reached. In V2-clauses the encounter of the finite verb leads to a postulation of a VP. The account of Konieczny et al. (1997) relies on the lexical subcategorization information. Hence, they must assume that the verb in the V2-position must be interpreted. An assumption that is unwarranted, as I have already argued and as will become more evident in the following.

5.3.3 Scope computing

Bott & Schlotterbeck (2015) investigate scope computation in German, more specifically the reconstruction of object quantifiers. As shown in (15), all their experimental sentences involved accusative-marked objects in clause-initial position. The accusative object has to be reconstructed. The unmarked base position of the object is located directly after the nominative subject and before the adverbial. The displaced object always contains a quantifier *jeden* 'each'. In (15a) the displaced object additionally contains a possesive pronoun *seiner* 'his' which is bound by the quantified subject *genau ein Lehrer* 'exactly one teacher'. This relation, in which the subject must take scope over the object, ensures the reconstruction of the object. Bott & Schlotterbeck (2015) contrast an *hypothesis of incremental scope computation*, which will determine the relative scope as soon as the quantifying expressions are encountered, with the *hypothesis of global interpretation*, which assumes that the determination of relative scope requires also the interpretation of the predicate, i. e. scope is computed for (minimal) clauses. By placing the lexical verb either in second (15a–15d) or in clause-final position (15e), the predictions of the two hypotheses can be contrasted. Although both clause types in (15) are clearly main clauses with V2-order, i. e. the finite verb in second position, I will nevertheless follow Bott & Schlotterbeck (2015) and call clauses with the lexical verb in second position *V2 condition* and clauses with the lexical verb in clause-final position *V-final condition*.

(15) a. QQ+BIND
Jeden seiner Schüler lobte genau ein Lehrer voller
[Each.Q of his pupils]ACC praised [exactly.Q one teacher]NOM full of
Wohlwollen.
goodwill.

b. QQ–BIND
Jeden dieser Schüler lobte genau ein Lehrer voller
[Each.Q of these pupils]ACC praised [exactly.Q one teacher]NOM full of
Wohlwollen.
goodwill.

c. QDEF+BIND
Jeden seiner Schüler lobte der neue Lehrer voller
[Each.Q of his pupils]ACC praised [the.DEF new teacher]NOM full of
Wohlwollen.
goodwill.

d. QDEF–BIND
Jeden dieser Schüler lobte der neue Lehrer voller
[Each.Q of these pupils]ACC praised [the.DEF new teacher]NOM full of
Wohlwollen.
goodwill.

e. V-final scheme
Jeden ... Schüler hat ... Lehrer voller Wohlwollen gelobt.
[Each pupils]ACC has [teacher]NOM full of goodwill praised.

(Bott & Schlotterbeck 2015: 64–65)

For the self-paced reading study, Bott & Schlotterbeck (2015) report a main effect with longer reading times for V2-clauses than for V-final clauses. The first spillover region *voller* 'full of' revealed a scope inversion effect only for V2-clauses, i. e. the condition in which the dislocated pronoun is bound by the subject (15a) elicited longer reading times only in the V2 condition. Additionally, at the clause-final region, a strong effect of DP-type turned up with longer reading times for the doubly quantified clauses (QQ). The effect seems to depend on the verb, because it does appear before the verb in the V-final condition. This indicates that the second spillover region is also the point at which the verb receives its full interpretation in the V2 condition. Bott & Schlotterbeck (2015) interpret this simply as a spillover effect. Under the V2-Reconstruction Hypothesis, however, this effect receives a principled explanation. After encountering the second argument, the processor invariably reconstructs the fronted object and the finite verb. In the V2 condition, the sentence is already complete and will be interpreted. In the V-final condition, however, the interpretation is delayed until the encounter of the clause-final verb.

For a parallel eye-tracking experiment, Bott & Schlotterbeck (2015) report increased reading times in late measures (go-past times and first-pass regression ratios) for both the doubly quantified condition and scope inversion. Both main effects are detectable only at the clause-final element, irrespective of the position of the lexical verb. Additionally, Bott & Schlotterbeck (2015) report longer second-pass times for the two arguments and the V2-position within the scope inversion condition. This indicates that in eye-tracking readers computed scope rather late, after reading the sentence.

In sum, the experiments on scope reconstruction revealed the same pattern as the processing of thematic structure. Processing effects that are dependent on the meaning of the verb show up at the end of the sentence, whether the verb is in V2 or in V-final position. This indicates that, in German, the interpretation of the verb is delayed until the base position of the verb (right edge of the VP).

5.3.4 Processing of the verb: Anticipation and integration

Now, I take a more direct look at the processing of the verb. Weyerts et al. (2002) report results from self-paced reading and ERP experiments which they interpret as providing evidence for the claim that German speakers process finite verbs in second position more easily than finite verbs in clause-final position. In light of the theoretical discussion above, these results seem quite surprising. A detailed inspection will show that these claims are unsubstantiated.

Weyerts et al. (2002) contrast coordinated matrix clauses with embedded clauses, as in (16).

(16) a. Hans facht das Lagerfeuer an, und Paul ⟨öffnet⟩ die Dosen ⟨*öffnet⟩.
Hans fans the camp fire PART and Paul opens the cans opens
'Hans fans the camp fire and Paul opens the cans.'

b. Die Leiterin des Kochkurses bestimmt, dass Erika ⟨*öffnet⟩ die
the director of the cookery course decides that Erika opens the
Dosen ⟨öffnet⟩.
cans opens
'The director of the cookery course decides that Heather the cans opens.'
(Weyerts et al. 2002: 219)

For the self-paced reading experiment, they report longer reading times for the object-verb region only within the coordinated main clauses with ungrammatical V-final order. Weyerts et al. (2002) interpret the absence of an ungrammaticality effect for the embedded V2-clause condition as evidence for a general processing preference of early finite verbs. It is, however, very likely that the absence of prolonged reading times is caused by syntactic priming, because all target clauses follow a main clause with V2-order. Consequently, we would expect that processing V2-order in the second clause is facilitated even if it is ungrammatical, whereas no facilitation is provided for V-final clauses in coordinated main clauses. Syntactic priming (parallel processing) has been shown to reduce reading times (Frazier et al. 1984, Weskott 2003).

For the ERP experiments with similar stimuli, Weyerts et al. (2002) report an early anterior negativity in OV clauses in contrast to VO clauses, which they interpret as an increased processing load for verb-final structures. However, Schlesewsky et al. (2002) argue that this effect is, in fact, an early *positivity* that stems from the comparison of a noun, i. e. the object of the verb-final clause, with the verb in the VO-clause. Schlesewsky et al. (2002) note that such word class differences that match in topography and latency have been reported for studies in English. Similar results from ERP responses to a lexical decision task that contrast nouns and verbs in German are also reported by Pulvermüller et al. (1999). The critical reexamination additionally explains why, in the self-paced reading study, the word order interacted with ungrammaticality (syntactic priming) whereas the ERP responses were independent of the grammaticality (word class difference). In sum, despite the claim that finite verbs are easier to process in an early clause position, the discussion of Weyerts et al. (2002) does not shed any light on the actual processing of the finite verb in the German clause, i. e. when and in which depth the finite verb is interpreted and whether or how it influences processing of other clausal constituents. For example, under the V2-Reconstruction Hypothesis, it is assumed that the first encounter of the displaced verb only involves a shallow parse. Hence, we would predict faster processing in comparison to clause-final verbs, but obviously we do not want to compare these instances. The discussion of reanalysis effects above have proven that clause-final verbs trigger several processing routines that relate to the preceding argument structure. Hence, a simple comparison between the two positions is unjustified.

Furthermore, the claim that clause-final verbs are generally harder to process is at best an oversimplification. Precisely for German, it has been argued that processing load varies as a function of preverbal material. Konieczny (2000) reports results from a self-paced reading study that became known as the *anti-locality effect*. In German verb-final clauses, reading times on the verb turned out to be shorter with increasing length of preverbal material. Konieczny (2000) takes this as an indication of a type reduction operation: The more elements precede the clause-final verb, the faster it will be processed. This effect is more pronounced for predictable elements, such as arguments, but also detectable for adjuncts (Konieczny 2000, Konieczny & Döring 2003, Levy & Keller 2013). The assumption of the *anticipation hypothesis*, as it was called later, is that the information of the arguments help to narrow down the verb to come and make it more expected. This essentially leads to the shorter processing time on the verb.

But are we bound to conclude that verbs in second position exhibit longer reading times than their clause-final correspondents, because they cannot be anticipated? On the contrary. Scheepers (1997) reports that verbs in V2-position are read faster than their corresponding counterparts in clause-final position. He attributes this to an opaque clause-final wrap-up process. Although I am not denying that clause-final wrap-up process may play a role here, I suggest that this effect may mask verb-specific processes. Under the assumption that the verb is not fully interpreted in the V2-position, it seems plausible that the processing time at this early point is rather short. A clause-final verb, on the other hand, can immediately integrate all its arguments and modifiers (except for complement clauses), and be immediately interpreted. Therefore processing of clause-final verbs is predicted to show longer processing time.

Finally, I present direct evidence for the fundamental assumption that verbal heads do reconstruct in a filler-gap-like fashion. Love & Swinney (1998) cite a cross-modal lexical priming study by Basilico et al. (1995)[12] that investigated reactivation priming effects for verbs in Spanish verb-initial structures, VSO and VOS. The rationale goes as follows: Spanish has a basic SVO structure. Both verb-initial orders are derived by fronting the pre-subject material, as shown in (17). Consequently we expect that the verb is reconstructed into a position between the subject and the object in the VSO structure in (17a), but not in the VOS structure in (17b).

12 Many thanks to Inés Antón-Méndez for rummaging up the paper and sharing it.

(17) a. VSO

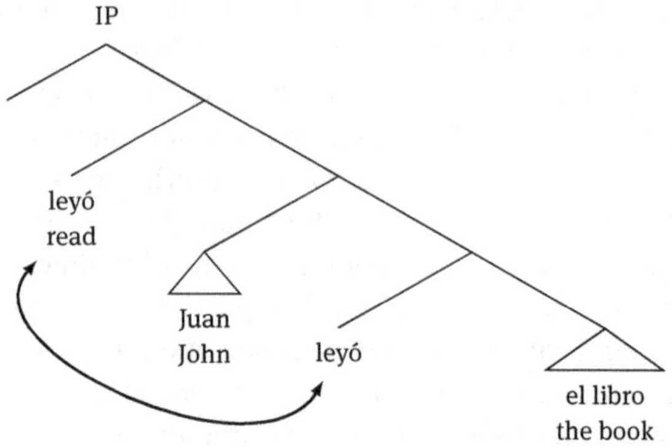

b. VOS

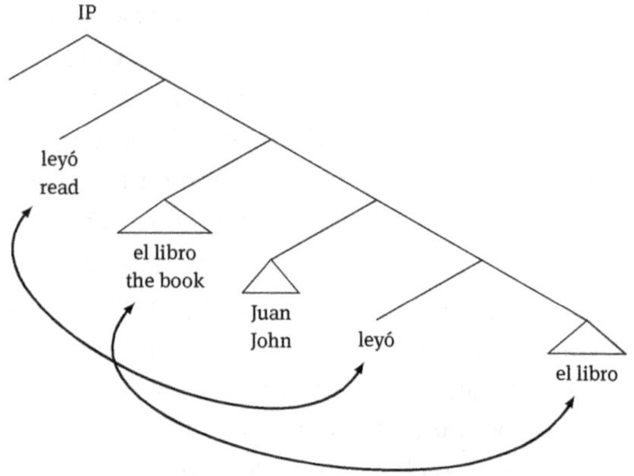

(18) a. VSO

Vieron$_1$ [tus vecinos, los de la casa rosa] ## t_1 [a todos sus
see your neighbors them from the house pink to all their
hijos, hijas y nietos] [el fin de semana pasado]?
sons daughters and grand children the end of week past
'Did your neighbors from the pink house see all their sons daughters and grand children last weekend?'

b. VOS

El fin de semana pasado vieron$_1$ a todos sus hijos, hijas y
[the end of week past] see [to all their sons daughters and
nietos ## tus vecinos, los de la casa rosa t_1?
grand children] [your neighbors them from the house pink]
'Last weekend, did you see all their sons daughters and grand children your neighbors from the pink house?'

c. prime position: ##, related prime: *mirar* 'look', unrelated prime: *lavar* 'wash'

Basilico et al. (1995) report trace reactivation effects of the verb between the subject and the object position (##) in VSO clauses in (18a) but none in the VOS structures in (18b). These results therefore provide positive evidence that also verbs, i. e. syntactic heads, may enter filler-gap dependencies in a similar way as it is widely accepted for dislocated phrasal constituents.

5.4 Chapter summary

In sum, the review of the experimental literature revealed that, clauses in which the lexical verb occurs in the V2-position do not reveal processing effects that are indicative of predictive parsing, although in German predicates show considerable variation with respect to number, case-marking, order, and syntactic category of the selected arguments. To the contrary, thematic effects are detectable at the clause-final position, irrespective of the surface position of the verb. Comparable temporal signatures are likewise found in experiments investigating scope reconstructions that require access to the verb meaning. The experimental results from attachment ambiguities also match the prediction that in V-final clauses, phrases remain open as attachment sites but in V2-clauses argument phrases are closed as early as possible. Additionally, I presented evidence from Spanish which indicates that verbs may enter filler-gap dependencies and hence support the view that they are reactivated at their base position. Taken together, the literature review provided empirical support for the V2-Reconstruction Hypothesis.

6 Experimental investigations of the V2-Reconstruction Hypothesis

In this chapter, I present four self-paced reading experiments on German that test the predictions of the V2-Reconstruction Hypothesis. The first two experiments make use of a verbal NPI to identify the temporal locus of interpretation. In an environment that does not license NPIs, the interpretation of such an NPI will lead to ungrammaticality which will result in increased reading times. The second experiment, in Section 6.2 is a follow-up study which eliminates potential confounds in the first experiment's design. The third experiment in Section 6.3 makes use of two verb groups that differ in their selectional requirements of infinitives. Violation of the selectional requirements will result in ungrammaticality which indicates the point at which these requirements are evaluated. The fourth experiment in Section 6.4 investigates argument order preferences dependent on the type of verb in the V2-position. The results of the first three experiments confirm the predictions of the V2-Reconstruction Hypothesis. The results of the fourth experiment are compatible with the V2-Reconstruction Hypothesis. Due to the fact that the last experiment does not involve a sharp contrast in grammaticality but only preferences, the results are less clear-cut and the interpretation is less evident.

6.1 Experiment 2: Reconstruction of the verbal NPI *brauchen* (self-paced reading)

In Section 3.3.2, I argued that the licensing of verbal NPIs in German has to be evaluated in their base position. This prediction is put to the test in an experimental setting. First, I summarize findings on correlates of (failed) NPI-licensing that were reported in the literature. Subsequently, I explicate how the rationale of the experiment makes use of those processing effects to evaluate the predictions of the V2-Reconstruction Hypothesis.

Previous research on processing NPIs showed that participants are sensitive to specific licensing condition, as predicted by grammatical accounts. In rating experiments, sentences which lack a licensor, as in (1b) receive comparably low acceptability ratings as do sentences in which the licensor is not in a c-command relation with the NPI, as in (1c) (Saddy et al. 2004, Xiang et al. 2013, Parker & Phillips 2016, Yanilmaz & Drury 2018).

https://doi.org/10.1515/9783110725018-006

(1) a. Kein$_{\text{LIC}}$ Mann, [der einen Bart hatte,] war jemals$_{\text{NPI}}$ glücklich.
no man who a beard had was ever happy
'No man who had a beard was ever happy.'

b. *Ein Mann, [der einen Bart hatte,] war jemals$_{\text{NPI}}$ glücklich.
a man who a beard had was ever happy
'*A man who had a beard was ever happy.'

c. *Ein Mann, [der [keinen Bart]$_{\text{LIC}}$ hatte,] war jemals$_{\text{NPI}}$ glücklich.
a man who no beard had was ever happy
'*A man who had no beard was ever happy.'

(Drenhaus et al. 2005: 146)

In on-line processing, participants showed immediate responses to licensing violations directly at the NPI (e. g. *jemals*). Violations yield prolonged reading times (RTs) for roughly three segments (Vasishth et al. 2008, Xiang et al. 2013, Parker & Phillips 2016). In ERP-experiments, NPI-licensing violations triggered N400 effects (Saddy et al. 2004, Drenhaus et al. 2005, 2007, Yanilmaz & Drury 2018) and P600 effects (Drenhaus et al. 2005, 2006, Xiang et al. 2009, Yanilmaz & Drury 2018). These immediate responses, which seems to be detectable robustly across languages, indicate that participants evaluate the licensing of an NPI as soon as the lexical item is interpreted. However, illusory licensors, such as in (1c) lead to significant deviations: more errors and longer response latencies in speeded acceptability judgments (Drenhaus et al. 2005: 148–149), delayed effects of reading time increase (Parker & Phillips 2016: 326–327), and a smaller N400 effect (Drenhaus et al. 2005: 155–157).

6.1.1 Rationale

Recall from the discussion in Section 3.3.2 that, in cases like (2a), the NPI can only be licensed in its base position and not in the surface position as illustrated in (2b). In order to check the licensing requirements of *brauchen* 'need to', it has to be reconstructed into its base position.

(2) a. Letztendlich *braucht*$_{\text{NPI}}$ der Autor den Roman nicht$_{\text{LIC}}$ zu drucken ~~braucht~~.
'Finally, the author doesn't have to print the novel.'

b.

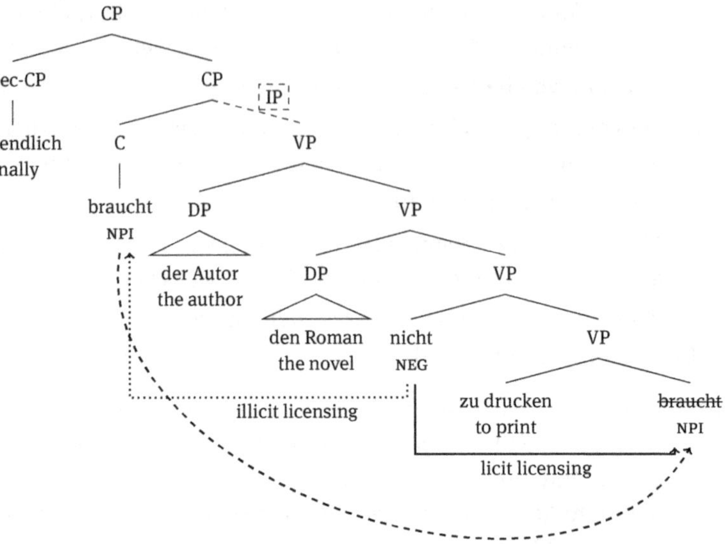

If the verbal NPI appears in the V2-position, it precedes its licensor. Nevertheless, no violation of NPI-licensing becomes apparent. According to the V2-Reconstruction Hypothesis, this is unproblematic because the position in which the V2-verb will be interpreted is its base position. Consequently, we expect that the above mentioned processing effects indicating NPI-licensing failure appear only in the base position of the NPI-verb, namely after the infinitive *zu drucken* 'to print'. I assume furthermore that the processor has a built-in preference to resolve such a pending dependency between the V2- and the base position as early as possible. For filler-gap dependencies (especially *wh*-movement), this has been thoroughly demonstrated and is widely accepted as the *active filler hypothesis* (see Frazier & Clifton 1989: 95). It builds on experimental evidence which indicates that the processor integrates the filler (displaced element) anticipatorily, i. e. before encountering explicit cues for the formation of the actual dependency. If the next incoming segment reveals that the position that was connected to the filler is filled by a surface element, a reanalysis process takes place. This reanalysis is reflected by increased processing load known as the *filled-gap effect* (Stowe 1986). Following this insight, the target sentences were extensions of sentences like (2), which provided for two possible positions into which the NPI *brauchen* could reconstruct, as illustrated in (3).[1] Both positions, #1 in (3a) and #2 in (3b) are licit positions

1 In the non-NPI-reading *brauchen* could also reconstruct after *Roman* yielding *The author needs the novel*. Searching for effects related to this reconstruction, which is, however, not dependent on a specific licensing configuration, would require a different experimental set-up.

for the NPI because they are verbal positions that are locally c-commanded by the negator *nicht*.

(3) a. Letztendlich *braucht* der Autor den Roman *nicht* zu drucken #1 ~~braucht~~ ...
finally needs the author the novel not to print

b. Letztendlich *braucht* der Autor den Roman zu drucken #1 unter Umständen *nicht* zu verbieten #2 ~~braucht~~ ...
finally needs the author the novel to print eventually not to forbid

If participants insert *brauchen* automatically in #1 in (3b), as expected under filler-gap parsing, the result is a temporarily ungrammatical structure.[2] The licensing conditions of the NPI are violated as seen in (4a) below. To measure such a potential effect we constructed control sentences, in which the NPI-verb *brauchen* was replaced by *beschließen* 'to decide', which appears in the same syntactic environment, selects *zu*-infinitives and constitutes a plausible replacement in the relevant contexts. Crucially, however, *beschließen* is not an NPI and therefore yields a grammatical structure if it is inserted in #1, as illustrated by the contrast between (4a) and (4b). On the other hand, *beschließen* is fully compatible with negation. The difference between the two verbs can therefore be paraphrased as follows: *brauchen* is ungrammatical in positions which are not in the scope of a negation whereas *beschließen* is grammatical whether in the scope of negation or not.

(4) a. * Letztendlich *braucht* der Autor den Roman zu drucken #1 ...
finally needs the author the novel to print

b. Letztendlich *beschließt* der Autor den Roman zu drucken #1 ...
finally decides the author the novel to print

6.1.2 Method

6.1.2.1 Materials

The material consisted of 32 experimental items interspersed with 35 fillers (20 from a different experiment) resulting in 67 stimuli per participant. The target sentences were preceded by a context sentence, as in (5), which introduced the agents

2 To be sure, there is no reason for the parser to hypothesize more than the minimally converging structure; this excludes the expectation of a converging structure that leads to the successful gap filling at #2.

and the scene of the item in order to render the target sentences more plausible and to reduce the number of accommodations that have to be made during the reading of the target sentence. The context sentences were not matched for length. The target sentences varied in a 2 × 2 × 2 design with the factors MATRIX.VERB, ILLUSORY.NEG, and LICENSING.NEG, which will be explicated hereafter. The finite matrix verb was either the modal NPI-verb *brauchen* 'need to', as in (6) or the polarity-neutral verb *beschließen* 'decide', as in (7). The factorial combination of the two negation positions results in four different negation patterns, which are first illustrated for the +NPI condition in (6): double negation (6a), only the late negation (6b), only the early negation (6c), and no negation at all (6d). Actually, only the second negation is relevant for the licensing of the NPI *brauchen* in the final structure, hence the term *licensing negation*. The first negation only appears to be relevant for the licensing of the NPI in the incomplete initial substring. In the final structure, however, the first negation is irrelevant for the licensing configuration because it does not c-command the head of the matrix clause VP/IP, hence the term *illusory negation*. Therefore the −LICENSOR.NEG conditions in (6c) and (6d) are finally ungrammatical which, however, does not affect measures at earlier points. The same negation patterns occur also with the −NPI verb in (7) with the difference that all four variants are grammatical.

The finite verb was followed by a subject DP and an object DP which were definite masculine singular and therefore unambiguously case marked. Between the two infinitives, i. e. following the first reconstruction site #1, a 2-word adverbial phrase such as *unter Umständen* 'possibly' was inserted to obtain a spillover region providing measure points for potential effects of the reconstruction of the finite verb. Similarly the second infinitive, i. e. the second reconstruction site #2, was followed by a 6-word infinitival clause introduced by the complementizer *um* 'for'. The potential reconstruction sites (#1 and #2) are indicated in the materials below only for illustrational purposes and to facilitate the comparison with the examples of the rationale-section above. These marking were not visible in the materials as they were presented to the participants. Half of the items were followed by a yes/no-comprehension question, as in (8), to evaluate whether participants paid attention to the task. All experimental items are given in the online appendix.

(5) CONTEXT:

Ein Autor hat wegen seines neuen Romans Ärger mit seinem Verlag. Er bespricht mit seinem Anwalt, ob er den Druck untersagen soll.

'An author has trouble with his publisher because of his new novel. He talks to his lawyer whether he should forbid the printing.'

(6) a. +NPI +ILLUSORY.NEG +LICENSOR.NEG
Letztendlich *braucht* der Autor den Roman *nicht* zu drucken #1 unter
finally NPI the author the novel not to print under
Umständen *nicht* zu verbieten #2, um das mediale Interesse zu
circumstances not to forbid for the medial interest to
wecken.
arouse
'Thus the author doesn't have to forbid to not print the novel this time in order to arouse the attention of the media.'

b. +NPI −ILLUSORY.NEG +LICENSOR.NEG
Letztendlich *braucht* der Autor den Roman zu drucken #1 unter
finally NPI the author the novel to print under
Umständen *nicht* zu verbieten #2, um das mediale Interesse zu
circumstances not to forbid for the medial interest to
wecken.
arouse
'Thus the author doesn't have to forbid to print the novel this time in order to arouse the attention of the media.'

c. +NPI +ILLUSORY.NEG −LICENSOR.NEG
*Letztendlich *braucht* der Autor den Roman *nicht* zu drucken #1 unter
finally NPI the author the novel not to print under
Umständen zu verbieten #2, um das mediale Interesse zu wecken.
circumstances to forbid for the medial interest to arouse

d. +NPI −ILLUSORY.NEG −LICENSOR.NEG
*Letztendlich *braucht* der Autor den Roman zu drucken #1 unter
finally NPI the author the novel to print under
Umständen zu verbieten #2, um das mediale Interesse zu wecken.
circumstances to forbid for the medial interest to arouse

(7) a. −NPI +ILLUSORY.NEG +LICENSOR.NEG
Letztendlich *beschließt* der Autor den Roman *nicht* zu drucken #1
finally decides the author the novel not to print
unter Umständen *nicht* zu verbieten #2, um das mediale Interesse
under circumstances not to forbid for the medial interest
zu wecken.
to arouse
'Thus the author decides not to forbid to not print the novel this time in order to arouse the attention of the media.'

b. –NPI –ILLUSORY.NEG +LICENSOR.NEG
Letztendlich *beschließt* der Autor den Roman zu drucken #1 unter Umständen *nicht* zu verbieten #2, um das mediale Interesse zu wecken.
'Thus the author decides not to forbid to print the novel this time in order to arouse the attention of the media.'

c. –NPI +ILLUSORY.NEG –LICENSOR.NEG
Letztendlich *beschließt* der Autor den Roman *nicht* zu drucken #1 unter Umständen zu verbieten #2, um das mediale Interesse zu wecken.
'Thus the author decides to forbid to not print the novel this time in order to arouse the attention of the media.'

d. –NPI –ILLUSORY.NEG –LICENSOR.NEG
Letztendlich *beschließt* der Autor den Roman zu drucken #1 unter Umständen zu verbieten #2, um das mediale Interesse zu wecken.
'Thus the author decides to forbid to print the novel this time in order to arouse the attention of the media.'

(8) COMPREHENSION QUESTION:
Hat der Autor mit seinem Anwalt gesprochen?
'Did the author talk to his lawyer'
correct answer = *Ja* 'Yes' wrong answer = *Nein* 'No'

6.1.2.2 Predictions

The predictions are as follows: Because reconstruction of the finite verb is an automated process, the finite verb will always be reconstructed into the earliest syntactically possible position. Consequently, longer reading times are predicted from #1 onwards, i. e. *drucken*, in the +NPI, –ILLUSORY.NEG-condition, in which an NPI is reconstructed into and interpreted in a position where it is not licensed. The same effect is predicted to appear in the extended sentence at #2, i. e. *verbieten*, except that longer reading times are expected in the +NPI, –LICENSOR.NEG-condition. Here again, the NPI is reconstructed into a position in which it is not licensed. According to previous findings, I expect that reading times at #2 may be influenced by the presence of an illusory licensor, i. e. a potentially licensing element which precedes the NPI, but is not in a structurally licit position to license the NPI. Additionally, prolonged reading times are also expected in conditions with two negations due to the increased complexity in interpretation. However, double negation should affect the +NPI and the –NPI condition equally.

6.1.2.3 Participants

We tested 41 participants (age 18–34 years, mean 23 year; 11 male), all students of the University of Konstanz, self-declared native speakers of German, and right-handed. Participants received a reimbursement of 5 € for participation.

6.1.2.4 Procedure

The experiment was carried out in a centered self-paced reading paradigm (Just et al. 1982) in which the segments were presented non-cumulatively in a stationary window. This mode of presentation provided no visual cues that would allow the participants to predict the length of the sentences. For each item, the participants saw the context sentences and the target sentence presented in a word-per-word fashion in the middle of the screen. Participant moved through the segments at their own pace by pressing the space bar. In approximately half of the stimuli a yes-no comprehension question was displayed after the final segment. Participants had to choose the correct answer by pressing the 'f' or 'j' key on a German keyboard. After each response the participants saw a feedback message whether their response was correct or not. Participants were instructed to read the sentences and to answer the questions as fast as possible in order to give correct responses.

The procedure was set up with the experiment software package *Linger*[3] and run on a Windows PC in a psycholinguistics lab. The experimental stimuli were randomized according to the Latin square design, such that each participant saw each of the 32 items in exactly one of the 8 experimental conditions. The total list of stimuli (experimental items plus fillers) were automatically randomized by the experiment software. Experiments took approximately 20 minutes.

6.1.2.5 Data analysis

Prior to the analysis, all data points with reading times larger than 2 seconds (n=48) have been excluded (0.2 % of the data). The data analysis was carried out by use of the statistical software package R (R Core Team 2015). I used linear mixed-effects models of the lme4 package (Bates et al. 2013) to analyze the log-transformed reading times.[4] Following arguments in Barr et al. (2013) and Bates et al. (2015), I fitted maximal justified random-effect structures for the LME-models. I performed a model criticism as recommended in Baayen & Milin (2010) by exclud-

3 Written by Doug Rhode available at http://tedlab.mit.edu/~dr/Linger/

4 Reading times were log-transformed to achieve a distribution of the data points that resemble a normal distribution.

ing absolute standardized residuals exceeding 2.5 standard deviations. I report the results of the criticized model, taking effects as significant if the respective t-value exceeds an absolute value of 2. I will report the fixed-effect coefficients of all analysis that showed significant effects below by indicating the exact model specifications.

The analysis of the reading times proceeded in two steps: The initial sequence of the target sentences including the adverbial *unter Umständen* was identical for the ±LICENSOR.NEG conditions. These two conditions are aggregated for the analysis of this region, resulting in a 2 × 2 analysis. Only for the remaining segments, a full 2 × 2 × 2 analysis including all 8 experimental condition were applied.

The participants' accuracy in response to the comprehension questions ranged from 71–100 % (mean 87 %). No participant was excluded from the analysis.

6.1.3 Results

First infinitive + adverb: The reading time results for the first region of interest are presented in Figure 6.1. No effects could be detected at the negation and the infinitive particle *zu* 'to'. At the following three segments, the infinitive *drucken* 'print', the first adverb segment *unter* 'under', and the second adverb segment *Umständen* 'circumstances', the 2 × 2 analysis revealed an interaction of both factors MATRIX.VERB and +ILLUSORY.NEG (t = −3.2511, t = −2.0309, and t = −1.6003 respectively) indicating that the +NPI −ILLUSORY.NEG condition shows longer reading times than all other conditions. Whereas the significance increases after model criticism for the first two segments, the t-value of the interaction term of the second adverb segment drops below significance. However, the direct comparison between the −NPI −ILLUSORY.NEG and the +NPI −ILLUSORY.NEG remains significant for all three segments (t = 2.8084, t = 3.2666, and t = 2.5077 respectively). Additionally, an analysis of the summed reading times for this 3-segment region also revealed a significant direct comparison (t = 3.6767) and a significant interaction (t = −3.0239). The exact model outputs of these analyses are given in Tables 6.1 to 6.4.

The reading times for the second region, i. e. the segments following the LICENSING.NEG are displayed in Figure 6.2. The results can be divided into two subregions, the second infinitive and the spillover region.

Second infinitive: No effects could be detected on the second negation. On the particle of the second infinitive *zu*, which followed directly after the LICENSING.NEG, the analysis revealed contrasts for both negations, the LICENSING.NEG (t = −2.3089) and the ILLUSORY.NEG (t = −2.6988), signaling that presence of the

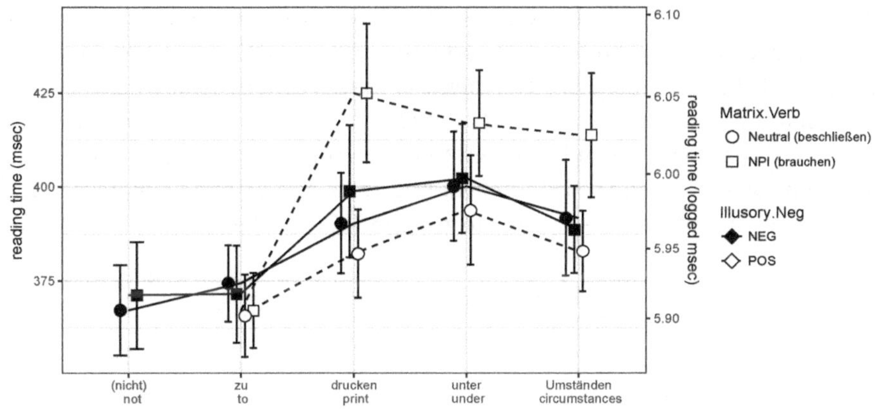

Figure 6.1: Mean reading times for the first infinitive + adverb region of Experiment 2 (95 % CI)

negations yields longer reading times. Additionally, the model revealed an interaction of the MATRIX.VERB and the ILLUSORY.NEG (t = 2.0343) which indicates that, for the −NPI matrix verb, both negations increase reading times whereas for the +NPI, only the directly preceding LICENSING.NEG affects reading times and the earlier ILLUSORY.NEG has no significant impact on the reading times. On the infinitive *verbieten* 'forbid' the model yielded only a contrast of LICENSING.NEG (t = −2.3346) with longer reading times for a present negation. The analysis of the aggregated reading times of the particle and the infinitive *zu verbieten* 'to forbid' revealed a significant contrast of LICENSING.NEG (t = −2.9335) and a strong tendency of ILLUSORY.NEG (t = −1.9718) for the −NPI verb. The exact model outputs for this subregion are given in Tables 6.5 to 6.7.

Spillover region: No effect could be detected on the first two segments of the spillover region, the complementizer *um* 'for' and the determiner *das* 'the'. On the adjective of the spillover region *mediale* 'medial', the analysis revealed an effect of MATRIX.VERB (t = −2.6226), LICENSING.NEG (t = −2.0702), and ILLUSORY.NEG (t = −2.5632) as well as an interaction of MATRIX.VERB and ILLUSORY.NEG (t = 2.1532). Essentially, this indicates that the ungrammatical condition in which the +NPI verb is preceded only by the ILLUSORY.NEG, yields longer reading times than all other conditions. On the noun *Interesse* 'interest' the model revealed an effect of LICENSING.NEG (t = 2.1943) for the −NPI verbs with longer reading times for the negation present. On the following infinitive particle *zu* 'to', the model revealed a 3-way interaction of MATRIX.VERB, LICENSING.NEG, and ILLUSORY.NEG (t = 2.1173), indicating a significant contrast between the non-negated −NPI condition with shortest reading times and the doubly-negated +NPI condition with longest reading times. On the final segment, i. e. the infinitive *wecken* 'arouse', the model revealed several significant contrasts which indicate that the non-negated −NPI condition shows shorter reading times than all other condition, as clearly visible in Figure 6.2. The analysis of the aggregated reading times of the three final segments *Interesse zu wecken* 'interest to arouse' yielded the same combination of contrasts, which have been found on the final segment, namely that the non-negated −NPI showed shorter reading times than all other conditions. The exact model outputs for this region are given in Tables 6.8 to 6.12.

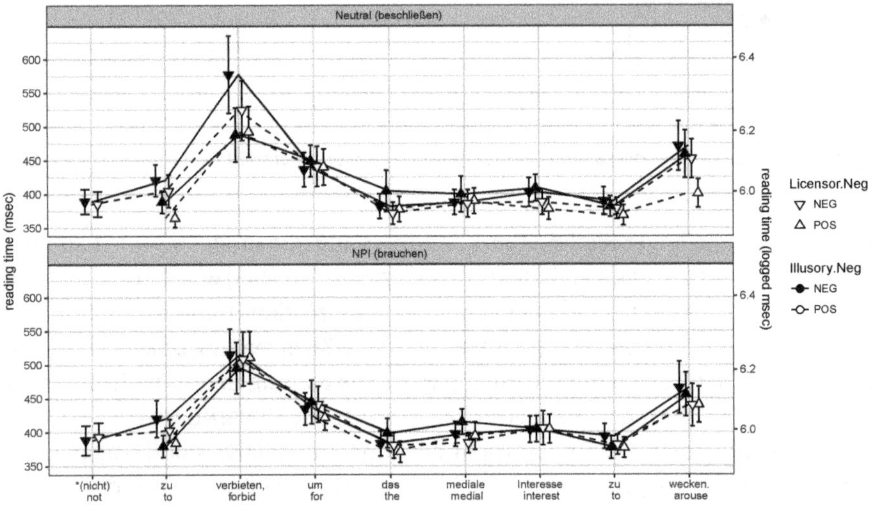

Figure 6.2: Mean reading times for the high VP + spillover region of Experiment 2 (95 % CI)

6.1.4 Discussion

In line with the predictions of the V2-Reconstruction Hypothesis, the results show increased reading times for non-licensed NPI from the first infinitive *drucken* onwards. As illustrated for the materials in (6) and (7), this is the segment which directly precedes the first reconstruction site. This indicates that, after integrating *drucken* into the parse, the finite verb will be automatically reconstructed and interpreted. If the finite verb is the NPI *brauchen*, it must be properly licensed at this point. In the +NPI −ILLUSORY.NEG condition, no such licensor is present. This temporary licensing failure results in prolonged reading times which extend to the two following segments, showing the same effect profile with respect to polarity and temporal extension as in previous studies of non-licensed NPIs in surface position (e. g. Parker & Phillips 2016).

At the second infinitive region *zu verbieten*, the result did not indicate an immediate effect of NPI-licensing in contrast to the predictions above. For both verb types, the presence of an immediately preceding LICENSING.NEG led to longer reading times. However, at the particle of the second infinitive *zu*, a statistical interaction turned up which indicates that NPI-licensing does affect reading times at this point: For the −NPI verb *beschließen* reading times are shortest in the condition without negation, and the presence of each negation increases reading times in an additive fashion. For the +NPI verbs only the directly preceding negation, the LICENSING.NEG, increased reading times. The non-negated condition, being ungrammatical, shows comparably longer reading times, i. e. as long as all singly negated conditions.

In the spillover region, the analysis revealed a correlate of NPI-licensing failure. At the adjective *mediale*, the model detected significantly longer reading times for the +NPI verb that was preceded only by the illusory negation (+NPI, +ILLUSORY.NEG, −LICENSOR.NEG). In contrast to the predictions, this effect was very local and affected only one of two ungrammatical conditions. I assume that this effect reflects a delayed evaluation of the licensing conditions. Further, I assume that the delay is due to the complexity of the sentence with two embedded infinitives, which impedes the evaluation of the NPI-licensing. I suspect that the −ILLUSORY.NEG −LICENSOR.NEG condition, in which no possible NPI-licensor is present, is so demanding that the processor *gives up* and switches to a more shallow parsing mode which explains why no prolonged reading times corresponding to the ungrammaticality are observable at the spillover region. Interestingly, at the three clause-final segments, the results show a distance effect of negation. The non-negated −NPI verb condition showed the shortest reading times of all conditions, which indicate that simple and double negation does impact processing at the clause-final region. The non-negated +NPI condition, however, patterns with negated condition, due to its non-licensed NPI.

One weak point of the material is, that in the first region, where we found the predicted interaction, the distance between the position of the negation and the reconstruction site of the NPI is very small. An alternative explanation can therefore be that the prolonged reading times in the +NPI, −ILLUSORY.NEG condition is a consequence of the missing negation without resorting to a reconstruction analysis.[5] If the NPI is interpreted in the C-domain, a negation is expected. If this expectation is not satisfied, the reading times increase on the elements following

5 Thanks to Barbara Tomaszewicz for pointing this out.

the canonical position of the negation. In the next section, I report the results of a follow-up experiment which refutes the predictions of this alternative explanation. Additionally, I would expect that such an expectation-based effect would emerge in the same way at the second VP region (*nicht zu verbieten*), contrary to the results. The fact that the effect in the second region is delayed and sensitive to the illusory negation renders it more plausible that the effect is tied to an interpretative mechanism of NPI-licensing rather than a simple expectation of a negation. Moreover, an expectation-based approach is not able to explain the special status of the illusory licensing, which, however, has been reported in other experiments employing different experimental methods.

In sum, the results of the experiment closely match the predictions of the V2-Reconstruction Hypothesis in the first region. In the second region, the results are compatible with the V2-Reconstruction Hypothesis but the high complexity of the embedded clause structure seems to have attenuated the effect considerably.

Table 6.1: Output of the LME model for first inifinitive (*drucken*) in Experiment 2
```
lmer(log.RT~Matrix.Verb*Illusory.Neg+trial+segment.length+
(1+Matrix.Verb*Illusory.Neg|participant.ID)+
(1+Matrix.Verb*Illusory.Neg|stimulus.ID))
```

	criticized model			**raw model**		
	Estimate	SE	t	Estimate	SE	t
Intercept (−NPI −ILLUSORY.NEG)	5.7665	0.0431	133.8110	5.7966	0.0457	126.8162
MATRIX.VERB (+NPI)	0.0633	0.0225	2.8084	0.0733	0.0256	2.8607
+ILLUSORY.NEG (NEG)	0.0281	0.0157	1.7885	0.0141	0.0206	0.6820
trial	−0.0038	0.0003	−14.6113	−0.0042	0.0003	−12.3711
segment length	0.0130	0.0026	4.9311	0.0123	0.0033	3.7079
MATRIX.VERB:ILLUSORY.NEG	−0.0808	0.0249	−3.2511	−0.0707	0.0307	−2.3062

Table 6.2: Output of the LME model for first adverb segment (*unter*) in Experiment 2

```
lmer(log.RT~Matrix.Verb*Illusory.Neg+trial+segment.length+
(1+Matrix.Verb*Illusory.Neg|participant.ID)+
(1+Matrix.Verb*Illusory.Neg|stimulus.ID))
```

	criticized model			raw model		
	Estimate	SE	t	Estimate	SE	t
Intercept (−NPI −ILLUSORY.NEG)	5.9148	0.0338	175.1867	5.9347	0.0364	163.2562
MATRIX.VERB (+NPI)	0.0638	0.0195	3.2666	0.0478	0.0234	2.0414
+ILLUSORY.NEG (NEG)	0.0034	0.0165	0.2084	0.0067	0.0221	0.3051
trial	−0.0038	0.0003	−14.1245	−0.0034	0.0003	−9.9244
segment length	−0.0017	0.0033	−0.4993	−0.0018	0.0045	−0.4040
MATRIX.VERB:ILLUSORY.NEG	−0.0514	0.0253	−2.0309	−0.0435	0.0306	−1.4224

Table 6.3: Output of the LME model for second adverb segment (*Umständen*) in Experiment 2

```
lmer(log.RT~Matrix.Verb*Illusory.Neg+trial+segment.length+
(1+Matrix.Verb+Illusory.Neg|participant.ID)+
(1+Matrix.Verb+Illusory.Neg|stimulus.ID))
```

	criticized model			raw model		
	Estimate	SE	t	Estimate	SE	t
Intercept (−NPI −ILLUSORY.NEG)	5.8850	0.0408	144.1579	5.8854	0.0433	135.9400
MATRIX.VERB (+NPI)	0.0393	0.0157	2.5077	0.0617	0.0195	3.1591
+ILLUSORY.NEG (NEG)	−0.0055	0.0161	−0.3440	0.0084	0.0188	0.4455
trial	−0.0035	0.0003	−13.1883	−0.0033	0.0003	−10.3265
segment length	0.0019	0.0028	0.7003	0.0027	0.0031	0.8776
MATRIX.VERB:ILLUSORY.NEG	−0.0323	0.0202	−1.6003	−0.0583	0.0250	−2.3351

Table 6.4: Output of the LME model for first inifinitive + adverb region (*drucken unter Umständen*) in Experiment 2

```
lmer(log.RT~Matrix.Verb*Illusory.Neg+trial+segment.length+
(1+Matrix.Verb*Illusory.Neg|participant.ID)+
(1+Matrix.Verb*Illusory.Neg|stimulus.ID))
```

	criticized model			raw model		
	Estimate	SE	t	Estimate	SE	t
Intercept (−NPI −ILLUSORY.NEG)	6.9783	0.0429	162.8133	7.0083	0.0469	149.4134
MATRIX.VERB (+NPI)	0.0673	0.0183	3.6767	0.0651	0.0196	3.3113
+ILLUSORY.NEG (NEG)	0.0120	0.0128	0.9367	0.0126	0.0154	0.8199
trial	−0.0040	0.0002	−19.0776	−0.0037	0.0003	−14.3091
segment length	0.0015	0.0014	1.0568	0.0007	0.0017	0.4087
MATRIX.VERB:ILLUSORY.NEG	−0.0639	0.0211	−3.0239	−0.0616	0.0244	−2.5251

Table 6.5: Output of the LME model for second infinitive particle (*zu*) in Experiment 2

```
lmer(log.RT~Matrix.Verb*Licensor.Neg*Illusory.Neg+trial+
(1+Matrix.Verb*Licensor.Neg+Illusory.Neg|participant.ID)+
(1+Matrix.Verb*Licensor.Neg+Illusory.Neg|stimulus.ID))
```

	criticized model			raw model		
	Estimate	SE	t	Estimate	SE	t
Intercept (−npi +Lic.Neg+Ill.Neg)	5.9589	0.0384	155.2760	5.9777	0.0405	147.686
Matrix.Verb (+npi)	−0.0202	0.0213	−0.9485	−0.0027	0.0274	−0.099
−Licensor.Neg (pos)	−0.0506	0.0219	−2.3089	−0.0528	0.0282	−1.874
−Illusory.Neg (pos)	−0.0561	0.0208	−2.6988	−0.0480	0.0265	−1.815
trial	−0.0040	0.0003	−15.8086	−0.0036	0.0003	−10.997
Matrix.Verb:Licensor.Neg	−0.0096	0.0292	−0.3286	−0.0275	0.0380	−0.722
Matrix.Verb:Illusory.Neg	0.0561	0.0276	2.0343	0.0263	0.0352	0.746
Licensor.Neg:Illusory.Neg	0.0155	0.0275	0.5628	−0.0004	0.0352	−0.012
M.Verb:Lic.Neg:Ill.Neg	0.0017	0.0388	0.0443	0.0398	0.0497	0.799

Table 6.6: Output of the LME model for second infinitive (*verbieten*) in Experiment 2

```
lmer(log.RT~Matrix.Verb*Licensor.Neg*Illusory.Neg+trial+segment.length+
(1+Matrix.Verb*Licensor.Neg+Illusory.Neg|participant.ID)+
(1+Matrix.Verb+Licensor.Neg+Illusory.Neg|stimulus.ID))
```

	criticized model			raw model		
	Estimate	SE	t	Estimate	SE	t
Intercept (−npi +Lic.Neg+Ill.Neg)	5.8755	0.0860	68.2893	5.8683	0.0896	65.497
Matrix.Verb (+npi)	−0.0182	0.0378	−0.4821	−0.0493	0.0413	−1.193
−Licensor.Neg (pos)	−0.0836	0.0358	−2.3346	−0.0971	0.0430	−2.256
−Illusory.Neg (pos)	−0.0458	0.0365	−1.2544	−0.0463	0.0419	−1.106
trial	−0.0052	0.0004	−12.6238	−0.0051	0.0005	−10.494
segment.length	0.0251	0.0055	4.5857	0.0302	0.0058	5.245
Matrix.Verb:Licensor.Neg	0.0428	0.0507	0.8445	0.0585	0.0552	1.0592
Matrix.Verb:Illusory.Neg	0.0459	0.0441	1.0403	0.0483	0.0526	0.919
Licensor.Neg:Illusory.Neg	0.0509	0.0442	1.1505	0.0606	0.0526	1.1516
M.Verb:Lic.Neg:Ill.Neg	−0.0344	0.0622	−0.5530	−0.0400	0.0743	−0.538

Table 6.7: Output of the LME model for second infinitive region (*zu verbieten*) in Experiment 2

```
lmer(log.RT~Matrix.Verb*Licensor.Neg*Illusory.Neg+trial+segment.length+
(1+Matrix.Verb*Licensor.Neg+Illusory.Neg|participant.ID)+
(1+Matrix.Verb*Licensor.Neg+Illusory.Neg|stimulus.ID))
```

	criticized model			raw model		
	Estimate	SE	t	Estimate	SE	t
Intercept (−NPI +LIC.NEG+ILL.NEG)	6.5631	0.0695	94.4143	6.5559	0.0771	84.9951
MATRIX.VERB (+NPI)	−0.0226	0.0266	−0.8497	−0.0343	0.0314	−1.0936
−LICENSOR.NEG (POS)	−0.0763	0.0260	−2.9335	−0.0903	0.0328	−2.7512
−ILLUSORY.NEG (POS)	−0.0533	0.0270	−1.9718	−0.0548	0.0317	−1.7278
trial	−0.0046	0.0003	−15.0917	−0.0045	0.0004	−12.2199
segment.length	0.0167	0.0036	4.5958	0.0198	0.0044	4.4622
MATRIX.VERB:LICENSOR.NEG	0.0259	0.0360	0.7176	0.0321	0.0422	0.7610
MATRIX.VERB:ILLUSORY.NEG	0.0403	0.0329	1.2250	0.0392	0.0399	0.9845
LICENSOR.NEG:ILLUSORY.NEG	0.0540	0.0329	1.6443	0.0466	0.0399	1.1679
M.VERB:LIC.NEG:ILL.NEG	−0.0282	0.0463	−0.6096	−0.0125	0.0563	−0.2219

Table 6.8: Output of the LME model for the adjective of the spillover region (*mediale*) in Experiment 2

```
lmer(log.RT~Matrix.Verb*Licensor.Neg*Illusory.Neg+trial+segment.length+
(1+Matrix.Verb*Licensor.Neg+Illusory.Neg|participant.ID)+
(1+Matrix.Verb+Licensor.Neg+Illusory.Neg|stimulus.ID))
```

	criticized model			raw model		
	Estimate	SE	t	Estimate	SE	t
Intercept (+NPI −LIC.NEG+ILL.NEG)	5.8620	0.0456	128.4976	5.9030	0.0489	120.7331
MATRIX.VERB (−NPI)	−0.0623	0.0237	−2.6226	−0.0429	0.0286	−1.4970
+LICENSOR.NEG (NEG)	−0.0467	0.0226	−2.0702	−0.0412	0.0270	−1.5292
−ILLUSORY.NEG (POS)	−0.0560	0.0218	−2.5632	−0.0508	0.0269	−1.8903
trial	−0.0042	0.0003	−15.0489	−0.0040	0.0003	−11.9231
segment.length	0.0092	0.0022	4.1973	0.0065	0.0027	2.4600
MATRIX.VERB:LICENSOR.NEG	0.0439	0.0304	1.4440	0.0141	0.0375	0.3762
MATRIX.VERB:ILLUSORY.NEG	0.0651	0.0302	2.1532	0.0444	0.0368	1.2045
LICENSOR.NEG:ILLUSORY.NEG	0.0488	0.0301	1.6213	0.0326	0.0368	0.8856
M.VERB:LIC.NEG:ILL.NEG	−0.0655	0.0427	−1.5342	−0.0257	0.0521	−0.4926

Table 6.9: Output of the LME model for the noun of the spillover region (*Interesse*) in Experiment 2

```
lmer(log.RT~Matrix.Verb*Licensor.Neg*Illusory.Neg+trial+segment.length+
(1+Matrix.Verb*Licensor.Neg+Illusory.Neg|participant.ID)+
(1+Matrix.Verb*Licensor.Neg+Illusory.Neg|stimulus.ID))
```

	criticized model			raw model		
	Estimate	SE	t	Estimate	SE	t
Intercept (−NPI −LIC.NEG−ILL.NEG)	5.7349	0.0422	135.8538	5.7375	0.0433	132.5118
MATRIX.VERB (+NPI)	0.0394	0.0233	1.6882	0.0535	0.0272	1.9655
+LICENSOR.NEG (NEG)	0.0556	0.0253	2.1943	0.0725	0.0289	2.5117
+ILLUSORY.NEG (NEG)	0.0006	0.0213	0.0262	0.0159	0.0272	0.5840
trial	−0.0034	0.0003	−12.6887	−0.0036	0.0003	−10.8754
segment.length	0.0152	0.0020	7.6812	0.0156	0.0021	7.3593
MATRIX.VERB:LICENSOR.NEG	−0.0523	0.0315	−1.6618	−0.0732	0.0376	−1.9441
MATRIX.VERB:ILLUSORY.NEG	−0.0087	0.0288	−0.3010	−0.0177	0.0360	−0.4919
LICENSOR.NEG:ILLUSORY.NEG	−0.0205	0.0288	−0.7136	−0.0547	0.0361	−1.5168
M.VERB:LIC.NEG:ILL.NEG	0.0338	0.0407	0.8309	0.0577	0.0510	1.1316

Table 6.10: Output of the LME model for the infinitive particle of the spillover region (*zu*) in Experiment 2

```
lmer(log.RT~Matrix.Verb*Licensor.Neg*Illusory.Neg+trial+
(1+Matrix.Verb+Licensor.Neg+Illusory.Neg|participant.ID)+
(1+Matrix.Verb+Licensor.Neg+Illusory.Neg|stimulus.ID))
```

	criticized model			raw model		
	Estimate	SE	t	Estimate	SE	t
Intercept (−NPI −LIC.NEG−ILL.NEG)	5.8796	0.0295	199.6061	5.8879	0.0287	204.9369
MATRIX.VERB (+NPI)	0.0130	0.0179	0.7277	0.0121	0.0224	0.5394
+LICENSOR.NEG (NEG)	0.0184	0.0185	0.9911	0.0230	0.0231	0.9991
+ILLUSORY.NEG (NEG)	0.0061	0.0189	0.3247	0.0153	0.0229	0.6663
trial	−0.0027	0.0002	−11.5572	−0.0028	0.0003	−9.8815
MATRIX.VERB:LICENSOR.NEG	−0.0311	0.0252	−1.2329	−0.0273	0.0313	−0.8714
MATRIX.VERB:ILLUSORY.NEG	−0.0057	0.0253	−0.2248	−0.0010	0.0314	−0.0306
LICENSOR.NEG:ILLUSORY.NEG	−0.0413	0.0254	−1.6286	−0.0165	0.0313	−0.5258
M.VERB:LIC.NEG:ILL.NEG	0.0758	0.0358	2.1173	0.0393	0.0443	0.8875

Table 6.11: Output of the LME model for the verb of the spillover region (*wecken*) in Experiment 2
```
lmer(log.RT~Matrix.Verb*Licensor.Neg*Illusory.Neg+trial+segment.length+
(1+Matrix.Verb+Licensor.Neg+Illusory.Neg|participant.ID)+
(1+Licensor.Neg|stimulus.ID))
```

	criticized model			raw model		
	Estimate	SE	t	Estimate	SE	t
Intercept (−NPI −LIC.NEG−ILL.NEG)	5.8449	0.0561	104.1871	5.8542	0.0615	95.1699
MATRIX.VERB (+NPI)	0.0712	0.0274	2.6016	0.0750	0.0328	2.2854
+LICENSOR.NEG (NEG)	0.0772	0.0258	2.9915	0.1006	0.0335	3.0020
+ILLUSORY.NEG (NEG)	0.0896	0.0257	3.4810	0.0896	0.0332	2.7001
trial	−0.0040	0.0003	−11.9502	−0.0039	0.0004	−9.2995
segment.length	0.0078	0.0035	2.2231	0.0087	0.0044	1.9860
MATRIX.VERB:LICENSOR.NEG	−0.0661	0.0356	−1.8548	−0.0962	0.0456	−2.1091
MATRIX.VERB:ILLUSORY.NEG	−0.1085	0.0357	−3.0411	−0.1024	0.0457	−2.2423
LICENSOR.NEG:ILLUSORY.NEG	−0.0920	0.0358	−2.5667	−0.0804	0.0456	−1.7617
M.VERB:LIC.NEG:ILL.NEG	0.1120	0.0506	2.2140	0.1065	0.0645	1.6501

Table 6.12: Output of the LME model for the final 3-segments-region of the spillover region (*Interesse zu wecken*) in Experiment 2
```
lmer(log.RT~Matrix.Verb*Licensor.Neg*Illusory.Neg+trial+segment.length+
(1+Matrix.Verb*Licensor.Neg+Illusory.Neg|participant.ID)+
(0+Matrix.Verb*Licensor.Neg+Illusory.Neg|stimulus.ID))
```

	criticized model			raw model		
	Estimate	SE	t	Estimate	SE	t
Intercept (−NPI −LIC.NEG−ILL.NEG)	6.8719	0.0463	148.3777	6.8899	0.0483	142.7712
MATRIX.VERB (+NPI)	0.0455	0.0177	2.5709	0.0487	0.0213	2.2874
+LICENSOR.NEG (NEG)	0.0616	0.0175	3.5227	0.0716	0.0221	3.2397
+ILLUSORY.NEG (NEG)	0.0466	0.0169	2.7602	0.0467	0.0218	2.1404
trial	−0.0037	0.0002	−16.8791	−0.0035	0.0003	−12.7953
segment.length	0.0063	0.0014	4.5722	0.0060	0.0015	3.8688
MATRIX.VERB:LICENSOR.NEG	−0.0470	0.0238	−1.9747	−0.0659	0.0301	−2.1895
MATRIX.VERB:ILLUSORY.NEG	−0.0562	0.0233	−2.4100	−0.0478	0.0300	−1.5937
LICENSOR.NEG:ILLUSORY.NEG	−0.0436	0.0233	−1.8702	−0.0492	0.0300	−1.6411
M.VERB:LIC.NEG:ILL.NEG	0.0561	0.0330	1.7001	0.0651	0.0424	1.5369

6.2 Experiment 3: Follow-up study on the NPI *brauchen* (self-paced reading)

This experiment is a follow-up study designed to test the predictions of an alternative explanation of the findings of Experiment 2.

6.2.1 Rationale

As noted in Section 6.1.4, the alternative explanation of the increased reading times in Experiment 2 is valid only because the canonical position of the negation and the position at which increased reading times start to emerge (*drucken* 'print') are separated only by the short infinitive particle *zu* 'to', as shown in (9a). To contrast the predictions of the two hypotheses, the distance between the canonical position of the negation and the reconstruction position has to be increased. This is achieved by inserting a prepositional phrase between the negation and the infinitive, such as the *an den Verlag* 'to the publisher' in (9b).[6]

(9) a. Letztendlich *braucht* der Autor den Roman (nicht) zu drucken #1 unter
finally needs the author the novel not to print under
Umständen ...
circumstances

b. Letztendlich *braucht* der Autor den Roman (nicht) [an den Verlag]
finally needs the author the novel not at the publisher
zu schicken #1 unter Umständen ...
to send under circumstances

In the extended structure (9b), the positions at which the different hypothesis predict longer reading times are now distinguishable. The expectation-based approach predicts that increased reading times due to a non-licensed NPI should appear on the segments following the canonical position of the negation, i. e. on the PP *an den Verlag* 'at the publisher'. The V2-Reconstruction Hypothesis, on the other hand, predicts that the licensing of the NPI will only be evaluated after reconstruction, i. e. reading times will not increase before the element directly preceding the reconstruction site, i. e. the verb *schicken* 'send'.

6 Thanks to Daniel Gutzmann for pointing out this possibility of extending the materials.

6.2.2 Method

6.2.2.1 Participants

We tested 48 participants (age 19–37 years, mean 22.9 years; 8 male; 4 left-handed), all self-declared German native speakers (5 bilinguals) and students of the University of Cologne. Participants either received course credits or a reimbursement of 4 €.

6.2.2.2 Materials

The materials consisted of 32 items interspersed with 34 fillers (8 from Experiment 4) resulting in 66 stimuli per participants. All stimuli consisted of an introductory context of 1–2 sentences, a declarative target sentence and a comprehension question (50 % polar interrogatives and 50 % constituent questions).

An example of an experimental item is given in (10). The target items varied in a 2 × 3 design with the factors MATRIX.VERB and NEGATION. The finite verb was either the modal NPI-verb *brauchen* 'need to', as in (10b), (10d), and (10f) or the polarity-neutral verb *beschließen* 'decide', as in (10c), (10e), and (10g). The materials contained a LOW.NEGATION directly preceding the first infinitive as in (10b–10c), a HIGH.NEGATION preceding the second infinitive, as in (10d–10e), or no negation at all (NO.NEGATION), as in (10f–10g). Generally, the target sentences were very similar to the one from Experiment 2 above. The first major difference is that the materials of this experiment exhibited a PP, such as *an den Verlag* 'to the publishing company' between the canonical position of the negation and the first infinitive *zu schicken* 'to send'. As a consequence, the sentences also contained different predicates, namely such that take low argumental or adverbial PPs which canonically follow the sentential negation. Additionally, in comparison to Experiment 2, the number of conditions were reduced by dropping the doubly negated condition in order to eliminate a source of processing difficulty from the materials. Furthermore, I chose to use a different continuation for the conditions with a low negation, in (10b) and (10c). Those structures are not extended by an superordinate VP that would require an additional negation to render the NPI-condition grammatical. Now, only one of the six conditions is ungrammatical, namely (10f) with the NPI *brauchen* 'need to' and no negation in the sentence. All experimental items are given in the online appendix.

(10) a. CONTEXT:

Ein Autor hat wegen seines neuen Romans Ärger mit seinem Verlag. Er bespricht mit seinem Anwalt, ob er das Manuskript auch an anderer Stelle veröffentlichen kann.

'An author has trouble with his publisher because of his new novel. He talks to his lawyer whether he could publish the manuscript also somewhere else.'

b. +NPI LOW.NEGATION

Letztendlich braucht der Autor den Roman nicht an den Verlag zu
finally NPI the author the novel not at the publisher to
schicken #1 unter Umständen aber an ein Internetportal.
send under circumstances however at an internet portal

'Thus the author doesn't have to send the novel to the publisher perhaps however to an internet portal.'

c. −NPI LOW.NEGATION

Letztendlich beschließt der Autor den Roman nicht an den Verlag
finally decides the author the novel not at the publisher
zu schicken #1 unter Umständen aber an ein Internetportal.
to send under circumstances however at an internet portal

'Thus the author decides to not send the novel to the publisher perhaps however to an internet portal.'

d. +NPI HIGH.NEGATION

Letztendlich braucht der Autor den Roman an den Verlag zu
finally NPI the author the novel at the publisher to
schicken #1 unter Umständen nicht sofort zu verbieten #2
send under circumstances not immediately to forbid
um die rechtlichen Bestimmungen zu wahren.
for the legal regulations to preserve

'Thus the author doesn't have to immediately forbid to print the novel this time to preserve the legal regulations.'

e. −NPI HIGH.NEGATION

Letztendlich beschließt der Autor den Roman an den Verlag zu
finally decides the author the novel at the publisher to

schicken #1 unter Umständen nicht sofort zu verbieten #2
send under circumstances not immediately to forbid
um die rechtlichen Bestimmungen zu wahren.
for the legal regulations to preserve

'Thus the author decides to not immediately forbid to print the novel this time to preserve the legal regulations.'

f. +NPI NO.NEGATION
*Letztendlich braucht der Autor den Roman an den Verlag zu
finally NPI the author the novel at the publisher to
schicken #1 unter Umständen sofort zu verbieten #2 um die
send under circumstances immediately to forbid for the
rechtlichen Bestimmungen zu wahren.
legal regulations to preserve

g. −NPI NO.NEGATION
Letztendlich beschließt der Autor den Roman an den Verlag zu
finally decides the author the novel at the publisher to
schicken #1 unter Umständen sofort zu verbieten #2 um die
send under circumstances immediately to forbid for the
rechtlichen Bestimmungen zu wahren.
legal regulations to preserve

'Thus the author decides to immediately forbid to print the novel this time to preserve the legal regulations.'

h. COMPREHENSION QUESTION:
Wer spricht mit seinem Anwalt?

'Who talks to his/its lawyer'
correct answer = *Der Autor* 'the author' wrong answer = *Der Verlag* 'the publishing company'

6.2.2.3 Procedure

The context was presented as one text block. The presentation of the target sentence began with a fixation cross and conformed to the centered self-paced reading paradigm (Just et al. 1982) in which the segments were presented non-cumulatively in a stationary window, i. e. participants saw only one word at a time at the center of the screen and had no visual cues that would allow them to predict the length of the sentences. Participant moved through the segments at their own pace by pressing the space bar. Each item contained a comprehension question, as in (10h), to control whether participants paid attention to the task. Answers to the comprehension questions were presented in the bottom left and right of the screen and were chosen by pressing the 'd' or 'k' key on a German keyboard respectively. After each response the participants saw a feedback message indicating whether their response was correct or not. Participants were instructed to read the sentences and to answer the questions as fast as possible in order to give correct responses.

The procedure was programmed in the python experiment suite PsychoPy (Peirce 2007) and run on a Windows PC in a psycholinguistics lab. The experimental stimuli were randomized according to the Latin square design, such that each participant saw each of the 32 items in exactly one of the 6 experimental conditions. The position of the correct answer to the comprehension question (left or right) was balanced across the items. The total list of stimuli (experimental items plus fillers) was automatically randomized by the experiment software. Experiments took approximately 25 minutes.

6.2.2.4 Data analysis

Prior to the analysis, all reading times larger than 2 seconds (n=43) have been excluded (0.06 % of the data). The participants' accuracy in response to the comprehension questions ranged from 78–100 % (mean 91 %). No participant was excluded from the analysis but all trials with a false response to the comprehension question were excluded (9.2 % of the data). The statistical handling of the data was identical to the procedure described for Experiment 2.

Data analysis proceeded in two steps: The initial sequence of the target sentences including the adverbial *unter Umständen* was identical for the HIGH.NEGATION and the NO.NEGATION condition. These two conditions were aggregated for the analysis of this region and contrasted to the LOW.NEGATION condition, resulting in a 2 × 2 analysis. The continuations for the LOW.NEGATION conditions differ from the continuation of the remaining four conditions. Hence the analyses for the continuations were carried out separately in a 1 × 2 and a 2 × 2 fashion respectively.

6.2.3 Results

A graphical summary of the result for the initial sequence is given in Figure 6.3. No effects could be detected on the negation and the two following segments of the PP *an* and *den*. On the noun of the PP *Verlag* the analysis revealed a simple effect of MATRIX.VERB ($t = -2.0090$) with longer reading times for the +NPI condition. On the infinitive particle *zu*, an interaction of MATRIX.VERB and NEGATION turned up indicating that the +NPI LOW.NEGATION condition received shorter reading times than all other conditions. On first infinitive *schicken* 'send', the statistical analysis revealed a significant effect of NEGATION (t = −2.2931) with longer reading times for non-negated sentences. An analysis of the aggregated reading times of the infinitive region (*zu schicken*) yielded only a significant effect of NEGATION (t = −3.1992) with longer reading times for non-negated sentences. On the first adverbial segment *unter*, the analysis revealed a significant contrast in the non-negated sentences with longer reading times for the non-licensed +NPI condition (t = −2.5087). On the second adverbial segment *Umständen* the analysis revealed a similar contrast, however, in the negated sentences indicating longer reading times for the +NPI condition (t = −2.0064). The analysis of the aggregated reading times of the adverb region did not yield significant results. The exact model outputs of the analyses are given in Tables 6.13 to 6.18.

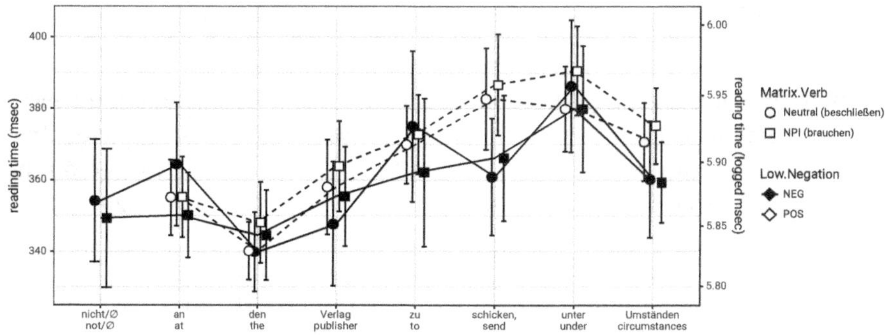

Figure 6.3: Mean reading times for the uniform initial region of interest in Experiment 3 (95 % CIs)

A graphical summary of the spillover region of the LOW.NEGATION conditions is given in Figure 6.4. No effects of the experimental conditions could be detected in this region. Even the contrast on the determiner *ein* 'an', which appears largest in Figure 6.4, did not reach significance in the raw model and decreased even further after model criticism.

A graphical summary for the continuation of the remaining conditions is presented in Figure 6.5. On the adverbial *sofort* directly following the negation, the analysis revealed a significant simple effect of NEGATION (t = −2.3413) with longer reading times for the HIGH.NEGATION conditions. On the adjective of the spillover region *rechtlichen* 'legal', the model revealed a significant contrast for MATRIX.VERB (t = 2.4666) and close to significant tendencies for NEGATION (t = 1.9786) and the interaction term (t = −1.9326). This indicates that reading times for the −NPI conditions are longer than for the +NPI conditions. Additionally,

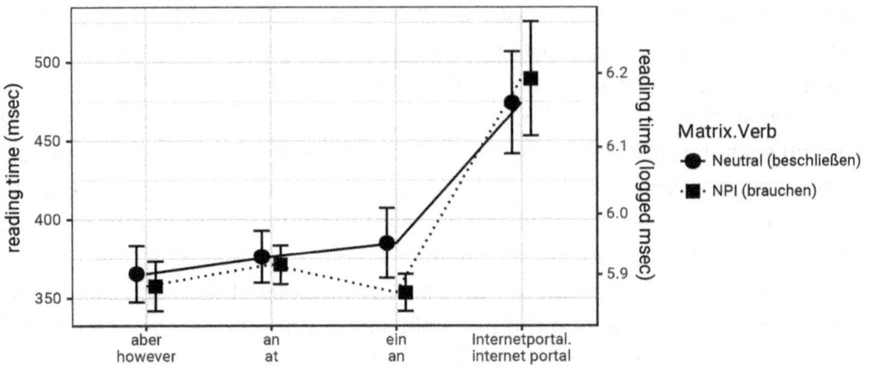

Figure 6.4: Mean reading times for the continuation of the LOW.NEGATION conditions in Experiment 3 (95 % CIs)

negation did not affect the –NPI condition. Within the +NPI condition, however, the ungrammatical NO.NEGATION condition showed longer reading times than the grammatical HIGH.NEGATION condition. No effects could be detected on the other segments. The exact model outputs are given in Tables 6.19 to 6.20.

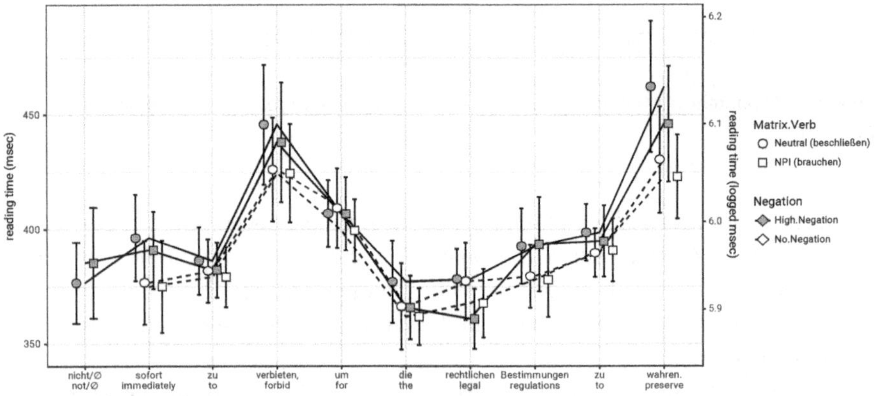

Figure 6.5: Mean reading times for the continuation with the second VP structure in Experiment 3 (95 % CIs)

6.2.4 Discussion

The results of this experiment did not replicate the clean interaction pattern of MATRIX.VERB and NEGATION on the first infinitive and the following two segments that was found in Experiment 2. Instead, the results indicated an effect at an earlier position preceding the infinitive, namely at the noun *Verlag*. Although the temporal profile matches the prediction of the expectation-based account, the form of the effect does not. Remember, this account predicts that an NPI in V2-position triggers an expectation for a negation. If this expectation is violated, we should observe prolonged reading times for the non-licensed +NPI. However, what we observed was longer reading times for NPI-verbs irrespective of negation. This indicates that, at this point, only the content of the V2-position is relevant. The negation seems to impact processing only on the following segments, the infinitive region *zu schicken*. Again, the result do not indicate that the processor expected a negation only for the NPI-verbs but the results indicate a general effect of negation. However, it is surprising that the presence of negation led to shorter reading times and not to longer ones, as we would plausibly expect. Interestingly, on the two subsequent segments the results showed specific interactions involving longer reading times for the NPI-verbs. This contrast appears on the first adverbial *unter* only in non-negated sentences and on the second adverbial *Umständen* only in negated sentences. It seems as if the presence of negation delayed the evaluation of the content of the verb. Although the results are not as predicted, they can receive an explanation under the V2-Reconstruction Hypothesis. The general verb-type effect that shows up at the noun *Verlag* might be a reflection of an automated reconstruction process. The finite verb is reconstructed and its content is reactivated. This reactivation seems to be more demanding for the +NPI verb *brauchen* 'need to'. Subsequently, with encounter of the infinitive, the finite verb is reconstructed into a potential base position. At this point, a negation-related process seems to apply. As noted above, it is surprising that this leads to faster processing in the negated sentences. Only on the subsequent segments, the lexical content of the reconstructed verb will be interpreted triggering longer reading times, first in the non-negated sentences and subsequently in the negated sentences.

The remainder of the sentence showed two effects. The first one, on the the adverbial *sofort*, is most likely a spillover effect from the preceding element. A preceding negation lead to prolonged reading times due to additional semantic processing. The second effect turned up on the adjective of the spillover region *rechtliche* 'legal'. The interaction at this point indicates that the content of the V2-verbs are interpreted with respect to the second negation. The ungrammatical +NPI NO.NEGATION condition showed longer reading times than the grammatical +NPI HIGH.NEGATION condition. This indicates that licensing of the NPI is reflected three segments after the second infinitive. Note that a comparable effect was found on the same segment in Experiment 2. This supports the assumption that this is an evaluation of the licensing requirements at the second reconstruction site, that appears a slightly delayed due to the relative complexity of the sentence.

Although the results are not as clear-cut as in Experiment 2, they clearly favor the V2-Reconstruction Hypothesis over the expectation-based approach. Remember that the latter predicted that negation-related effects should appear at the segments directly following the canonical position of the negation, i. e. the PP *an den Verlag* 'to the publisher'. However, no such effects could be detected at those segments. Distant effects of the negation did not show up until the reconstruction position of the finite verb, i. e. the directly preceding infinitive *schicken* 'send', as predicted by the V2-Reconstruction Hypothesis.

Table 6.13: Output of the LME model for noun of the PP (*Verlag*) in Experiment 3
`lmer(log.RT~Matrix.Verb*Low.Negation+segment.length+trial+`
`(1+segment.length+trial|participant.ID)+(1|stimulus.ID))`

	criticized model			raw model		
	Estimate	SE	t	Estimate	SE	t
Intercept (+NPI −LOW.NEGATION)	5.7416	0.0331	173.7189	5.7324	0.0377	152.0945
MATRIX.VERB (−NPI)	−0.0253	0.0126	−2.0090	−0.0246	0.0168	−1.4596
+LOW.NEGATION (NEG)	0.0147	0.0153	0.9607	−0.0073	0.0206	−0.3544
segment length	0.0067	0.0029	2.3430	0.0116	0.0033	3.4795
trial	−0.0056	0.0006	−9.8937	−0.0059	0.0006	−9.7096
MATRIX.VERB:LOW.NEGATION	−0.0149	0.0219	−0.6796	−0.0095	0.0293	−0.3255

Table 6.14: Output of the LME model for particle of the first infinitive (*zu*) in Experiment 3
`lmer(log.RT~Matrix.Verb*Low.Negation+segment.length+trial+`
`(1+trial|participant.ID)+(1|stimulus.ID))`

	criticized model			raw model		
	Estimate	SE	t	Estimate	SE	t
Intercept (+NPI −LOW.NEGATION)	5.8490	0.0308	190.0450	5.8701	0.0329	178.2923
MATRIX.VERB (−NPI)	−0.0088	0.0119	−0.7385	−0.0127	0.0157	−0.8073
+LOW.NEGATION (NEG)	−0.0319	0.0145	−2.1995	−0.0302	0.0192	−1.5761
trial	−0.0050	0.0005	−9.7793	−0.0052	0.0006	−9.3646
MATRIX.VERB:LOW.NEGATION	0.0198	0.0207	0.9550	0.0359	0.0273	1.3146

Table 6.15: Output of the LME model for first infinitive (*schicken*) in Experiment 3
`lmer(log.RT~Matrix.Verb*Low.Negation+segment.length+trial+`
`(1+Matrix.Verb+segment.length+trial|participant.ID)+(1|stimulus.ID))`

	criticized model			raw model		
	Estimate	SE	t	Estimate	SE	t
Intercept (+NPI −LOW.NEGATION)	5.8420	0.0445	131.1401	5.8563	0.0492	119.0898
MATRIX.VERB (−NPI)	−0.0177	0.0146	−1.2163	−0.0147	0.0177	−0.8313
+LOW.NEGATION (NEG)	−0.0374	0.0163	−2.2931	−0.0390	0.0201	−1.9349
segment length	0.0024	0.0039	0.6204	0.0026	0.0043	0.6079
trial	−0.0061	0.0006	−9.7544	−0.0064	0.0007	−9.7246
MATRIX.VERB:LOW.NEGATION	0.0078	0.0233	0.3363	0.0059	0.0287	0.2064

Table 6.16: Output of the LME model for first infinitive region (*zu schicken*) in Experiment 3
`lmer(log.RT~Matrix.Verb*Low.Negation+segment.length+trial+`
`(1+trial|participant.ID)+(1|stimulus.ID))`

	criticized model			raw model		
	Estimate	SE	t	Estimate	SE	t
Intercept (+NPI −LOW.NEGATION)	6.5306	0.0587	111.3367	6.5454	0.0671	97.5947
MATRIX.VERB (−NPI)	−0.0163	0.0111	−1.4593	−0.0123	0.0137	−0.8955
+LOW.NEGATION (NEG)	−0.0434	0.0136	−3.1992	−0.0310	0.0168	−1.8499
segment length	0.0031	0.0041	0.7458	0.0029	0.0049	0.5931
trial	−0.0057	0.0006	−10.3249	−0.0059	0.0006	−10.0857
MATRIX.VERB:LOW.NEGATION	0.0196	0.0194	1.0126	0.0169	0.0239	0.7065

Table 6.17: Output of the LME model for first segment of the adverbial (*unter*) in Experiment 3
`lmer(log.RT~Matrix.Verb*Low.Negation+segment.length+trial+`
`(1+trial|participant.ID)+(1|stimulus.ID))`

	criticized model			raw model		
	Estimate	SE	t	Estimate	SE	t
Intercept (+NPI −LOW.NEGATION)	5.8981	0.0366	161.1577	5.9220	0.0412	143.5940
MATRIX.VERB (−NPI)	−0.0314	0.0125	−2.5087	−0.0320	0.0157	−2.0415
+LOW.NEGATION (NEG)	−0.0226	0.0153	−1.4807	−0.0192	0.0192	−1.0010
segment length	−0.0029	0.0050	−0.5763	−0.0030	0.0067	−0.4497
trial	−0.0049	0.0005	−9.6943	−0.0050	0.0006	−8.9305
MATRIX.VERB:LOW.NEGATION	0.0305	0.0218	1.3988	0.0270	0.0273	0.9897

Table 6.18: Output of the LME model for second segment of the adverbial (*Umständen*) in Experiment 3
`lmer(log.RT~Matrix.Verb*Low.Negation+segment.length+trial+`
`(1+trial|participant.ID)+(1|stimulus.ID))`

	criticized model			raw model		
	Estimate	SE	t	Estimate	SE	t
Intercept (+NPI +LOW.NEGATION)	5.8319	0.0411	141.9282	5.8501	0.0435	134.3574
MATRIX.VERB (−NPI)	−0.0343	0.0171	−2.0064	−0.0174	0.0221	−0.7878
−LOW.NEGATION (POS)	0.0036	0.0145	0.2452	0.0239	0.0189	1.2682
segment length	0.0018	0.0027	0.6558	−0.0006	0.0032	−0.1868
trial	−0.0050	0.0006	−8.9633	−0.0051	0.0006	−8.0745
MATRIX.VERB:LOW.NEGATION	0.0191	0.0209	0.9138	−0.0024	0.0269	−0.0882

Table 6.19: Output of the LME model for the adverbial of the second VP (*sofort*) in Experiment 3
`lmer(log.RT~Matrix.Verb*Negation+segment.length+trial+`
`(1+segment.length+trial|participant.ID)+(1|stimulus.ID))`

	criticized model			raw model		
	Estimate	SE	t	Estimate	SE	t
Intercept (−NPI HIGH.NEGATION)	5.8101	0.0374	155.1934	5.8243	0.0409	142.3883
MATRIX.VERB (+NPI)	−0.0093	0.0175	−0.5294	−0.0124	0.0219	−0.5662
NEGATION (NO.NEGATION)	−0.0416	0.0178	−2.3413	−0.0311	0.0221	−1.4069
segment length	0.0104	0.0037	2.7672	0.0099	0.0041	2.4013
trial	−0.0061	0.0006	−10.1179	−0.0064	0.0007	−9.3876
MATRIX.VERB:NEGATION	0.0011	0.0250	0.0460	0.0062	0.0312	0.1988

Table 6.20: Output of the LME model for the adjective of the spillover region (*rechtliche*) in Experiment 3
`lmer(log.RT~Matrix.Verb*Negation+segment.length+trial+(1+Matrix.Verb*Negation|participant.ID)+(1+Negation|stimulus.ID))`

	criticized model			raw model		
	Estimate	SE	t	Estimate	SE	t
Intercept (+NPI HIGH.NEGATION)	5.8029	0.0432	134.4415	5.8010	0.0473	122.5629
MATRIX.VERB (−NPI)	0.0409	0.0166	2.4666	0.0534	0.0202	2.6463
NEGATION (NO.NEGATION)	0.0331	0.0167	1.9786	0.0429	0.0203	2.1128
segment length	0.0015	0.0036	0.4012	0.0015	0.0041	0.3642
trial	−0.0059	0.0006	−9.6125	−0.0060	0.0007	−8.7448
MATRIX.VERB:NEGATION	−0.0459	0.0238	−1.9326	−0.0401	0.0287	−1.3954

6.3 Experiment 4: Reconstruction of infinitive-embedding verbs (self-paced reading)

6.3.1 Rationale

The rationale of this experiments makes use of selectional properties of German verbs that embed infinitival verb phrases. Those verbs split into two groups. The majority of embedding verbs select infinitives which are preceded by the particle *zu* 'to', like the verb *versuchen* 'try' in (11a). Few verbs, however, embed bare infinitives, like the modal verb *müssen* 'must' in (11b).

(11) a. Uwe versucht den Zug *(zu) nehmen.
Uwe tries the train to take
'Uwe tries to take the train.'

b. Uwe muss den Zug (*zu) nehmen.
Uwe must the train to take
'Uwe must to take the train.'

Each of the embedding verbs may also embed a member of the other group which, in turn, selects an infinitive. The selection requirement, i. e. bare infinitive vs. particle, thereby applies strictly hierarchical from the embedding verb to the directly embedded verb, as indicated by the contrast between the V-final clauses in (12a) and (12b).

(12) a. ..., dass Uwe [[den Zug (*zu) nehmen] *(zu) müssen] versucht.
that Uwe the train to take to must tries
'... that Uwe tries to must take the train.'[7]

b. ..., dass Uwe [[den Zug *(zu) nehmen] (*zu) versuchen] muss.
that Uwe the train to take to try must
'... that Uwe must try to take the train.'

In V2-clauses, the finite verb moves to the left periphery. If the finite verb is automatically reconstructed after the first infinitive (#1), the string is temporarily ungrammatical because the first infinitive does not match the requirements of the finite verb as illustrated in (13) and (14).

(13) a. Uwe versucht [[den Zug nehmen] #1 zu müssen] #2 ~~versucht~~.
Uwe tries the train take to must

---

7 Clearly, the meaning of this combination is quite unusual. Assume that Uwe intentionally creates a situation, in order to set himself under pressure, in which he has no choice but to take a certain train.

b. * Uwe versucht [[den Zug nehmen] ~~versucht~~] ...
Uwe tries the train take

(14) a. Uwe muss [[den Zug zu nehmen] #1 versuchen] #2 ~~muss~~.
Uwe must the train to take try

b. * Uwe muss [[den Zug zu nehmen] ~~muss~~] ...
Uwe must the train to take

6.3.2 Method

6.3.2.1 Participants and procedure

Participants and procedure are identical to Experiment 3 because both experiments have been combined in one experimental run.

6.3.2.2 Materials

Materials consisted of 8 experimental items interspersed with 58 fillers (32 from Experiment 3) resulting in 66 stimuli per participant. All stimuli consisted of an introductory context of 1–2 sentences, a declarative target sentence and a comprehension question (50 % polar interrogatives and 50 % constituent questions).

An example item is given in (15). All target clauses have an adverbial in the sentence-initial position. The V2-position was filled with an infinitive-embedding verb which varied according to the experimental condition MATRIX.VERB, either selecting an infinitive with a particle (PARTICLE), like *beabsichtigen* 'intend' in (15b), or selecting a bare infinitives (BARE) like *müssen* 'must' in (15c). In both conditions, the identical ditransitive non-finite VP followed the V2-position. The infinitive of this VP, *zu navigieren* 'to navigate', was always preceded by the infinitive particle *zu* 'to'. Consequently, the sentence could be a well-formed structure only in the PARTICLE condition but not in the BARE condition as indicated by the starred reconstruction position (#1) in (15c). Only after a 2-segment adverbial, like *am Anfang* 'in the beginning', a second infinitive was presented, which corresponded to the selectional requirements of the respective matrix verbs rendering all items well-formed. A 6-segment embedded clause followed the infinitive to detect potential spillover effects.

(15) a. CONTEXT:
Ein Bauarbeiter hat den Arbeitgeber gewechselt. Hier müssen nun die Fahrzeuge jeden Abend in die engen Garagen geparkt werden.

'A construction worker changed his employer. Here, the vehicles now have to pulled into the narrow garages every evening.'

b. PARTICLE

Logischerweise beabsichtigt der Bauarbeiter den Lastwagen
logically intends the construction worker the truck
in die Garage zu navigieren #1 am Anfang erst zu lernen, damit
into the garage to navigate at the beginning first to learn so that
das teure Fahrzeug heil bleibt.
the expensive vehicle undamaged remains

'Naturally, the construction worker intends to learn how to navigate the truck into the garage first, so that the expensive vehicle will remain undamaged.'

c. BARE

Logischerweise muss der Bauarbeiter den Lastwagen in die
logically must the construction worker the truck into the
Garage zu navigieren *#1 am Anfang erst lernen, damit das
garage to navigate at the beginning first to learn so that
teure Fahrzeug heil bleibt.
the expensive vehicle undamaged remains

'Naturally, the construction worker must learn how to navigate the truck into the garage first, so that the expensive vehicle will remain undamaged.'

d. COMPREHENSION QUESTION:

Von welchem Fahrzeug war hier die Rede?

'What kind of vehicle was talked about?'
correct answer = *von einem Laster* 'about a truck' wrong answer = *von einem Bagger* 'about an excavator'

According to the V2-Reconstruction Hypothesis, the finite verbs will be automatically reconstructed and interpreted after the first infinitive *navigieren*. In the BARE condition, however, the infinitive does not match the selectional requirements of the finite matrix verb. Hence, I predict longer reading times for the BARE condition at this segment.

The low number of items is a consequence of the low number of verbs selecting a bare infinitive overall. I could not come up with more verbs that could be paired with a canonical cluster verb that is either synonymous or at least replaceable in the same context. The verb pairs of the materials are given Table 6.21, all experimental items are given in the online appendix.

Table 6.21: Pairs of cluster verb in Experiment 4

BARE	PARTICLE
muss 'must'	*beabsichtigt* 'intends'
soll 'should'	*probiert* 'tries'
darf 'is allowed'	*gedenkt* 'intends'
möchte 'wants'	*plant* 'plans'
lässt 'lets'	*intendiert* 'intends'
kommt 'comes to'	*versucht* 'tries'
kann 'can'	*verlangt* 'demands'
sieht 'sees'	*verpflichtet* 'obligates'

6.3.2.3 Data analysis

Prior to the analysis, all reading times larger than 2 seconds (n=43) have been excluded (0.06 % of the data). The participants' accuracy in response to the comprehension questions ranged from 63–100 % (mean 87 %). No participant was excluded from the analysis but all trials with a false response to the comprehension question were excluded (13 % of the data). The statistical handling of the data was identical to the procedure described for Experiment 2.

6.3.3 Results

A graphical summary of the reading times of the region of interest, ranging from the V2-position until the spillover region, is given in Figure 6.6. On the subject determiner *der* 'the', the model revealed longer reading times for the PARTICLE condition ($t = -2.1779$). On the first infinitive *navigieren* 'navigate' the analysis indicated longer reading times for the PARTICLE condition only in the first model. After model criticism, the effect decreased below significance ($t = -1.7229$) indicating that the effect was mostly driven by extreme values. The analysis revealed longer reading times for the BARE condition only on the first adverbial segment *am* ($t = 2.1286$) but no effect on the second segment *Anfang*. The analysis of the aggregated reading times for the region *am Anfang* 'at the beginning' indicated longer reading times for the BARE condition ($t = 2.8873$). On the second infinitive *lernen*, the analysis revealed longer reading times for the PARTICLE condition ($t = -2.3438$). No effects could be detected on the other segments. The exact model outputs of the analyses are given in Tables 6.22 to 6.26.

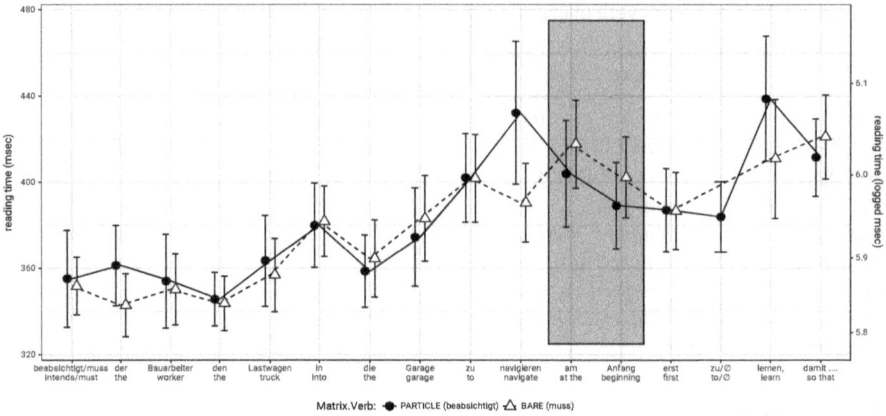

Figure 6.6: Mean reading times in from the V2-position until the spillover region in Experiment 4 (95 % CIs)

6.3.4 Discussion

In line with the predictions above, the results indicated longer reading times for the BARE condition on the two segments following the first possible reconstruction site of the matrix verb *am Anfang* 'at the beginning', i. e. the dark-gray area in Figure 6.6. I assume that with the encounter of the infinitive *navigieren* 'navigate' the matrix verb is automatically reconstructed and interpreted. In the BARE condition, the resulting representation is ill-formed because the infinitive is accompanied by the infinitive particle *zu* 'to', which violates the selectional requirements of matrix verbs like *müssen* 'must' which select a bare infinitive. The response to this temporary ungrammaticality is reflected by the longer reading times on the two adverb segments *am Anfang* 'at the beginning'. Note that an alternative explanation based on an incremental interpretation would predict the opposite effect. Assume that incoming material is integrated in the parse strictly from left to right without resorting to reconstruction. In the PARTICLE condition, the parse could be completed after the first infinitive *navigieren*. Hence the encounter of the adverbial *am Anfang* would indicate that the structure is not yet complete which should trigger a reanalysis reflected by prolonged reading times. In the BARE condition, on the other hand, the first infinitive does not match the selectional requirements of the matrix verb. Therefore, the parse could not be completed at this point. The encounter of the adverbial does not trigger a reanalysis but only continues the current structure. In sum, under a strictly incremental approach, we would expect longer reading times in the PARTICLE condition, contrary to the facts.

The results indicated longer reading times in the PARTICLE condition at three segments, i. e. the light-gray areas in Figure 6.6. Two of them are probably spillover effects caused by the directly preceding elements: The effect on the subject determiner is most likely caused by the previous segment, which consisted of the different lexical matrix verbs varying according to the experimental conditions. The effect on the second infinitive *lernen* might also be interpreted as a spillover effect. Remember that in the PARTICLE condition, the infinitive was preceded by the particle *zu* 'to' whereas, in the BARE condition, the infinitive was adjacent to the preceding adverbial. Only the tendency on the first infinitive *navigieren* 'navigate' is certainly a distant effect related to the matrix verb. Considering the linear distribution of these contrasts, I assume that all three effects stem from one underlying mechanism, i. e. they reflect lexical (re)activation processes. Initially, lexical access of the verbs in the PARTICLE condition is more demanding than for the verbs in the BARE condition which induces longer reading times at the first encounter of the verbs, i. e. on the segment following the V2-position. According to the V2-Reconstruction Hypothesis, the matrix verb is reactivated at the segments directly preceding its potential base position, i. e. at the two infinitives *navigieren* and *lernen* (see also the results of experiments 2 and 3). At these position, the lexical reactivation of the verbs of the PARTICLE condition is also more costly; again reflected by locally prolonged reading times. Additionally, this explanation matches the temporal profile of the intended experimental effect. The mismatch effect of the infinitive selection directly follows the lexical reactivation of the matrix verb at the first infinitive, because evaluation of selectional requirements depends on the lexical information.

In sum, the experiment yielded the predicted results, i. e. a mismatch effect directly following a potential reconstruction site, thereby supporting the V2-Reconstruction Hypothesis. Additionally, the results indicate that lexical reactivation precedes the evaluation of selectional requirements of embedding verbs at their reconstruction sites.

Table 6.22: Output of the LME model for determiner of the subject (*der*) in Experiment 4
`lmer(log.RT~Matrix.Verb+trial+(1|participant.ID)+(1|stimulus.ID))`

	criticized model			raw model		
	Estimate	SE	t	Estimate	SE	t
Intercept (PARTICLE)	5.7966	0.0392	147.9671	5.8143	0.0410	141.8559
MATRIX.VERB (BARE)	−0.0461	0.0212	−2.1779	−0.0503	0.0262	−1.9211
trial	−0.0042	0.0006	−6.8288	−0.0048	0.0008	−6.3209

Table 6.23: Output of the LME model for the first infinitive (*navigieren*) in Experiment 4
`lmer(log.RT~Matrix.Verb+segment.length+trial+(1+segment.length+trial|participant.ID)+(1|stimulus.ID))`

	criticized model			raw model		
	Estimate	SE	t	Estimate	SE	t
Intercept (PARTICLE)	5.6763	0.0940	60.3957	5.6235	0.0855	65.7551
MATRIX.VERB (BARE)	−0.0397	0.0230	−1.7229	−0.0715	0.0288	−2.4802
segment.length	0.0260	0.0099	2.6165	0.0361	0.0093	3.8913
trial	−0.0055	0.0009	−6.1586	−0.0059	0.0010	−5.7025

Table 6.24: Output of the LME model for the first adverb segment (*am*) in Experiment 4
`lmer(log.RT~Matrix.Verb+segment.length+trial+(1+trial|participant.ID)+(1|stimulus.ID))`

	criticized model			raw model		
	Estimate	SE	t	Estimate	SE	t
Intercept (PARTICLE)	5.7774	0.0460	125.6477	5.8078	0.0543	106.8798
MATRIX.VERB (BARE)	0.0490	0.0230	2.1286	0.0454	0.0275	1.6494
segment.length	0.0457	0.0120	3.8110	0.0409	0.0154	2.6540
trial	−0.0045	0.0009	−4.7716	−0.0051	0.0009	−5.7851

Table 6.25: Output of the LME model for the second 2-segment adverb region (*am Anfang*) in Experiment 4
`lmer(log.RT~Matrix.Verb+segment.length+trial+(1|participant.ID)+(1|stimulus.ID))`

	criticized model			raw model		
	Estimate	SE	t	Estimate	SE	t
Intercept (PARTICLE)	6.5201	0.1117	58.3604	6.5371	0.1150	56.8254
MATRIX.VERB (BARE)	0.0571	0.0198	2.8873	0.0382	0.0232	1.6479
segment.length	0.0065	0.0107	0.6023	0.0067	0.0111	0.6084
trial	−0.0051	0.0006	−8.7960	−0.0051	0.0007	−7.5005

Table 6.26: Output of the LME model for the second infinitive (*lernen*) in Experiment 4
`lmer(log.RT~Matrix.Verb+segment.length+trial+(1+Matrix.Verb+trial|participant.ID)+(1|stimulus.ID))`

	criticized model			raw model		
	Estimate	SE	t	Estimate	SE	t
Intercept (PARTICLE)	5.8328	0.0875	66.6348	5.8028	0.1248	46.5084
MATRIX.VERB (BARE)	−0.0646	0.0275	−2.3438	−0.0529	0.0380	−1.3938
segment.length	0.0108	0.0073	1.4781	0.0160	0.0115	1.3930
trial	−0.0060	0.0009	−6.5301	−0.0071	0.0011	−6.1781

6.4 Experiment 5: Verb reconstruction and word order preferences (self-paced reading)

6.4.1 Rationale

The rationale of this experiment connects closely to the findings about thematic processing, which have been discussed in Section 5.3.1. There, I have summarized that effects related to the thematic structure of the verb are only found at the assumed base position of the finite verb, irrespective whether the lexical verb specifying the thematic structure of the clause appears in the V2-position or in its base position. Previous experiments, however, included additional factors that influence thematic processing such as case-ambiguity, two animate arguments, and dative case. In this experiment, we[8] investigate the influence of the thematic information of the verb in V2-position on the processing of the arguments in relatively unmarked structures. We contrast the *experiencer-first* preference of experiencer object (EO) verbs with the *subject-first* preference which assumably holds for the default processing routine as well as non-experiencer verbs (non-Exp). The abstract schematics in (16)–(18) illustrate the linear ordering of the critical configurations. Consider (16), if the V2-position is occupied by an auxiliary like *haben* 'have', no information about the thematic roles of the arguments is available to the processor by the time the arguments are processed. The processor must rely on the default *subject-first* preference until it reaches the lexical verb. Hence, we expect that the subject<object order is processed faster than the object<subject order, as indicated by the pointing glyph.

(16)	a. ☞	XP	Auxiliary	Subject	Object	|	EO/non-Exp verb ~~Auxiliary~~
	b.	XP	Auxiliary	Object	Subject	|	EO/non-Exp verb ~~Auxiliary~~
		PREFIELD	V2	DP1	DP2		V(+I)

The same pattern is expected for non-Exp verbs. If the thematic information of the lexical verb influences argument processing, we expect a preference for the subject<object order in (17). If the finite verb is only interpreted in its base position, we expect the same effect although caused by the default processing routine analogously to the V2-auxiliary cases in (16).

8 This experiment presents collaborative work with Anne Temme. I will therefore use *we* in this chapter purposely.

(17)	a. ☞	XP	non-Exp verb	Subject$_{AGENT}$	Object$_{THEME}$	~~non-Exp verb~~
	b.	XP	non-Exp verb	Object$_{THEME}$	Subject$_{AGENT}$	~~non-Exp verb~~
		PREFIELD	V2	DP1	DP2	V(+I)

Clauses with an experiencer object verb in the V2-position, however, constitute critical test cases. There, the experiencer-first preference conflicts with the subject-first preference. Objects of experiencer verbs are more likely to precede the subject, than objects of non-experiencer verbs, as experimentally confirmed by Temme & Verhoeven (2016: 783-790). We assume that the experiencer-first preference also affects online-processing directly in such a way that the object<subject order is processed faster, as indicated in (18). Crucially, this only holds under the assumption that the information about the thematic roles encoded in a verb in V2-position is immediately activated at its surface position, where it precedes its arguments. Under the V2-Reconstruction Hypothesis, however, we expect that the lexical meaning of the verb in V2-position, including the information about the thematic roles, is only interpreted in its base position, which follows its arguments. Thus, initially, the experiencer object structures in (18) will be processed with the same default subject<object preference that we predict for the V2-auxiliary structures in (16). We expect that verb-type-specific effects will occur only right-adjacent to the second argument in transitive structures, similar to the results of Scheepers et al. (2000).

(18)	a.	XP	EO-verb	Subject$_{STIM}$	Object$_{EXP}$	~~EO-verb~~
	b. ☞	XP	EO-verb	Object$_{EXP}$	Subject$_{STIM}$	~~EO-verb~~
		PREFIELD	V2	DP1	DP2	V(+I)

Additionally, two hypotheses apply to the V-final condition, corresponding to scheme (16) above. First, thematic role assignment may apply anticipatorily: In absence of a lexical verb that specifies the thematic roles, the processor assigns thematic roles by default, maybe guided by properties of the arguments such as animacy and case (see Bornkessel & Schlesewsky 2006a). If, however, two verbs which assign different thematic roles follow the identical argument configuration, we expect that at least for one verb the roles have to be reassigned, which should be reflected in increased processing costs. Alternatively thematic role assignment may be delayed in absence of an assigner. Following this path the assignment of thematic roles remains underspecified until the lexical verb is encountered. In principle, both assignment procedures are compatible with the V2-Reconstruction Hypothesis and an incremental processing hypothesis. However, we assume the delayed assignment to be the more economic variant if applied to V2-cases.

Otherwise, the processor would assign incorrect thematic roles by default even though the information about the assigner would, in principle, be available.

To sum up, this experiment uses three factors to diagnose the influence of thematic information of lexical verbs on on-line processing. If the lexical verb is presented late, in its base position, as in (16), the verb cannot influence the processing of the arguments and the default processing routine must take place, preferring subject<object order. If, however, the lexical verb appears in V2-position, the information about the thematic roles is principally available. Under a strict incremental processing hypothesis, we expect that the information about the thematic roles will decrease the subject-first preference for experiencer object verbs immediately after the encounter of the lexical verb. In contrast, under the V2-Reconstruction Hypothesis, we expect that the processing of the arguments always proceeds according to the default mechanism because the lexical meaning of the verb in V2-position will only be interpreted in its base position. Thus, we expect an interaction of verb type and argument order in any case but two different temporal profiles according to respective hypotheses.

6.4.2 Method

6.4.2.1 Participants

We tested 48 participants (age 19–50 years, mean 24 years; 7 male; 4 left-handed), all self-declared German native speakers (6 bilinguals) and students of the University of Cologne. Participants either received course credits or a reimbursement of 4 €.

6.4.2.2 Procedure

The self-paced reading procedure was almost identical to Experiment 3 above. The only difference was that the target sentences were not presented strictly word per word but also larger phrases were presented at once, as indicated for the material below.

The context was presented as one text block. The presentation of the target sentence began with a fixation cross and conformed to the centered self-paced reading paradigm (Just et al. 1982) in which the segments were presented non-cumulatively in a stationary window, i. e. participants saw only one segment at a time at the center of the screen and had no visual cues that would allow them to predict the length of the sentences. Participant moved through the segments at their own pace by pressing the space bar. Each item contained a comprehension question to control whether participants paid attention to the task. Answers to the comprehension questions were presented in the bottom left and right of the screen and were chosen by pressing the 'd' or 'k' key on a German keyboard respectively. After each response the participants saw a feedback message whether their response was correct or not. Participants were instructed to read the sentences and answer the question as fast as possible in order to give correct responses.

The procedure was programmed in the python experiment suite PsychoPy (Peirce 2007) and run on a Windows PC in a psycholinguistics lab. The experimental stimuli have been randomized according to the Latin square design, such that each participant saw each of the 32 items in exactly one of the 6 experimental conditions. The position of the correct answer to the comprehension question (left or right) was balanced across the items. The total list of stimuli (experimental items plus fillers) were automatically randomized by the experiment software. Experiments took approximately 20 minutes.

6.4.2.3 Materials

The materials consisted of 32 experimental items interspersed with 32 filler items resulting in 64 stimuli per participant. The 32 filler items included two sets of control structures with 8 items each, which are explicated below. All stimuli consisted of a context of 1–2 sentences, a declarative target sentence and a comprehension question (50% polar interrogatives and 50% constituent questions).

The target sentences varied in a 2 × 2 × 2 design with the factors V-Type, V-Position, and Word Order. An example item is given in (19). The context sentences, such as (19a), introduced two concepts which are supersets to the subject and object of the target sentence, such as *traditional methods* for *the woven coat*, and *people who work with bees* for *the beekeeper*. This unspecific introduction should avoid increased reading times especially for information structurally marked object<subject (OS) orders (see Weskott 2003: 62–76). The target sentences were presented in segments as indicated in (19b). The sentence-initial segment was a sentence adverbial. By filling the prefield, we ensured that all arguments would follow the V2-position. The V2-position (C) was either filled by the auxiliary *hat* 'has' in the V-final conditions such as (19b), or by the lexical verb in the simple past form, such as *verblüffte* 'baffled', in the V2 conditions, see (19d). The subsequent positions of DP1 and DP2 are separated by a high temporal adverb, such as *letztens* 'recently'.[9] The two DP-positions are filled by the subject *der gewebte Mantel* 'the woven coat' and the object *den vorsichtigen Imker* 'the cautious beekeeper' corresponding to the subject<object (SO) and OS condition

9 See Frey & Pittner (1998) or Frey (2003) for an overview of base positions of adverbials in German.

respectively. The nominative subject was always inanimate and the accusative object was always animate. Both nouns were always masculine singular such that they exhibit unambiguous case marking in German. A low process-related adverbial, such as *total* 'totally', separated the lower argument from the clause-final position (V) which was filled only in the V-FINAL condition, namely by the participle of the lexical verb, such as *verblüfft* 'baffled' in (19b). The two clause-internal adverbials have been inserted to separate the critical DP-regions and the clause-final verb so that effects of one region would not immediately spill over onto the next region. All conditions contained an embedded clause as a final spillover region, which was divided into four segments: a subordination, a definite DP, and two segments that showed larger variation between items in order to create meaningful continuations for all scenarios. The lexical verb was either an experiencer object verb in the EXPERIENCER conditions, such as *verblüffen* 'baffle' in (19b–19e), or a non-experiencer verb in the NON-EXPERIENCER conditions, such as *schützen* 'protect' in (19f–19g). The non-experiencer verbs do not form a natural class, however, many of them are causative verbs. They have in common that they are non-psych verbs which take inanimate subjects (stimulus) and animate objects (theme/patient). In some of the items, the low adverb and the spillover regions differed between the two verb classes in order to maintain plausibility.

(19) a. CONTEXT:
Traditionelle Methoden sind immer noch das Mittel der Wahl für Leute, die mit Bienen arbeiten.

'Traditional methods are still the means of choice for people who work with bees.'

b. EXPERIENCER–V-FINAL–SO

Offenbar	| hat	| der	gewebte	Mantel	| letztens	| den	vorsichtigen
apparently	has	the	woven	coat	recently	the	cautious
PREFIELD	C	DP1			HIGHADV	DP2	

Imker	| total	| verblüfft,	| obwohl	| die	Bienen	| ziemlich
beekeeper	totally	baffled	although	the	bees	quite
	LOWADV	V	SPILL1	SPILL2		SPILL3

angriffslustig	| waren.
aggressive	were
	SPILL4

'Apparently, the woven coat recently baffled the cautious beekeeper totally although the bees were quite aggressive.'

c. EXPERIENCER–V-FINAL–OS
Offenbar hat den vorsichtigen Imker letztens der gewebte Mantel
apparently has the cautious beekeeper recently the woven coat
total verblüfft, obwohl die Bienen ziemlich angriffslustig waren.
totally baffled although the bees quite aggressive were

d. EXPERIENCER–V2–SO
Offenbar verblüffte der gewebte Mantel letztens den vorsichtigen
apparently baffled the woven coat recently the cautious
Imker total, obwohl die Bienen ziemlich angriffslustig waren.
beekeeper totally although the bees quite aggressive were

e. EXPERIENCER–V2–OS
Offenbar verblüffte den vorsichtigen Imker letztens der gewebte
apparently baffled the cautious beekeeper recently the woven
Mantel total, obwohl die Bienen ziemlich angriffslustig waren.
coat totally although the bees quite aggressive were

f. NON-EXPERIENCER–V-FINAL/V2–SO
Offenbar hat/ schützte der gewebte Mantel letztens den vorsichtigen
apparently has/ protected the woven coat recently the cautious
Imker genug geschützt/∅, obwohl die Bienen ziemlich angriffslustig
beekeeper enough protected although the bees quite aggressive
waren.
were
'Apparently, the woven coat recently protected the cautious beekeeper sufficiently although the bees were quite aggressive.'

g. NON-EXPERIENCER–V-FINAL/V2–OS
Offenbar hat/ schützte den vorsichtigen Imker letztens der
apparently has/ protected the cautious beekeeper recently the
gewebte Mantel genug geschützt/ ∅, obwohl die Bienen ziemlich
woven coat enough protected although the bees quite
angriffslustig waren.
aggressive were

h. COMPEHENSION QUESTION:
Werden neue Methoden bevorzugt bei der Arbeit mit Bienen?
'Are novel methods preferred in beekeeping?'
correct answer = *Nein* 'No' wrong answer = *Ja* 'Yes'

The factor V-TYPE differs from the other two factors in so far as the individual lexical verbs are fixed with respect to the different lexicalizations. Each EO-verb was paired with a corresponding non-experiencer verb, such as *verblüffen* 'baffle' with *schützen* 'protect'. Moreover, the number of suitable verb pairs is rather restricted so that we only used 16 different verb pairs in this experiment. Each of these pairs appeared twice in the experimental material, although with different accompanying lexical material. However, we ensured that each participant saw each lexicalization and each lexical verb of the pair only once during the experiment, e. g. the EXPERIENCER verb with lexicalization A and the NON-EXPERIENCER verb with lexicalization B. Apart from that, the factors varied according to a Latin square design.

The AGENTIVE control structures, illustrated in (20), consisted of the same number and types of segments as the experimental items in (19). In contrast to the experimental items, they contained verbs that select an agent, such as *zerreißen* 'rip' and more prototypical arguments: The nominative subject was animate and the accusative object was inanimate. Like in the experimental items, the DPs were always definite, masculine, singular and contained an adjectival modifier. These control structures were constructed only in the canonical SO order. They provide a baseline for a prototypical subject-first preference and allow to gauge whether the non-prototypical animacy properties of the experimental items led to a deviation of this preference.

(20) AGENTIVE-controls

a. CONTEXT:
Die Arbeiter auf der Baustelle leiden oft darunter, dass zu wenig Material für die anstehenden Arbeiten vorhanden ist.

'The workers on the construction site often suffer from the fact that too little material for the upcoming work is available.'

b. V-FINAL–SO
Deswegen | hat | der dicke Maler | heute | den alten Lappen |
hence has the fat painter today the old rag
kurzerhand | zerissen, | damit | die Lehrlinge | beide etwas |
quickly ripped so that the apprentices both something
zum Abwischen | hatten.
to wipe had

'Hence the fat painter ripped up the old rag today so that both apprentices had something to wipe.'

c. V2–SO
Deswegen zeriss der dicke Maler heute den alten Lappen kurzerhand,
hence ripped the fat painter today the old rag quickly
damit die Lehrlinge beide etwas zum Abwischen hatten.
so that the apprentices both something to wipe had

d. COMPREHENSION QUESTION:
Haben die Bauarbeiter zu wenig Material?
'Did the construction workers lack material?'
correct answer = *Ja* 'Yes' wrong answer = *Nein* 'No'

The CONFIGURATIONAL control structures, illustrated in (21), also consisted of the same number and types of segments, as the experimental items. These control structures contain *configurational* verbs, such as *umgeben* 'surround', and two inanimate arguments. This verb class resembles experiencer object verbs in two respects, which makes them useful control structures: First, they take inanimate nominative subjects, and second, they also show a relatively unmarked object<subject order. However, the unmarked object<subject order depends on the definiteness of the subject. Therefore, the nominative subject of these verbs was always an indefinite DP. The accusative object, however, was always definite. Both DPs were masculine singular and contained an adjectival modifier. Like the experimental items, these control structures varied according to the two factors V-POSITION and WORD ORDER as shown in (21). All stimuli are given in the online appendix.

(21) CONFIGURATIONAL-controls

a. CONTEXT:
Die Archäologen untersuchen die auffälligen Steinformationen in der Nähe des alten Klosters. Etwas war hier besonders.
'The archaeologists investigate the peculiar stone formation in the vicinity of the old monastery. Something was special here.'

b. V-FINAL–SO
Offenbar | hat | ein hoher Schutzwall | damals | den weiten
apparently has a high protective barrier back then the large
Acker | vollständig | umgeben, | damit | die Ernte | in unruhigen
field completely surrounded so that the harvest in turbulent
Zeiten | verteidigt werden konnte.
times protected be could
'Apparently, a large protective barrier surrounded the large field entirely back then so that the harvest could be protected in turbulent times.'

c. V-FINAL–OS
Offenbar hat den weiten Acker damals ein hoher Schutzwall
apparently has the large field back then a high protective barrier

vollständig umgeben, damit die Ernte in unruhigen Zeiten
completely surrounded so that the harvest in turbulent times
verteidigt werden konnte.
protected be could

d. V2–SO
Offenbar umgab ein hoher Schutzwall damals den
apparently surrounded a high protective barrier back then the
weiten Acker vollständig, damit die Ernte in unruhigen Zeiten
large field completely so that the harvest in turbulent times
verteidigt werden konnte.
protected be could

e. V2–OS
Offenbar umgab den weiten Acker damals ein hoher
apparently surrounden the large field back then a high
Schutzwall vollständig, damit die Ernte in unruhigen Zeiten
protective barrier completely so that the harvest in turbulent times
verteidigt werden konnte.
protected be could

f. COMPREHENSION QUESTION:
Umgab der Schutzwall nur den Marktplatz?
'Did the protective barrier surround the market square?'
correct answer = *No* 'No' wrong answer = *Ja* 'Yes'

6.4.2.4 Data analysis

We removed all data points with reading times larger than 3 seconds (0.018 % of the data). The participants' accuracy in response to the comprehension questions ranged from 78–97 % (mean 90 %). No participant was excluded but we dismissed all trials of the experimental items with a falsely answered comprehension question (8.4% of the data). The statistical handling of the data was identical to the procedure described for Experiment 2.

The statistical analysis proceeded in four steps: The first analysis covered only the initial segments from the V2-position until the high adverb. The V-FINAL conditions of both verb types are identical because for both verbs the auxiliary *hat* 'has' appears in the V2-position. Hence, we analyzed this region with a 3 × 2 analysis, featuring three types of verbs in the V2-position, auxiliaries, EXPERIENCER and NON-EXPERIENCER and the two levels of WORD ORDER, SO and OS. In a second step, we analyzed the clause-final verb and the spillover region. This analysis was carried out with two separate models for the V2 and the V-FINAL condition respectively. In the third step, we compared the SO conditions with the AGENTIVE controls. In the fourth step, we analyzed the CONFIGURATIONAL controls.

6.4.3 Results and Discussion

6.4.3.1 Experimental items

6.4.3.1.1 Main clause

A graphical summary of the reading times of the main clause segments is given in Figure 6.7. On the DP1-segment, the analysis revealed that the AUXILIARY conditions showed significantly shorter reading times than the EXPERIENCER condition ($t = 3.7550$), and than the NON-EXPERIENCER condition ($t = 2.4896$). These differences are robust for both WORD ORDER conditions. Whereas the EXPERIENCER condition showed numerically the longest reading times, the contrast to the NON-EXPERIENCER condition is non-significant. On the high adverb *letztens*, we detected a significant contrast between the EXPERIENCER-SO and the NON-EXPERIENCER-SO condition ($t = 2.0207$) with longer reading times for the latter. Additionally, the model also revealed a significant interaction ($t = -2.1677$), which indicates that the SO-order caused longer reading times in the NON-EXPERIENCER condition, whereas the opposite holds for the EXPERIENCER condition and the AUXILIARY condition, in which the OS-order led to longer reading times. On the DP2-segment, the analysis revealed a significant contrast of WORD ORDER for the EXPERIENCER verbs ($t = 4.5269$) with longer reading times for the OS-order. Additionally, the interaction terms indicate that the WORD ORDER effect is smaller for the AUXILIARY and the NON-EXPERIENCER condition. Subsequent analyses revealed that reading times for the OS condition are significantly longer in the AUXILIARY condition too, whereas they are only numerically longer in the NON-EXPERIENCER condition and did not reach significance. On the low adverb *total*, we found a significant contrast between the NON-EXPERIENCER-SO and the AUXILIARY-SO condition ($t = -2.1027$) with longer reading times for the former. The exact model outputs of these analyses are given in Tables 6.27 to 6.30.

Note that for the V-FINAL conditions (AUXILIARY), which we consider the baseline with respect to default processing of arguments, we have found an effect of WORD ORDER only on a single segment: On the DP2-segment, reading times for the OS condition were longer than in the SO condition ($t = 3.0534$), see Table 6.31.

6.4.3.1.2 Verb + Spillover

The reading times for the clause-final verb and the following spillover region are displayed in Figure 6.8. On the clause-final verb, the analyses revealed the shortest

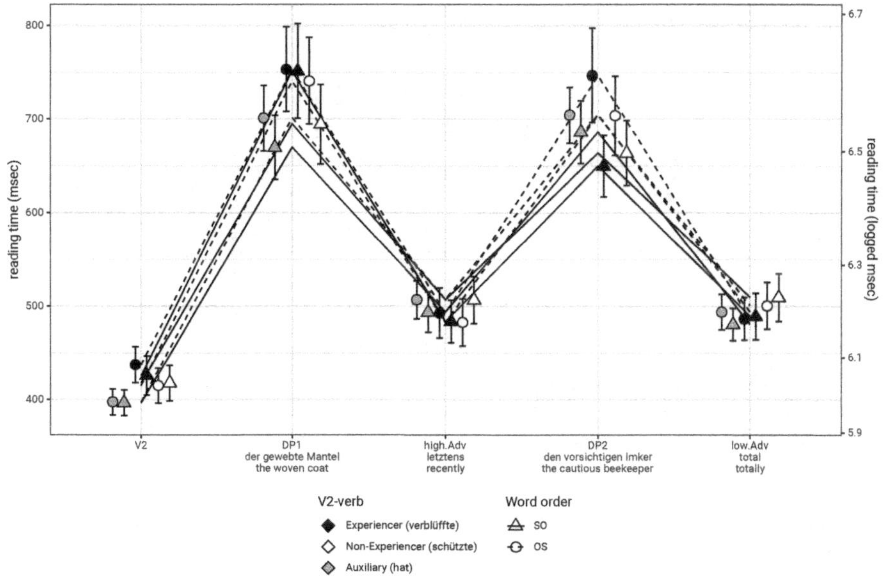

Figure 6.7: Mean reading times for the initial part of Experiment 5 (95 % CIs)

reading times for the EXPERIENCER-SO conditions with significant contrasts to the NON-EXPERIENCER (t = 2.0361) and to the OS condition (t = 2.3428). Within the NON-EXPERIENCER condition the WORD ORDER difference is non-significant, see Table 6.32.

The respective analyses of the spillover region of the V2 condition and the V-FINAL condition indicated only non-significant tendencies for segment 1–3 and a significant contrast only on the final segments, see Tables 6.33 to 6.36. We summarized the reading times for spillover segment 1 and 2, as well as for spillover segment 3 and 4 to obtain a more robust pattern, as displayed in Figure 6.9. In the V2 subset (small icons), we found a significant interaction of V-TYPE and WORD ORDER (t = −2.0100) in the first region, indicating that OS-order causes longer reading times for the EXPERIENCER verbs, whereas OS-order causes shorter reading times for NON-EXPERIENCER-verbs. In the final region, the analysis revealed two main effects, with longer reading times for EXPERIENCER-verbs (t = 3.3371) and OS-order (t = 2.0726). In the V-FINAL subset (large icons), no effect could be found on the first spillover region. In the final region, however, the analysis revealed a significant contrast of V-TYPE (t = 3.8937) indicating that the EXPERIENCER-SO condition showed longer reading times than the NON-EXPERIENCER-SO condition, see Tables 6.37 to 6.39.

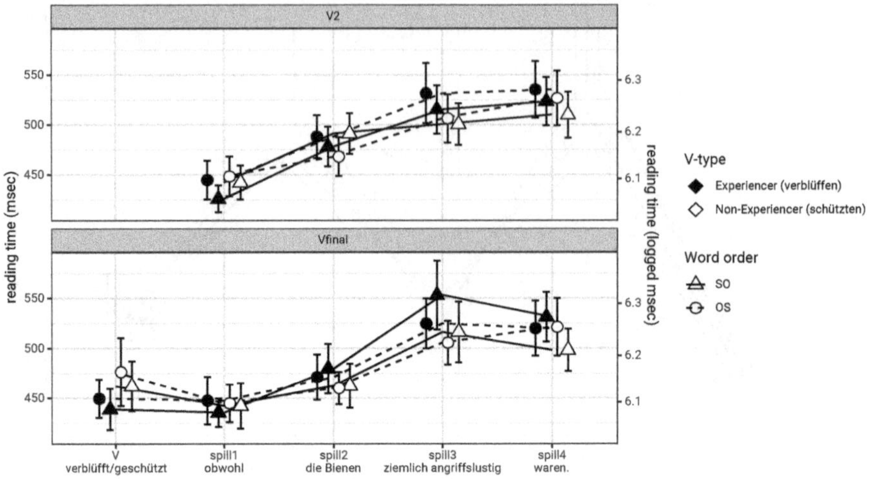

Figure 6.8: Mean reading times for the clause-final verb and the spillover region in Experiment 5 (95 % CIs)

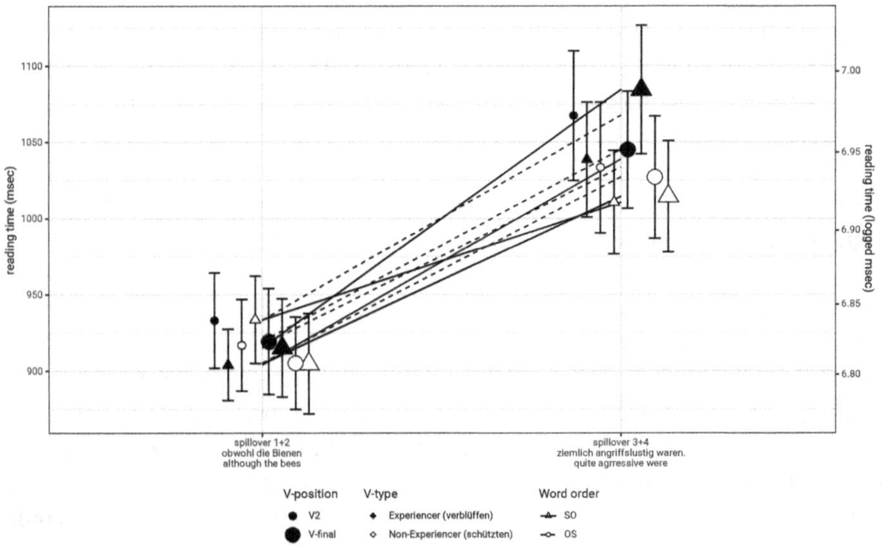

Figure 6.9: Mean reading times for the summarized regions of the spillover are in Experiment 5 (95 % CIs)

6.4.3.1.3 Interim discussion

On the first DP, we found only a categorial contrast between the auxiliaries and longer reading times for the lexical verbs. This effect is present on subjects and objects alike. We assume that this is most likely a spillover effect from the preceding segment, the V2-position, reflecting differences of the initial processing such as lexical access, due to length and frequency. On the high adverb *letztens*, the NON-EXPERIENCER-SO condition shows prolonged reading times in comparison to the other conditions. This indicates that, in this condition, some additional or demanding process is initiated. Two possibilities come to our mind: First, the subject is incrementally integrated into the parse and some incongruity or implausibility triggers prolonged reading times. Second, the finite verb is reconstructed with the encounter of the subject, as it would be the case for intransitive verbs, and the prolonged reading times are a reflection of the initiated interpretation process. However, visual inspection of individual items did not support either of this hypothesis. Therefore, we must leave open what the reason for this effect is. On the second DP, we found longer reading times for the non-canonical OS order across verb types. However, the strength of this reading time difference was modulated as a function of the verb in the V2-position. The baseline group with the auxiliary in the V2-position showed a robust reading time difference between SO and OS order. This difference is approximately twice as large in the EXPERIENCER-V2 condition whereas, in the NON-EXPERIENCER-V2 condition, it is smaller than in the baseline condition. This modulation indicates that the different verb classes interact with the word order which must reflect verb-related processing. Interestingly, the modulation seems to affect the slow-down of OS and the speed-up of SO uniformly, i. e. for all verb classes the two orders seem to be distanced from a potential zero value, see Figure 6.7. On the low adverb *total*, we found longer reading times of the NON-EXPERIENCER-SO in comparison to the respective V-FINAL baseline condition. This effect looks similar to the one that appeared on the high adverb. Moreover, this penalty for the NON-EXPERIENCER-SO condition continues into the first summarized spillover region but reverses in the final spillover region. At the clause-final verb, we found effects of verb type and word order. This matches the predictions for anticipatory assignment of thematic roles in that it probably reflects a reranking of the thematic roles after the lexical verb was encountered. In the spillover region, we found that, in the V2 condition, the penalty for the NON-EXPERIENCER-SO continues on the first two spillover segments, which we also interpret as a reflection of a thematic reranking process. On the two final segments, the factors V-TYPE and WORD ORDER affect the reading times uniformly, which we assume to reflect discourse integration costs, which are higher for experiencer verbs and non-canonical object<subject order. In the V-FINAL condition, on the hand, no ef-

fect turned up on the first two spillover segments, indicating that the thematic reranking is completed on the clause-final verb. Only on the last two segments, we find again an interaction of V-TYPE and WORD ORDER. We assume that this interaction also reflects discourse integration, like in the V2 condition. However, we must leave open why the SO order seems to be dispreferred in the V-FINAL condition only.

6.4.3.2 Agentive controls

A graphical summary of the main clause segments of the AGENTIVE controls and the SO subset of the experimental items is given in Figure 6.10.[10] The analysis of the AGENTIVE controls revealed only one significant contrast: On the DP1-segment, which was always the subject, we found a simple effect of V-POSITION with longer reading times for the V2 condition. This was confirmed by a combined analysis of the DP1-segment for the AGENTIVE controls and the SO subset of the experimental items, which revealed a significant contrast for V-POSITION with longer reading times for the V2 condition (t = 3.3680) that remains significant across verb types, see Table 6.40.

Like in previous analysis, we aggregated the reading times for the spillover segments 1+2, and 2+3, as shown in Figure 6.11. The analysis of the spillover regions did not reveal any new contrast in addition to the primary analysis above. Generally, the AGENTIVE controls pattern with the EXPERIENCER verbs. No contrast to the experimental conditions reaches significance, see Tables 6.41 to 6.42.

6.4.3.2.1 Interim discussion

The comparison with the AGENTIVE controls strengthened the assumption that the V-POSITION effect on the DP1-segment is a general contrast of auxiliaries and lexical verbs and not verb-type-specific. Furthermore, the comparison with the corresponding conditions of the experimental items did not yield any significant contrasts which indicates that the non-prototypical animacy properties of the arguments of the experimental items did not induce serious differences in reading times.

---

10 Note that the content of the respective segments of the experimental items and the AGENTIVE controls are not identical and therefore contain length differences, especially the larger segments such as DP1 and DP2. These differences are accounted for in the statistical analysis. Note also that the V-FINAL condition of the EXPERIENCER condition and the NON-EXPERIENCER condition are identical until the final segment of this plot. They are represented by two different points for technical reasons.

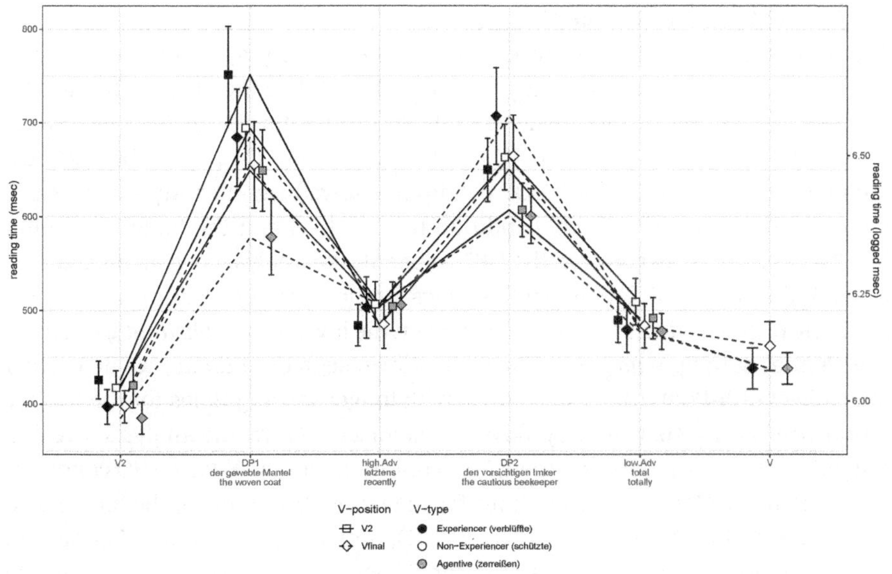

Figure 6.10: Mean reading times of the main clause segments for the experimental items of Experiment 5 and the AGENTIVE controls in the SO order only (95 % CIs)

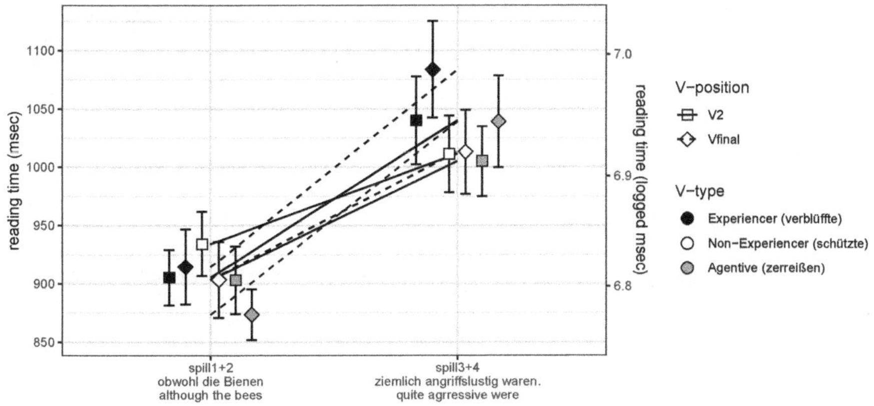

Figure 6.11: Mean reading times for the summed spillover regions of Experiment 5 with the AGENTIVE controls (95 % CIs)

6.4.3.3 Configurational controls

The reading times of the CONFIGURATIONAL controls are graphically summarized in Figure 6.12. The statistical analysis revealed the following effects: On the DP1-segment, we found two main effects with shorter reading times for the V-FINAL condition (t = −2.3378) and the SO condition (t = −3.2434), see Table 6.43. On the high adverb *damals*, the V2-OS condition showed significantly shorter reading times than the V-FINAL-OS condition (t = 2.7019) and the V2-SO condition (t = 2.8287), see Table 6.44. On the DP2-segment, the analysis revealed a main effect of V-POSITION with longer reading times for the V-FINAL condition (t = 3.8157), see Table 6.45. No effects could be detected on the low adverb *vollständig* or on the clause-final participle *umgeben*. On the spillover segment 1 *damit*, we detected a main effect of V-POSITION (t = −3.1641) with longer reading times for the V2 condition, see Table 6.46. On the spillover segment 2 *die Ernte*, the analysis revealed a significant contrast between the V2-SO condition and the V-FINAL-SO condition (t = 2.2100) with longer reading times for the latter. Additionally, the model also yielded a significant interaction (t = −2.5702), indicating that in the V2 condition OS showed longer reading times than the SO whereas the opposite holds in the V-FINAL condition, see Table 6.47. No effects could be detected on the remaining two segments.

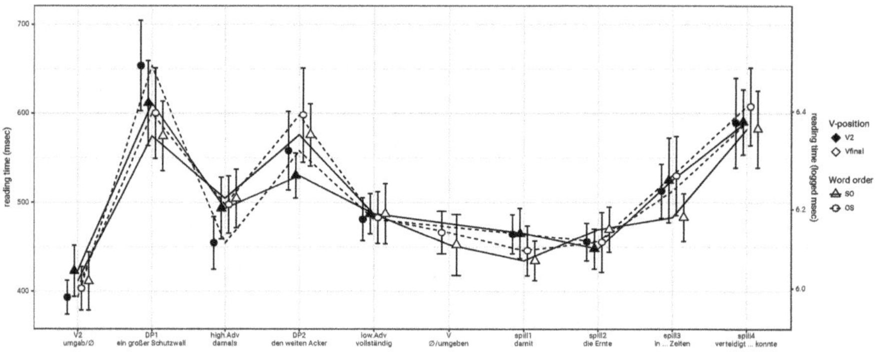

Figure 6.12: Mean reading times for the CONFIGURATIONAL controls in Experiment 5 (95 % CIs)

6.4.3.3.1 Interim discussion

On the DP1-segment, we found the same contrast with shorter reading times for the V-FINAL condition which was present for the other verb types above. This further strengthens the assumption that this effect is a spillover effect from the preceding segment, which reflects the smaller processing demand for the initial activation of the auxiliary. Additionally, we found shorter reading times for the SO conditions on this segment. However, considering that this effect reached significance only for this verb class, it is likely that this is a definiteness effect. Remember that, only for the CONFIGURATIONAL controls, the arguments differed in definiteness. On the high adverb *damals*, we found an interaction that shows the profile of an object-first preference only when the lexical verb appeared in the V2-position. This effect appears to be very local. In contrast to the other verb types, we didn't find a reading time difference corresponding to WORD ORDER on the second DP but only a contrast of V-TYPE. Additionally, it is rather unexpected that the V2 conditions show longer reading times. We suspect that the speed-up of the V2 condition on this segment stands in a relation with the relative slow-down on the first spillover segment. Similarly, the interaction on the spillover segment 2 indicates that, in the V-FINAL condition, some main clause related processing is still going on whereas the argument order related aspects are already completed in the V2 condition.

6.4.4 General discussion

In line with our predictions, we found a subject-first preference in the V-FINAL baseline condition. This preference manifested itself on the DP2-segment with shorter reading times for the SO condition and is the signature of the default argument processing. Also in line with the predictions of the V2-Reconstruction Hypothesis, the EXPERIENCER condition patterned with the V-FINAL baseline (except for DP1) and the AGENTIVE controls, as if the arguments are processed by the default routine despite the lexical verb surfaced in the V2-position. Only at the second argument, we found the expected verb-type dependent modulation of the WORD ORDER preference. This is the first segment where the V2-Reconstruction Hypothesis predicts verb-related processing effects to appear because with the encounter of the DP2-segment the reconstruction site of the verb can be postulated. In contrast to our predictions, however, the EXPERIENCER verbs did not reflect an OS preference (experiencer-first) but instead showed a stronger subject-first preference than the V-FINAL baseline and the NON-EXPERIENCER condition. The NON-EXPERIENCER verbs, on the other hand, showed a penalty for the canonical SO order that surfaces after both arguments and extends to the first half of the spillover region. We interpreted the latter effect as a thematic reranking process that is likewise observable at the clause-final participles in the V-FINAL condition. The prolonged reading times on the high adverb, directly following the first argument in the NON-EXPERIENCER-SO condition indicates that a verb-related process may start directly after the subject. As for now, it remains unclear, what causes this effect and why it only appears for NON-EXPERIENCER-verbs and neither for the EXPERIENCER verbs nor for the AGENTIVE verbs. A similar indication for a immediate argument structure processing is observable for the CONFIGURATIONAL controls, for which V2-OS shows shorter reading times, maybe reflecting an object-first preference. However, effects for these verb classes have to be interpreted with care because the two arguments also involved a definiteness difference. The profile of these early effects match the predictions of the incremental processing hypothesis and constitutes a problem for the V2-Reconstruction Hypothesis. One possibility: Even under the V2-Reconstruction Hypothesis, we need some routine that keeps track of the incoming material which decides when the finite verb must be reconstructed and the interpretation process will be initiated. The early effects could then be interactions with this monitoring process. As for now, we must leave this issue to further research.

Our experiments reproduced some results of previous studies. Like Scheepers et al. (2000), we found a modulation of the S<O-preference involving experiencer object verbs. In contrast to their results, we detected an increase of this preference rather than a mitigation. However, our study used only unambiguously marked arguments which could influence the anticipatory assignment of thematic roles, as could the fact that our material involved an animacy contrast. Furthermore, Scheepers et al. (2000) found the mitigation effect in late eye tracking measures. Therefore the correlates of their effect might have to be searched in the spillover region. Although we detected some residuals of verb-argument processing in the spillover region, the effects are not uniform for V2 and V-FINAL sentences and thus not straightforwardly identifiable. A further contrast that may influence the timing of the results is that Scheepers et al. (2000) contrasted main clauses with embedded clauses whereas we contrasted only main clauses but with different verb forms. In relation to Temme & Verhoeven (2016), it seems that the experiencer-first preference may only be reflected in higher order processing routines related to the discourse structure which might be indicated towards the end of the spillover region. At least in the final region of the EXPERIENCER-V-FINAL condition, an OS-preference showed up. This indicates that the experiencer-first preference might not originate from structural properties but relates to higher order semantico-pragmatic aspects.[11]

In sum, the results of this experiment support the main predictions of the V2-Reconstruction Hypothesis. However, we also identified an effect that appeared

11 This assumption is restricted to accusative experiencer objects. Datives experiencers are certainly different and may be structurally exceptional too.

earlier than expected. Clearly, follow-up studies are in need to provided a more detailed picture of the processing routines in relation to the thematic structure.

Table 6.27: Output of the LME model for DP1-segment in Experiment 5
`lmer(log.RT~V2.verb*word.order+segment.length+trial+`
`(1+segment.length+trial|participant.ID)+(1+word.order|stimulus.ID))`

	criticized model			raw model		
	Estimate	SE	t	Estimate	SE	t
Intercept (AUXILIARY SO)	5.7785	0.0975	59.2692	5.8477	0.1054	55.4920
V2.VERB (EXPERIENCER)	0.1126	0.0300	3.7550	0.1210	0.0337	3.5948
V2.VERB (NON-EXPERIENCER)	0.0739	0.0297	2.4896	0.0676	0.0336	2.0129
WORD ORDER (OS)	0.0294	0.0303	0.9696	0.0312	0.0331	0.9416
segment length	0.0262	0.0042	6.2237	0.0234	0.0047	4.9997
trial	0.0000	0.0008	−0.0023	−0.0003	0.0008	−0.3744
EXPERIENCER:OS	−0.0027	0.0426	−0.0636	−0.0172	0.0479	−0.3587
NON-EXPERIENCER:OS	−0.0012	0.0421	−0.0293	0.0086	0.0475	0.1805

Table 6.28: Output of the LME model for high adverb *letztens* in Experiment 5
`lmer(log.RT~V2.verb*word.order+segment.length+trial+`
`(1+word.order+trial|participant.ID)+(1|stimulus.ID))`

	criticized model			raw model		
	Estimate	SE	t	Estimate	SE	t
Intercept (EXPERIENCER SO)	6.1446	0.0670	91.6861	6.1473	0.0723	85.0240
V2.VERB (AUXILIARY)	−0.0029	0.0179	−0.1637	0.0032	0.0226	0.1424
V2.VERB (NON-EXPERIENCER)	0.0412	0.0204	2.0207	0.0452	0.0259	1.7475
WORD ORDER (OS)	0.0186	0.0244	0.7602	0.0198	0.0287	0.6892
segment length	−0.0029	0.0098	−0.2964	−0.0009	0.0105	−0.0818
trial	−0.0026	0.0004	−6.5404	−0.0031	0.0005	−5.9256
AUXILIARY:OS	0.0169	0.0256	0.6608	0.0200	0.0322	0.6200
NON-EXPERIENCER:OS	−0.0635	0.0293	−2.1677	−0.0602	0.0370	−1.6263

Table 6.29: Output of the LME model for DP2-segment in Experiment 5
`lmer(log.RT~V2.verb*word.order+segment.length+trial+(1+segment.length+trial|participant.ID)+(1|stimulus.ID))`

	criticized model			raw model		
	Estimate	SE	t	Estimate	SE	t
Intercept (EXPERIENCER SO)	5.8360	0.0699	83.4730	5.8697	0.0802	73.1514
V2.VERB (NON-EXPERIENCER)	0.0358	0.0284	1.2620	0.0230	0.0333	0.6909
V2.VERB (AUXILIARY)	0.0197	0.0248	0.7945	0.0374	0.0291	1.2851
WORD ORDER (OS)	0.1312	0.0290	4.5269	0.1218	0.0340	3.5815
segment length	0.0243	0.0033	7.4820	0.0230	0.0035	6.4936
trial	−0.0022	0.0007	−3.1249	−0.0022	0.0007	−3.2238
AUXILIARY:OS	−0.0773	0.0407	−1.9004	−0.0603	0.0477	−1.2655
NON-EXPERIENCER:OS	−0.0467	0.0354	−1.3187	−0.0654	0.0415	−1.5739

Table 6.30: Output of the LME model for the low adverb *total* in Experiment 5
`lmer(log.RT~V2.verb*word.order+segment.length+trial+(1+trial|participant.ID)+(1+word.order|stimulus.ID))`

	criticized model			raw model		
	Estimate	SE	t	Estimate	SE	t
Intercept (NON-EXPERIENCER SO)	6.0754	0.0330	184.1343	6.1037	0.0379	161.1473
V2.VERB (AUXILIARY)	−0.0348	0.0166	−2.1027	−0.0476	0.0209	−2.2758
V2.VERB (EXPERIENCER)	−0.0321	0.0189	−1.7035	−0.0386	0.0238	−1.6226
WORD ORDER (OS)	−0.0080	0.0224	−0.3594	−0.0137	0.0279	−0.4903
segment length	0.0113	0.0024	4.6134	0.0109	0.0030	3.6628
trial	−0.0031	0.0004	−7.2363	−0.0030	0.0006	−5.2831
AUXILIARY:OS	0.0255	0.0232	1.1005	0.0412	0.0293	1.4049
EXPERIENCER:OS	0.0038	0.0269	0.1424	0.0101	0.0340	0.2965

Table 6.31: Output of the LME model for DP2-segment in the V-FINAL condition in Experiment 5
`lmer(log.RT~word.order+segment.length+trial+(1|participant.ID)+(1|stimulus.ID))`

	criticized model			raw model		
	Estimate	SE	t	Estimate	SE	t
Intercept (SO)	5.8881	0.0994	59.2222	5.9624	0.1094	54.5052
WORD ORDER (OS)	0.0679	0.0222	3.0534	0.0487	0.0255	1.9065
segment length	0.0233	0.0039	5.9571	0.0205	0.0044	4.6460
trial	−0.0019	0.0006	−3.0726	−0.0021	0.0007	−2.8609

Table 6.32: Output of the LME model for clause-final verb in Experiment 5
`lmer(log.RT~verb.type+word.order+segment.length+trial+`
`(1+segment.length|participant.ID)+(1|stimulus.ID))`

	criticized model			raw model		
	Estimate	SE	t	Estimate	SE	t
Intercept (EXPERIENCER SO)	6.0326	0.0583	103.5089	5.9586	0.0721	82.6040
V-TYPE (NON-EXPERIENCER)	0.0388	0.0190	2.0361	0.0531	0.0237	2.2407
WORD ORDER (OS)	0.0437	0.0187	2.3428	0.0342	0.0234	1.4627
segment length	−0.0023	0.0052	−0.4377	0.0066	0.0070	0.9429
trial	−0.0021	0.0004	−5.6392	−0.0025	0.0005	−5.2200
V-TYPE:WORD ORDER	−0.0292	0.0271	−1.0789	−0.0214	0.0340	−0.6315

Table 6.33: Output of the LME model for spillover segment 1 *obwohl* of the V2-subgroup in Experiment 5
`lmer(log.RT~verb.type*word.order+segment.length+trial+`
`(1+segment.length+trial|participant.ID)+(1|stimulus.ID))`

	criticized model			raw model		
	Estimate	SE	t	Estimate	SE	t
Intercept (EXPERIENCER SO)	5.9718	0.0412	145.0120	5.9511	0.0446	133.3687
V-TYPE (NON-EXPERIENCER)	0.0310	0.0159	1.9461	0.0371	0.0191	1.9457
WORD ORDER (OS)	0.0103	0.0162	0.6375	0.0273	0.0193	1.4133
segment length	0.0095	0.0059	1.6200	0.0130	0.0064	2.0135
trial	−0.0013	0.0004	−3.1935	−0.0014	0.0005	−2.8916
NON-EXPERIENCER:OS	−0.0232	0.0228	−1.0188	−0.0289	0.0271	−1.0645

Table 6.34: Output of the LME model for spillover segment 2 *die Bienen* of the V2-subgroup in Experiment 5
`lmer(log.RT~verb.type*word.order+segment.length+trial+`
`(1+segment.length|participant.ID)+(1|stimulus.ID))`

	criticized model			raw model		
	Estimate	SE	t	Estimate	SE	t
Intercept (EXPERIENCER SO)	5.9718	0.0412	145.0120	5.9511	0.0446	133.3687
V-TYPE (NON-EXPERIENCER)	0.0310	0.0159	1.9461	0.0371	0.0191	1.9457
WORD ORDER (OS)	0.0103	0.0162	0.6375	0.0273	0.0193	1.4133
segment length	0.0095	0.0059	1.6200	0.0130	0.0064	2.0135
trial	−0.0013	0.0004	−3.1935	−0.0014	0.0005	−2.8916
NON-EXPERIENCER:OS	−0.0232	0.0228	−1.0188	−0.0289	0.0271	−1.0645

Table 6.35: Output of the LME model for spillover segment 4 *waren* of the V2-subgroup in Experiment 5
`lmer(log.RT~verb.type*word.order+segment.length+trial+(1+segment.length+trial|participant.ID)+(1|stimulus.ID))`

	criticized model			raw model		
	Estimate	SE	t	Estimate	SE	t
Intercept (EXPERIENCER OS)	6.0971	0.0388	157.1231	6.0962	0.0433	140.8018
V-TYPE (NON-EXPERIENCER)	−0.0522	0.0216	−2.4194	−0.0383	0.0257	−1.4928
WORD ORDER (SO)	−0.0502	0.0212	−2.3665	−0.0365	0.0254	−1.4393
segment length	0.0096	0.0027	3.5166	0.0105	0.0029	3.5912
trial	−0.0033	0.0006	−5.3642	−0.0031	0.0006	−4.9109
NON-EXPERIENCER:SO	0.0418	0.0298	1.4009	0.0135	0.0356	0.3782

Table 6.36: Output of the LME model for spillover segment 4 *waren* of the V-FINAL-subgroup in Experiment 5
`lmer(log.RT~verb.type*word.order+segment.length+trial+(1+trial|participant.ID)+(1|stimulus.ID))`

	criticized model			raw model		
	Estimate	SE	t	Estimate	SE	t
Intercept (EXPERIENCER SO)	6.1101	0.0484	126.1970	6.1389	0.0511	120.1603
V-TYPE (NON-EXPERIENCER)	−0.0518	0.0243	−2.1268	−0.0679	0.0290	−2.3380
WORD ORDER (OS)	−0.0030	0.0240	−0.1238	−0.0332	0.0284	−1.1695
segment length	0.0071	0.0024	2.9559	0.0063	0.0027	2.3290
trial	−0.0021	0.0007	−3.1663	−0.0020	0.0008	−2.5204
NON-EXPERIENCER:OS	0.0149	0.0341	0.4363	0.0623	0.0405	1.5365

Table 6.37: Output of the LME model for spillover segment 1+2 *obwohl die Bienen* of the V2-subgroup in Experiment 5
`lmer(log.RT~verb.type*word.order+segment.length+trial+(1+segment.length+trial|participant.ID)+(1|stimulus.ID))`

	criticized model			raw model		
	Estimate	SE	t	Estimate	SE	t
Intercept (EXPERIENCER SO)	6.6258	0.0566	117.0060	6.6388	0.0602	110.3324
V-TYPE (NON-EXPERIENCER)	0.0264	0.0155	1.7041	0.0322	0.0176	1.8280
WORD ORDER (OS)	0.0252	0.0156	1.6190	0.0291	0.0177	1.6411
segment length	0.0079	0.0031	2.5330	0.0075	0.0033	2.2926
trial	−0.0016	0.0004	−4.0063	−0.0015	0.0004	−3.5846
NON-EXPERIENCER:OS	−0.0442	0.0220	−2.0100	−0.0512	0.0249	−2.0528

Table 6.38: Output of the LME model for spillover segment 3+4 *ziemlich angriffslustig waren* of the V2-subgroup in Experiment 5
`lmer(log.RT~verb.type+word.order+segment.length+trial+(1+segment.length+trial|participant.ID)+(1|stimulus.ID))`

	criticized model			raw model		
	Estimate	SE	t	Estimate	SE	t
Intercept (NON-EXPERIENCER SO)	6.5867	0.0607	108.5453	6.5806	0.0668	98.5427
V-TYPE (EXPERIENCER)	0.0418	0.0125	3.3371	0.0376	0.0150	2.5013
WORD ORDER (OS)	0.0255	0.0123	2.0726	0.0251	0.0148	1.6909
segment length	0.0094	0.0017	5.6427	0.0101	0.0019	5.3069
trial	−0.0026	0.0006	−4.7164	−0.0026	0.0006	−4.3485

Table 6.39: Output of the LME model for spillover segment 3+4 *ziemlich angriffslustig waren* of the V-FINAL-subgroup in Experiment 5
`lmer(log.RT~verb.type*word.order+segment.length+trial+(1+segment.length+trial|participant.ID)+(1|stimulus.ID))`

	criticized model			raw model		
	Estimate	SE	t	Estimate	SE	t
Intercept (NON-EXPERIENCER SO)	6.5969	0.0611	107.8891	6.6318	0.0644	103.0088
V-TYPE (EXPERIENCER)	0.0708	0.0182	3.8937	0.0669	0.0216	3.1030
WORD ORDER (OS)	0.0205	0.0181	1.1335	0.0090	0.0216	0.4146
segment length	0.0090	0.0017	5.3134	0.0085	0.0018	4.6829
trial	−0.0024	0.0006	−4.1899	−0.0024	0.0006	−3.9285
EXPERIENCER:OS	−0.0437	0.0254	−1.7192	−0.0403	0.0302	−1.3333

Table 6.40: Output of the LME model for the DP1-segment with the AGENTIVE controls in Experiment 5
`lmer(log.RT~verb.type*verb.position+segment.length+trial+(1+trial|participant.ID)+(1|stimulus.ID))`

	criticized model			raw model		
	Estimate	SE	t	Estimate	SE	t
Intercept (AGENTIVE V-FINAL)	5.6993	0.1036	55.0359	5.7177	0.0992	57.6183
V-TYPE (EXPERIENCER)	0.0758	0.0460	1.6487	0.0568	0.0514	1.1062
V-TYPE (NON-EXPERIENCER)	0.0603	0.0463	1.3004	0.0471	0.0519	0.9072
V-POSITION (V2)	0.1058	0.0314	3.3680	0.0999	0.0363	2.7484
segment length	0.0271	0.0049	5.5694	0.0270	0.0055	4.8951
trial	−0.0003	0.0007	−0.4045	−0.0003	0.0008	−0.3403
EXPERIENCER:V2	−0.0178	0.0453	−0.3926	0.0215	0.0523	0.4118
NON-EXPERIENCER:V2	−0.0318	0.0454	−0.7005	−0.0298	0.0528	−0.5652

Table 6.41: Output of the LME model for spillover segment 1+2 with the AGENTIVE controls in Experiment 5

`lmer(log.RT~verb.type*verb.position+segment.length+trial+(1+segment.length+trial|participant.ID)+(1|stimulus.ID))`

	criticized model			raw model		
	Estimate	SE	t	Estimate	SE	t
Intercept (NON-EXPERIENCER V2)	6.6408	0.0501	132.5052	6.6687	0.0529	126.1178
V-TYPE (AGENTIVE)	−0.0303	0.0218	−1.3880	−0.0269	0.0232	−1.1581
V-TYPE (EXPERIENCER)	−0.0362	0.0155	−2.3370	−0.0343	0.0181	−1.8881
V-POSITION (V-FINAL)	−0.0513	0.0157	−3.2578	−0.0428	0.0183	−2.3327
segment length	0.0087	0.0025	3.5065	0.0077	0.0027	2.8311
trial	−0.0018	0.0004	−4.9448	−0.0015	0.0004	−3.8620
AGENTIVE:V-FINAL	0.0357	0.0217	1.6429	0.0135	0.0253	0.5343
EXPERIENCER:V-FINAL	0.0505	0.0222	2.2748	0.0501	0.0259	1.9332

Table 6.42: Output of the LME model for the region consisting of spillover segment 3+4 with the AGENTIVE controls in Experiment 5

`lmer(log.RT~verb.type*verb.position+segment.length+trial+(1+trial|participant.ID)+(1|stimulus.ID))`

	criticized model			raw model		
	Estimate	SE	t	Estimate	SE	t
Intercept (EXPERIENCER V-FINAL)	6.6105	0.0548	120.6926	6.6485	0.0561	118.4244
V-TYPE (NON-EXPERIENCER)	−0.0736	0.0175	−4.2200	−0.0680	0.0206	−3.3047
V-TYPE (AGENTIVE)	−0.0353	0.0260	−1.3614	−0.0397	0.0263	−1.5101
V-POSITION (V2)	−0.0482	0.0171	−2.8266	−0.0403	0.0202	−1.9946
segment length	0.0112	0.0015	7.6682	0.0104	0.0015	6.8627
trial	−0.0022	0.0005	−4.2187	−0.0023	0.0006	−4.1039
NON-EXPERIENCER:V2	0.0525	0.0244	2.1508	0.0374	0.0288	1.2961
AGENTIVE:V2	0.0267	0.0237	1.1238	0.0192	0.0281	0.6832

Table 6.43: Output of the LME model for DP1-segment of the CONFIGURATIONAL controls in Experiment 5

`lmer(log.RT~verb.position+word.order+segment.length+trial+(1+segment.length+trial|participant.ID)+(1|stimulus.ID))`

	criticized model			raw model		
	Estimate	SE	t	Estimate	SE	t
Intercept (V2 OS)	5.4138	0.3270	16.5549	5.6271	0.3468	16.2235
V-POSITION (V-FINAL)	−0.0649	0.0278	−2.3378	−0.0693	0.0305	−2.2700
WORD ORDER (SO)	−0.0932	0.0287	−3.2434	−0.0932	0.0328	−2.8407
segment length	0.0531	0.0190	2.8041	0.0422	0.0203	2.0765
trial	−0.0001	0.0012	−0.0918	−0.0002	0.0013	−0.1512

Table 6.44: Output of the LME model for the high adverb segment of the CONFIGURATIONAL controls in Experiment 5
`lmer(log.RT~verb.position+word.order+segment.length+trial+(1|participant.ID)+(1|stimulus.ID))`

	criticized model			raw model		
	Estimate	SE	t	Estimate	SE	t
Intercept (V2 OS)	6.0328	0.0387	156.0507	6.0731	0.0471	129.0500
V-POSITION (V-FINAL)	0.0695	0.0257	2.7019	0.0762	0.0343	2.2178
WORD ORDER (SO)	0.0729	0.0258	2.8287	0.0732	0.0344	2.1262
segment length	0.0058	0.0038	1.5277	0.0022	0.0051	0.4387
trial	−0.0018	0.0005	−3.4285	−0.0011	0.0007	−1.6399
V-FINAL:SO	−0.0616	0.0366	−1.6816	−0.0610	0.0487	−1.2527

Table 6.45: Output of the LME model for DP2-segment of the CONFIGURATIONAL controls in Experiment 5
`lmer(log.RT~verb.position+word.order+segment.length+trial+(1|participant.ID)+(1|stimulus.ID))`

	criticized model			raw model		
	Estimate	SE	t	Estimate	SE	t
Intercept (V2 SO)	6.4494	0.2597	24.8315	6.1417	0.3272	18.7707
V-POSITION (V-FINAL)	0.0874	0.0229	3.8157	0.0673	0.0294	2.2930
WORD ORDER (OS)	0.0230	0.0245	0.9384	0.0315	0.0315	1.0017
segment length	−0.0138	0.0146	−0.9449	0.0037	0.0185	0.2000
trial	−0.0011	0.0007	−1.7069	−0.0019	0.0008	−2.2551

Table 6.46: Output of the LME model for spillover segment 1 of the CONFIGURATIONAL controls in Experiment 5
`lmer(log.RT~verb.position+word.order+segment.length+trial+(1+segment.length+trial|participant.ID)+(1|stimulus.ID))`

	criticized model			raw model		
	Estimate	SE	t	Estimate	SE	t
Intercept (V2 SO)	5.9005	0.0520	113.3904	5.9042	0.0578	102.1478
V-POSITION (V-FINAL)	−0.0499	0.0158	−3.1641	−0.0482	0.0190	−2.5418
WORD ORDER (OS)	0.0260	0.0157	1.6510	0.0096	0.0190	0.5060
segment length	0.0260	0.0064	4.0859	0.0284	0.0071	3.9850
trial	−0.0007	0.0005	−1.2844	−0.0006	0.0006	−0.9003

Table 6.47: Output of the LME model for spillover segment 2 of the CONFIGURATIONAL controls in Experiment 5

```
lmer(log.RT~verb.position*word.order+segment.length+trial+(1|participant.ID)+
(1|stimulus.ID))
```

	criticized model			raw model		
	Estimate	SE	t	Estimate	SE	t
Intercept (V2 SO)	5.8149	0.1486	39.1347	5.7732	0.1623	35.5796
V-POSITION (V-FINAL)	0.0564	0.0255	2.2100	0.0548	0.0313	1.7496
WORD ORDER (OS)	0.0462	0.0255	1.8131	0.0303	0.0313	0.9657
segment length	0.0197	0.0123	1.5932	0.0241	0.0135	1.7800
trial	−0.0010	0.0005	−1.8773	−0.0010	0.0006	−1.5344
V-FINAL:OS	−0.0927	0.0361	−2.5702	−0.0663	0.0443	−1.4977

6.5 Summary of the experimental investigations

In this chapter, I presented four self-paced reading experiments designed to test the prediction of the V2-Reconstruction Hypothesis about the processing of the finite verb in on-line sentence comprehension. Experiment 2 used the verbal NPI *brauchen* 'need to' whose grammaticality/interpretability hinges on a proper NPI-licensor. The results indicate that the NPI-verb in V2-position triggers prolonged reading times at the potential base position of the finite verb if this position is not in the scope of an NPI-licensor. This matches the predictions of the V2-Reconstruction Hypothesis, namely that the finite verb is automatically reconstructed into potential base positions, comparable to filler-gap parsing. Experiment 3 was a follow-up study designed to diagnose whether the NPI-violation effect of experiment 2 was really tied to the base position of the finite verb, or whether the effect was actually related to the base position of the negation, which was almost adjacent to the one of the verb. Although the results are less pronounced than in experiment 2, they clearly favor the V2-Reconstruction Hypothesis over the alternative hypothesis.

Experiment 4 applied a similar logic as the preceding experiments. Two verb classes were contrasted in the V2-position, which selected bare infinitives and *zu*-infinitives respectively. The first potential reconstruction site followed a *zu*-infinitive. In line with the V2-Reconstruction Hypothesis, the results showed longer reading times for the matrix verb whose selection requirement are not satisfied at this point. This indicates that the finite verb is automatically reconstructed into a potential base position before the selection requirement are evaluated. This was supported by the observation that the selection mismatch effect was directly preceded by another effect, which probably reflects lexical reactivation.

Experiment 5 was intended to tap into the verb-related argument processing by contrasting verb classes with different thematic roles and corresponding argument-order preferences. The main result showed a modulation of the subject-first preference as a function of the V2-verb at the position directly preceding the reconstruction site. Additionally, the results also included potential verb-related effects at earlier points which indicate that thematic processing might starts prior to the reconstruction of the finite verb.

In sum, this chapter presented a series of experiments which investigated three properties which depend on the interpretation of the lexical content of a verb in the V2-position and tested whether their processing correlates can be diagnosed at a distant position in the sentence as predicted by the V2-Reconstruction Hypothesis. The expectations have been met for polarity-sensitive properties, which trigger an immediate response to the licensing requirement at the reconstruction site. The predictions could also be confirmed for the evaluation of selection requirements of the V2-verb, although these seem to be evaluated only shortly after lexical reactivation took place. Concerning the evaluation of thematic structure of the V2-verb, the result are compatible with the V2-Reconstruction Hypothesis. However, the result are less clear-cut than for the other two phenomena. This is not very surprising considering that argument order does not induce strict ungrammaticality but only preferences, which also strongly interact with discourse-properties. Taken together, the experiments showed that the V2-Reconstruction Hypothesis yields very accurate predictions concerning the temporal locus at which the lexical information of the V2-verb is evaluated during the on-line processing of V2-clauses in German.

7 Peculiarities of processing V2-clauses: Specifying the V2-Reconstruction Hypothesis

Based on the three previous chapters about the general properties of the processing device (Chapter 4), the review of the literature on sentence processing in German (Chapter 5), and the experimental results (Chapter 6), this chapter provides a more elaborated inspection of the processing of V2-clauses under the V2-Reconstruction Hypothesis. I will discuss how the verbs in V2-position are processed and elaborate on consequences of the relation of grammar and processing. I will begin by discussing three important issues of V2-parsing under the V2-Reconstruction Hypothesis: the special status of subject-initial clauses, the point at which the interpretation of the reconstructed verb will be initiated, and a comparison of two different ways of implementing phrase structure buildup with verb reconstruction, i. e. cascading structures vs. structure insertion. The second part then evaluates the assumed proportions of the parsing mechanism by contrasting V2-structures with English head-initial structures. Temporary constituency, diagnosed by Right Node Raising constructions, indicates that V-initial parsing builds cascading structures, whereas V2-parsing uses the insertion strategy. Furthermore, I will show that the base position of the finite verb divides the German clause into two areas with distinct interpretation potentials. Finally, I will present a speculative idea about the cross-linguistic impact of generalized application of reconstruction as an explanation for unattested phrase structure patterns.

7.1 Properties of V2-processing

Following Haider (2012), I assume that verbal heads in German license only to the left. Based on that, I conclude that the processor may only integrate arguments and adjuncts on the left of the verb, and cannot generate predictions pointing to the right. Consequently in a left-to-right structure building process the verb has to be lowered successively, as in (1), to license and interpret complements and adjuncts.

https://doi.org/10.1515/9783110725018-007

(1) Successive lowering of the finite verb (to be revised)

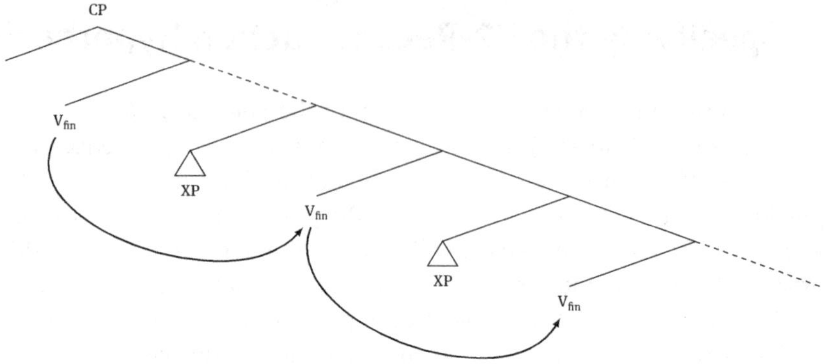

The discussion in the following sections will reveal that the successive lowering of the verb is not the only possibility. In fact, I will show that an alternative structure building procedure is empirically more accurate. Before I turn to the structure building mechanism, I will discuss two prerequisites, namely the special status of subject-initial V2-clauses and the effect of immediate access of the meaning of the reconstructed verb.

7.1.1 The special status of subject-initial V2-clauses

Subject-initial V2-clauses constitute a special case of V2-clauses. I assume that these are processed more efficiently than non-subject-initial clauses, see the discussion of (non-subject) XP-fronting in Section 5.2. The reason for the processing advantage is that subject-initial V2-clauses can dispense with at least one reordering step in contrast to non-subject-initial V2-clauses. Subject-initial V2-clauses are (partially) string identical to the base order of the respective elements in the middle field (VP). This can be illustrated most clearly with an intransitive predicate, as in (2). The subject-initial V2-clause in (2a) is string-identical to its V-final counterpart in (2b), as long as no further modifying material is present, such as the adverbial *seit zwei Stunden* 'for two hours' in brackets. If additional material is present, the verb has to be rearranged with respect to this material and has to be reconstructed into the clause-final position. However, the order of subject and verb remains the same, in contrast to non-subject-initial clauses, as in (2c). Here the preverbal constituent and the finite verb have to be rearranged with respect to the subject.

(2) a. Der Junge schläft (seit zwei Stunden).
the boy sleeps since two hours

b. ... dass der Junge (seit zwei Stunden) schläft.
that the boy since two hours sleeps

c. [Seit zwei Stunden]$_1$ schläft$_2$ der Junge t_1 t_2.
since two hours sleeps the boy
'The boy sleeps for two hours.'

To recapitulate, the special property of subject-initial V2-clauses is that the order of the subject and the finite verb remains stable during the parse. Therefore, there is no need to assume that the processor induces a reordering of the subject and the finite verb in a subject-initial clause. The result of such an operation would be string-identical to the initial sequence, as shown in (3).

(3) String-identical reconstruction of subject and finite verb

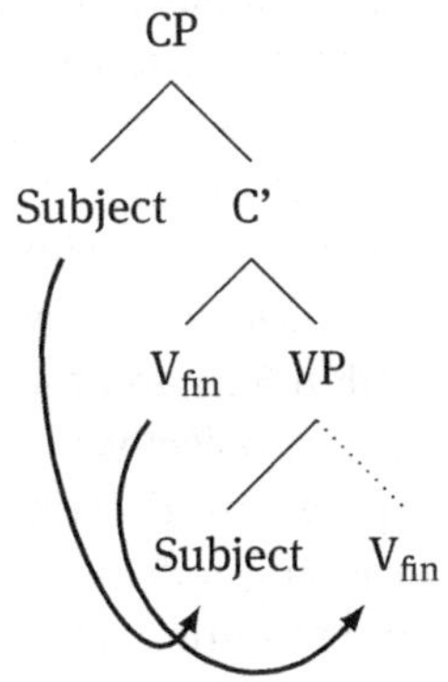

Instead, I assume the following for subject-initial V2-parsing: When the parser encounters a clause-initial nominative phrase, it immediately induces a procedure to which I will refer as *projection matching* (following Haider 1988 who proposed this based solely on theoretical arguments). Thereby, the parser relabels the subject in Spec-CP as a Spec-VP element. The subsequent finite verb will consequently be integrated as the head of the VP. The procedure is illustrated in (4).

(4) Projection matching operation

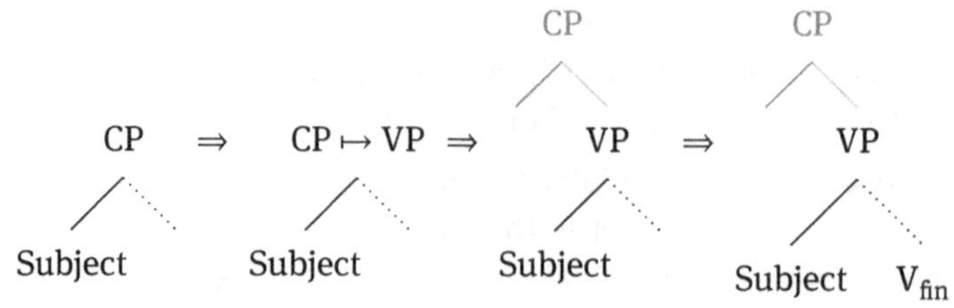

The projection matching procedure presupposes that the hierarchical layer receives labels by the processor. There is, however, no a priori reason to assume this. Assuming that the processor constructs unlabeled hierarchies, there is not even a need for relabeling. Subject-initial clauses therefore allow a more efficient processing, such that more properties can be assigned on-line and less properties have to be delayed.

This peculiarity might explain the subject-object asymmetry for the unstressed pronoun *es* in German (Kathol 1990, Travis 1991) that is observable under certain conditions (see Frey 2006b, Meinunger 2007). Only as a subject, the pronoun does not have to be reordered but can be integrated into the VP. It is unclear whether the processing advantage generalizes to other (pragmatically) unmarked prefield elements that are assumed to be fronted by *formal movement* (Frey 2006a). However, the review of the experimental results in Section 5.3.1 and the results of Experiment 5 indicated that initial objects of experiencer object verbs induce local reordering effects although theses orderings are (pragmatically) unmarked. To my knowledge, no study has investigated the processing differences of V2-clauses with initial subjects vs. sentence adverbs or frame setting adverbs. For now, I will assume that the special status for processing V2-clauses is restricted to initial subjects.

7.1.2 Aspects of (immediate) interpretation

Based on the experimental evidence reviewed in Section 5.3 and Chapter 6, I assume that the processor does not access the information about the verb frame immediately at the V2-position. Consequently, the processor simply does not "know" whether the verb is intransitive, as in (2) or not. This will be evaluated only after the integration of the subject and a (partial) interpretation. Therefore, the reconstruction of the finite verb has to begin immediately after the encounter of the subject. This assumption is supported by the findings of Schlesewsky et al. (2000), who report that a verb which immediately follows a case ambiguous *wh*-element which does not agree in number, as in (5a), results in longer reading times on the verb and subsequent segments, in contrast to a number matching verb, as in (5b). Crucially, the effect emerges before the disambiguating second noun phrase has been encountered. This indicates that the first noun phrase is immediately integrated as the clausal subject and the verb is immediately integrated as head of the VP, either by projection matching as in (6a) or by reconstruction as in (6b). Thus, whereas the verb does not induce an input-predicting process, all potential arguments that appear to the right of the verb will be integrated and (partially) interpreted as early as possible.

(5) a. Object-initial
Welche Frauen sah der Mann am Freitag?
[which woman].PL saw.SG [the man]NOM on Friday
'which woman did the man see on Friday?'

b. Subject-initial
Welche Frauen sahen den Mann am Freitag?
[which woman].PL saw.PL [the man]ACC on Friday
'which woman saw the man on Friday?'

(Schlesewsky et al. 2000: 77)

(6) a.

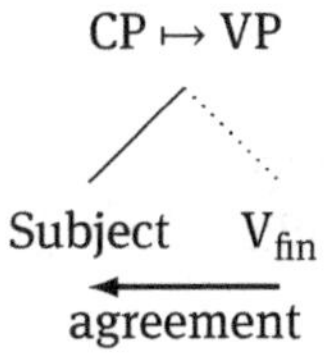

b.

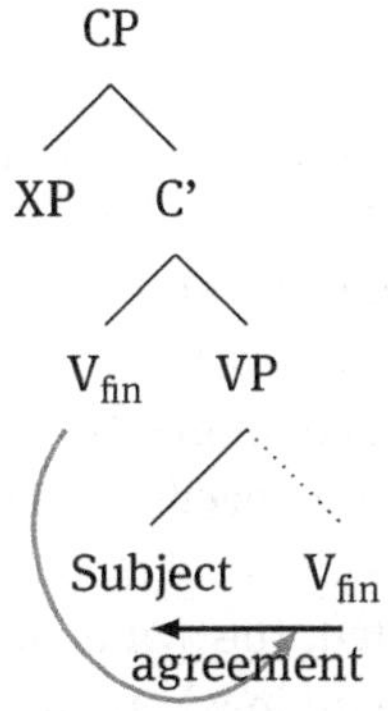

This immediate response to temporary agreement mismatches, however, leaves open whether the processor only validates morphosyntactic features or also initiates a full interpretation process. There is supporting evidence for the latter, namely that the processor starts an integration, linking and interpretation process immediately after inserting a phrase into the current phrase structure. Results indicating immediate interpretation processes have been reported by Friederici & Frisch (2000). They investigate three types of violation in V2-clauses and V-final clauses, as illustrated in (7).

(7) a. Well-formed
Heute ⟨besuchte⟩ der Cousin den Geiger im
today visited [the cousin]NOM [the violinist]ACC [in the
Krankenhaus ⟨besuchte⟩.
hospital] visited
'Today, the cousin visited the violinist in the hospital.'

b. Semantic violation
*Heute ⟨beizte⟩ der Cousin den Geiger am Mittag ⟨beizte⟩.
today stained [the Cousin]NOM [the violinist]ACC at noon stained

c. Number of argument violation
*Heute ⟨trödelte⟩ der Cousin den Geiger am Aufzug
today dawdled [the cousin]NOM [the violinist]ACC [at the lift]
⟨trödelte⟩.
dawdled

d. Type of argument violation (case marking)
*Heute ⟨besuchte⟩ der Cousin dem Geiger im
today visited [the Cousin]NOM [the violinist]DAT [in the
Krankenhaus ⟨besuchte⟩.
hospital] visited

(Friederici & Frisch 2000: 481, 490)

In verb-final clauses, the responses to the violations in (7) were detected at the clause-final verb, consisting of an early negativity (N400/left lateralized negativity) and a later positivity (P600). The negative components are interpreted as a semantic or syntactic violation, followed by a repair process, which is indicated by the positive component. In V2-clauses, however, the components which emerged immediately at the second NP, showed more violation-specific variation. The semantic violation (7b) only evoked an N400, which is a typical response to semantic violations. I assume that the verb is reconstructed, the syntactic structure is built and the whole VP is pushed further to interpretation where the violation becomes evident. The number-of-argument violation in (7c) confronts the processor with a surplus argument for an intransitive verb. After the syntactic integration of the surplus element, the interpretation procedure will result in a violation of the argument structure or the modifier structure. This results in a N400, followed by structural reanalyses, reflected by the P600. The type of argument violation in (7d) does not show an immediate negative component in the V2-clauses because the clause is not necessarily ungrammatical at this point but there exist acceptable continuations[1]. The P600 therefore might only reflect structural delay without semantic anomaly. While Friederici & Frisch (2000) assume that, in V2-clauses, the arguments are checked against the predictions of the verbs, I assume the opposite: In V2-clauses, the processor tries to complete the clause after every potential argument and pushes it to interpretation. In V-final clauses, the argument structure creates a prediction for the verb. Because the verb distinctively marks the end of the clause, the content will automatically be pushed to interpretation. There, all mismatches result in immediate negativities followed by a repair mechanism, which is indicated by positivities.

I summarize that the processor integrates all potential arguments to the left of the reconstructed verb as soon as possible.

7.1.3 Structural build-up and verb reconstruction: Cascades vs. insertion

In this section, I will take a closer look at the mechanism of reconstructing the finite verb. To set the scene for this discussion, I make two basic assumptions: First, in non-subject-initial clauses, the preverbal phrase will be held in working memory for later integration, which is in accordance with filler-gap processing. Second, the finite verb will be rearranged with respect to the subject. This yields the initial situation for regular V2-parsing, as it is illustrated in (8). This configuration is presumed for subject-initial and non-subject-initial clauses alike, except that, in the latter, the integration of the prefield element is pending until the gap site.

---

1 These continuations include benefactive constructions as in (i) and dative possesive structures as in (ii), which are common in many German variants.

(i) *Heute besuchte der Cousin dem Geiger zuliebe eine Freundin im*
today visited [the Cousin]NOM [[the violinist]DAT for the sake] a friend in the
Krankenhaus.
hospital
'Today visited the cousin a friend in the hospital for the sake of the violinist.'

(ii) *Heute besuchte der Cousin dem Geiger seine Frau im Krankenhaus.*
today visited [the Cousin]NOM [[the violinist]DAT his wife] in the hospital
'Today visited the cousin the violinist's wife in the hospital.'

(8)

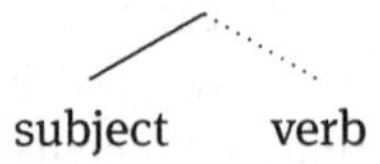

I will review two different strategies of integrating new strings into the structure. The first strategy extends the structure cyclically to the right, which results in a cascading structure with multiple copies of the verb, as shown in (9). This strategy is assumed by Phillips (1996) for the left-to-right derivation of English sentences (based on Pesetsky 1995).

(9) V2-parsing: cascading structure

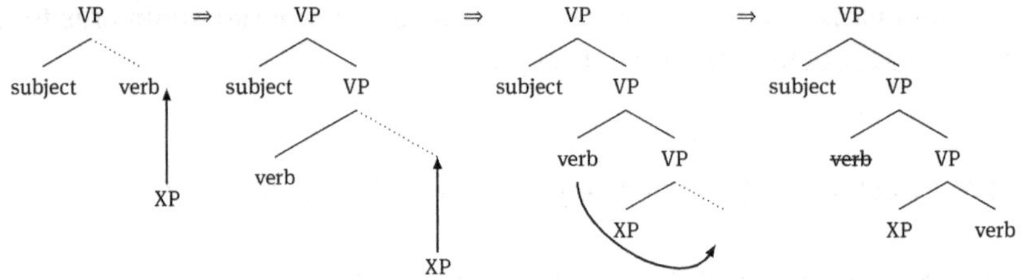

The second strategy extends the structure by inserting incoming parts before the verb, as in (10). The process resembles the mechanisms of the tree adjoining grammar formalism (Rambow & Joshi 1994: 274-275).

(10) V2-parsing: insertion strategy

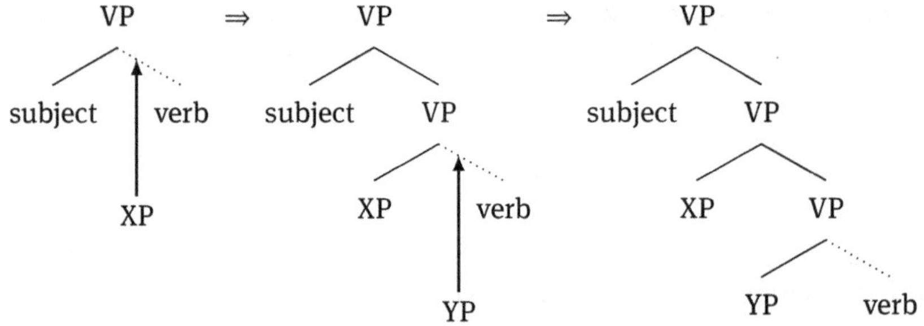

This second strategy is basically identical to the parsing of V-final structures, as illustrated in (11).

(11) V-final parsing

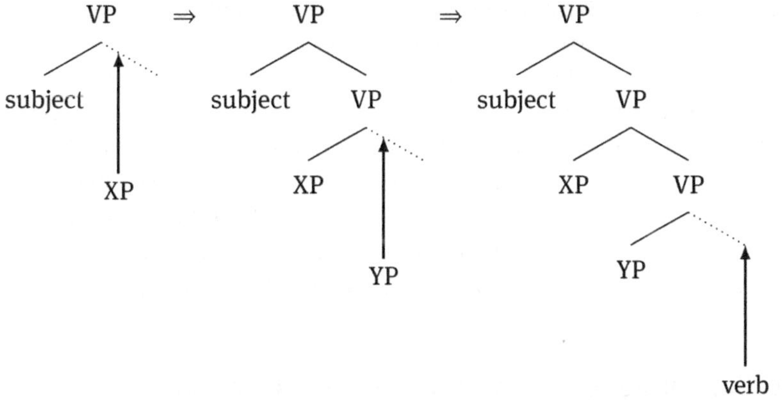

V2-parsing and V-final parsing result in identical phrase structure configurations of the argument structure: In V2-parsing the most deeply embedded element of the clause, the finite verb, is overtly present while the structure is extended with every input item. Structure building of V-final clauses is identical, except that the most deeply embedded element is typically the last input item. Furthermore, clauses may contain more than one verbal element and all but one are non-finite. In OV-languages such as German and Dutch, the verbal elements form a verb cluster which has two important properties: It is compact, i. e. no non-verbal elements, such as adjuncts, intervene between the verbal elements of the cluster (Haider 2010: 274–282). Second, the order of the elements in the cluster may vary (Haider 2010: 286–292). German exhibits a head-final base order, i. e. the selecting verb follows the head of the VP it selects (its complements), as in (12a). Dutch and Swiss German, in contrast, linearize verbs in verb clusters preferably in the inverted order (Bresnan et al. 1982, Shieber 1985, Bach et al. 1986). Although German does not allow the fully inverted order, it allows variants in which the finite auxiliary is semi or fully shifted to the left, as in (12b) and (12c).

(12) a. ... dass er uns nicht mitfahren lassen *hat*.
that he us not ride let has
'... that he didn't let us join the ride.'

b. ... dass er uns nicht mitfahren *hat* lassen.
that he us not ride has let

c. ... dass er uns nicht *hat* mitfahren lassen.
that he us not has ride let

Irrespective of the linear order, the hierarchical order (scope) of the verbal elements must be identical in all permutations of (12). Consequently, the processor must be able to map non-canonical orders onto an interpretable hierarchy and simultaneously resolve crossing dependencies (see Culicover 2014 for a detailed discussion of verb clusters in Continental West Germanic).

The comparison of cascades in (9) and insertion in (10) shows that the differences between the resulting structures are rather subtle. The main difference is that the cascading structure exhibits copies of the finite verb in VP-internal positions (*copy and paste*).[2] If such copies have any noticeable effect, they should only appear in V2-clauses but not in V-final clauses.[3] In the following section, I will discuss three aspects that provide arguments in favor of the insertion strategy and against a cascading structure building process in German.

7.2 Consequences and diagnostics for V2-parsing

In this section, I evaluate the predictions of the structure building mechanism for V2-parsing that I discussed in the previous section, *cascades* vs. *insertion*. The first argument builds on implications about the (temporary) constituency which we can draw from Right Node Raising constructions: Intermediate copies of the finite verb should take part in temporary constituents parallel to cascading phrase structure constructions in English, a prediction that is not borne out. The second and third argument concentrate on the distinctive properties of the areas preceding and following the base position of the verb. I will specify an interpretation domain and discuss its relation to extraposition patterns in German. In the final subsection, I will generalize the idea of reconstruction and relate it to cross-linguistically unattested/excluded phrase structure configurations.

7.2.1 Temporary constituency: Right Node Raising with the exclusion of C

In this section, I motivate why I assume the *insertion* strategy for German, rather than the *cascade* strategy. One diagnostic that taps into incremental structure building processes is the identification of temporary constituency, as proposed by Phillips (2003) and introduced in Section 4.2.3. In a nutshell, the two right-

2 If the lowering process doesn't leave copies behind, but applies a *cut and paste* strategy, I cannot see in which way it differs from the insertion strategy and take it to be identical with it.

3 Theoretically, it would be possible to assume that in V-final structures an empty V-head is anticipated which will be lowered with any incoming element until the V-head is encountered. However, I cannot think of any supporting evidence for such an assumption nor of any desirable consequences.

most constituents of any substring form a temporary constituent. Because of this, such a temporary constituent can be coordinated whereas it may not pass other constituent tests, such as topicalization. The examples in (13)–(15) illustrate that, in English, the two constituents at the right edge of a partial phrase marker form a temporary constituent which may serve as a conjunct of a coordination.

(13) a. [Wallace will]
b. [Wallace will] and [Wendolene probably won't] give Gromit crackers before breakfast.
(Phillips 2003: 47)

(14) a. [Wallace [will give]]
b. [Wallace will give] and [Wendolene will send] some crackers to Gromit for his birthday.
c. Wallace [will design] but [won't actually build] an exciting new invention for his dog's birthday.
(Phillips 2003: 48)

(15) a. [Wallace [will [give Gromit]]]
b. [Wallace will give Gromit] and [Wendolene will give Preston] a shining new collar for walking about town.
c. Wallace [will give Gromit] and [(will) send Preston] a shining new collar for walking about town.
(Phillips 2003: 48)

Coordinations such as (13)–(15) are known as *Right Node Raising* constructions. These differ from "simple" coordinations in the following respects: In a simple coordination, such as in (16a), the coordinated NPs yield a complex element that functions like a plural NP, in the same way as *the fairies* in (16b).

(16) a. [Paul and Mary] are walking through the prairie.
b. [The fairies] are walking through the prairie.

In Right Node Raising construction, the conjuncts are incomplete, e. g. exhibit an unfilled argument slot, such as the object slots in (17a). This missing part, which usually appears right peripheral, here *the prairie*, is connected to both conjuncts, i. e. the conjuncts "share" one continuation.[4] Constructions of this sort pose a serious problem for classic phrase structure theories, due to the non-monotonic dominance relations. One popular class of accounts assume an ellipsis analysis as

4 The term *Right Node Raising*, introduced by Postal (1974: 125-129), refers to a specific type of analysis which assumes an accross-the-board extraction of the right peripheral continuation with subsequent adjunction to the right of the coordinated phrase.

indicated in (17b), in which the "shared" material is elided in the first conjunct. In contrast, I will assume an approach in which the right peripheral material is really *shared*, as will be illustrated below. For a brief overview of Right Node Raising analyses see Sabbagh (2014), and Citko (2017) for a more extensive one.[5]

(17) a. [[Mary loves $\_\__1$] and [the fairy detests $\_\__1$]] [the prairie]$_1$.
b. [Mary loves ~~the prairie~~] and [the fairy detests the prairie].

At first glance, German subject-initial clauses show a pattern similar to the English examples in (13)–(15). The examples in (18) seem to indicate that the subject and the finite verb build a temporary constituent.[6]

(18) a. [Ich werde] und [du wirst nicht] gewinnen.
I will and you will not win
'I will win and you won't win.'
b. [Peter muss] und [Maria darf] zu Hause bleiben.
Peter must and Maria may at home stay
'Peter has to stay at home and Maria is allowed to stay at home.'

Parallel to English, strings of VP-internal material, such as subject and indirect object may also form temporary constituents which allow coordination but resist topicalization because only one (phrasal) constituent may move to the prefield. This is illustrated by the acceptable coordinations in (19a) and (20a), and the corresponding ungrammatical topicalizations in (19b) and (20b). Note that, in (20), even an adjunct is part of the temporary constituent string.

(19) a. Dann hat [die Sängerin ihrem Bruder] und [die Ärztin ihrem Vater]
then has the singer her brother and the physician her father
das Geschenk überreicht.
his present hand over
'Then singer gave her brother and the physician gave her father the present.'
b. *[Die Sängerin ihrem Bruder]$_1$ hat t_1 das Geschenk überreicht
the singer her brother has the present hand over

5 It should be noted that in Right Node Raising constructions neither the contrasted nor the shared material have to be constituents in classical phrase structure analysis, as noted in Hartmann (2000: 55–60). Thanks to Sophie Repp for pointing that out.

6 Unfortunately, no alternative constituency diagnostics can be conducted for the subject-verb string in German. Clearly this string cannot be moved without violating the V2-constraint because it contains the finite verb. The same logic applies to deletion diagnostics. Substitution by an alternative (pronominal) element is also not an option.

(20) a. Dann hat [die Sängerin ihrem Bruder im Park] und [die Ärztin
then has the singer her brother in the park and the physician
ihrem Vater im Garten] das Geschenk überreicht.
her father in the garden his present hand over
'Then singer gave her brother the present in the park and the physician gave her father the present in the garden.'

b. *[Die Sängerin ihrem Bruder im Park]$_1$ hat t_1 das Geschenk
the singer her brother in the park has the present
überreicht.
hand over

Closer inspection, however, reveals significant differences between German and English, and indicates that the finite verb in V2-position is not part of a temporary constituent. Subject-initial V2-clauses constitute a special case because they are temporarily string identical with V-final clauses, see Section 7.1.1. I assume that this is the reason why it is possible to coordinate the subject-verb string in (21) with the exclusion of other VP-internal material. In (22), the subject follows the finite verb. The resulting verb-subject string cannot be coordinated, which indicates that it does not form a temporary constituent.[7] These verb-subject strings can only be coordinated as elliptical clauses (gapping), as in (23).[8]

(21) a. [Ich werde] und du wirst nicht bezahlen.
I will and you will not pay
'I will and you won't pay.'

---

7 Sophie Repp (p. c.) pointed out that there exist acceptable variants of the examples in (22), such as (i).

(i) a. *Zur Belohnung koche ich und isst du superleckeres Apfelmus.*
for reward cook I and eat you scrummy apple sauce

b. *Zu allem Überfluss besteigt unsere Katze und beschnüffelt unser Hund in diesem*
to make matters worse climbs our cat and noses at our dog in this
Moment auch noch eine der überaus wertvollen Vasen neben der Vitrine links
moment even also on of the extremely precious vases next to the cabinet left
hinten an der Wand.
rear at the wall

8 Josef Bayer provided the example in (i) which I and Max Bonke (p. c.) consider considerably marked. As illustrated by the indices, I assume that the topicalized object is inserted in both coordinated clauses, which each constitute *comments* on the *aboutness topic* in the sense of Krifka (2007). I further assume that the markedness is the result from such a construal being interpretable but only analyzable by "bending" syntactic rules.

b. [Ich koche] und du isst Apfelmus.
I cook and you eat apple sauce
'I cook and you eat the apple sauce.'

c. [Peter darf] und Julia muss Hausaufgaben machen.
Peter may and July must homework make
'Peter may and July must do the homework.'

(22) a. * Dann [werde ich] und wirst du nicht bezahlen.
then will I and will you not pay

b. * Dann [koche ich] und isst du Apfelmus.
then cook I and eat you apple sauce

c. * Dann [darf Peter] und muss Julia Hausaufgaben machen.
then may Peter and must Julia homework make

(23) a. Dann werde ich bezahlen und du nicht.
then will I pay and you not
'Then I will pay and you won't.'

b. Dann koche ich Apfelmus und du isst es.
then cook I apple sauce and you eat it
'Then I cook apple sauce and you will eat it.'

c. Dann darf Peter Hausaufgaben machen und Julia muss (sie machen).
then may Peter homework make and Julia must them make
'Then Peter may do the homework and Julia must.'

The same effect has been observed for other constituents that follow the finite verb, such as objects and adjuncts. They too do not form a temporary constituent with the finite verb, as shown in (24). In cascading structures, temporary constituents of this sort are expected, and actually attested, as the English sentences in (14) and (15) illustrate. The impossibility of such coordinations in German indicates that no intermediate copies of the finite verb are present in the phrase structure analysis.[9]

(i) ?? *[Diesen Hasen]$_1$ [schoss$_2$ der Jäger gestern* t$_1$*] und [wird$_3$ seine Frau morgen* t$_1$
this hare shot the hunter yesterday and will his wife tomorrow
zubereiten] t$_3$.
prepare
'This hare, the hunter shot today and his will prepare it tomorrow.'

9 Sophie Repp (p. c.) pointed out that the structures in (24) can be changed to acceptable variants, as in (i).

(24) a. * Der Professor [wird das Buch] und wird die Zeichnung nicht
the professor will the book and will the drawing not
verkaufen.
sell

b. * Die Lehrlinge [reinigen heute] und verarbeiten morgen die Fische.
the apprentices clean today and process tomorrow the fish

c. * Der Dieb [stahl der Gräfin] und schenkte den Kindern die Diamanten.
the thief stole the countess and gave the children the diamonds

d. * Peter [darf Schokolade] und muss grünen Salat einkaufen.
Peter may chocolate and must green lettuce buy

Additionally, if a string is coordinated that encompasses the finite verb, the finite verb itself does not seem to be part of the conjunct because it can be left out of the second conjunct, as shown in (25).

(25) a. [Der Professor |hat| einen Studenten] und [der Lehrer einen Schüler]
the professor has a student and the teacher a pupil
zu dem Vernetzungstreffen geschickt.
to the networking meeting sent
'The professor sent a student and the teacher sent a pupil to the network meeting.'

b. [Der Professor |hat| einen Studenten zu der Konferenz] und [der Lehrer
the professor has a student to the conference and the teacher
einen Schüler zu dem Vernetzungstreffen] geschickt.
a pupil to the network meeting sent
'The professor sent a student to the conference and the teacher sent a pupil to the network meeting.'

(i) a. *Die Lehrlinge reinigen heute und verarbeiten morgen die Fische, die der alte*
the apprentices clean today and process tomorrow the fish REL the old
Kutter heute morgen mitgebracht hat.
cutter today morning brought have
'The apprentices clean the fish today that the old cutter brought this morning today and process it tomorrow.'

b. *Peter darf zwar Schokolade, muss aber auch grünen Salat einkaufen.*
Peter may PRT chocolate must however also green lettuce buy
'Peter may buy chocolate but he has to buy green lettuce.'

c. [Die Nachbarin |hat| ihrem Sohn eine Sonnenbrille] und [Herr Müller
the neighbor has her son a sunglasses and Mr. Müller
seiner Tochter eine Gitarre] geschenkt.
his daughter a guitar donated
'The neighbor has donated her son sunglasses and Mr. Müller donated his daughter a guitar.'

The exclusion of the finite verb from temporary constituents matches the predictions of the insertion strategy. In particular, it follows from the assumption that the finite verb is initially reconstructed as clause-final element. As a consequence, the finite verb does not take part in the intermediate structure building and is therefore not part of temporary constituents. As expected, we observe that V-final embedded clauses exhibit the same coordination structure, as in (25), which is shown in (26).

(26) a. ... dass [der Professor einen Studenten] und [der Lehrer einen Schüler]
that the professor a student and the teacher a pupil
zu dem Vernetzungstreffen geschickt hat.
to the networking meeting sent has
'... that the professor sent a student and the teacher sent a pupil to the network meeting.'

b. ... dass [der Professor einen Studenten zu der Konferenz] und [der
that the professor a student to the conference and the
Lehrer einen Schüler zu dem Vernetzungstreffen] geschickt hat.
teacher a pupil to the network meeting sent has
'... that the professor sent a student to the conference and the teacher sent a pupil to the network meeting.'

c. ... dass [die Nachbarin ihrem Sohn eine Sonnenbrille] und [Herr Müller
that the neighbor her son a sunglasses and Mr. Müller
seiner Tochter eine Gitarre] geschenkt hat.
his daughter a guitar donated has
'... that the neighbor has donated her son sunglasses and Mr. Müller donated his daughter a guitar.'

I therefore assume that, in sentences like (25), the finite verb is suspended from clause-internal structure building. For those sentences, I assume a Right Node Raising analysis as proposed in Phillips (2003: 65) i. e. with a multiple dominance account for structure sharing (Moltman 1992, de Vries 2009), as illustrated in (27).

(27) a.

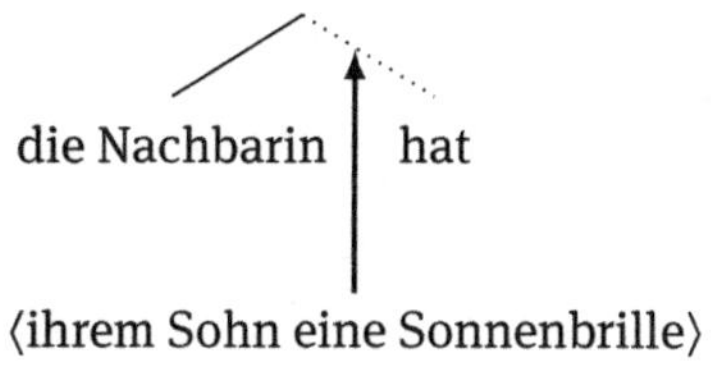
die Nachbarin
hat
⟨ihrem Sohn eine Sonnenbrille⟩

b.

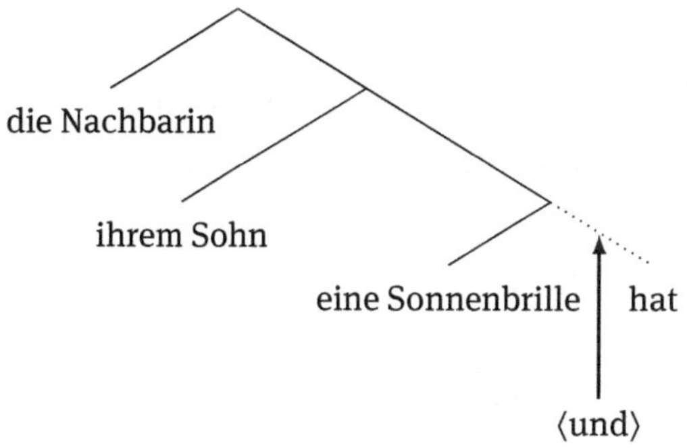
die Nachbarin
ihrem Sohn
eine Sonnenbrille
hat
⟨und⟩

c.

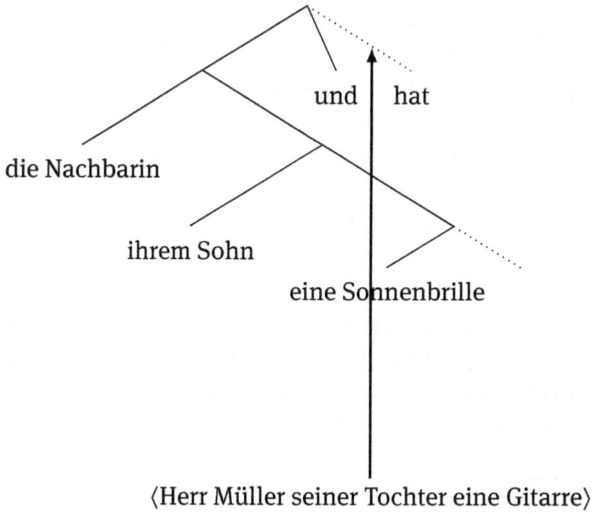
und
hat
die Nachbarin
ihrem Sohn
eine Sonnenbrille
⟨Herr Müller seiner Tochter eine Gitarre⟩

d.

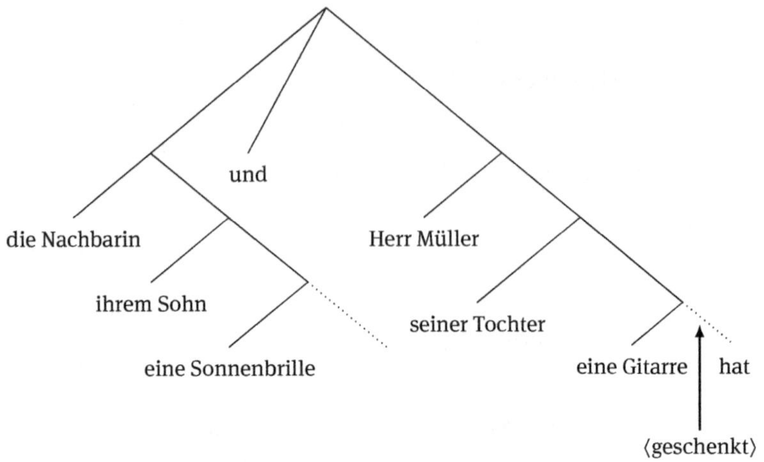

e.

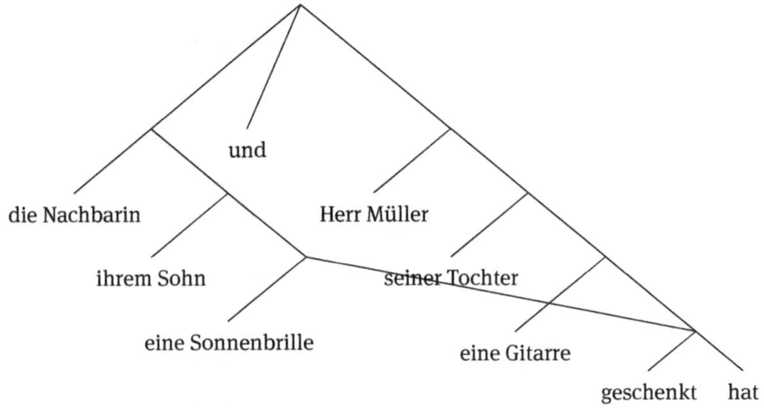

It is crucial for my argument that the examples above are analyzed as instances of *Right Node Raising/non-gapping coordination* (Osborne 2006). Therefore, I will show that the relevant examples are not instances of gapping, presupposing that the three properties in (28) are constitutive of gapping.

(28) Constitutive properties of gapping

a. Gapping only functions forward, i. e. the antecedent appears in the initial conjunct and the elided material is located in the subsequent conjunct. Other variants of structure sharing may also allow the shared content to appear after the non-initial conjunct. (Maling 1972, Osborne 2006: 321)

b. In gapping construction, the shared material must be contained inside the coordinated structure, i. e. the initial conjunct according to (28a). In other variants of structure sharing, the shared material may appear outside of the coordinated structure (Osborne 2006: 321).

c. In gapping constructions, the phonological identity of the shared material is lenient. Agreement mismatches are tolerated. In other variants of structure sharing, the requirement on phonological identity is strict (Osborne 2006: 321).

English allows gapping sentences as in (29a). Eliding only the finite auxiliary and retaining the lexical verb, as in (29b), is significantly degraded, although to varying degrees. Clearly impossible, however, is a structure corresponding to the German clause in (25a), here repeated as (30), with only the finite auxiliary present in the initial conjunct and the lexical verb only present in the final conjunct, as in (29c). The gapping of *scrub* in the first conjunct violates the restriction on forward sharing, which is formulated in (28a).

(29) a. [Tom will scrub the sink] and [Bill ~~will scrub~~ the tub].
b. ?/* [Tom will scrub the sink] and [Bill ~~will~~ scrub the tub].
c. * [Tom will ~~scrub~~ the sink] and [Bill ~~will~~ scrub the tub].
(Osborne 2006: 325)

(30) [Der Professor hat einen Studenten ~~zu dem Vernetzungstreffen geschickt~~]
the professor has a student to the network meeting sent
und [der Lehrer ~~hat~~ einen Schüler zu dem Vernetzungstreffen geschickt].
and the teacher has a pupil to the network meeting sent

Second, if the German sentences in (25) would be instances of gapping, they would also violate the requirement that shared material must be inside the coordinated structure, see (28b). In the analysis above, however, both the right-peripheral non-finite verb and the reconstructed finite verb, are outside of the coordinated structure, as illustrated in (27).

Third, in gapping structures, the elided material must be phonologically identical, see (28c). This is best demonstrated by agreement incompatibilities of the finite verb with subjects in two conjuncts. If the subjects of the two conjuncts match in their agreement features the auxiliary is preferably elided in the second conjunct, as indicated in (31). If the subjects do not agree in their respective features, structure sharing is degraded, as in (32).

(31) a. What is [he saying] and [she doing]?
b. (?) What [is he saying] and [is she doing]?
(see Osborne 2006: 321)

(32) a. ?? What is [he saying] and [you doing]?
b. What [is he saying] and [are you doing]?
(Osborne 2006: 321)

In classical gapping structures the phonological identity is known to be relaxed, as shown in (33) for English and in (34) for German.

(33) [I *am doing* the windows] and [you the tables]
a. [I *am doing* the windows] and [you (*are doing*) the tables]
b. [I *am doing* the windows] and [you (**am doing*) the tables]
(see Osborne 2006: 321)

(34) ... dass [ich meinen Vater besucht habe] und [du deine Mutter].
that I my father visited have and you your mother
'... that I visited my father and you your mother.'
a. ... dass [ich meinen Vater besucht habe] und [du deine Mutter
that I my father visited have.1SG and you your mother
(besucht hast)].
visited have.2SG
b. ... dass [ich meinen Vater besucht habe] und [du deine Mutter
that I my father visited have.1SG and you your mother
(besucht *habe)].
visited have.1SG

Note the contrast with the non-gapping coordination in (35a). The verb cluster on the right is shared by both conjuncts and must therefore agree with both subjects, which is impossible in (35a) but necessarily so in (35b).

(35) a. ... dass [ich meinen Vater] und [du deine Mutter] besucht *habe/
that I my father and you your mother visited have.1SG
*hast.
have.2SG
b. ... dass [das Mädchen ihren Vater] und [der Junge seine Mutter] besucht
that the girl her father and the boy his mother visited
hat.
has.3SG
'that the girl visited her father and the boy visited his mother.'

Now, I apply this diagnostic to the examples in (25), repeated here as (36). If one of the subjects is altered to obtain a mismatch with the finite verb, the judgments significantly degrade, as shown in (37). The observation that the phonological identity of the shared element is required provides further evidence in favor of a Right Node Raising analysis and against a gapping analysis.

(36) a. [Der Professor |hat| einen Studenten] und [der Lehrer einen Schüler]
the professor has a student and the teacher a pupil
zu dem Vernetzungstreffen geschickt.
to the networking meeting sent
'The professor sent a student and the teacher sent a pupil to the network meeting.'

b. [Der Professor |hat| einen Studenten zu der Konferenz] und [der Lehrer
the professor has a student to the conference and the teacher
einen Schüler zu dem Vernetzungstreffen] geschickt.
a pupil to the network meeting sent
'The professor sent a student to the conference and the teacher sent a pupil to the network meeting.'

c. [Die Nachbarin |hat| ihrem Sohn eine Sonnenbrille] und [Herr Müller
the neighbor has her son a sunglasses and Mr. Müller
seiner Tochter eine Gitarre] geschenkt.
his daughter a guitar donated
'The neighbor has donated her son sunglasses and Mr. Müller donated his daughter a guitar.'

(37) a. * [Der Professor |hat| einen Studenten] und [wir einen Schüler] zu
the professor has.3SG a student and we a pupil to
dem Vernetzungstreffen geschickt.
the networking meeting sent

b. * [Die Professoren |haben| einen Studenten zu der Konferenz] und
the professors have.3PL a student to the conference and
[der Lehrer einen Schüler zu dem Vernetzungstreffen] geschickt.
the teacher a pupil to the network meeting sent

c. * [Ihr |habt| eurem Sohn eine Sonnenbrille] und [ich meiner Tochter
you have.2PL your son a sunglasses and I my daughter
eine Gitarre] geschenkt.
a guitar donated

In German, two strings that each include a finite verb can be coordinated, too, as shown in (38). Along the lines of the V2-Reconstruction Hypothesis, I predict that the analysis of the coordination in (38) involves two full clauses. In both clauses, the finite verb is reconstructed. In the first conjunct, the locative phrase and the participle are elided rather than shared, as illustrated in (39).

(38) a. [Der Professor hat einen Studenten] und [der Lehrer hat einen Schüler]
the professor has a student and the teacher has a pupil
zu dem Vernetzungstreffen geschickt.
to the networking meeting sent
'The professor sent a student and the teacher sent a pupil to the network meeting.'

b. [Der Professor hat einen Studenten] und [wir haben einen
the professor has.3SG a student and we have.1PL a
Schüler] zu dem Vernetzungstreffen geschickt.
pupil to the networking meeting sent
'The professor sent a student and we sent a pupil to the network meeting.'

(39) [Der Professor hat$_1$ einen Studenten ~~zu dem Vernetzungstreffen geschickt~~
the professor has a student to the networking meeting sent
~~hat$_1$~~] und [der Lehrer hat$_2$ einen Schüler zu dem Vernetzungstreffen
has and the teacher has a pupil to the networking meeting
geschickt ~~hat$_2$~~].
sent has
'The professor sent a student and the teacher sent a pupil to the network meeting.'

The paradigm in (40) provides further evidence that the predictions of the V2-Reconstruction Hypothesis are borne out and that the analysis in (39) is adequate. The Right Node Raising sentence in (40a) relates the external shared material with the conjuncts. Hence, a collective reference to the direct object of the two conjuncts by a plural pronoun is preferred. In the coordination of the two full clauses in (40b) however, each clause only allows a singular pronoun reference. Hence, the collective reading is unavailable.

(40) a. [Der Lehrer |hat| den jüngeren Bruder] und [die Trainerin den älteren
the teacher has the younger brother and the coach the older
Bruder] zu ?seinen/ deren Eltern begleitet.
brother to his their parents accompanied
'The teacher accompanied the younger brother and the coach accompanied the older bother to their parents.'

b. [Der Lehrer hat den jüngeren Bruder] und [die Trainerin hat den
the teacher has the younger brother and the coach has the
älteren Bruder zu seinen/ *deren Eltern begleitet].
older brother to his their parents accompanied
'The teacher accompanied the younger brother and the coach accompanied the older bother to their parents.'

Finally, I note that I judge sentences as in (38) to be clearly dispreferred in comparison to alternatives that involve *canonical* gapping, as in (41).

(41) a. [Der Professor hat einen Studenten] zu dem Vernetzungstreffen
the professor has a student to the networking meeting
geschickt und [der Lehrer einen Schüler].
sent and the teacher a pupil
'The professor sent a student to the network meeting and the teacher a pupil.'

b. [Der Professor hat einen Studenten] zu dem Vernetzungstreffen
the professor has.3SG a student to the networking meeting
geschickt und [wir einen Schüler].
sent and we a pupil
'The professor sent a student to the network meeting and we a pupil.'

The obligatory reconstruction of the finite verb has further consequences. German V2-clauses that contain only one verbal element, i. e. the finite verb, are ambiguous between gapping and non-gapping coordinations, as in (42).

(42) Josef schließt seine Tür und seine Schublade.
'Josef closes his door and his drawer.'

a. Gapping
[Josef schließt seine Tür ~~schließt~~] und [~~Josef~~ seine Schublade ~~schließt~~].
Josef closes his door and his drawer

b. Non-gapping
Josef schließt [seine Tür] und [seine Schublade] ~~schließt~~.
Josef closes his door and his drawer

The base position of the verb can be identified unambiguously by augmenting the verb with a particle. In the non-gapping coordination, the shared material outside of the coordination is identical for both conjuncts. Therefore the coordinated material must fulfill the same function, e. g. being subject or object. In gapping structures on the other hand, restrictions on the elided material are much less restrictive. In (43), the verbal particle may appear in the either one of the potential base positions of the particle verbs, parallel to (42). If the overt element of the second conjunct is simply a potential alternative for the subject of the first conjunct, as in (44), only the gapping analysis is licit. Hence the verbal particle that marks the base position of the finite verb, is only valid in the first conjunct.

(43) Josef schließt seine Tür ⟨ab⟩ und seine Schublade auch ⟨ab⟩.
'Josef locks his door and also his drawer.'

a. Gapping
[Josef schließt seine Tür ab~~schließt~~] und [~~Josef~~ seine Schublade auch
Josef closes his door from and his drawer too
~~abschließt~~].

b. Non-gapping
Josef schließt [seine Tür] und [seine Schublade auch] ab~~schließt~~.
Josef closes his door and his drawer too from

(44) Josef schließt seine Tür ⟨ab⟩ und seine Kollegin auch ⟨*ab⟩.
'Josef locks his door and his colleague too.'

a. Gapping
[Josef schließt seine Tür ab~~schließt~~] und [seine Kollegin ~~ihre Tür~~
Josef closes his door from and his colleague
auch ~~abschließt~~].
too

b. Non-gapping
*Josef schließt [seine Tür] und [seine Kollegin auch] ab~~schließt~~.
Josef closes his door and his colleague too from

The rhetorical figure *zeugma* employs similar ellipses which combine verbs with arguments of different types, whereby the lexical meaning of the verb changes.[10] It seems, however, that these lexical differences do not differentiate between gapping and non-gapping structures. Although Right Node Raising (non-gapping) requires phonological identity, it does not seem to require lexical identity, as illustrated by the examples in (45)–(47). Even though the judgments are subtle, I consider the gapping cases (b-examples) harder to understand than the non-gapping cases.

10 Many thanks to Laura Dörre for bringing this to my attention.

(45) a. Non-gapping (Right Node Raising)
Ich fror vor mich hin, denn nicht nur [meine Mutter], sondern
I froze before REFL along since not only my mother but
auch [der Ofen] war ausgegangen.
also the stove was went out
'I was freezing because not only my mother went out but also the stove extinguished.' (Heinz Erhardt, *Wieso ich Dichter wurde*, http://www.heinz-erhardt.de/html/dichtkunst.html)

b. Gapping
Ich fror vor mich hin, denn nicht nur [meine Mutter war
I froze before REFL along since not only my mother was
ausgegangen], sondern auch [der Ofen ~~war ausgegangen~~].
went out but also the stove

(46) a. Non-gapping (Right Node Raising)
Unverzüglich werde ich [mich bei der Prüfungskommission] und [die
immediately will I REFL at the examination board and the
Blätter mit einem Ziegelstein] beschweren.
sheets with a brick complain/weight
'Immediately I will complain at the examination board and weight the sheets with a brick.'

b. Gapping
Unverzüglich [werde ich mich bei der Prüfungskommission beschweren]
immediately will I REFL at the examination board complain/weight
und [~~werde ich~~ die Blätter mit einem Ziegelstein ~~beschweren~~].
and the sheets with a brick

(47) a. Non-gapping (Right Node Raising)
Maria hat [zuerst mit ihrem Mann] und [dann tief und fest]
Maria has first with her husband and then deep and firm
geschlafen.
slept
'Maria first had sex with her husband and then was sound asleep.'

b. Gapping
[Maria hat zuerst mit ihrem Mann geschlafen] und [dann ~~hat Maria~~
Maria has first with her husband slept and then
tief und fest ~~geschlafen~~].
deep and firm

To summarize, the discussion of coordinated structures has revealed that German V2-clauses show significant structural differences in comparison to English clauses. In particular, I have argued that the finite verb in V2-position does not take part in temporary constituents. This, in turn, disfavors an analysis of cascading structure buildup and favors the insertion strategy as the preferred analysis of parsing of V2-structures.

7.2.2 The preverbal area: Licensing direction and core interpretation domain

Following Haider (2012), I assume that languages with head-initial VPs (VSO and SVO languages) have anterograde[11] licensing heads. As a consequence, head-initial VPs show two main properties: *compactness* and *strict serialization* (Haider 2010: 10–14). Compactness means that no element may intervene between the verbal head and its object, as in (48a), or between two objects, as in (48b). Strict serialization is the absence of scrambling, as shown in (48c). The corresponding German examples in (49) illustrate that the head-final V-domain in German differs with respect to both of these properties.

(48) ENGLISH

a. We will [prepare (*carefully) this dish].

b. You have [told (*humorously) your students (*humorously) personal stories].

c. * You have [told personal stories$_1$ your students t_1].

(49) GERMAN

a. Wir werden (sorgfältig) dieses Gericht (sorgfältig) zubereiten.
we will carefully this dish carefully prepare

b. Du hast (humorvoll) deinen Studenten (humorvoll) persönliche
you have humorously your students humorously personal
Geschichten (humorvoll) erzählt.
stories humorously told

c. Du hast persönliche Geschichten$_1$ deinen Studenten t_1 erzählt.
you have personal stories your students told

Haider (2012) demonstrates that the properties compactness and strict-serialization are consequences of head-initial and head-final phrases across domains, i. e. these regularities are not restricted to verbal projections but hold also for NPs, APs etc. I assume that processing mechanisms differ as a function of the headedness of a phrase. Parsing of head-initial phrases is *predictive* with respect to

11 *Anterograde* means progressing in the forward direction, locally and temporally.

the thematic structure, whereas parsing of head-final phrases is *integrative*. Thus, the processor employs the cascading strategy for head-initial phrases, a simple right-branching extension for head-final phrases, and the insertion strategy for head-final V2-structures.

In V2-clauses, the insertion strategy requires some kind of decision mechanism whether to insert incoming phrases preverbally or postverbally, i. e. higher than the verbal head of the clause or lower. Superficial cues for the clause-final position are, for example, provided by the non-finite parts of the verb cluster, complementizers of subordinate clauses and intonation. A similar decision mechanism must also be assumed for the cascade strategy, namely a decision whether the verb has to be lowered or not. This could be triggered by the valency of the verb.

Phrase structures built by both strategies, insertion and cascading, seem to have a *core interpretation domain*. In the cascading structure this domain consists of the postverbal area, i. e. the adjacent arguments. Since the verb precedes its arguments, the representation that results from the identification of a verb is likely to be incomplete in the sense of (20) in Section 4.1.4, i. e. its particular interpretation depends on the arguments and hence may be revised. The two properties of head-initial phrases *compactness* and *strict serialization* enforce that the verb meaning will be completed as early as possible.

Carlson & Tanenhaus (1988) report an informal experiment that investigates the processing difficulty of thematic and lexical ambiguity in English. In (50) the string *Bill set the alarm clock* is ambiguous with respect to the lexical meaning of *set*. The sentences are disambiguated by the final phrase in (50a) and (50c). Sentences (50b) and (50d) form unambiguous control conditions. Similarly, the clauses in (51) contain a thematic ambiguity. The initial string *Bill loaded the truck* is ambiguous with respect to the thematic role of the NP *the truck* which can either be goal as in (51a) or a theme as in (51c). Again the clauses in (51b) and (51d) represent unambiguous control sentences.

(50) Lexical ambiguity[12]

a. Bill set the alarm clock for six in the morning.

---

12 Joseph Bayer pointed out that the two meanings of *set* must ultimately receive different analyses. In ditransitive structures, the verb has to be lowered in order to license the indirect argument *onto the shelf*, as in (i.a), whereas the adjunct *for six in the morning* in (i.b) can be adjoined to the VP without lowering of the verb. This resembles the mirror image of the VP shell analysis of Larson (1988).

(i) a. *Bill [~~set~~ [the alarm clock] [set [onto the shelf]]].*

b. *Bill [[set the alarm clock] [for six in the morning]].*

b. Bill reset the alarm clock for six in the morning.
c. Bill set the alarm clock onto the shelf.
d. Bill put the alarm clock onto the shelf.
(Carlson & Tanenhaus 1988: 274)

(51) Thematic ambiguity
a. Bill loaded the truck with bricks.
b. Bill filled the truck with bricks.
c. Bill loaded the truck onto the ship.
d. Bill drove the truck onto the ship.
(Carlson & Tanenhaus 1988: 274)

Carlson & Tanenhaus (1988) conducted a decision task experiment in which the participants had to decide whether the sentence *makes sense* as quickly as possible. Lexical ambiguity evokes longer reaction times and a lower percentage of positive answers (*makes sense*) than thematic ambiguities and unambiguous control conditions. A post hoc analysis revealed that the reaction time difference is caused by cases of lexical ambiguity which are disambiguated towards the less-preferred sense. They report a similar but weaker effect for disambiguation towards the less-preferred thematic structure. Carlson & Tanenhaus (1988) assume that only one of several possible meanings of an ambiguous verb, namely the contextually most appropriate, will remain active during on-line processing. Later reaccess of an alternative meaning is comparably costly, whereas readjustment of thematic roles is comparably easy.

Assuming that the processing mechanism of German resembles the English procedure, we expect that German shows severe problems with resolving lexical ambiguities, caused by homonymous predicates, polysemous predicates, or incomplete particle verbs (see Section 4.3.4). However, those potential garden-path sentences are typicality unproblematic, which indicates that the semantic interpretation of these predicates is delayed. I suggest that the core interpretation domain of head-final insertion structures consists of the preverbal area. Upon reaching the verb, the VP's content will be chunked and sent to interpretation. This chunk has to be interpretational complete, as was defined in (20) of Section 4.1.4, i. e. the meaning of the predicate must not change after this point. Therefore, all parts that are required for the identification of the interpretational properties of the predicate must be available at this point. The intuition behind this assumption is the following: Imagine an incomplete structure is sent to interpretation prematurely. First, the processor activates a particular verb meaning. Subsequently, an incompatible element is encountered and the structure has to be reanalyzed.

Reanalysis of meaning involves the reaccess of lower level elements (phonetic or morphology), which is costly because the activation level of the lower level representation have faded and must be reactivated. Depending on the distance and thereby the temporal decay, the processor may not be able to reactivate the lower level representations at all and may only be able to reconstruct the content partially. Depending on the headedness of the VP, we observe one of the two instances for processing incomplete structures: Head-initial phrases employ the anticipation strategy and activate the contextually most appropriate meaning as soon as the verb is encountered. This decision may have to be revised. Head-final phrases also initiate the interpretation process at the verb. At this point, however, the arguments are already accessible and the mapping is complete. In V2-clauses of verb-final languages, such as German, the processor adheres to the integrative licensing of VP-internal material to the left of the verb. This results in delayed interpretation of the finite verb at the clause-final position.

7.2.3 The postverbal area: Extraposition and its restrictions

Extraposition seems to be an exception to the requirement that the core interpretation domain must be complete. Closer inspection of the restrictions on extraposition, however, will reveal that extraposition is only apparently an exception. The discussion will lead to a more precise understanding of the core interpretation domain. I will first discuss the difference between extraposition of nominal and clausal complements before I take a closer look at the extraposition of PPs.

Extraposition is another instance of non-linear parsing. We might describe extraposition as delayed pronunciation of a certain constituent. Verb-final languages exhibit complex center embedded patterns, as illustrated in (52a). Especially for selected clauses, as in (52b), and relative clauses, it has been proposed that extraposition is a structural option that facilitates parsing because the dependents (arguments) of the matrix verb *versprochen* 'promised' can be assigned earlier in the extraposed variant (52b), namely after *Lehrerin* 'teacher', in contrast to the in-situ variant in (52a), in which the assignment is delayed until the sentence-final position (Hawkins 2004: 142–146).

(52) a. Gestern hat [der Vater$_i$ der Lehrerin [PRO$_i$ seinen Sohn
yesterday has [the father]NOM [the teacher.F].DAT [his son]ACC
der Tochter des Hausmeisters vorzustellen] versprochen].
[the daughter [of the janitor]GEN]DAT introduce.INF promised
'Yesterday the father promised to the teacher to introduce his son to the daughter of the janitor.'

b. Gestern hat [der Vater$_i$ der Lehrerin t_1 versprochen] [PRO$_i$
yesterday has [the father]NOM [the teacher.F].DAT promised
seinen Sohn der Tochter des Hausmeisters vorzustellen]$_1$.
[his son]ACC [the daughter [of the janitor]GEN]DAT introduce.INF
'Yesterday the father promised to the teacher to introduce his son to the daughter of the janitor.'

I presume that not all instances of right dislocation have a homogeneous cause. Within the limit of this publication, I cannot address the phenomenon of extraposition thoroughly. Instead, I will focus on the restrictions of extraposition. Extraposition in German is severely restricted and only observed for embedded clauses and PPs (Haider 2010: 188–196).[13] Extraposition of clausal complements is always possible and even strongly preferred for finite clauses. Non-clausal complements of the verb must not be extraposed. I assume the cause for the ban on non-clausal arguments is that the meaning of the predicate is specified by its non-clausal arguments. Here is an example: The verbs *versuchen/probieren* are polysemous with a base meaning of 'try' as in (53a). With an NP argument, denoting edible things, the verbs have an alternative meaning 'taste', as in (53b).

(53) a. Heute hat Julius im Kindergarten [das Eis mit Erdbeergeschmack
Today has Julius in the kindergarten the ice with strawberry flavor
selbst herzustellen] versucht/probiert.
self make tried
'Today in kindergarten Julius tried to make the ice cream with strawberry flavor.'

b. Heute hat Julius im Kindergarten [das Eis mit Erdbeergeschmack]
Today has Julius in the kindergarten the ice with strawberry flavor
versucht/probiert.
tasted
'Today in kindergarten Julius tasted the ice cream with strawberry flavor.'

The DP argument is crucial for the specific verb meaning. Therefore it must be contained in the core interpretation domain. Indeed, extraposition of the non-finite clause in (54a) is fine, whereas extraposition of the DP in (54b) is out.[14]

---

13 I will not consider the extraposition of heavy DP arguments as presentend in Haider (2010: 192). They seem to be subject to additional constraints, which cannot be discussed here.

14 A restricted class of cluster verbs in German also allow the so called *third construction*, as in (i), in which the argument (*the ice ...*) of the lower verb (*make*) appears before the clustering verb (see Haider 2010: 284–286 and references therein).

(54) a. Heute hat Julius im Kindergarten versucht/probiert [das Eis
Today has Julius in the kindergarten tried the ice
mit Erdbeergeschmack selbst herzustellen].
with strawberry flavor self make
'Today in the kindergarten, Julius tried to make the ice cream with strawberry flavor.'

b. *Heute hat Julius im Kindergarten versucht/probiert [das Eis
Today has Julius in the kindergarten tasted the ice
mit Erdbeergeschmack].
with strawberry flavor

A similar contrast can be illustrated with the verb *ärgern*, which is ambiguous between the agentive meaning 'tease' and the experiencer object meaning 'annoy'. The subject in the agentive use in (55a) is expressed by a DP. In the experiencer object use in (55b), on the other hand, the subject is expressed by a clausal complement. The contrast in (56) shows that the DP in (56a) cannot occur postverbally, whereas the clausal subject in (56b) can.

(55) a. [Der Junge aus der Nachbarschaft] hat meinen Bruder geärgert.
the boy from the neighborhood has my brother teased
'The boy from the neighborhood teased my brother.'

b. [Dass wir schon nach Hause gehen] hat meinen Bruder geärgert.
that we already at home go has my brother annoyed
'That we already go home annoyed my brother.'

(56) a. Meinen Bruder hat ⟨der Junge aus der Nachbarschaft⟩ geärgert
[my brother]ACC has the boy from the neighborhood teased
⟨*der Junge aus der Nachbarschaft⟩.
the boy from the neighborhood
'The boy from the neighborhood teased my brother.'

(i) *Heute hat Julius im Kindergarten [das Eis mit Erdbeergeschmack] versucht/probiert*
Today has Julius in the kindergarten the ice with strawberry flavor tried
selbst herzustellen.
self make
'Today in the kindergarten, Julius tried to make the ice cream with strawberry flavor.'

b. Meinen Bruder hat (es) geärgert, [dass wir schon nach Hause
[my brother]ACC has EXPL annoyed that we already at home
gehen].
go
'That we already go home annoyed my brother.'

The stimulus subject can alternatively be expressed as a DP on the surface. This DP however is a representative for a propositional argument, as in (57). In such uses the DP stands for the event of giving the answer, or the fact that the answer has some specific property, such as *dass die Antwort so grob war* 'that the answer was so rude'.[15]

(57) Die Antwort des Lehrers ärgerte den fleißigen Schüler.
the answer of the teacher annoyed the diligent student
'The answer of the teacher annoyed the diligent student.'

The extraposition data show that the restrictions apply to the syntactic category. The extraposed DP in (58a) is ungrammatical even though it represents a clausal element. Only the spelled out clause can be extraposed, as shown in (58b).

(58) a. * Den fleißigen Schüler hat (es) geärgert die Antwort des Lehrers.
the diligent student has EXPL annoyed the answer of the teacher
'The answer of the teacher annoyed the diligent student.'

b. Den fleißigen Schüler hat (es) geärgert, dass die Antwort des
the diligent student has EXPL annoyed that the answer of the
Lehrers so grob war.
teacher so rude was
'That the answer of the teacher was so rude annoyed the diligent student.'

The restrictions on PPs, on the other hand, are not specified formally but functionally. PPs (and DPs) appear at the right edge only if they are adverbial, as in (59).

(59) a. Ich habe gestern noch im Büro gearbeitet [bis spät in die Nacht].
I have yesterday still in-the office worked till late in the night

b. wenn sie nicht geheiratet hätte [letztes Jahr] /*seinen Nachbarn.
if she not married had last year his neighbour
(Haider 2010: 191–192)

15 Thanks to Anne Temme for bringing this to my attention.

If the PP functions as a secondary predicate, i. e. if it specifies the meaning of the predicate, as in (60), then the PP has to be contained in the core interpretation domain and must not be extraposed.

(60) a. Resultative predicate
*Er hat es geschnitten [in kleine Stücke].
he has it cut into small pieces
'He cut it into small pieces.'

b. Directional predicate
*Er hat sie gestellt [in eine Ecke].
he has her put into a corner
'He put her into a corner.'

c. Predicative PP
*Es ist gewesen [in einem schlechten Zustand].
it is been in a bad shape
'It has been in a bad shape.'

(Haider 2010: 192)

The generalization that we can draw about extraposition (and its restrictions) is the following: The core interpretation domain must be complete. Information which is necessary for the interpretation of the event must appear preverbally because at the clause-final position, i. e. the base position of the finite verb, the structure is mapped onto the semantic representation. Any postverbal information that alters the meaning of the verb, enforces the processor to reanalyze the VP. Structures that violate this principle are good candidates to be excluded by grammatical conventions because they are highly error prone. This does not exclude that additional information is added later on, but such additions are typically only allowed for adjuncts which do not alter the interpretation of the event.

I will conclude the discussion of extraposition with a remark concerning the violation of restrictions on extraposition. There are actually grammatical possibilities to add argumental information in the postverbal area. This is shown in (61a), an extension of (59b), and (61b). The examples involve coordinative-restrictive elements such as *oder zumindest* 'or at least' and *und zwar* 'and in fact', that trigger gapping structures that permit extensions of the gapped (duplicated) predicate. The parallel examples in (61c) and (61d) show that such extension are only permissible if the initial string is already acceptable.

(61) a. Wenn sie nicht geheiratet hätte oder zumindest nicht seinen
if she not married had or at least not his
Nachbarn.
neighbour

b. Sie hat geheiratet und zwar ihren Nachbarn.
she has married and in fact her neighbor

c. * Sie hat angelächelt und zwar ihren Nachbarn.
she has smiled at and in fact her neighbor

d. * Den Schüler hat (es) geärgert und zwar die Antwort des Lehrers.
the student has EXPL annoyed and in fact the answer of the teacher

The processing routine, as it has been sketched above, does not rule out that predicates may be specified postverbally but it predicts that such cases are considerably demanding. Indeed, we find rhetorical figures in which those restrictions on postverbal complementation are intentionally violated. Examples of that sort are the zeugmata in (45)–(47) above or the one in (62), in which the two meanings *ausgehen* 'go out' and *von etwas ausgehen* 'assume something' are contrasted. The argumental PP *davon* 'thereoff' in the second part is extraposed.

(62) Ich gehe aus, Baptist! Vor allem davon, dass Sie mir auf meine Talerchen
I go out Baptist above all thereof that you me for my coins
achten!
watch
'I go out Baptist. And I assume that you will watch my money.'
[https://de.wikipedia.org/wiki/Zeugma_(Sprache), accessed 19.04.2021]

I mentioned above that these constructions appear to be more degraded in the gapping analysis in contrast to the Right Node Raising analysis, in (45)–(47). Within the current perspective, this receives a principled explanation: In the gapping analysis, the first conjunct is complete and sent to interpretation as soon as the finite verb is encountered. During the processing of the second conjunct the content of the first conjunct is copied. Due to the incompatibility of the two argument structures, lower level representations of the copied content (phonological representation, syntactic representation) have to be accessed. In the Right Node Raising analysis, on the other hand, the core interpretation domain remains incomplete until the end of the sentence. At the clause-final position the meanings of the two conjuncts are computed in parallel[16].

16 The term *parallel* is not used in a temporal sense here, rather it should mean that the meaning of each conjunct will be computed independent of the meaning of the other.

7.2.4 Speculations about crosslinguistic generalizations

I argued above that elements which are displaced into a higher functional projection are reconstructed into their base position for interpretation. This holds for phrasal movement such as *wh*-movement and topicalization, but also for displaced heads, such as the finite verb in V2-clauses. In canonical cases, leftward movement adds a meaning component to the moved item, such as scope to *wh*-elements, or information structural aspects, such as topic and focus. In case of V2-movement, I assumed that the movement is driven by some abstract requirement for finiteness, and the verb is solely pied-piped. But irrespective of the trigger, the dislocated element has to be reconstructed into the base position for proper interpretation. This reconstruction requirement may be the key to understand left-right asymmetries in phrase structure analyses. One prominent observation concerns the asymmetry of movement patterns: Wh-movement, for instance, seems to proceed only to the left (see *Filler First* principle Hawkins 2004: 203–205). The explanation is obvious: Movement to the left, allows on-line interpretation at the gap site, because the gap follows the filler. Movement to the right, however, will either delay the interpretation or even result in a serious misparse that requires reanalysis.

I will assume that a lexical head can only be interpreted within its functional extension[17], for example, the VP and its extension, the IP. The functional extension specifies properties that situate the event, such as tense. If the lexical verb moves to a higher functional position, it must reconstruct into its base position to be in the c-command domain of, for instance, sentence negation. If the functional extension of the verb is realized without movement, i. e. by an unbound morpheme, it takes the verb in its core interpretation domain. Accepting these assumptions, it becomes clear why one combination of functional extensions of lexical phrases is apparently absent in natural languages: head-initial lexical phrases that are dominated by a head-final functional extension as illustrated in Haider (2012: 67–81), a configuration that has also been discussed under the term *Final-Over-Final Constraint* (FOFC) (Biberauer et al. 2008)[18]. If higher functional categories have to be reconstructed into their lexical base position, these elements must either precede the base position or they must be adjacent, enabling a cluster formation (for peculiarities of head adjacency see Bayer 1999, Bayer et al. 2005,

---

17 Functional extensions are functional projections in which lexical content of the head is derived by movement or feature attraction. Lexical complementizers or determiners do not qualify as derived heads (Haider 2012: 71).

18 See Haider (2012: 132–135) for a direct comparison of the binary branching conjecture (BBC) and the FOFC.

Haider 2010). Thus, patterns with a head-initial phrase dominated by a head-final one are ruled out, as illustrated in (63) vs. (64). Reconstruction cannot apply to the left, because it involves reprocessing the structure from the base position of the VP onward. In a recursive grammar, the object can be of arbitrary length and so would be the distance between the base position of the verb and its dislocated position in the functional extension.

(63)

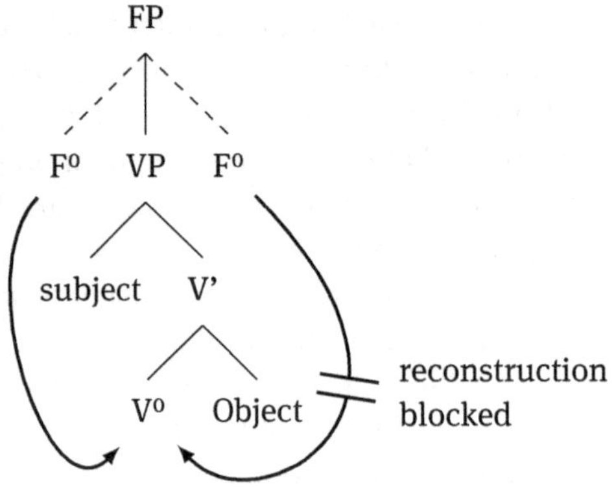

(64)

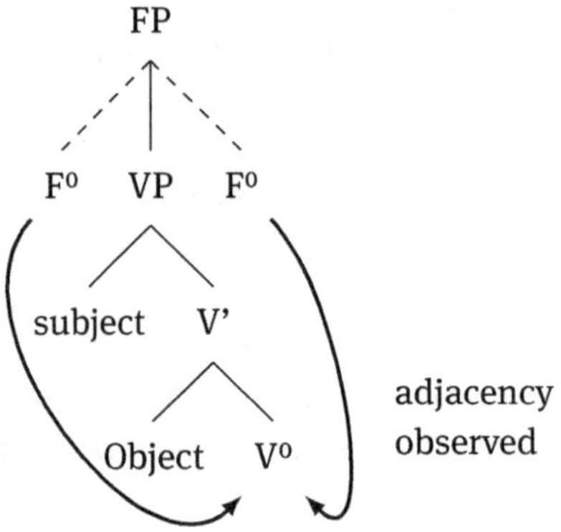

In a strictly head-final language, we could also encounter a generalized V-to-C movement. However, this would not result in V2-clauses but in V-final clauses because the movement would be string-vacuous, as can be illustrated in (65). And indeed there exists a discussion about string-vacuous verb movement in head-final languages, such as Japanese and Korean, see Koisumi (2000) and Hatakeyama et al. (2008) for arguments in favor of verb movement, and Kobayashi (2016) for arguments against it. Expectedly, the arguments are based on indirect evidence and are rather complex. Future research will show which position will prevail.

(65)

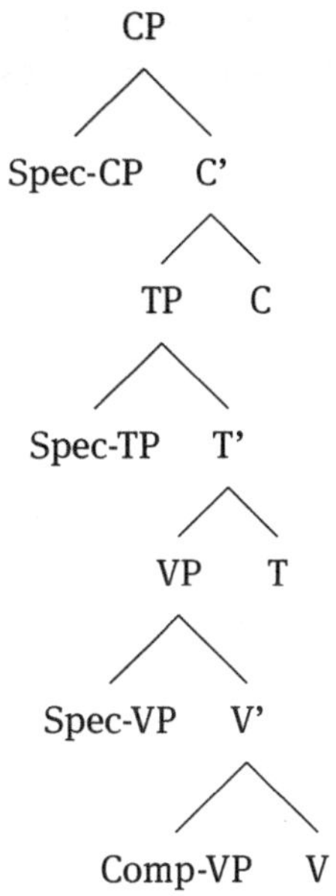

7.3 Chapter summary

In this chapter, I have provided a detailed description of the mechanics of the V2-Reconstruction Hypothesis. I have argued that V2-parsing does not involve a successive lowering of the verb with multiple instances (copies) of it. In contrast, I have argued that the parser places the finite verb in clause-final position very early and inserts incoming phrases before the verb. I cited experimental results which indicate that the resulting structure will be interpreted as soon as it is potentially complete. Following Phillips (2003), I employed Right Node Raising structures to identify temporary constituents of the German clause during incremental parsing. The results indicated that the finite verb does not take part in temporary constituents, as predicted by the V2-Reconstruction Hypothesis. I have also considered the consequences for the interpretation process of verb-final clauses. The clause-final verb marks the end of the core interpretation domain. This matches with extraction facts that only allow non-argumental constituents and clausal complements to be extraposed. Finally, I have speculated that reconstruction of functional heads might be the cause for the absence of non-adjacent functional heads succeeding their lexical heads.

In sum, I have specified the incremental procedure of V2-parsing in German and identified crucial contrasts to SVO structure building as it has been described for English.

8 Grand summary and conclusion

This monograph makes two major contributions to the investigation of the V2-phenomenon which build on the well-established insight that the V2-order is a derived word order establishing a dependency between the base position and the surface position of the finite verb. First, the investigation provides empirical evidence from linguistic and psycholinguistic investigations for the hypothesis that the lexical content of the V2-verb is reconstructed into and only interpreted in its base position. Verb reconstruction, therefore, provides a case in which language comprehension closely follows grammatical principles. Second, the discussion refines some details of the reconstruction process and relates it to other general properties of language processing in German.

In the following, I briefly summarize the chapters and recapitulate the main conclusions and open issues.

Part I set the scene with an introduction into the broader phenomenon of V2-movement and the presentation of the V2-Reconstruction Hypothesis – the core idea on which this publication is based.

In Chapter 2, I illustrated the main properties of the V2-phenomenon. First, there must be a movement dependency between the base position of the finite verb and the V2-position with the latter being a derived position because, under certain conditions, specific verbs may only appear in the base position but not in the V2-position, whereas the reverse pattern is unattested. Second, V2-movement applies exceptionless, i. e. it cannot be suspended. In some cases, the application of V2-movement conflicts with another rule of grammar and would result in an ungrammatical structure. Crucially, however, the non-application of V2-movement in such cases also leads to ungrammaticality. The only possibility is to alter the sentence, e. g. by using a different verb form, such that both grammatical requirements can be satisfied. Third, V2-movement targets one specific position in the left periphery of the clause. While the filling of the prefield shows larger variation giving rise to V1- or V3-pattern, these patterns are very restricted in their interpretation and use conditions.

Chapter 3 introduced the central assumption, namely the V2-Reconstruction Hypothesis, according to which V2-movement affects only the finiteness features while the lexical part of the verb is pied-piped. Consequently, the lexical part has to be reconstructed into its base position, which is is also the only locus at which the lexical content of the verb is interpreted. Two groups of evidence were presented in support of the V2-Reconstruction Hypothesis: First, I showed that the V2-position is systematically filled with surface elements that are insufficient for

https://doi.org/10.1515/9783110725018-008

interpretation (particle verbs), semantically empty (periphrastic *tun*), or outright ungrammatical if interpreted at this point (verb doubling). Second, using semantic operators which require a c-command relation, such as association with focus, verbal NPIs and sentence negation, I provided evidence that the finite verb must be interpreted in its base position. Taken together, the results strongly support the V2-Reconstruction Hypothesis.

All in all, Part I provided the empirical and theoretical background to understand the significance and the implications of the V2-Reconstruction Hypothesis. Additionally, it also provided an empirical basis for the validity of the V2-Reconstruction Hypothesis whose predictions concerning language processing were applied in the next part. The discussion of Part I has shown that V2-movement is a rather abstract mechanism that attracts only the finiteness features or, as the data from complementizer agreement indicates, only the subset of subject-agreement features. However, it still remains unclear, why these features have to be realized in the left periphery in V2-languages. There exist several sophisticated accounts that connect V2-movement with the illocutionary potential of main clauses. As mentioned in Chapter 2, for now, these accounts seem to be language-specific. They may not be generalizable for all V2-languages and, moreover, do not explain why such a feature movement seems to be unnecessary in the majority of languages.

Part II provided a general introduction to language processing and sentence processing in German, followed by a series of on-line experiments which tested the predictions of the V2-Reconstruction Hypothesis. Finally, I explored some specifics of the reconstruction process based on theoretical arguments.

In Chapter 4, I sketched the basic properties of an on-line language comprehension model with a focus on the syntactic domain. I illustrated that deviations from strict on-line processing, as assumed by the V2-Reconstruction Hypothesis, occur regularly and are handled by one of two different processing strategies: anticipatory analysis with potential subsequent repairs, or delayed processing. Comparison with well-established manifestations of these two strategies in other languages and domains, especially the absence of garden paths effects, indicated that V2-clauses adhere to delayed processing. Additionally, a delayed processing as assumed under the V2-Reconstruction Hypothesis is also preferable for reasons of economy because the V2-position is frequently occupied by verbs that are either uninformative (auxiliaries, modals, etc.) or misleading with respect to the meaning of the predicate (particle verbs).

Chapter 5 reviewed previous findings regarding the processing of the core argument structure in German sentences. The review showed that argument orders that deviate from the canonical NOM<ACC<DAT order give rise to immediate pro-

cessing responses, which are more local for scrambling and long-lasting for topicalization. These findings provided the background for experimental investigations of the influence of lexical V2-verbs on the processing of arguments. In this light, I reviewed on-line processing experiments on thematic structure, attachment ambiguities and scope computing in German. The results indicated that potentially verb-related effects only appeared rather late in the clauses as predicted by the V2-Reconstruction Hypothesis.

In Chapter 6, I presented four self-paced reading experiments that tested predictions of the V2-Reconstruction Hypothesis concerning on-line sentence processing. The experiments on verbal NPIs and the one on infinitive selection showed that the finite verb is automatically reconstructed into the first potential base position. Only subsequent interpretation could reveal whether insertion of the verb led to ungrammaticality, e. g. in case of non-licensed NPIs or mismatching infinitive forms, which was reflected by increased reading times. The experiment on the interaction of verb types and argument order showed a verb-specific modulation of the argument-order preference at the reconstruction site of the verb. Additionally, the experimental manipulation led to other, less clear-cut, correlates appearing later and also earlier in the clause which must be further investigated to allow a clear interpretation.

In Chapter 7, I examined three aspects of how the reconstruction process should look like. First, subject-initial V2-clauses are special in that their structural representation can be generated with fewer restructuring operations. Second, I contrasted two realizations of verb reconstruction: lowering the verb cascadically after every incoming unit, or inserting incoming units directly before the verb. By applying the logic of temporary constituency to Right Node Raising structures in German V2-clauses, I constructed an argument against the cascading analysis and in favor of the insertion approach. Third, I argued that only the subject-verb agreement features on the finite verb are immediately interpreted. Other aspects of the verb are only interpreted after every incoming argument. The interpretation may be extended or altered during the course of the processing. However, once unambiguous cues for the clause-final base position are encountered, the parse is completed and the core meaning cannot be altered again, as evidenced by restrictions on extraposition.

Based on explicit assumptions about a human processing device, I explicated in this part how the predictions of the V2-Reconstruction Hypothesis are reflected in previous research on sentence comprehension in German. Furthermore, I presented the results of four specifically designed studies as additional support of the V2-Reconstruction Hypothesis. Finally, I discussed some details of the structural analysis and its relation to semantic interpretation in on-line processing. The experimental investigation of the V2-Reconstruction Hypothesis is the major contribution of this work. The results support the hypothesis that there is an asymmetry between the syntactic realization of the finite verb and the semantic interpretation. While I have shown in Part I that this asymmetry is operative in the realm of grammar, the findings of this part showed that this asymmetry also holds on the level of language processing. This may provide the strongest case of grammar overruling inherent principles of on-line processing. It is clear that the investigations here can only be regarded as the beginning of an experimental endeavor aiming in a detailed understanding of how the linguistic representations are constructed in V2-environments. After all, the experimental results presented here indicate that at least some meaning components of the verb, such as polarity-sensitivity and infinitive selection, are activated at a position different from the surface occurrence. This is an important result for any research on sentence processing in V2-languages because until now it has mostly been assumed, implicitly or explicitly, and without positive evidence that V2-sentences are processed/interpreted strictly incrementally. While future research must show which aspects enter the sentence processing routine immediately, the findings of this study indicate that some information is only evaluated at the reconstruction site of the verb.

Taken together, this investigation presented evidence which shows that German V2-order is derived from an underlying V-final order. Moreover, I presented a hypothesis according to which the underlying base position is not only of relevance for grammar models but it is also the locus where the lexical content of the V2-moved verb will be interpreted. In support of this hypothesis, I have offered empirical evidence from grammatical regularities and from on-line processing experiments, confirming the psychological reality of the hypothesis.

Finally, I would like to add two remarks, one about the nature of V2-movement and one about the generality of the findings: First, the findings indicate that V2-movement is the consequence of the requirement to realize subject-verb agreement features in the left periphery. It remains open why these features have to be realized in the V2-position in V2-languages only. However, whereas the findings reveal that the lexical content of the V2-verb only enters the processing at a later point, it has been noted that the realization of the agreement features immediately impacts language processing. This shows that V2-movement is best characterized as I-to-C movement, which also becomes evident in languages that realize agreement features exclusively by clitics (Warpiri) or auxiliaries (O'odham) – these languages never move lexical verbs. Having this in mind, I must clearly oppose to the claim that V2-movement is non-syntactical in nature, as e. g. argued in Zwart (2017). As stated above, the pied-piping of other material, such as the lexical verb, is due to extrasyntactic factors whereas the movement of the agreement features is purely syntactic. In this way, deeming V2-movement as a whole non-syntactic misses crucial details of its nature. Second, the argumentation of this contribution was mainly based on German. At numerous points, however, I drew comparisons to other V2-languages. Generally, I assume that the cause of V2-movement is identical in all V2-languages, namely that subject-verb agreement features must be realized in the left periphery. Consequently, the V2-Reconstruction Hypothesis applies to all other V2-languages as well. However, VO-languages, such as the Scandinavian languages, differ not only in the locus of the base position of the finite verb but, as I mentioned above, VO-parsing assumably differs parametrically from OV-parsing. This must certainly be considered if the findings of this investigation will be adapted to those languages.

Bibliography

Abraham, Werner & Annette Fischer. 1998. Das grammatische Optimalisierungsszenario von *tun* als Hilfsverb. In Karin Donhauser & Ludwig M. Eichinger (eds.), *Deutsche Grammatik – Thema in Variationen: Festschrift für Hans-Werner Eroms zum 60. Geburtstag*. Heidelberg: Winter.

Anderson, John R., Daniel Bothell, Michael D. Byrne, Scott Douglas, Christian Lebiere & Yulin Qin. 2004. An integrated theory of the mind. *Psychological Review* 111(4). 1036–1060.

Antomo, Mailin & Markus Steinbach. 2010. Desintegration und Interpretation: *Weil*-V2-Sätze an der Schnittstelle zwischen Syntax, Semantik und Pragmatik. *Zeitschrift für Sprachwissenschaft* 29. 1–37.

Baayen, Harald R. & Petar Milin. 2010. Analyzing reaction times. *International Journal of Psychological Research* 3(2). 12–28.

Bach, Emmon. 1962. The order of elements in a transformational grammar of German. *Language* 38(2). 263–269.

Bach, Emmon, Colin Brown & William Marslen-Wilson. 1986. Crossed and nested dependencies in German and Dutch: A psycholinguistic study. *Language and Cognitive Processes* 1(4). 249–262.

Bader, Markus & Josef Bayer. 2006. *Case and linking in language comprehension: Evidence from German*. Dordrecht: Springer.

Bader, Markus & Ingeborg Lasser. 1994. German verb-final clauses and sentence processing: Evidence for immediate attachment. In Charles Clifton, Lyn Frazier & Keith Rayner (eds.), *Perspectives on sentence processing*, 225–242. Hillsdale, NJ: Lawrence Erlbaum Associates.

Bader, Markus & Michael Meng. 1999. Subject-object ambiguities in German embedded clauses: An across-the-board comparison. *Journal of Psycholinguistic Research* 28(2). 121–143.

Barr, Dale J., Roger Levy, Christoph Scheepers & Harry J. Tily. 2013. Random effects structure for confirmatory hypothesis testing: Keep it maximal. *Journal of Memory and Language* 68(3). 255–278.

Bartsch, Renate & Theo Vennemann. 1972. *Semantic structures: A study in the relation between semantics and syntax*. Frankfurt am Main: Athenaeum Verlag.

Basilico, David, Pilar Piñar & Inès Antòn-Mèndez. 1995. Canonical word order and the processing of verbal traces in Spanish. The Proceedings of the Eighth Annual CUNY Conference on Human Sentence Processing, Tucson, Arizona.

Bates, Douglas, Reinhold Kliegl, Shravan Vasishth & Harald Baayen. 2015. Parsimonious mixed models. Unpublished manuscript, eprint arXiv:1506.04967.

Bates, Douglas, Martin Maechler & Ben Bolker. 2013. *lme4: Linear mixed-effects models using S4 classes*. R package version 0.999999-2.

Bayer, Josef. 1984. COMP in Bavarian syntax. *The Linguistic Review* 3(3). 209–274.

Bayer, Josef. 1993. V(p)-topicalization and the role of traces. Unpublished manuscript, Universität Stuttgart.

Bayer, Josef. 1996. *Directionality and logical form: On the scope of focusing particles and* wh-*in-situ*. Dordrecht: Kluwer.

Bayer, Josef. 1999. Final complementizers in hybrid languages. *Journal of Linguistics* 35(2). 233–271.

https://doi.org/10.1515/9783110725018-009

Bayer, Josef. 2004. Decomposing the left periphery: Dialectal and cross-linguistic evidence. In Horst Lohnstein & Susanne Trissler (eds.), *The syntax and semantics of the left periphery*, 59–95. Berlin: De Gruyter Mouton.

Bayer, Josef. 2008. What is verb second? Unpublished manuscript, Universität Konstanz.

Bayer, Josef. 2014. Syntactic and phonological properties of *wh*-operators and *wh*-movement in Bavarian. In Günther Grewendorf & Helmut Weiss (eds.), *Bavarian syntax: Contributions to the theory of syntax*, 23–50. Amsterdam: John Benjamins.

Bayer, Josef & Markus Bader. 2007. On the syntax of prepositional phrases. In Andreas Späth (ed.), *Interfaces and interface conditions*, 157–179. Berlin: De Gruyter.

Bayer, Josef & Probal Dasgupta. 2016. Emphatic topicalization and the structure of the left periphery: Evidence from German and Bangla. *Syntax* 19(4). 309–353.

Bayer, Josef & Constantin Freitag. 2020. How much verb moves to second position? In Horst Lohnstein & Antonios Tsiknakis (eds.), *Verb second: Grammar internal and grammar external interfaces*, 77–122. Berlin: De Gruyter Mouton.

Bayer, Josef & William Marslen-Wilson. 1992. Configurationality in the light of language comprehension: The order of arguments in German. Unpublished manuscript Friedrich-Schiller-Universität Jena/Birkbeck College London.

Bayer, Josef, Tanja Schmid & Markus Bader. 2005. Clause union and clausal position. In Marcel den Dikken & Christina M. Tortora (eds.), *The function of function words and functional categories*, 79–113. John Benjamins.

Bayer, Josef & Volker Struckmeier (eds.). 2017a. *Discourse particles: Formal approaches to their syntax and semantics*. Berlin: De Gruyter.

Bayer, Josef & Volker Struckmeier. 2017b. The status quo of research on discourse particles in syntax and semantics. In Josef Bayer & Volker Struckmeier (eds.), *Discourse particles: Formal approaches to their syntax and semantics*, 1–14. Berlin: De Gruyter.

Bayer, Josef & Andreas Trotzke. 2015. The derivation and interpretation of left peripheral discourse particles. In Josef Bayer, Roland Hinterhölzl & Andreas Trotzke (eds.), *Discourse-oriented syntax*. Amsterdam: John Benjamins.

Bech, Gunnar. 1955. *Studien über das deutsche Verbum infinitum*. København: Munksgaard.

Bennis, Hans & Liliane Haegeman. 1984. On the clause status of agreement and relative clauses in West-Flemish. In Wim de Geest & Yvan Putseys (eds.), *Sentential complementation: Proceedings of the international conferenceheld at UFSAL, Brussels, June, 1983*, 33–53. Dordrecht: Foris.

den Besten, Hans. 1983. On the interaction of root transformation and lexical deletive rules. In Werner Abraham (ed.), *On the formal syntax of the Westgermania*, 47–131. Amsterdam: John Benjamins.

den Besten, Hans. 1985. The ergative hypothesis and free word order in Dutch and German. In Jindrich Toman (ed.), *Studies in German grammar*, 23–64. Dordrecht: Foris.

Bever, Thomas G. 1970. The cognitive basis for linguistic structures. In John R. Hayes (ed.), *Cognition and the development of language*, 279–362. New York: Wiley & Sons.

Bever, Thomas G. & Brian McElree. 1988. Empty categories access their antecedents during comprehension. *Linguistic Inquiry* 19(1). 35–43.

Bhatt, Rajesh. 1995. Verb movement in Kashmiri. *University of Pennsylvania Working Papers in Linguistics* 2(1). Article 2, 1–10.

Bhatt, Rakesh Mohan. 1994. Word order, configurationality and the structure of the Kashmiri clause. In Miriam Butt, Tracy Holloway King & Gillian Ramchand (eds.), *Theoretical perspectives on word order in South Asian languages*, 31–65. Stanford: CSLI Publication.

Bhatt, Rakesh Mohan & James Yoon. 1991. On the composition of COMP and parameters of V2. In Dawn Bates (ed.), *The proceedings of the tenth West Coast Conference on Formal Linguistics (WCCFL)*, 41–53. Stanford, CA: CSLI Publications.

Biberauer, Theresa, Anders Holmberg & Ian Roberts. 2008. Structure and linearization in disharmonic word orders. In Charles B. Chang & Hannah J. Haynie (eds.), *Proceedings of the 26th West Coast Conference on Formal Linguistics*, 96–104. Somerville, MA: Cascadilla Proceedings Project.

Bidese, Ermenegildo, Andrea Padovan & Alessandra Tomaselli. 2012. A binary system of complementizers in Cimbrian relative clauses. *Working Papers in Scandinavian Syntax* 90. 1–21.

Bidese, Ermenegildo, Andrea Padovan & Alessandra Tomaselli. 2013. Bilingual competence, complementizer selection and mood in Cimbrian. In Werner Abraham & Elisabeth Leiss (eds.), *Dialektologie in neuem Gewand: Zu Mikro-/Varietätenlinguistik, Sprachenvergleich und Universalgrammatik*, 47–58. Hamburg: Buske.

Bierwisch, Manfred. 1963. *Grammatik des deutschen Verbs*. Berlin: Akademie Verlag.

Bierwisch, Manfred. 1983. How on-line is language processing? In Giovanni B. Flores d'Arcais & Robert J. Jarvella (eds.), *The process of language understanding*, 113–168. Chichester: John Wiley & Sons.

Bonke, Maximilian. 2017. *Die linke Peripherie im Kiezdeutschen*. Humboldt-Universität zu Berlin. (Master's thesis).

Booij, Geert. 1990. The boundary between morphology and syntax: Separable complex verbs in Dutch. In Geert Booij & Jaap von Marle (eds.), *Yearbook of Morphology 1990*, 45–64. Dordrecht: Foris.

Bornkessel, Ina. 2002. *The argument dependency model: A neurocognitive approach to incremental interpretation*. Leipzig: Max Planck Institute of Cognitive Neuroscience.

Bornkessel, Ina & Matthias Schlesewsky. 2006a. The extended argument dependency model: A neurocognitive approach to sentence comprehension across languages. *Psychological Review* 113(4). 787–821.

Bornkessel, Ina & Matthias Schlesewsky. 2006b. The role of contrast in the local licensing of scrambling in German: Evidence from online comprehension. *Journal of Germanic Linguistics* 18(1). 1–43.

Bornkessel, Ina, Matthias Schlesewsky & Angela Friederici. 2002. Grammar overrides frequency: Evidence from the online processing of flexible word order. *Cognition* 85. B21–B30.

Bornkessel, Ina, Matthias Schlesewsky & Angela D. Friederici. 2003a. Contextual information modulates initial processes of syntactic integration: The role of inter- versus intrasentential predictions. *Journal of Experimental Psychology: Learning, Memory, and Cognition* 29(5). 871–882.

Bornkessel, Ina, Matthias Schlesewsky & Angela D. Friederici. 2003b. Eliciting thematic reanalysis effects: The role of syntax-independent information during parsing. *Language and Cognitive Processes* 18(3). 269–298.

Bott, Oliver & Fabian Schlotterbeck. 2015. The processing domain of scope interaction. *Journal of Semantics* 32(1). 39–92.

Brandner, Ellen. 2004. Head-movement in minimalism, and V2 as FORCE-marking. In Horst Lohnstein & Susanne Trissler (eds.), *The syntax and semantics of the left periphery*, 97–138. Berlin: De Gruyter Mouton.

Bresnan, Joan, Ronald M. Kaplan, Stanley Peters & Annie Zaenen. 1982. Cross-serial dependencies in Dutch. *Linguistic Inquiry* 13(4). 613–635.

Bruening, Benjamin. 2014. Precede-and-command revisited. *Language* 90(2). 342–388.

Bücker, Jörg. 2012. *Mit die schönsten und heitersten Stunden*: System und Gebrauch der Partikelvorkommen von *mit* im gesprochenen Deutsch. *Zeitschrift für Sprachwissenschaft* 31(2). 207–233.

Büring, Daniel & Katharina Hartmann. 2001. The syntax and semantics of focus-sensitive particles in German. *Natural Language & Linguistic Theory* 19(2). 229–281.

Cable, Seth. 2004. Predicate clefts and base-generation: Evidence from Yiddish and Brazilian Portuguese. Unpublished manuscript, MIT.

Carlson, Greg N. & Michael K. Tanenhaus. 1988. Thematic roles and language comprehension. In Wendy Wilkins (ed.), *Thematic relations*, 263–288. New York: Academic Press.

Carstens, Vicki. 2003. Rethinking complementizer agreement: Agree with a case-checked goal. *Linguistic Inquiry* 34(3). 393–412.

Cheng, Lisa Lai-Shen. 1991. *On the typology of* wh-*questions*. Cambridge, MA: MIT. (Doctoral dissertation).

Chilla, Solveig, Stefanie Haberzettl & Nadja Wulff. 2013. Dummy verbs in first and second language acquisition in German. In Elma Blom, Ineke van de Crats & Josje Verhagen (eds.), *Dummy auxiliaries in first and second language acquisition*, 209–250. Berlin: De Gruyter Mouton.

Chomsky, Noam. 1964. Degrees of grammaticalness. In Jerry A. Fodor & Jerrold J. Katz (eds.), *The structure of language: Readings in the philosophy of language*, 384–389. Englewood Cliffs, NJ: Prentice-Hall.

Chomsky, Noam. 1976. Conditions on rules of grammar. *Linguistic Analysis* 2(4). 303–351.

Chomsky, Noam. 1981. *Lectures on government and binding: The Pisa lectures*. Berlin: De Gruyter Mouton.

Chomsky, Noam. 1995. *The minimalist program*. Cambridge, MA: MIT Press.

Citko, Barbara. 2017. Right node raising. In Martin Everaert & Henk van Riemsdijk (eds.), *The Wiley Blackwell companion to syntax, second edition*, 1–33. Oxford: John Wiley & Sons.

Clahsen, Harald & Sam Featherston. 1999. Antecedent priming at trace positions: Evidence from German scrambling. *Journal of Pycholinguistic Research* 28(4). 415–437.

Clifton, Charles & Lyn Frazier. 1989. Comprehending sentences with long-distance dependencies. In Greg N. Carlson & Michael K. Tanenhaus (eds.), *Linguistic structure in language processing*. Dordrecht: Kluwer.

Clifton, Charles, Lyn Frazier & Keith Rayner (eds.). 1994. *Perspectives on sentence processing*. Hillsdale, NJ: Lawrence Erlbaum Associates.

Coenen, José & Wolfgang Klein. 1992. The acquisition of Dutch. In Wolfgang Klein & Clive Perdue (eds.), *Utterance structure: Developing grammars again*, 189–224. Amsterdam: John Benjamins.

van de Craats, Ineke. 2009. The role of *is* in the acquisition of finiteness by adult Turkish learners of Dutch. *Studies in Second Language Acquisition* 31 (1). 59–92.

Crain, Stephen & Janet Dean Fodor. 1985. How can grammar helps parsers? In David R. Dowty, Lauri Karttunen & Arnold M. Zwicky (eds.), *Natural language parsing: Psychological, computational, and theroretical perspectives*, 94–128. Cambridge: Cambridge University Press.

Crain, Stephen & Mark Steedman. 1985. On not being led up the garden path: The use of context by the psychological syntax processor. In David R. Dowty, Lauri Karttunen & Arnold M.

Zwicky (eds.), *Natural language parsing: Psychological, computational, and theroretical perspectives*, 320–358. Cambridge: Cambridge University Press.

Crocker, Mathew W. 1994. On the nature of the principle-based sentence processor. In Charles Clifton, Lyn Frazier & Keith Rayner (eds.), *Perspectives on sentence processing*, 245–266. Hillsdale, NJ: Lawrence Erlbaum Associates.

Culicover, Peter W. 2014. Constructions, complexity and word order variation. In Frederick J. Newmeyer & Laurel B. Preston (eds.), *Measuring linguistic complexity*, 148–178. Oxford: Oxford University Press.

Czypionka, Anna. 2013. *The interplay of object animacy and verb class in representation building*. Humboldt-Universität zu Berlin. (Doctoral dissertation).

Czypionka, Anna, Felix Golcher, Carsten Eulitz & Josef Bayer. 2016. Discontinuous particle verbs in German sentence comprehension. Poster presented at the 22nd AMLaP conference, 1–3 September 2016, Bilbao.

Davidson, Donald. 1967. The logical form of action sentences. In Nicholas Rescher (ed.), *The logic of decision and action*, 81–95. Pittsburgh, PA: University of Pittsburgh Press.

De Kuthy, Kordula & Walt Detmar Meurers. 2003. The secret life of focus exponents, and what it tells us about fronted verbal projections. In Stefan Müller (ed.), *Proceedings of the tenth international conference on HPSG*, 88–96. Stanford, CA: CSLI Publication.

Diesing, Molly. 1992. *Indefinites*. Cambridge, MA: The MIT Press.

Dowty, David R., Lauri Karttunen & Arnold M. Zwicky (eds.). 1985. *Natural language parsing: Psychological, computational, and theroretical perspectives*. Cambridge: Cambridge University Press.

Drach, Erich. 1937. *Grundgedanken der deutschen Satzlehre*. Frankfurt am Main: Diesterweg.

Drenhaus, Heiner, Peter beim Graben, Douglas Saddy & Stefan Frisch. 2006. Diagnosis and repair of negative polarity constructions in the light of symbolic resonance analysis. *Brain and Language* 96(3). 255–268.

Drenhaus, Heiner, Joanna Błaszcak & Juliane Schütte. 2007. Some psycholinguistic comments on NPI licensing. In Estela Puig-Waldmüller (ed.), *Proceedings of Sinn und Bedeutung 11*, 180–193. Barcelona: Universitat Pompeu Fabra.

Drenhaus, Heiner, Stefan Frisch & Douglas Saddy. 2005. Processing negative polarity items: When negation comes through the backdoor. In Stefan Kepser & Marga Reis (eds.), *Linguistic evidence: Empirical, theoretical and computational perspectives*, 145–164. Berlin: De Gruyter Mouton.

Drubig, Hans Bernhard. 1994. *Island constraints and the syntactic nature of focus and association with focus*. Arbeitspapiere des Sonderforschungsbereichs 340 Nr. 51. Tübingen: Universität Tübingen.

Emonds, Joseph E. 1970. *Root and structure-preserving transformations*. Cambridge, MA: MIT. (Doctoral dissertation).

Emonds, Joseph E. 1976. *A transformational approach to English syntax: Root, structure-preserving, and local transformations*. New York: Academic Press.

Erb, Marie Christine. 2001. *Finite auxiliaries in German*. Tilburg: Katholieke Universiteit Brabant. (Doctoral dissertation).

Erdmann, Oskar. 1886. *Grundzüge der deutschen Syntax nach ihrer geschichtlichen Entwicklung*. Stuttgart: Cotta.

Erdocia, Kepa, Itziar Laka, Anna Mestres-Missé & Antoni Rodriguez-Fornells. 2009. Syntactic complexity and ambiguity resolution in a free word order language: Behavioral and electrophysiological evidences from Basque. *Brain and Language* 109(1). 1–17.

Eroms, Hans-Werner. 1984. Indikativische periphrastische Formen mit doã im Bairischen als Beispiel für latente und virulente syntaktische Regeln. In Peter Wiesinger (ed.), *Beiträge zur Bairischen und Ostfränkischen Dialektologie*, 123–135. Göppingen: Kümmerle.

Everaert, Martin & Henk van Riemsdijk (eds.). 2006. *The Blackwell companion to syntax*. Oxford: Blackwell Publishing.

Fanselow, Gisbert. 1987. *Konfigurationalität: Untersuchungen zur Universalgrammatik am Beispiel des Deutschen*. Tübingen: Narr.

Fanselow, Gisbert. 1993. Die Rückkehr der Basisgenerierer. *Groninger Arbeiten zur Germanistischen Linguistik* 36. 1–74.

Fanselow, Gisbert, Reinhold Kliegl & Matthias Schlesewsky. 1999. Processing difficulty and principles of grammar. In Susan Kemper & Reinhold Kliegl (eds.), *Constraints on language: Aging, grammar and memory*, 171–201. Dordrecht: Kluwer.

Fanselow, Gisbert & Thomas Weskott. 2010. A short note on long movement in German. *Linguistische Berichte* 222. 129–140.

Featherston, Samuel. 2001. *Empty categories in language processing*. Amsterdam: John Benjamins.

Featherston, Samuel. 2008. Thermometer judgments as linguistic evidence. In Claudia Maria Riehl & Astrid Rothe (eds.), *Was ist linguistische Evidenz?*, 69–90. Aachen: Shaker Verlag.

Featherston, Samuel. 2009. A scale for measuring well-formedness: Why syntax needs boiling and freezing points. In Sam Featherston & Susanne Winkler (eds.), *The fruits of empirical linguistics*, 47–74. Berlin: De Gruyter.

Felser, Claudia, Harald Clahsen & Thomas F. Münte. 2003. Storage and integration in the processing of filler-gap dependencies: An ERP study of topicalization and *wh*-movement in German. *Brain and Language* 87(3). 345–354.

Fiebach, Christian J., Matthias Schlesewsky & Angela D. Friederici. 2001. Syntactic working memory and the establishment of filler-gap dependencies: Insights from ERPs and fMRI. *Journal of Psycholinguistic Research* 30(3). 321–338.

Fischer, Annette. 2001. Diachronie und Synchronie von auxiliarem *tun* im Deutschen. In Sheila Watts, Jonathan West & Hans-Joachim Solms (eds.), *Zur Verbmorphologie germanischer Sprachen*, 137–154. Tübingen: Niemeyer.

Fleischer, Jürg. 2008. Zur topikalisierenden Infinitivverdopplung in deutschen Dialekten: *Trinken trinkt er nich, aber rauchen raucht er* (mit einem Exkurs zum Jiddischen). In Peter Ernst & Franz Patocka (eds.), *Dialektgeographie der Zukunft: Akten des 2. Kongresses der Internationalen Gesellschaft für Dialektologie des Deutschen (IGDD) am Institut für Germanistik der Universität Wien, 20. bis 23. September 2006*, 243–268. Stuttgart: Steiner.

Fodor, Janet Dean. 1978. Parsing strategies and constraints on transformations. *Linguistic Inquiry* 9(3). 427–473.

Fodor, Jerry A. 1983. *The modularity of mind*. Cambridge, MA: MIT Press.

Fortmann, Christian. 2007. Bewegungsresistente Verben. *Zeitschrift für Sprachwissenschaft* 26. 1–40.

Fourquet, Jean. 1959. Strukturelle Syntax und Inhaltsbezogene Grammatik. In Helmut Gipper (ed.), *Sprache, Schlüssel zur Welt: Festschrift für Leo Weisgerber*. Düsseldorf: Schwann.

Frazier, Lyn. 1978. *On comprehending sentences: Syntactic parsing strategies*. Storrs, CT: University of Connecticut. (Doctoral dissertation).

Frazier, Lyn & Charles Clifton. 1989. Successive cyclicity in the grammar and the parser. *Language and Cognitive Processes* 4(2). 93–126.

Frazier, Lyn & Janet Dean Fodor. 1978. The sausage machine: A new two-stage parsing model. *Cognition* 6. 291–325.

Frazier, Lyn, Lori Taft, Tom Roeper, Charles Clifton & Kate Ehrlich. 1984. Parallel structure: A source of facilitation in sentence comprehension. *Memory & Cognition* 12(5). 421–430.

Freitag, Constantin. 2012. *A processing account of syntactic islands and grammaticalness: Towards a reduction of grammar*. Humboldt-Universität zu Berlin. (Master's thesis).

Frey, Werner. 2003. Syntactic conditions on adjunct classes. In Ewald Lang, Claudia Maienborn & Catherine Fabricius-Hansen (eds.), *Modifying adjuncts*, 163–209. Berlin: De Gruyter Mouton.

Frey, Werner. 2004. The grammar-pragmatics interface and the German prefield. *Sprache und Pragmatik* (52). 1–39.

Frey, Werner. 2006a. Contrast and movement to the German prefield. In Valèria Molnàr & Susanne Winkler (eds.), *The architecture of focus*, 235–264. Berlin: De Gruyter.

Frey, Werner. 2006b. How to get an object-*es* into the German prefield. In Patrick Brandt & Eric Fuß (eds.), *Form, structure, and grammar: A festschrift presented to Günther Grewendorf on occasion of his 60th birthday*, 159–185. Berlin: Akademie Verlag.

Frey, Werner. 2012. On two types of adverbial clauses allowing root-phenomena. In Lobke Aelbrecht, Liliane Heageman & Rachel Nye (eds.), *Main clause phenomena: New horizons*, 405–429. Amsterdam: John Benjamins.

Frey, Werner & Karin Pittner. 1998. Zur Positionierung der Adverbiale im deutschen Mittelfeld. *Liguistische Berichte* 176. 489–534.

Freywald, Ulrike. 2014. *Parataktische Konjunktionen: Zur Syntax und Pragmatik der Satzverknüpfung im Deutschen – am Beispiel von* obwohl, wobei, während, wogegen *und* dass. Humboldt-Universität zu Berlin. (Doctoral dissertation).

Freywald, Ulrike, Leonie Cornips, Natalia Ganuza, Ingvild Nistov & Toril Opsahl. 2015. Beyond verb second – a matter of novel information-structural effects? Evidence from Norwegian, Swedish, German and Dutch. In Jacomine Nortier & Bente A. Svendsen (eds.), *Language, youth and identity in the 21st century: Linguistic practices across urban spaces*, 73–92. Cambridge: Cambridge University Press.

Freywald, Ulrike & Horst J. Simon. 2007. Wenn die Wortbildung die Syntax stört: Über Verben, die nicht in V2 stehen können. In Maurice Kauffer & René Métrich (eds.), *Verbale Wortbildung im Spannungsfeld zwischen Wortsemantik, Syntax und Rechtschreibung*, 181–194. Tübingen: Stauffenburg.

Friederici, Angela D. & Stefan Frisch. 2000. Verb argument structure processing: The role of verb-specific and argument-specific information. *Journal of Memory and Language* 43(3). 476–507.

Friederici, Angela D., Axel Mecklinger, Kevin M. Spencer, Karsten Steinhauer & Emanuel Donchin. 2001. Syntactic parsing preferences and their on-line revisions: A spatio-temporal analysis of event-related brain potentials. *Cognitive Brain Research* 11. 305–323.

Frisch, Stefan, Matthias Schlesewsky, Douglas Saddy & Annegret Alpermann. 2002. The P600 as an indicator of syntactic ambiguity. *Cognition* 85(3). B83–B92.

Fuß, Eric. 2014. Complementizer agreement (in Bavarian): Feature inheritance or feature insertion? In Günther Grewendorf & Helmut Weiss (eds.), *Bavarian syntax: Contributions to the theory of syntax*. Amsterdam: John Benjamins.

Gärtner, Hans-Martin. 2013. Infinite Hauptsatzstrukturen. In Jörg Meibauer, Markus Steinbach & Hans Altmann (eds.), *Satztypen des Deutschen*. Berlin: De Gruyter.

Glaser, Elvira & Natascha Frey. 2007. Doubling phenomena in Swiss German dialects. In Sjef Barbiers, Margreet van der Ham & Marika Lekakou (eds.), *European dialect syntax project: Papers presented at the workshop on syntactic doubling, Amsterdam, March 2006.*

Grewendorf, Günther. 2013. Satztypen und die linke/rechte Peripherie. In Jörg Meibauer, Markus Steinbach & Hans Altmann (eds.), *Satztypen des Deutschen*. Berlin: De Gruyter.

Grewendorf, Günther & Helmut Weiss (eds.). 2014. *Bavarian syntax: Contributions to the theory of syntax*. Amsterdam: John Benjamins.

Gunlogson, Christine. 2002. Declarative questions. In Brendan Jackson (ed.), *Proceedings from Semantics and Lignustic Theory XII*, 124–143. Ithaca, NY: Cornell University.

de Haan, Germen J. 2010. Complementizer agreement. In Jarich Hoekstra, Willem Visser & Goffe Jensma (eds.), *Studies in West Frisian grammar: Selected papers by Germen J. de Haan*, 215–232. Amsterdam: John Benjamins.

Haberzettl, Stefanie. 2003. "Tinkering" with chunks: Form-oriented strategies and idiosyncratic utterance patterns without functional implications in the IL of Turkish speaking children learning German. In Christine Dimroth & Marianne Starren (eds.), *Information structure and the dynamics of language acquisition*, 45–63. Amsterdam: John Benjamins.

Haegeman, Liliane. 1992. *Theory and description in generative syntax: A case study in West Flemish*. Cambridge: Cambridge University Press.

Haegeman, Liliane & Marjo van Koppen. 2012. Complementizer agreement and the relation between C^0 and T^0. *Linguistic Inquiry* 43(3). 441–454.

Haider, Huber. 2010. *The syntax of German*. Cambridge: Cambridge University Press.

Haider, Hubert. 1985. V-second in German. In Hubert Haider & Martin Prinzhorn (eds.), *Verb second phenomena in Germanic languages*, 49–75. Dordrecht: Foris.

Haider, Hubert. 1988. Matching projections. In Anna Cardinaletti, Guglielmo Cinque & Giuliana Giusti (eds.), *Constituent structure*, 101–121. Dordrecht: Foris.

Haider, Hubert. 1993. *Deutsche Syntax – generativ: Vorstudien zur Theorie einer projektiven Grammatik*. Tübingen: Narr.

Haider, Hubert. 2000a. Adverb placement: Convergence of structure and licensing. *Theoretical Linguistics* 26. 65–134.

Haider, Hubert. 2000b. Branching and discharge. In Peter Coopmans, Martin Everaert & Jane Grimshaw (eds.), *Lexical specification and insertion*, 135–164. Amsterdam: John Benjamins.

Haider, Hubert. 2012. *Symmetry breaking in syntax*. Cambridge: Cambridge University Press.

Hale, Ken. 1983. Warlpiri and the grammar of non-configurational languages. *Natural Language & Linguistic Theory* 1(1). 5–47.

Hartmann, Katharina. 2000. *Right node raising and gapping: Interface conditions on prosodic deletion*. Amsterdam: John Benjamins.

Hatakeyama, Yuji, Kensuke Honda & Kosuke Tanaka. 2008. Verb movement in Japanese revisited. *Journal of Japanese Linguistics* 24. 89–103.

Hawkins, John A. 2004. *Efficiency and complexity in grammars*. Oxford: Oxford University Press.

Hemforth, Barbara. 1993. *Kognitives Parsing: Repräsentation und Verarbeitung sprachlichen Wissens*. Sankt Augustin: infix.

Hemforth, Barbara & Lars Konieczny (eds.). 2000. *German sentence processing*. Dordrecht: Kluwer.

Hemforth, Barbara, Lars Konieczny & Christoph Scheepers. 2000. Modifier attachment: Relative clauses and coordinations. In Barbara Hemforth & Lars Konieczny (eds.), *German sentence processing*. Dordrecht: Kluwer.

Heycock, Caroline. 1995. Asymmetries in reconstruction. *Linguistic Inquiry* 26(4). 547–570.
Heycock, Caroline. 2006. Embedded root phenomena. In Martin Everaert & Henk van Riemsdijk (eds.), *The Blackwell companion to syntax*, 174–209. Oxford: Blackwell Publishing.
Higgins, F. R. 1973. On J. Emond's analysis of extraposition. In John P. Kimball (ed.), *Syntax and semantics*. New York: Seminar Press.
Hoekstra, Eric & Caroline Smits. 1998. Everything you always wanted to know about complementizer agreement. In Elly van Gelderen & Vida Samiian (eds.), *Proceedings of the twenty-seventh Western Conference On Linguistics (WECOL 98)*. Fresno, CA: California State University Press.
Hoekstra, Jarich. 2016. Beyond *do*-support and *tun*-periphrasis: The case of finite verb doubling in Karrharde North Frisian. *Journal of Germanic Linguistics* 28(4). 317–348.
Höhle, Tilman N. 2018. Projektionsstufen bei V-Projektionen: Bemerkungen zu Frey/Tappe (1991). In Stefan Müller, Marga Reis & Frank Richter (eds.), *Beiträge zur deutschen Grammatik: Gesammelte Schriften von Tilman N. Höhle*, 369–379. Formerly unpublished manuscript from 1991, Universität Tübingen. Berlin: Language Science Press.
Holmberg, Anders. 2015. Verb second. In Tibor Kiss & Artemis Alexiadou (eds.), *Syntax – theory and analysis: An international handbook*, 342–383. Berlin: De Gruyter.
Hooper, Joan B. & Sandra A. Thompson. 1973. On the applicability of root transformations. *Linguistic Inquiry* 4(4). 465–497.
Hornstein, Norbert & Amy Weinberg. 1981. Case theory and preposition stranding. *Linguistic Inquiry* 12(1). 55–91.
Huang, Cheng-Teh James. 1993. Reconstruction and the structure of VP: Some theoretical consequences. *Linguistic Inquiry* 24(1). 103–138.
Iatridou, Sabine & Spyridola Varlokosta. 1998. Pseudoclefts crosslinguistically. *Natural Language Semantics* 6(1). 3–28.
Jacobs, Joachim. 1983. *Fokus und Skalen: Zur Syntax und Semantik der Gradpartikeln im Deutschen*. Tübingen: Niemeyer.
Jouitteau, Mélanie. 2012. Verb doubling in Breton and Gungbe: Obligatory exponence at the sentence level. In Enoch O. Aboh, Norval Smith & Anne Zribi-Hertz (eds.), *The morphosyntax of reiteration in creole and non-creole languages*, 135–174. Amsterdam: John Benjamins.
Julien, Marit. 2015. The force of V2 revisited. *The Journal of Comparative Germanic Linguistics* 18(2). 139–181.
Just, Marcel Adam, Patricia A. Carpenter & Jacqueline D. Woolley. 1982. Paradigms and processes in reading comprehension. *Journal of Experimental Psychology: General* 111(2). 228–238.
Kaan, Edith. 1997. *Processing subject-object ambiguities in Dutch*. University of Groningen. (Doctoral dissertation).
Kaan, Edith, Anthony Harris, Edward Gibson & Phillip Holcomb. 2000. The P600 as an index of syntactic integration difficulty. *Language and Cognitive Processes* 15(2). 159–201.
Källgren, Gunnel & Ellen F. Prince. 1989. Swedish VP-topicalization and Yiddish verb-topicalization. *Nordic Journal of Linguistics* 12. 47–58.
Karagjosova, Elena & Katja Jasinskaja. 2015. Predicate clefts in Bulgarian. In Gerhild Zybatow, Petr Biskup, Marcel Guhl, Claudia Hurtig, Olav Mueller-Reichau & Maria Yastrebova (eds.), *Slavic grammar from a formal perspective*, 231–244. Frankfurt am Main: Peter Lang.

Kathol, Andreas. 1990. A uniform approach to V2 in German. In Juli Carter, Rose-Marie Déchaine, Bill Philip & Tim Sherer (eds.), *Proceedings of NELS 20*, 244–254. Amherst, MA: GLSA.

Kawasha, Boniface. 2007. Subject-agreeing complementizers and their functions in Chokwe, Luchazi, Lunda, and Luvale. In Doris L. Payne & Jaime Peña (eds.), *Selected proceedings of the 37th Annual Conference on African Linguistics*. Somerville, MA: Cascadilla Proceedings Project.

Kayne, Richard S. 1994. *The antisymmetry of syntax*. Cambridge, MA: The MIT Press.

Kim, Jaegwon. 1976. Events as property exemplifications. In Myles Brand & Douglas Walton (eds.), *Action theory: Proceedings of the Winnipeg conference on human action*, 159–177. Dordrecht: Reidel.

Kimball, John P. 1973. Seven principles of surface structure parsing in natural language. *Cognition* 2(1). 15–47.

Kluender, Robert & Maria Kutas. 1993a. Bridging the gap: Evidence from ERPs on the processing of unbounded dependencies. *Journal of Cognitive Neuroscience* 5(2). 196–214.

Kluender, Robert & Marta Kutas. 1993b. Subjacency as a processing phenomenon. *Language & Cognitive Processes* 8(4). 573–633.

Kobayashi, Ryoichiro. 2016. Against V-to-T-to-C movement in Japanese and Korean non-constituent coordination. In Patrick Farrell (ed.), *Proceedings of the 2016 annual meeting of the Linguistic Society of America*, vol. 1, 1–14. Linguistic Society of America.

Koisumi, Masatoshi. 2000. String vacuous overt verb raising. *Journal of East Asian Linguistics* 9(3). 227–285.

Kölligan, Daniel. 2004. Zur präteritalen *tun*-Periphrase im Ripuarischen. In Franz Patocka & Peter Wiesinger (eds.), *Morphologie und Syntax deutscher Dialekte und Historische Dialektologie des Deutschen: Beiträge zum 1. Kongress der Internationalen Gesellschaft für Dialektologie des Deutschen, Marburg/Lahn, 5.–8. März 2003*, 429–452. Wien: Praesens Verlag.

Konieczny, Lars. 1996. *Human sentence processing: A semantics-oriented parsing approach*. Albert-Ludwigs-Universität zu Freiburg. (Doctoral dissertation).

Konieczny, Lars. 2000. Locality and parsing complexity. *Journal of Psycholinguistic Research* 29(6). 627–645.

Konieczny, Lars & Philipp Döring. 2003. Anticipation of clause-final heads: Evidence from eye-tracking and SRNs. In Peter Slezak (ed.), *Proceedings of the 4th international conference on cognitive science and the 7th conference of the Australasian society for cognitive science*, 330–335.

Konieczny, Lars, Barbara Hemforth, Christoph Scheepers & Gerhard Strube. 1997. The role of lexical heads in parsing: Evidence from German. *Language and Cognitive Processes* 12(2-3). 307–348.

Konieczny, Lars & Nicole Völker. 2000. Referential biases in syntactic attachment. In Barbara Hemforth & Lars Konieczny (eds.), *German sentence processing*, 137–160. Dordrecht: Kluwer.

König, Ekkehard. 1993. Focus particles. In Joachim Jacobs, Arnim von Stechow, Wolfgang Sternefeld & Theo Vennemann (eds.), *Syntax: Ein internationales Handbuch zeitgenössischer Forschung*, 978–987. Berlin: De Gruyter.

Koopman, Hilda. 1984. *The syntax of verbs: From verb movement rules in the Kru languages to Universal Grammar*. Dordrecht: Foris.

Koopman, Hilda. 1995. On verbs that fail to undergo V-second. *Linguistic Inquiry* 26(1). 137–163.

Koster, Jan. 1975. Dutch as an SOV language. *Linguistic Analysis* 1. 111–136.

Koul, Omkar N. & Kashi Wali. 2015. *Kashmiri*. München: LINCOM.

Kratzer, Angelika. 1995. Stage-level and individual-level predicates. In Gregory N. Carlson & Francis Jeffry Pelletier (eds.), *The generic book*. Chicago: University of Chicago Press.

Kremers, Joost. 2009. A prosodic approach to particle verbs. *Linguistische Berichte* 217. 81–96.

Kretzschmar, Franziska, Ina Bornkessel-Schlesewsky, Adrian Staub, Dietmar Roehm & Matthias Schlesewsky. 2012. Prominence facilitates ambiguity resolution: On the interaction between referentiality, thematic roles and word order in syntactic reanalysis. In Monique Lamers & Peter de Swart (eds.), *Case, word order and prominence: Interacting cues in language production and comprehension*, 239–271. Dordrecht: Springer.

Krifka, Manfred. 2006. Association with focus phrases. In Valèria Molnàr & Susanne Winkler (eds.), *The architecture of focus*. Berlin: De Gruyter.

Krifka, Manfred. 2007. Basic notions of information structure. In Gisbert Fanselow, Caroline Féry & Manfred Krifka (eds.), *The notions of information structure*, 13–55. Potsdam: Universitätsverlag Potsdam.

Kural, Murat. 2005. Tree traversal and word order. *Linguistic Inquiry* 36. 367–387.

Larson, Richard K. 1988. On the double object construction. *Linguistic Inquiry* 19(3). 335–391.

Legate, Julie Anne. 2008. Warlpiri and the theory of second position clitics. *Natural Language & Linguistic Theory* 26(1). 3–60.

Lenerz, Jürgen. 1994. Pronomenprobleme. In Brigitta Haftka (ed.), *Was determiniert Worstellungsvariation? Studien zu einem Interaktionsfeld von Grammatik, Pragmatik und Sprachtypologie*, 161–173. Opladen: Westdeutscher Verlag.

Levy, Roger & Frank Keller. 2013. Expectation and locality effects in German verb-final structures. *Journal of Memory and Language* 68. 199–222.

Lewis Jr., Robert Eugine. 2013. *Complementizer agreement in Najdi Arabic*. Lawrence: University of Kansas. (Master's Thesis).

Lin, Jing, Fred Weerman & Hedde Zeijlstra. 2015. Emerging NPIs: The acquisition of Dutch *hoeven* 'need'. *The Linguistic Review* 32(2). 333–347.

Lohnstein, Horst. 2020. The grammatical basis of verb second: The case of German. In Rebecca Woods & Sam Wolfe (eds.), *Rethinking verb second*, 177–207. Oxford: Oxford Universtity Press.

Love, Tracy E. & David A. Swinney. 1998. The influence of canonical word order on structural processing. In Dieter Hillert (ed.), *Sentence processing: A crosslinguistic perspecive*, 153–166. New York: Academic Press.

MacDonald, Maryellen C. 1989. Priming effects from gaps to antecedents. *Language and Cognitive Processes* 4(1). 35–56.

MacWhinney, Brian, Elizabeth Bates & Reinhold Kliegl. 1984. Cue validity and sentence interpretation in English, German, and Italian. *Journal of Verbal Learning and Verbal Behavior* 23(2). 127–150.

Maienborn, Claudia. 2003. *Die logische Form von Kopula-Sätzen*. Berlin: Akademie-Verlag.

Maienborn, Claudia. 2005. On the limits of the Davidsonian approach: The case of copula sentences. *Theoretical Linguistics* 31(3). 275–316.

Maienborn, Claudia. 2007. On Davidsonian and Kimian states. In Ileana Comorovski & Klaus von Heusinger (eds.), *Existence: Semantics and syntax*. Dordrecht: Kluwer.

Maling, Joan M. 1972. On "gapping and the order of constituents". *Linguistic Inquiry* 3(1). 101–108.

Matzke, Mike, Heinke Mai, Wido Nager, Jascha Rüsseler & Thomas Münte. 2002. The costs of freedom: An ERP-study of non-canonical sentences. *Clinical Neurophysiology* 113(6). 844–852.

Mecklinger, Axel, Herbert Schriefers, Karsten Steinhauer & Angela D. Friederici. 1995. Processing relative clauses varying on syntactic and semantic dimensions: An analysis with event-related potentials. *Memory & Cognition* 23(4). 477–494.

Meibauer, Jörg, Markus Steinbach & Hans Altmann (eds.). 2013. *Satztypen des Deutschen*. Berlin: De Gruyter.

Meinunger, Andé. 2007. About the object *es* in the German Vorfeld. *Linguistic Inquiry* 38. 553–563.

Meinunger, André. 2004. Interface restrictions on verb second. In Ralf Vogel (ed.), *Three papers on German verb movement*, 51–81. Potsdam: Universitätsverlag.

Miestamo, Matti. 2007. Negation: An overview of typological research. *Language and Linguistics Compass* 1(5). 552–570.

Miyamoto, Edson T. & Shoichi Takahashi. 2002. The processing of *wh*-phrases in Japanese. *Scientific Approaches to Language* 1. 133–172.

Miyashita, Mizuki. 2006. Tohono o'odham. In Keith Brown (ed.), *Encyclopedia of language & linguistics*, Second Edition, 735–737. Oxford: Elsevier.

Mollica, Fabio. 2014. Der *Dativus ethicus* im Deutschen aus konstruktionsgrammatischer Sicht. *Zeitschrift für germanistische Linguistik* 42(3). 349–378.

Molnàr, Valèria & Susanne Winkler (eds.). 2006. *The architecture of focus*. Berlin: De Gruyter.

Moltman, Friederike. 1992. *Coordination and comparatives*. Cambridge, MA: MIT. (Doctoral dissertation).

Müller, Gereon. 2004. Verb-second as vP-first. *The Journal of Comparative Germanic Linguistics* 7(3). 179–234.

Müller, Stefan. 2003. Mehrfache Vorfeldbesetzung. *Deutsche Sprache* 31(1). 29–62.

Müller, Stefan. 2005. Zur Analyse der scheinbar mehrfachen Vorfeldbesetzung. *Linguistische Berichte* 203. 297–330.

Nolda, Andreas. 2004. Topics detached to the left: On 'left dislocation', 'hanging topic', and related constructions in German. In Benjamin Shaer, Werner Frey & Claudia Maienborn (eds.), *Proceedings of the Dislocated Elements Workshop, ZAS Berlin, November 2003*. Berlin: ZAS.

Omaki, Akira, Ellen F. Lau, Imogen Davidson White, Myles Louis Dakan, Aaron Apple & Colin Phillips. 2015. Hyper-active gap filling. *Frontiers in Psychology* 6(384).

Oppenrieder, Wilhelm. 2013. Deklarativsätze. In Jörg Meibauer, Markus Steinbach & Hans Altmann (eds.), *Satztypen des Deutschen*, 20–50. Berlin: De Gruyter.

Osborne, Timothy. 2006. Gapping vs. non-gapping coordination. *Linguistische Berichte* 207. 307–338.

Osterhout, Lee & David Swinney. 1993. On the temporal course of gap-filling during comprehension of verbal passives. *Journal of Psycholinguistic Research* 22(2). 273–286.

Ott, Dennis. 2018. VP-fronting: Movement vs. dislocation. *The Linguistic Review* 35(2). 243–282.

Parker, Dan & Colin Phillips. 2016. Negative polarity illusions and the format of hierarchical encodings in memory. *Cognition* 157. 321–339.

Parodi, Teresa. 2000. Finiteness and verb placement in second language acquisition. *Second Language Research* 16(4). 355–381.

Pechmann, Thomas, Hans Uszkoreit, Johannes Engelkamp & Dieter Zerbst. 1996. Wortstellung im deutschen Mittelfeld. In Christopher Habel, Siegfried Kanngießer & Gert Rickheit (eds.), *Perspektiven der Kognitiven Linguistik*, 257–299. Wiesbaden: VS Verlag für Sozialwissenschaften.

Peirce, Jonathan W. 2007. PsychoPy: Psychophysics software in Python. *Journal of Neuroscience Methods* 162(1-2). 8–13.

Penka, Doris. 2011. *Negative indefinites*. Oxford: Oxford University Press.

Pesetsky, David. 1995. *Zero syntax: Experiencers and cascades*. Cambridge, MA: MIT Press.

Phillips, Colin. 1996. *Order and structure*. Cambrigde, MA: MIT. (Doctoral dissertation).

Phillips, Colin. 2003. Linear order and constituency. *Linguistic Inquiry* 34(1). 37–90.

Pickering, Martin & Guy Barry. 1991. Sentence processing without empty categories. *Language and Cognitive Processes* 6(3). 229–259.

Platzack, Christer. 1986. COMP, INFL, and Germanic word order. In Lars Hellan & Kirsti Koch Christensen (eds.), *Topics in Scandinavian syntax*, 185–234. Dordrecht: Reidel.

Poletto, Cecilia. 2002. The left-periphery of V2-Rhaetoromance dialects: A new view on V2 and V3. In Sjef Barbiers, Leonie Cornips & Susanne van der Kleij (eds.), *Syntactic microvariation*, 214–242. Amsterdam: Meertens Institute.

Postal, Paul M. 1974. *On raising: One rule of English grammar and its theoretical implications*. Cambridge, MA: The MIT Press.

Progovac, Ljiljana. 1994. *Negative and positive polarity: A binding approach*. Cambridge: Cambridge University Press.

Pulvermüller, Friedemann, Werner Lutzenberger & Hubert Preissl. 1999. Nouns and verbs in the intact brain: Evidence from event-related potentials and high-frequency cortical responses. *Cerebral Cortex* 9(5). 497–506.

R Core Team. 2015. *R: A Language and Environment for Statistical Computing*. Vienna, Austria.

Rambow, Owen & Aravind K. Joshi. 1994. A processing model for free word-order languages. In Charles Clifton, Lyn Frazier & Keith Rayner (eds.), *Perspectives on sentence processing*, 267–301. Hillsdale, NJ: Lawrence Erlbaum Associates.

Reis, Marga. 1997. Zum syntaktischen Status unselbständiger Verbzweit-Sätze. In Christa Dürscheid, Karl Heinz Ramers & Monika Schwarz (eds.), *Sprache im Fokus. Festschrift für Heinz Vater zum 65. Geburtstag*, 121–144. Tübingen: Niemeyer.

Richter, Frank, Fabienne Fritzinger & Marion Weller. 2010. Who can see the forest for the trees? Extracting multiword negative polarity items from dependency-parsed text. *Journal for Language Technology and Computational Linguistics* 25(1). 83–110.

Richter, Frank & Janina Radó. 2014. Negative polarity in German: Some experimental results. *Journal of Semantics* 31(1). 43–65.

Rizzi, Luigi. 1997. The fine structure of the left periphery. In Liliane Haegeman (ed.), *Elements of grammar: Handbook in generative syntax*, 281–337. Dordrecht: Kluwer.

Röder, Brigitte, Tobias Schicke, Oliver Stock, Gwen Heberer, Helen Neville & Frank Rösler. 2000. Word order effects in German sentences and German pseudo-word sentences. *Sprache & Kognition* 19(1-2). 31–37.

Rooth, Mats. 1985. *Association with focus*. Amherst: University of Massachusetts. (Doctoral dissertation).

Rösler, Frank, Thomas Pechmann, Judith Streb, Brigitte Röder & Erwin Hennighausen. 1998. Parsing of sentences in a language with varying word order: Word-by-word variations of processing demands are revealed by event-related brain potentials. *Journal of Memory and Language* 38(2). 150–176.

Ross, John Robert. 1967. *Constraints on variables in syntax*. Cambridge, MA: MIT. (Doctoral dissertation).

Ross, John Robert. 1969. Auxiliaries as main verbs. In William Todd (ed.), *Studies in philosophical linguistics*, 77–102. Evanston, IL: Great Expectations Press.

Rothmayr, Antonia. 2009. *The structure of stative verbs*. Amsterdam: John Benjamins.

Sabbagh, Joseph. 2014. Right node raising. *Language and Linguistics Compass* 8(1). 24–35.

Saddy, Douglas, Heiner Drenhaus & Stefan Frisch. 2004. Processing polarity items: Contrastive licensing costs. *Brain and Language* 90. 495–502.

Sauerland, Uli & Paul Elbourne. 2002. Total reconstruction, PF movement, and derivational order. *Linguistic Inquiry* 33(2). 283–319.

Scheepers, Christoph. 1997. *Menschliche Satzverarbeitung: Syntaktische und thematische Aspekte der Wortstellung im Deutschen*. Albert-Ludwigs-Universität zu Freiburg. (Doctoral dissertation).

Scheepers, Christoph, Barbara Hemforth & Lars Konieczny. 2000. Linking syntactic functions with thematic roles: Psych-verbs and the resolution of subject-object ambiguity. In Barbara Hemforth & Lars Konieczny (eds.), *German sentence processing*, 95–135. Dordrecht: Kluwer.

Scheffler, Tatjana. 2013. *Two-dimensional semantics: Clausal adjuncts and complements*. Berlin: De Gruyter.

Scherf, Nathalie. 2017. The syntax of Swedish modal particles. In Josef Bayer & Volker Struckmeier (eds.), *Discourse particles: Formal approaches to their syntax and semantics*, 78–99. Berlin: De Gruyter.

Schlesewsky, Matthias & Ina Bornkessel. 2004. On incremental interpretation: Degrees of meaning accessed during sentence comprehension. *Lingua* 114(9–10). 1213–1234.

Schlesewsky, Matthias, Ina Bornkessel & Stefan Frisch. 2003. The neurophysiological basis of word order variations in German. *Brain and Language* 86(1). 116–128.

Schlesewsky, Matthias, Ina Bornkessel & Martin Meyer. 2002. Why a "word order difference" is not always a "word order" difference: A reply to Weyerts, Penke, Münte, Heinze, and Clahsen. *Journal of Psycholinguistic Research* 31(5). 437–445.

Schlesewsky, Matthias, Gisbert Fanselow, Reinhold Kliegl & Josef Krems. 2000. The subject preference in the processing of locally ambiguous wh-questions in German. In Barbara Hemforth & Lars Konieczny (eds.), *German sentence processing*, 65–93. Dordrecht: Kluwer.

Schönenberger, Manuela & Zvi Penner. 1995. Probing Swiss-German clause structure by means of placement of verbal explatives: *Tun* "do" insertion and verb doubling. In Zvi Penner (ed.), *Topics in Swiss German syntax*, 291–330. Bern: Peter Lang.

Schriefers, Herbert, Angela D. Friederici & Katja Kühn. 1995. The processing of locally ambiguous relative clauses in German. *Journal of Memory and Language* 34(4). 499–520.

Schwartz, Bonnie D. & Sten Vikner. 1989. All verb second clauses are CPs. *Working Papers in Scandinavian Syntax* 43. 27–49.

Schwartz, Bonnie D. & Sten Vikner. 1996. The verb always leaves IP in V2 clauses. In Adriana Belletti & Luigi Rizzi (eds.), *Parameters and functional heads: Essays in comparative syntax*, 11–62. New York: Oxford University Press.

Schwarz, Christian. 2004. *Die* tun-*Periphrase im Deutschen*. Ludwig-Maximilians-Universität München. (Magisterarbeit).

Seeliger, Heiko. 2015. "Surely that's not a negative declarative question?": Polar discourses in Swedish, German and English. In Eva Csipak & Hedde Zeijlstra (eds.), *Proceedings of Sinn und Bedeutung 19*, 571–589. Göttingen: Georg-August-Universität Göttingen.

Shaer, Benjamin & Werner Frey. 2004. 'Integrated' and 'non-integrated' left-peripheral elements in German and English. In Benjamin Shaer, Werner Frey & Claudia Maienborn (eds.), *Proceedings of the Dislocated Elements Workshop, ZAS Berlin, November 2003*, 465–502. Berlin: ZAS.

Shaer, Benjamin, Werner Frey & Claudia Maienborn (eds.). 2004. *Proceedings of the Dislocated Elements Workshop, ZAS Berlin, November 2003*. Berlin: ZAS.

Shannon, Claude E. & Warren Weaver. 1949. *The mathematical theory of communication*. Chicago: University of Illinois Press.

Shapiro, Lewis P. 2000. Some recent investigations of gap filling in normal listeners: Implications for normal and disordered language processing. In Yosef Grodzinsky, Lewis P. Shapiro & David Swinney (eds.), *Language and the brain: Representation and processing*, 357–376. San Diego, CA: Academic Press.

Shieber, Stuart M. 1985. Evidence against the context-freeness of natural language. *Linguistics and Philosophy* 8. 333–343.

Shlonsky, Ur. 1994. Agreement in Comp. *The Linguistic Review* 11(3-4). 351–357.

Speyer, Augustin. 2009. Das Vorfeldranking und das Vorfeld-*es*. *Linguistische Berichte* 219. 323–353.

Sportiche, Dominique. 2006. Reconstruction, binding, and scope. In Martin Everaert & Henk van Riemsdijk (eds.), *The Blackwell companion to syntax*, 35–93. Oxford: Blackwell Publishing.

Stowe, Laurie A. 1986. Parsing *wh*-constructions: Evidence for on-line gap location. *Language and Cognitive Processes* 1(3). 227–245.

Stowe, Laurie A., Michael K. Tanenhaus & Greg Calson. 1991. Filling gaps on-line: Use of lexical and semantic information in sentence processing. *Language and Speech* 34(4). 319–340.

Temme, Anne & Elisabeth Verhoeven. 2016. Verb class, case, and order: A crosslinguistic experiment on non-nominative experiencers. *Linguistics* 54(4). 769–813.

Thráinsson, Höskuldur. 2007. *The syntax of Icelandic*. Cambridge: Cambridge University Press.

Tomaselli, Alessandra. 1986. Das unpersönliche „es": Eine Analyse im Rahmen der Generativen Grammatik. *Linguistische Berichte* (102). 171–190.

Travis, Lisa deMena. 1991. Parameters of phrase structure and verb-second phenomena. In Robert Freidin (ed.), *Principles and parameters in comparative grammar*, 339–364. Cambridge, MA: The MIT Press.

Traxler, Matthew J. & Martin J. Pickering. 1996. Plausibility and the processing of unbounded dependencies: An eye-tracking study. *Journal of Memory and Language* 35(3). 454–475.

Trotzke, Andreas & Stefano Quaglia. 2016. Particle topicalization and German clause structure. *The Journal of Comparative Germanic Linguistics* 19(2). 109–141.

Trotzke, Andreas & Eva Wittenberg. 2017. Expressive particle verbs and conditions on particle fronting. *Journal of Linguistics* 53(2). 407–435.

Truckenbrodt, Hubert. 2006a. On the semantic motivation of syntactic verb movement to C in German. *Theoretical Linguistics* 32(3). 257–306.

Truckenbrodt, Hubert. 2006b. Replies to the comments by Gärtner, Plunze and Zimmermann, Portner, Potts, Reis, and Zaefferer. *Theoretical Linguistics* 32(3). 387–410.

Truckenbrodt, Hubert. 2013. In Jörg Meibauer, Markus Steinbach & Hans Altmann (eds.), *Satztypen des Deutschen*, 232–246. Berlin: De Gruyter.

Trutkowski, Ewa. 2016. *Topic drop and null subjects in German*. Berlin: De Gruyter.
Uszkoreit, Hans. 1986. Constraints on order. *Linguistics* 24. 883–906.
Vasishth, Shravan, Sven Brüssow, Richard L. Lewis & Heiner Drenhaus. 2008. Processing polarity: How the ungrammatical intrudes on the grammatical. *Cognitive Science* 32(4). 685–712.
Verhagen, Josje. 2009. *Finiteness in Dutch as a second language*. Vrije Universiteit Amsterdam. (Doctoral dissertation).
Verhoeven, Elisabeth. 2015. Thematic asymmetries do matter! A corpus study of German word order. *Journal of Germanic Linguistics* 27(1). 45–104.
Vikner, Sten. 1995. *Verb movement and expletive subjects in the Germanic languages*. New York: Oxford University Press.
Vikner, Sten. 2005. Immobile complex verbs in Germanic. *Journal of Comparative Germanic Linguistics* 8(1). 83–115.
de Vries, Mark. 2009. On mulitdominance and linearization. *Biolinguistics* 3(4). 344–403.
Wagers, Matthew W. & Colin Phillips. 2014. Going the distance: Memory and control processes in active dependency construction. *The Quarterly Journal of Experimental Psychology*. PMID: 24320939, 1–31.
Wagner, Michael. 2006. Association by movement: Evidence from NPI-licensing. *Natural Language Semantics* 14(4). 297–324.
Walkden, George. 2017. Language contact and V3 in Germanic varieties new and old. *The Journal of Comparative Germanic Linguistics* 20(1). 49–81.
Wechsler, Stephen. 1991. Verb second and illocutionary force. In Katherine Leffel & Denis Bouchard (eds.), *Views on phrase structure*, 177–191. Springer Netherlands.
Weiss, Helmut. 2005. Inflected complementizers in Continental West Germanic dialects. *Zeitschrift für Dialektologie und Linguistik* 72(2). 148–166.
Weskott, Thomas. 2003. *Information structure as a processing guide: The left periphery of German verb-second sentences and its interpretation in context*. Universität Leipzig. (Doctoral dissertation).
Weyerts, Helga, Martina Penke, Thomas F. Münte, Hans-Jochen Heinze & Harald Clahsen. 2002. Word order in sentence processing: An experimental study of verb placement in German. *Journal of Psycholinguistic Research* 31(3). 211–268.
Wiese, Heike. 2009. Grammatical innovation in multiethnic urban Europe: New linguistic practices among adolescents. *Lingua* 119(5). 782–806.
Williams, Edwin Samuel. 1974. *Rule ordering in syntax*. Cambridge, MA: MIT. (Doctoral dissertation).
Wolfe, Sam. 2016. On the left periphery of V2 languages: Evidence from Romance Fin and Force V2 systems. *Rivista di Grammatica Generativa* 38. 287–310.
Wöllstein-Leisten, Angelika, Axel Heilman, Peter Stepan & Sten Vikner. 1997. *Deutsche Satzstruktur: Grundlagen der syntaktischen Analyse*. Tübingen: Stauffenburg.
Xiang, Ming, Brian Dillon & Colin Phillips. 2009. Illusory licensing effects across dependency types: ERP evidence. *Brain and Language* 108(1). 40–55.
Xiang, Ming, Julian Grove & Anastasia Giannakidou. 2013. Dependency-dependent interference: NPI interference, agreement attraction, and global pragmatic inferences. *Frontiers in Psychology* 4(708).
Yanilmaz, Aydogan & John E. Drury. 2018. Prospective NPI licensing and intrusion in Turkish. *Language, Cognition and Neuroscience* 33(1). 111–138.

Zanuttini, Raffaella. 2001. Sentential negation. In Mark Baltin & Chris Collins (eds.), *The handbook of contemporary syntactic theory*, 511–535. Oxford: Blackwell.
Zeijlstra, Hedde. 2007. Negation in natural language: On the form and meaning of negative elements. *Language and Linguistics Compass* 1(5). 498–518.
Zeijlstra, Hedde. 2013. Not in the first place. *Natural Language & Linguistic Theory* 31(3). 865–900.
Zepeda, Ofelia. 1983. *A Papago grammar*. Tucson, AZ: The University of Arizona Press.
Zimmermann, Malte. 2011. Discourse particles. In Klaus von Heusinger, Claudia Maienborn & Pau Portner (eds.), *Semantics*, 2012–2038. Berlin: De Gruyter.
Zwart, Jan-Wouter. 1993. Clues from dialect syntax: Complementizer agreement. In Werner Abraham & Josef Bayer (eds.), *Dialektsyntax*. Opladen: Westdeutscher Verlag.
Zwart, Jan-Wouter. 1994. Dutch is head-initial. *The Linguistic Review* 11(3-4). 377–406.
Zwart, Jan-Wouter. 2017. An argument against the syntactic nature of verb movement. In Laura R. Bailey & Michelle Sheehan (eds.), *Order and structure in syntax I: Word order and syntactic structure*, 29–47. Berlin: Language Science Press.

Index

https://doi.org/10.1515/9783110725018-010